Frommer's

4th Edition

Honolulu, Waikiki & Oahu

by Faye Hammel

with Nature, Sports and Recreation Coverage
by Jeanette Foster

Macmillan • USA

ABOUT THE AUTHORS

Faye Hammel has been reporting on Hawaii for the last 30 years. When not in the islands, she lives in New York City. In addition to authoring *Frommer's Honolulu, Waikiki & Oahu* and *Frommer's Hawaii from $60 a Day* and co-authoring *Frommer's New York City*, Faye has also published *The Dream Theater* and *The New York Lunch*. **Jeanette Foster**, a resident of Hawaii, has skied the slopes of Mauna Kea—during a Fourth of July ski meet, no less—and scuba dived with manta rays off the Big Island's Kona coast. A prolific writer widely published in travel, sports, and adventure magazines, Jeanette is also a contributing writer to numerous travel guides, including *Frommer's Hawaii from $60 a Day*.

MACMILLAN TRAVEL

A Simon & Schuster Macmillan Company
1633 Broadway
New York, NY 10019

Copyright © 1996 by Simon & Schuster, Inc.

ISBN 0-02-860642-6
ISSN 1064-1238

Editor: Cheryl Farr
Map Editor: Douglas Stallings
Design by Michele Laseau
Digital Cartography by Devorah Wilkenfeld and Ortelius Design

SPECIAL SALES

Bulk purchases (10+ copies) of Frommer's travel guides are available to corporations at special discounts. The Special Sales Department can produce custom editions to be used as premiums and/or for sales promotion to suit individual needs. Existing editions can be produced with custom cover imprints such as corporate logos. For more information write to Special Sales, Simon & Schuster, 1633 Broadway, New York, NY 10019.

Manufactured in the United States of America

Contents

List of Maps

AN INVITATION TO THE READER

When researching this book, we discovered many wonderful places—hotels, restaurants, shops, and more. We're sure you'll find others. Please tell us about them so we can share the information with your fellow travelers in upcoming editions. If you were disappointed with a recommendation, we'd love to know that, too. Please write to:

Faye Hammel & Jeanette Foster
Frommer's Honolulu, Waikiki & Oahu, 4th Edition
Macmillan Travel
1633 Broadway
New York, NY 10019

AN ADDITIONAL NOTE

Please be advised that travel information is subject to change at any time—and this is especially true of prices. We therefore suggest that you write or call ahead for confirmation when making your travel plans. The authors, editors, and publisher cannot be held responsible for the experiences of readers while traveling. Your safety is important to us, however, so we encourage you to stay alert and be aware of your surroundings. Keep a close eye on cameras, purses, and wallets, all favorite targets of thieves and pickpockets.

WHAT THE SYMBOLS MEAN

✪ Frommer's Favorites

Accommodations, restaurants, attractions, and entertainment you should not miss.

Ⓢ Super-Special Values

Hotels and restaurants that offer great value for your money.

The following abbreviations are used for credit or charge cards:

AE	American Express	ER	enRoute
CB	Carte Blanche	JCB	Japan Credit Bank
DC	Diners Club	MC	MasterCard
DISC	Discover	V	Visa
EC	Eurocard		

The Best of Oahu

One of the hazards—and pleasures—of being a travel writer is that people are always calling on you for advice. A friend of a friend calls to say they're going to Hawaii; what are the most important things to do and see? Where should they stay? What restaurants can't be missed? They have just a few days or a week and they don't want to overlook anything that's really special. So, I've put together my own list of the island's bests. The list is subjective, personal, and admittedly idiosyncratic, but it should serve you well as a point of departure for the judgments you'll eventually formulate on your own.

1 The Best Beaches

Not all of the beaches on Oahu look like Waikiki—beach towel–to–beach towel, crowded by a wall of high-rise hotels—nor do all of them have the allure of a Hawaii Visitors Bureau poster—deserted, with creamy-white sand, strategically placed palms, and calm azure waves. Below is my list of the island's best beaches. In choosing them, I considered the overall beauty of the location, its ambience, and the range of ocean activities available there.

- **Waimea Bay.** This is where you'll find Hawaii big-wave surfing at its best. In the winter, monstrous waves, reaching more than 30 feet, come thundering into the bay and explode with such force that the ground shakes. During the summer the same curvaceous, white-sand beach borders a glassy, calm, gin-clear lake offering excellent swimming, snorkeling, kayaking, and even cliff diving.
- **Lanikai Beach.** Hidden by the residential area on Mokulua Drive, Lanikai is a mile-long sandy beach that's great for swimming and, with the prevailing trade winds, excellent for sailing and windsurfing. The hard-packed, corn starch–like sand along the shoreline is perfect for jogging. You can easily reach the two tiny offshore islands known as the Mokuluas (which are sea-bird sanctuaries) by kayak. Because Lanikai is off the main road, undeveloped, with no facilities, and surrounded by residential homes, it's less crowded than other beaches on the windward side and the perfect place to claim a remote, isolated spot to relax. Sun worshipers should arrive in the morning, as the shadow of the Koolau Range will block your access to the rays in the afternoon.

- **Kailua Beach.** This grand, two-mile-long beach is really three beaches in one: Kailua Beach, Kalama Beach, and Oneawa Beach. There's something for everyone here: For windsurfing, volleyball, swimming, and family-oriented activities, the 30-acre Kailua Beach Park is your best bet; the best waves are at Kalama Beach; and for those who want to get away from the crowds, Oneawa usually offers the most privacy.
- **Malaekahana Beach.** Located outside the town of Kahuku on the North Shore, this mile-long, seldom-used sandy beach is a hidden treasure. Protected for most of the year, Malaekahana is excellent for swimming, picnicking, and shore activities (fishing, beachcombing, etc.). In fact, at low tide you can wade from the beach to Moku'auia (Goat) Island, a bird refuge area, located just offshore. The beach backs up to the wooded Malaekahana State Recreational area, a tranquil state park offering camping, picnic areas, and plenty of public access.
- **Pokai Bay Beach Park.** Located outside the town of Waianae, this arid side of the island offers a different beach experience from that available on the windward side. The waters are calm enough for children inside this protected bay, and they offer excellent snorkeling—even when the rest of the Waianae shoreline is being battered by heavy surf. And on weekdays, when school is in session, this beach is deserted.

2 The Best Travel Experiences

You've only got a few days on Oahu, enough time to do just a handful of things. What should they be? Here's our list of terrific Oahu experiences that you shouldn't miss, if you can help it.

- **Visit the USS *Arizona* Memorial.** Take a boat, take the bus, or drive yourself—however you have to get there, do it. This impressive and deeply moving memorial commemorates December 7, 1941, the day the bombs fell on Pearl Harbor, catapulting the United States into World War II.
- **Snorkel Hanauma Bay.** Sure, it's crowded and filled with tourists, but the underwater experience at this marine life conservation district is spectacular. Be sure to go early.
- **Drive the North Shore.** It's hard to believe that such spectacular rural beauty is just a half-hour's drive from Honolulu. From Waikiki, follow the Pali Highway through the Koolaus and head north along the windward coast to Haleiwa. It's a different world on the other side of the mountains; you'll find one of the world's most beautiful coastlines and some of its most ferocious waves.
- **Take a Submarine Plunge.** You can marvel at Hawaii's brilliant underwater world even if you don't scuba, thanks to the submarine *Atlantis*. The high-tech sub descends to a depth of 100 feet just off the Waikiki shoreline giving you views of the coral reefs and kaleidoscopic fish otherwise available only to divers.
- **Visit the Buddha.** A magnificent gold carving of Amida, the Buddha of Western Paradise, serenely guards the Byodo-In Temple, located in the Valley of the Temples just outside Kaneohe. Surrounded by a fragrant and beautiful classical garden, this temple is an exact replica of the venerable Byodo-In in Uji, Japan. A visit here is a memorable aesthetic and spiritual experience.
- **Sail the Waikiki Shoreline.** Watching the sunset from a small, intimate sailboat off Waikiki is a perfect way to end a day in paradise.

3 The Best Outdoor Adventures

Thrill seekers, Oahu is the place for you. The island offers an array of activities that will get your adrenalin pumping, your heart pounding—and others wondering about your sanity.

- **Soar the Thermals in a Glider.** Soaring in the thermals over Oahu's craggy Waianae mountain range has been described as a religious experience by many who have chosen to take a glider flight from Oahu's Dillingham Air Field. For more than 20 years, 1- and 2-passenger gliders have been towed aloft from the Mokuleia Field and set adrift in the thermal—with a certified glider pilot at the controls, assuring safety—to soar effortlessly on long, gossamer-like wings.

- **Kayak Along the North Shore from Waimea River to Haleiwa.** Gliding through the calm waters of the Waimea River, the only sounds you'll hear are the singing of the birds and the gentle splash of your paddle in the water. Once you reach the ocean, the shallow draft kayak allows you close access to the shoreline as well as to the marine world, alive with endangered green sea turtles, playful dolphins, and schools of multihued fish; you'll see the North Shore of Oahu from an entirely different perspective.

- **Canoe Surf Waikiki.** When the South Pacific swells roll into Waikiki and the summertime surf is up, experience the thrill of surfing in a Hawaiian outrigger canoe. Numerous beach concessions offer outrigger canoe surfing; an experienced canoe steersman will guide your novice effort. As you paddle, enjoy the offshore view of the world-famous beach and thrill to catching a wave, accelerating, and gliding over the water. It's an electrifying experience that will remain with you long after the ride is over.

- **Scuba Dive into the Mystical World of Kahuna Canyon.** Near Mokuleia, on the North Shore, is a summer dive spot the locals call Kahuna Canyon. In Hawaiian, *kahuna* means priest, wise man, or sorcerer, this underwater site is definitely something a sorcerer might conjure up. Walls rising from the ocean floor, resembling an underwater Grand Canyon, define an amphitheater with crabs, octopuses, and slipper and spiny lobsters sitting in the audience and giant trevally, parrotfish, and unicorn fish as the entertainment—with an occasional shark making a surprise appearance. For this experience of a lifetime, be sure to get scuba-certified before you come to Hawaii, so you don't "waste time" in a swimming pool getting trained on your vacation.

- **Hike the Makiki-Manoa Cliffs Trail.** Sojourn through a Hawaiian rain forest to the top of a ridge offering spectacular views of Honolulu. This trail takes you over mountain streams, through dense jungle, and over several peaks. Soft tropical breezes carry whiffs of sweet-smelling flowers mixed with the lusty, earthy smell of the rain forest. The whispering of the stream and fluttering trees provide background for the high-pitched song of the forest birds. The views are captivating, but the experience of a Hawaiian rain forest is the true reward— it's bewitching.

4 The Best Luxury Hotels & Resorts

- **The Halekulani.** This remake of an old classic is as good as the original, maybe even better. Perhaps it's the refinement, the impeccable service, the luxurious rooms, the orchid mosaic sparkling on the floor of the beachside swimming pool, the miraculous food at La Mer and Orchids—or all the details that combine to create such a fabulous whole—that keeps this place right at the top of the list.

- **Hilton Hawaiian Village.** The sheer beauty of the landscaped grounds—with ponds, botanical gardens, waterfalls, fragrant flowers, singing birds—makes just walking from your room to the beach—one of the very best stretches in Waikiki—sheer pleasure. This 20-acre resort offers plenty of water sports (it even has its own dock), beautifully decorated rooms, and two award-winning restaurants: the serene Bali By The Sea and the dramatic Golden Dragon.
- **The Royal Hawaiian.** The legendary "Pink Palace of the Pacific" has been a Waikiki landmark since 1927, and it's as regal, lush, and romantic as ever. Gorgeous grounds, a fine strip of beach, handsome period-style rooms in the old building, the Surf Room for lavish oceanside buffets—it all adds up to a feast for the senses.
- **Ihilani Resort & Spa.** As sumptuous as any neighbor island resort, with its own world-championship golf and tennis, a gentle swimming beach, plus a state-of-the-art European health spa, all in an atmosphere of rarefied beauty and exquisite taste.

5 The Best Moderately Priced Hotels

- **Hawaiiana Hotel.** One of the very few garden hotels still left in Waikiki, the Hawaiiana is wonderfully located a half-block from the wide sandy beach in front of the Reef Hotel and Fort DeRussy Park. Rustic, cozy units, all with kitchenettes, are situated around a tropical garden and two swimming pools, where comfy chairs are situated for serious relaxation.
- **The Royal Garden at Waikiki.** This newcomer close to the Ala Wai Canal offers beauty, luxury, great service and every amenity—plus a gourmet chef in residence at Cascada—all at very affordable prices. It's about a 10-minute walk to the beach, but don't worry: There are two swimming pools and two whirlpools right at home.
- **Waikiki Joy.** This boutique hotel is a secluded oasis in the heart of Waikiki, just a block from the beach. An extremely solicitous staff takes good care of the guests here—they've been known to send chicken soup when one came down with the flu. Every room has its own Jacuzzi and a Bose entertainment center. Cappuccino's offers exotic coffees and chat downstairs.

6 The Best Places to Stay Beyond Waikiki

- **New Otani Kaimana Beach Hotel.** Ideally located at the foot of Diamond Head, this hotel is perfect for those who want to be close to Waikiki, but not in the heart of its madness. It's right on Sans Souci Beach—which means wonderful swimming in gentle waves, kayaking, and snorkeling—and across from Kapiolani Park, with all its facilities for golf, tennis, kite flying, jogging, and bicycling. And the Hau Tree Lanai, a delightful indoor-outdoor beachfront restaurant, is one of the most romantic spots on Oahu.
- **The Manoa Valley Inn.** This three-story gingerbread house listed in the National Register of Historic Places, is one of the grand old mansions of Honolulu. It's also Oahu's most romantic bed-and-breakfast inn. Each of the

unique guest rooms, are furnished with period antiques. In addition to breakfast in the morning, fruits, wine, and cheese are offered in the evening, and the lanai offers guests a hypnotic view of Honolulu's city lights.

- **Schrader's Windward Marine Resort.** Here's something definitely off the beaten path: a small, rural resort on the shores of Kaneohe Bay. The accommodations are older and not at all fancy; but where else can you rent an apartment so close to the water that you can fish from your lanai? You could also sail or windsurf or go kayaking; lessons, boat trips, and rentals are available from the resort's own pier.

7 The Best Culinary Experiences

If you like to eat, you'll love Oahu. From the most innovative and sophisticated bastions of Hawaiian Regional cuisine to local saimin stands and simple country restaurants, the dining scene is an ongoing adventure. These are some of my favorites:

- **Roy's,** in Hawaii Kai. You'll have to drive eight miles from Waikiki to the suburbs to get to Roy's, but it's definitely worth the trip. Roy Yamaguchi is the wunderkind chef of the new East-West style of cooking known as Hawaiian Regional cuisine. His innovative creations, offered from a menu that changes every night, always include original appetizers, salads, pastas, wood-fire individual pizzas, and many fresh fish dishes, including spiny lobster. New wonders never stop emerging from the open display kitchen. And the show-biz crowd can be a show in itself.

- **The Secret,** in the Hawaiian Regent Hotel. This is one of Honolulu's special-occasion restaurants—elegant, expensive, but worth every dollar. In a setting that could be Camelot—open-beamed ceilings, magnificent copper chandeliers, multicolored banners, rippling fountains flowing over black river rocks—you'll dine on superb continental fare. The evening's finale should be the Grand Marnier soufflé and then (compliments of the house) chocolate-covered ice cream bonbons, served on white clouds of dry ice.

- **Ciao Mein,** in the Hyatt Regency Hotel. It's a Chinese restaurant and an Italian restaurant in one: gourmet fare from both cuisines and a mix-and-match menu, served in an appealing, casually elegant bistro-style setting. The atmosphere is up, the price range is moderate to expensive, and the eggplant Szechuan, the chicken broth with lobster wontons, the risotto and cake noodles are all terrific. Desserts are embarrassingly decadent.

- **Ahi's,** in Kahuku. The shrimp served at this modest restaurant, halfway down a country road on the windward coast, is so fresh—it comes from an aquaculture farm close by—and so good that people drive from all over the island to partake. You can have it lightly tempuraed, deep-fried, or as shrimp cocktail. The prices are modest, and the atmosphere at Roland Ahi's family place couldn't be friendlier.

- **Kua'Aina,** in Haleiwa. Known for serving the best sandwiches on the North Shore—possibly on the entire island—this is a sparkling little place where you'll have a chance to meet the surfing set and other local folk. The gigantic sandwiches are a meal in themselves, and so reasonable that a recent Zagat survey hailed Kua'Aina as the second best "Bang for the Buck" in the entire state.

8 The Best Snorkeling

The best snorkeling spots can be defined not only by the quality of the marine life found there, but also by the water clarity, the geological formations, the ease of access, even by the way the light dances across the water, adding to the mystical experience of the Neptunian world. All you'll need is a mask, snorkel, fins—and an open mind—for your Oahu snorkeling adventures.

- **Hanauma Bay.** It can be crowded and the parking lot fills up by 10am, but this usually is the best single snorkeling area on Oahu, all things considered. Calm, clear, warm water populated by thousands of fish and other marine life draw people to Hanauma Bay every day. There are so many different species that you'll feel like you're floating in an aquarium, and the fish are generally so tame they'll swim right up to your face mask. The inside reef is calm and shallow (mostly less than 10 feet deep); the outside reef is deeper and generally used by scuba divers. This is a good place to see schools of colorful butterfly fish and tangs; a few trumpetfish and spotted pufferfish will often flitter by.
- **Queen's Surf Beach.** Actually part of Waikiki's Kapiolani Park Beach Center, Queen's Surf Beach is located between the Natatorium and the Waikiki Aquarium. The reef shelf in front of the Aquarium is best for snorkeling; there's easy access from the sandy shoreline and the waters are nearly always calm. The adjacent Waikiki Aquarium can answer any questions you may have about the marine flora and fauna you observe in the water.
- **Pupukea Marine Life Conservation District.** In 1983, Pupukea Beach was made a Marine Life Conservation District. It's easy to see why the people of Hawaii wanted to protect the ocean off this popular North Shore 80-acre beach park; Pupukea is abundant in marine life, from its tide pools to its many ledges, arches, and lava tubes (in the deeper water). The best snorkeling is during the calm summer months at the southern end of the beach, in an area called Three Tables, named after the three flat sections of reef visible at low tide. The shallow (about 15 feet deep) area is perfect for viewing marine life.
- **Laie Beach.** Although there's no direct public access, this white-sand beach is worth seeking out. Fronting North Shore residential and vacation homes, it's uncrowded and, in the calm summer months, the shallow waters and nearby reefs can keep a snorkeler happy for hours. Recommended for experienced snorkelers only, as there is no lifeguard on duty.

9 The Best Walks

The beautiful weather and surroundings make Oahu eminently suited to walking, whether it's poking around downtown Honolulu, strolling along a deserted beach, or hiking along a lush mountain trail.

- **Chinatown.** The sights, sounds, and smells of this Asian quarter will fascinate you—you can examine the gift shops, the grocery and fish stalls, stop in at a bakery to try a traditional moon cake, visit the art galleries, watch lei makers at work, even look in on an herbal doctor or acupuncturist. Be sure to stroll by the newly restored art deco Hawaii Theater; then pick up your pace and walk a few more blocks to the exotic Kuan Yin Buddhist Temple.
- **Malaekahana Beach to Hukilau Beach on the North Shore.** The wonderful white sand is packed hard enough to walk on, making it perfect for a stroll. A

walk along this usually empty stretch lined with ironwoods offers great views, wind in your hair, and lots of peace and quiet. When the tide is out, you can even walk out to tiny Goat Island, a veritable beachcomber's paradise.

- **The University of Hawaii.** The garden-like campus is full of flowers, trees, impressive architecture (note I. M. Pei's Jefferson Hall at the East West Center), and lively student life. Chances are you'll see rainbows in Manoa Valley. After your stroll, it's only a short bus ride or drive to the Waioli Tea Room for afternoon tea.
- **Diamond Head.** An easy walk around this Hawaii landmark and to the 760-foot summit will reward you with spectacular ocean views; you'll even have a great vantage for watching Waikiki surfers hang-ten. It will also take you through lush Kapiolani Park and Oahu's ritziest neighborhoods, at the edge of Waikiki, and past the Honolulu Zoo.
- **Hawaii Trail and Mountain Club.** The members invite you to hike with them on Saturday and Sunday mornings along one of the beautiful trails near Honolulu. It's safer and more fun to go with a group—particularly one that knows the area—rather than solo, and they often have access to private lands you couldn't visit on your own.

10 The Best of Natural Hawaii

Want to view Hawaii the way Mother Nature created it? Even though Oahu is home to urban Honolulu as well as most of the population of the Hawaiian Islands, much of the island is still home to the same natural beauty that enchanted the Polynesian explorers many hundreds of years ago.

- **Foster Botanical Gardens.** This is a quiet, meditative oasis in the heart of Honolulu. The gardens date back to the 1850s, when German immigrant Dr. William Hillebrand started a botanical garden at his Nuuanu Street home. This was no ordinary garden; the doctor imported exotic plants from around the world. His estate was later sold to Captain and Mrs. Foster, who expanded the garden,filling it with even more exotic plants. When Mrs. Foster died in 1930, she donated the lush gardens to the people of Hawaii. You'll find some 4,000 species of tropical plants and flowers, including a special collection of palms, bromeliad, and wild orchids, on the immaculate 20-acre site; it's a perfect place to sit and reflect on paradise.
- **Tantalus-Manoa Trails.** Step back in time with a visit to Oahu's rain forest jungles, whispering waterfalls, and clear mountain streams. Myriad trails interconnect off Tantalus-Round Top Drive, leading you to a world far from urban Honolulu. This is a chance to see it all, from breathtaking views of the Honolulu skyline to untouched verdant tropical forest.
- **Nuuanu Pali.** The *pali* (cliff) is steeped in history and shrouded in greenery. The drive up Nuuanu Pali Drive traverses native forests and passes the Upside Down Waterfall (which got its name because continuous winds blowing the water create an upward veil of tear-like mist as it thunders down). According to legend, the water from these falls is the tears of a Hawaiian princess who continually weeps for her fallen lover. At the summit is the Pali Lookout, offering one of Oahu's most extraordinary views of the windward side. Blustery winds at the Pali are occasionally so powerful that you can literally stand at a 45-degree angle and be held up by the winds. This is a site of a massive battle, where

Kamehameha the Great trounced the armies of the chiefs of Oahu by pushing them over the cliff, thus uniting the Hawaiian Islands under one leader for the first time.

- **Kahana Valley State Park/Kahana Bay Beach Park.** On the windward side lies this jungle-robed, chiseled valley, flowing into a deep, placid bay, offering glimpses into an ancient Hawaiian world, from the dense mountain jungle to the man-made fishponds on the edge of the bay. Sparsely developed, protected from intrusion, you can hike over fern-filled trails, stop for awe-inspiring views, and swim in the azure ocean off a salt-and-pepper beach. This vestige of old Oahu is both a healing and a relaxing place.

- **Sunrise at Malaekahana.** On the North Shore, watch the pencil-thin orange line appear out of the inky darkness as the sun slowly makes its appearance behind Moku'auia (Goat) Island. Smell the *ehukai* (salty, sea breeze) as you either sit quietly, nestled in the soft ironwood needles of the woody state park, or stand in the soft sands of the deserted crescent-shaped beach. Listen to the song of the early morning birds, the murmur of the trade winds over the land, and the faint lap of the ocean on the shore. This is an experience that nourishes the soul and satiates the senses.

11 The Best Views

There's no two ways about it—Oahu's majestic beauty is breathtaking. Below are some vistas with particularly awe-inspiring views:

- **Nuuanu Pali.** This is Oahu's number-one view spot. Some claim that these jagged cliffs are haunted (it was here that Kamehameha the Great vanquished his enemies in 1795, toppling thousands to their deaths on the peaks below). The scenery below is enough to take your breath away: a view of Oahu's windward Coast, its mountains looking like Gothic spires, the craft of Kaneohe Bay looking like toy boats. It's beautiful at night, too, with the lights of Kailua and Kaneohe winking below.

- **Pu'u Ualakaa Park.** Noted for sunrise, sunset, and night views—or anytime in between—the view halfway up Tantalus Mountain, at Pu'u Ualakaa Park on Round Top Drive, is an unobstructed one, sweeping from Diamond Head to Pearl Harbor. And the air, rich with ginger and night-blooming jasmine, smells heavenly. The well-paved road goes through the Round Top Forest Reserve.

- **Diamond Head Crater.** You can't help but see Diamond Head from Waikiki Beach. From its 760-foot summit—reached by a short but steep hike to the top—you'll view a splendid panorama of Waikiki, and half of the island as well.

- **Halona Blowhole.** Geysers shoot into the air through an underground vent in the lava cliffs. The views, of ocean on one side, mountain peaks on the other, are breathtaking. Just below the Blowhole is Halona Cove, where you may be lucky enough to spot whales in winter.

- **Pupukea Heiau.** Some of the most sweeping views of the wild and windy North Shore can be seen from this ancient temple.

12 The Best Spots for Romance

Hawaii and romance are almost synonymous in the minds of many—and rightly so. Here are a few of Oahu's extra-magical spots:

- **The Sands of Waikiki at Night.** A barefoot walk, with the water lapping at your feet, the stars winking above, and the strains of music from the shows at the big hotels drifting in from afar—what could be sweeter?
- **The House Without a Key,** at the Halekulani. This is what you always dreamed Hawaii would be like. This open-air waterfront cocktail lounge is the perfect place to hold hands as the sun sinks over the water, the moon slowly rises, the palm trees sway, and an exquisite hula girl dances the languid strains of the music of her islands.
- **Hanohano Room of the Sheraton Waikiki.** It's hard to imagine a more romantic spot than this spectacular dining room with huge picture windows, from which the view is unbroken from Diamond Head to Pearl Harbor and the sunset is unforgettable. You might get to see whales and dolphins if you're on the ocean side of the room, maybe a rainbow or two over Manoa Valley from the mountain side.
- *Navatek I* **Skyline Dinner Cruise.** How's a candlelight dinner aboard a sunset cruise to set the scene for romance? Watch the moon rise over Diamond Head, enjoy a good meal, and listen to some of Hawaii's best jazz—they toss a free flower blossom onto the waves as you make your wish.
- **Nuuanu Pali Lookout.** As dusk falls and the lights begin to sparkle along the Windward Coast far below, that old island magic descends, and romance is in the air.

13 The Best of Oahu for Kids

Oahu is a great place for a family holiday. There's no shortage of activities to keep the keikis amused.

- **The Beach.** Waikiki Beach and Ala Moana Beach Park both offer safe swimming and plenty of potential playmates. Waikiki Beach gets the visitor crowd, Ala Moana Beach Park is the place local families like best.
- **Sea Life Park.** This is Oahu's top family attraction. It's hard to tear the kids away from this place. They like everything about it, especially the shows where the dolphins and penguins—and even a killer whale—do amazing tricks.
- *Bowfin* **Submarine Museum Park.** Close to the USS *Arizona* Memorial at Pearl Harbor, this museum gives kids a chance to explore below the decks of the *Bowfin* submarine, to see where its 80-man crew served during some of the fiercest naval battles of World War II.
- **Fireboat Cruises.** Kids love the tours of historic Honolulu Harbor on the retired fireboat *Abner T. Longley,* especially if they get a chance to operate one of the water cannons on the nighttime cruises.
- **Playing with Dolphins.** The frolicking dolphins at the Kahala Mandarin Oriental are always big kid-pleasers, particularly at feeding times.
- **A Rainy Day Possibility.** Kids love the big Pearlridge Shopping Center out in Aiea, about a half-hour's drive from Waikiki. They can ride Oahu's only monorail train and play electronic games galore.

14 The Best Places to Discover Historic Oahu

Hawaii has come out of the Stone Age and into the Space Age in 200 years—for both better and worse. To miss seeing how and where and when this happened is to miss one of the main reasons for journeying so far—after all, if you came just for the beach, there's probably one a lot closer to home. Below are the prime spots reliving Hawaii's fascinating historical and cultural heritage.

- **Pre-Contact Hawaii: The Bishop Museum.** The Polynesian past comes alive in this vibrant cultural and natural history museum's Hawaiian Hall: outrigger canoes, a model *heiau*, the fabulous feather cloaks of the *alii*, war weapons, and wooden calabashes tell the story. Take the kids: a Please Touch gallery in the Hall of Discovery enhances the absorbing exhibits throughout the museum.
- **The Missionary Period: The Mission Houses Museum and Kawaiahao Church.** The day-to-day toils and triumphs of the 19th-century New England missionaries and their historic encounter with the Polynesians, one that would change the shape of Hawaii forever, is deftly chronicled at the Mission Houses Museum by descendants of the missionary families. This is a fascinating look at a key aspect of Hawaiian history. There are guided tours, exhibits, living-history programs, and more. Michener did much of his research for his novel here.

  Just across from the Mission Houses Museum is the Kawaiahao Church, built by the original missionaries. Since its dedication in 1842, the "Westminster Abbey of Hawaii" has been the scene of pomp and ceremony, coronations and celebrations. Come on a Sunday morning at 8 or 10:30am to hear a Hawaiian-English service accompanied by beautiful Hawaiian singing.
- **The Monarchy Period: Iolani Palace.** Restored to its architectural grandeur of 1842, Iolani Palace is once again open. The American-Florentine building is the only royal palace on American soil, built by King David Kalakaua in 1842. It was here that his sister and successor, Queen Liliuokalani, was kept under house arrest after an abortive coup to restore the monarchy that had been overthrown by American sugar interests in 1893. Guided tours are available and are highly recommended. Because of rising sentiments in favor of Hawaiian sovereignty, many Islanders consider the palace reverential ground.
- **The Age of the Immigrant: Hawaii's Plantation Village.** Without the thousands of immigrant laborers—Chinese, Japanese, Portuguese, Filipino, Puerto Rican, Okinawan, and Korean—who came to work the great sugar plantations in the second half of the 19th century, Hawaii's economy could not have thrived. Their descendants mingled with and married the native Hawaiians and the *haoles* (Caucasians) to create the multicultural society that is Hawaii today. Their poignant story is told in this living museum in Waipahu (not far from Pearl Harbor).
- **The Japanese Contribution: The Japanese Tea Ceremony at the Urasenke Foundation.** The *nisei*, the Japanese American descendants of the 19th-century sugar plantation workers, are now perhaps the most powerful ethnic group in the islands, in both politics and the professions. Modern Japanese investors and Japanese visitors, of course, play a significant part in the economy. How appropriate, then, that the first authentic tea house outside of Japan is right here in Honolulu. Visitors can attend twice-weekly demonstrations of the Japanese tea ceremony here. The Urasenke Foundation-of Japan is a non-profit group whose goal is "to find peacefulness through a bowl of tea."

15 The Best Shopping

Oahu abounds with wonderful, uniquely Hawaiian things to bring home—so you'll always have at hand your own little bit of Oahu.

- **Arts and Crafts: Nohea Gallery,** at Ward Warehouse. Showing the work of more than 450 island artists and craftspeople, Nohea offers just about the widest and best selection in the Islands. You'll find handcrafted jewelry, paintings, koa boxes, chests and furniture, basketry, feather work, quilts, pottery, glass and sculpture, and much more here.
- **Hawaiian and Polynesian Arts and Crafts: The Little Hawaiian Craft Shop and Wood Gallery,** at the Royal Hawaiian Shopping Center. Almost everything in this engaging shop is handmade in Hawaii by craftspeople using natural island materials and working in both traditional and contemporary styles. You'll find authentic kukui-nut leis, feather hatbands, sandalwood beads, Niihau shell necklaces, Hawaiian quilting pillows and patterns, and much more. The Wood Gallery specializes in hand-carved replicas of Hawaiian artifacts, as well as collector's items from throughout the South Pacific.
- **Antiques: Claire de Lune,** at Ward Warehouse. Nostalgia buffs seek out Claire de Lune, where they snap up everything from rattan furniture to outrigger canoe models, framed prints, old sheet music and books, antique aloha shirts, dishes, boxes, candlesticks, and much more vintage Hawaiiana.
- **Vintage Aloha Shirts: Bailey's Antique Clothes & Aloha Shirts,** 517 Kapahulu Ave. Vintage rayon shirts ("silkies") from the 1930s, 40s, and early 50s have become hot collectors items; they can command prices from $100 to $1,000, and Bailey's has more of them than anybody else. They're snatched up quickly by folks like Robin Williams, Tom Selleck, and Steven Spielberg, to drop just a few names. Bailey's also has plenty of shirts for those who only want to spend $20 or less. Whether you choose to buy or not, it's great fun browsing among literally thousands of shirts, as well as other collectibles, including art deco and retro jewelry.
- **Designer Muumuus: Mamo Howell,** at Ward Warehouse. The most beautiful muumuus in Hawaii are made by Mamo Howell, a Christian Dior model who takes the inspiration for her stunning garments from Hawaiian quilt motifs. Her elegant creations (which can run up to $200) are worn by the best-dressed women in Honolulu. (A tip for bargain-hunters: Mamo's muumuus sometimes turn up, barely used, at **The Ultimate You,** Hawaii's best consignment shop, for as little as $25).
- **Hawaiian Quilts: Kwilt's 'n Koa,** in Kamuki. This charming shop features quilt patterns, already made quilts, and quilts on commission, as well as demonstrations and lessons. In Kailua, **Elizabeth's Fancy** offers superb quilts as well as many quilt-design items—jewelry, ready-made pillows, wall-hangings, kits, and more—all created by Elizabeth, a nationally known quilt designer whose work is seen in shops throughout the Islands. This is the source.
- **Most Imaginative One-Stop Shopping: Aloha Tower Marketplace.** Visit the new Aloha Tower Marketplace on the Honolulu waterfront. Shops and kiosks offer lots of tasteful items; there's not a bit of "tourist junk" in the lot.

16 The Best of Oahu After Dark

With one notable exception—The Brothers Cazimero, below—almost all of the nightlife activity takes place in Waikiki; even residents who swear they never go near the "gilded ghetto" come to Waikiki once in a while to see a show or a singer or to catch a great jazz musician. Venues change frequently, but you can almost surely count on the following:

- **The Brothers Cazimero,** at the Bishop Museum. These beloved champions of authentic Hawaiian music and dance are tops on just about everybody's list. After many years as headliners at the Royal Hawaiian Hotel, the Brothers made the move to the Bishop Museum's Hawaiian Hall last year—and they're better than ever in these very Hawaiian surroundings.
- **Frank DeLima,** at the Polynesian Palace Showroom. A huge favorite with the local people, DeLima is a singing comedian whose outrageous parodies on every ethnic group in the Islands only endear him to everyone more; he's a man with a heart as big as his generous girth.
- **Don Ho,** at the Waikiki Beachcomber Hotel. Yes, Don is still around, still professing he hates to sing "Tiny Bubbles" before he does, and still beloved by myriads of mostly silver-haired fans.
- **Maharaja,** at the Waikiki Trade Center. The most lavish disco club in town, Maharaja is known for an incredible sound-and-light system, an international crowd, and an opulent mood.
- **Sheraton's Spectacular Polynesian Revue,** at the Princess Kailuani Hotel. You've got to see at least one of these shows while you're in Hawaii; this is one of the best. The sensational Tahitian shimmy, the gentle Maori slap dances, the heart-stopping Samoan fire dance, and the languid Hawaiian hulas are performed by top artists.

17 The Best-Kept Secrets of Oahu

Not many tourists know about these off-the-beaten-path adventures, but they're some of the best of what Oahu has to offer.

- **Ho'omaluhia Regional Park,** in Kaneohe. This is a perfect retreat for nature lovers; it's got waterfalls and mountains, wild flowers and trees, a beautifully planted garden, and a manmade lake. It's spectacular for a moonlight walk. Free, two-hour, two-mile long guided nature walks are held every weekend.
- **Kaneaki Heiau,** in Makaka Valley. Because it's tucked away deep in a secluded valley and an hour's drive from Waikiki, and because it's on private land and open only for limited hours, few visitors make it out here. That's a pity: It's the best-restored heiau on Oahu, a temple dating back to the 15th century where human sacrifice was practiced to appease the angry gods of war.
- **Ulupo Heiau,** in Kailua. Few people know about this one—even those who've lived in Kailua for many years. What appears at first glance to be just piled rocks are actually the ruins of an ancient temple, believed to have been built by the Menehunes (a race of "little folk" who pre-dated the Polynesians) and imbued with a magical, mystical power for those who can tune in.
- **Old-time Train Rides.** Out in Ewa Beach, railroad buffs can take a 13-mile round-trip ride on a restored train of the old Oahu Railway and Land Company. The private parlor car once carried such luminaries as Queen Liliuokalani, Prince Kuhio, and President William Howard Taft.
- **Hart, Tagami & Powell Gallery and Gardens.** This is a rare opportunity to enter a private world of beauty that art lovers shouldn't miss. You can make an appointment to visit this combination art gallery and botanical gardens, the home of two of Hawaii's leading painters, Hiroshi Tagami and Michael Powell.

Introducing Oahu, the Gathering Place

2

Allow me to introduce you to one of the world's most extraordinary islands—Oahu. Introductions may be necessary because, while everyone has heard of Waikiki Beach, and most people know Honolulu, the capital city of the 50th American state, the rest of the island may be a blur. And that's a pity, because Oahu is one of the most vibrant, diverse, and—with two volcanic mountain ranges and a shoreline edged with emerald waters and ringed with one white sandy beach after another—beautiful places on earth. The visitor who stays on Oahu only to change planes at Honolulu International Airport to head for a neighboring island (or points beyond) is missing something. The other Hawaiian Islands are wonderful, each in their own way, but Oahu has it all.

Oahu is unusual in that it is at once very different from the rest of the United States, and at the same time, very much a part of it. You almost have the feeling of being in a foreign land, but everybody speaks your language. The faces—they're different. The unique comingling in Hawaii of the original Polynesian settlers with immigrants from China, Japan, Korea, Europe, the Mainland, and elsewhere has produced a melting pot like no other in the world. Not only are the faces of Oahu different, so is the air—a perfumed bouquet of tropical blossoms and ocean breezes. The pace is slower, for sure; there's a musical lilt to the way people speak, a general slowing down of tone and the rhythms of life. Of course, there are plenty of go-getter businesspeople in Honolulu, but on Aloha Fridays even round-the-clock lawyers and CEO types relax in Aloha shirts and flowing muumuus.

You'll find everything you want to see and do in Oahu. You can relive Hawaii's pre-industrial past at ancient Hawaiian temples or in museums that bring alive the days of the 19th-century missionaries. You can honor Pacific war heroes at the USS *Arizona* Memorial or at an ancient "Hill of Sacrifice" now known as Punchbowl Memorial Cemetery. You can "travel" to far-flung islands at the Polynesian Cultural Center. You can partake in the ancient Japanese tea ceremony at a serene tea house right in the heart of busy Waikiki. You can sample the foods that Hawaii's various ethnic groups brought to their new island home—poi and kim chee, saimin and malasadas, dim sum and hamburgers—and try the astonishing hybrid cuisine created by Hawaii's wunderkind chefs. You can shop till you drop for island art and crafts, bargain at bazaars, scour flea markets for finds. You can watch the best Polynesian shows, listen to first-class jazz, learn to hula, dance the night away at world-class discos, or enjoy moonlit strolls along the beach.

Of course, if you're into the great outdoors, there's plenty to keep you happy on Oahu. That's why you came here, right? For the bright blue skies, the turquoise waters, the white sands? You can hike gorgeous nature trails or ride horseback through the hills, snorkel or scuba or sky dive, surf big waves or small, learn to windsurf or parasail or Snuba. And then you can do what most people like to do best in Oahu—simply lie on an island beach beneath swaying palms and dream. Feel that sweet Polynesian paralysis taking over. You may be tempted to tear up your return ticket or go back home and make plans to move here permanently— it happens all the time.

1 A Look at Hawaii's Past

The very earliest settlers to the Hawaiian islands arrived from various parts of Polynesia, probably Tahiti and Bora Bora, about A.D. 750. They crossed thousands of miles of oceans in pairs of large double-hulled canoes connected by long bamboo poles that supported a tiny hut between the hulls. They brought with them their animals and plants, introducing such foods as the sweet potato into a climate that had never yet supported it.

They settled primarily on the largest islands of the archipelago—Hawaii, Kauai, Maui, Molokai, and Oahu. The islands were fragmented into little kingdoms, each ruled by its own leader and with its own *kapus* (taboos) and customs. Power belonged to the strongest, and the bloody overthrow of leaders was quite common. But life was generally stable and probably even comfortable. None of the settlers ever tried to return to the places from which they had come. In the warmth of the sun, these people lived relatively uncomplicated lives and kept their old ways of life. They remained undisturbed by outsiders until the 18th century.

CAPTAIN COOK VISITS   In 1778, Capt. James Cook, looking for the Northwest Passage, stumbled on the island of Kauai. The islanders, who had long believed that their great god Lono would one day return, mistook Cook and his crew for the god and a full entourage of lesser deities. At first Cook received a god's reception, but soon fighting broke out between the islanders and the sailors. When Cook returned to the islands in early 1779, he was clubbed by Islanders and drowned off the Kona shore of the island of Hawaii. But from that time on, the Sandwich Islands, as Cook had named them (in honor of the earl of Sandwich) when he claimed them for Great Britain, became part of the greater world.

By 1790, King Kamehameha the Great, operating from his home island of Hawaii, had conquered the other islands in the chain in a series of bloody forays (except Kauai and Niihau, which surrendered) and united them under his rule. Consequently, Hawaii was already one nation when the first emissaries from the Western world—merchants, fur traders, and whalers—arrived.

THE MISSIONARIES ARRIVE   In 1820, a band of New England missionaries arrived in Hawaii, determined to save the heathen Islanders from the devil. They brought industry and Christianity to the Islanders—and speeded the end of the old Hawaiian life. They smashed the idols, continued the destruction of the

The Hawaiian Islands

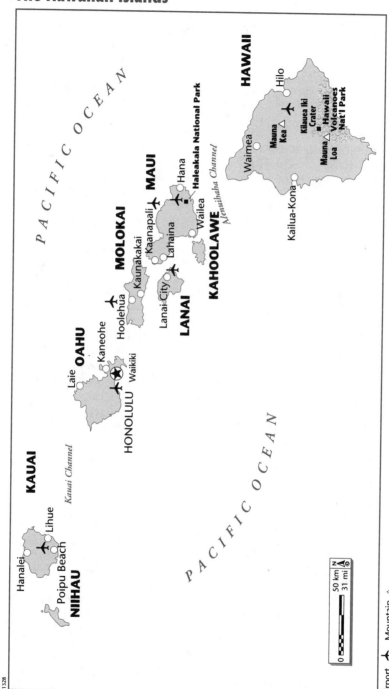

Airport ✈   Mountain △

Famous Islanders

Hiram Bingham (1789–1869)   The model for Abner Hale in James Michener's *Hawaii*, Bingham and his wife, Sybil, were among the missionaries who arrived on the brig *Thaddeus* in 1820. Popular with the Hawaiian rulers but extremely unpopular with the whaling captains, Bingham helped create the written Hawaiian alphabet, which was used to translate the Bible into Hawaiian. He was the first pastor of Kawaiahao Church.

Bernice Pauahi Bishop (1831–84)   Married to the American Charles Reed Bishop, this great-granddaughter of Kamehameha I declined the 1872 offer by Kamehameha V to succeed him on the throne. But her name lives on today in the Bishop Museum and the Bishop Estate, which administers the Kamehameha lands she inherited—almost 9% of the entire area of the Hawaiian Islands. The Kamehameha School, which educates children of Hawaiian blood, was established by the terms of her will.

Princess Kaiulani (1875–99)   The widely beloved princess, named heiress apparent to the throne on the accession of her aunt, Queen Liliuokalani, died at the age of 24. She traveled to Washington, D.C., to argue unsuccessfully for the restoration of the monarchy after it was overthrown. Her estate, Ainahau, in Waikiki, where in 1889 she entertained and enchanted Robert Louis Stevenson, is now the site of the Princess Kaiulani Hotel.

Juliette May Fraser (1887–1983)   The dean of the island painters in her time, she studied mural and fresco painting under Jean Charlot. Her works can be seen at Bilger Hall at the University of Hawaii, as well as many other places on the Island. She worked in many mediums and, at the time of her death (at age 96), was busy creating a ceramic mural for the district court building in downtown Honolulu. She was named a "living treasure" of Hawaii.

Madge Tennent (1889–1972)   An important figure in the arts in Hawaii, Madge Tennent came to the islands in the 1920s via South Africa and Paris; she broke away from the academy and its conventions to record on canvas her massive portraits of the Hawaiian people. The Tennent Art Foundation, still open, was a showplace for the work of island artists.

Duke Kahanamoku (1890–1968)   Hawaii's most famous athlete, Kahanamoku won Olympic swimming medals in 1912, 1920, 1924, and 1928. He has been honored by the Swimming Hall of Fame and the Surfing Hall of Fame. The Invitational Surfing Championships of Hawaii are named in his honor. There is a statue of him at Kuhio Beach in Waikiki.

rigid *kapus* (already weakened by the king prior to their arrival), taught the people to read and write (they created the first written version of the Hawaiian language), and westernized the Islanders. Many Islanders have never forgiven the missionaries for doing so well, as the saying goes. It was the missionaries' children who became businesspeople, bought land, thrived as planters, and started industries. Their descendants are still among the elite of Hawaii's corporate empires.

Along with the missionaries' religious teachings, the Hawaiians imbibed a bitter catechism of shame and self-loathing: They were inferior and always would

Jean Charlot (1898–1979)   Born in Paris, he worked with the great Mexican muralists Diego Rivera and David Siqueiros. His work in that medium can be seen in Hawaii, Fiji, Mexico, and the U.S. mainland. He came to Hawaii in 1946, published plays in both English and Hawaiian, and taught at the University of Hawaii until 1967, where the Hamilton Library houses the remarkable Jean Charlot Collection.

Rev. Abraham Akaka (b. 1917)   Since 1957 the pastor of Hawaii's oldest and most prestigious church, Kawaiahao in Honolulu, Akaka, whom the Islanders affectionately call "Kahu," delivered the keynote address at the Statehood Service of Dedication, linking the spirit of aloha with the spirit of Christianity in a sermon that has since become a classic in the writings of Hawaii.

Daniel K. Inouye (b. 1924)   Hawaii's senior senator in the U.S. Congress, Daniel Inouye won national fame in 1974 as a member of the Watergate committee and again in 1987 as chairperson of the committee to investigate the Iran–Contra affair. He continues to hold major positions among Senate Democrats. Inouye has been reelected to the U.S. Senate five times. The grandson of Japanese immigrants who came to Hawaii to work on the sugar plantations, Inouye was born in Honolulu and graduated from the University of Hawaii at Manoa and the George Washington University Law School. During World War II, he was a member of the distinguished 442nd Regimental Combat Team, perhaps the most decorated unit in U.S. military history.

Wally Amos (b. 1936)   This unofficial ambassador of Hawaii is an adopted son: He has lived in the islands since 1977 and claims he'd "rather be a beggar in Hawaii than a king anywhere else." King of the designer cookie market, Uncle Amos promotes his cookies when he's not busy traveling around the country as a motivational speaker. For more than a decade, he's been national spokesperson for Literacy Volunteers of America. Amos and his wife and daughter live in Lanikai, on the island of Oahu.

Bette Midler (b. 1945)   Hawaii's gift to show business was born and raised in Hawaii (and named after Bette Davis by her mother, a movie buff). Active in local community theatre, she was chosen to play a missionary wife in the movie *Hawaii* when she was 18. She saved her movie money, moved to New York, got a job as an understudy in *Fiddler on the Roof,* appeared on "The Tonight Show," started making records—and the rest is history.

be; they would always be treated as spiritual children, never as equals. That sense of inferiority left an indelible mark, one that has begun to be addressed only in the past few decades.

Even on concrete terms, the indigenous Hawaiians never adjusted to the *haole's* (white man's) world. They refused to work his plantations and died from his diseases in horrendous epidemics. Today, just a few thousand pure-blooded Hawaiians remain. The rest are a mixture of Hawaiian and other ethnic groups—mostly Japanese and Chinese—who came to work the plantations.

Asians began to arrive around the 1850s, when the whaling trade was dropping off and sugar plantations were becoming big business. Chinese came first, then Japanese and Filipinos; the Hawaiian melting pot began to simmer.

MONARCHY WEAKENS   Meanwhile, the reign of Kamehameha II had been short: He and his queen died of measles in London in 1824. Kamehameha III reigned for 30 years, during which time the islands declared their independence from Great Britain. An English-language newspaper was started and a public school opened at that time, both in the islands' capital, Lahaina, on the island of Maui. But the capital remained there only until 1845, when the king and his court moved to Honolulu. Commerce was picking up in the Honolulu harbors, and in 1850 that city was declared the capital of the 19th-century kingdom.

The Kamehameha line ended in 1872, after the death of Kamehameha V. William Lunalilo was elected successor by the legislature, but he died within a year; David Kalakaua succeeded him. Queen Emma, the widow of Kamehameha IV, appeared to have a rightful claim to the throne; to put her there, her supporters staged a number of riots. American and British marines were called in to restore calm.

THE AMERICAN AGE   In the latter part of the 19th century, industry continued to boom, with sugar the leading crop and coffee a close second. In 1875, Hawaiian sugar planters worked out a reciprocal agreement with the U.S. government by which Hawaiian sugar was assured an American market and America obtained use of Pearl Harbor as a coaling station; the American age began. The United States annexed the Republic of Hawaii in 1898. Statehood was not achieved until more than a half a century later, in 1959.

King Kalakaua, "The Merrie Monarch," was followed by Queen Liliuokalani, the last reigning monarch of the islands. When her plans for a new constitution met strong opposition, she was removed from office in the bloodless uprising of 1893 and replaced by Sanford B. Dole, a *haole* representing U.S. commercial interests. While under house arrest, Queen Liliuokalani wrote the poignant "Aloha Oe," now a song of good-bye to those leaving the islands. It was also a lament, a farewell to the days when kings and queens—and even an occasional god—walked the earth.

THE EARLY 20TH CENTURY   These years saw the booming of the pineapple industry in Hawaii. U.S. armed forces moved into the area and made Hawaii an independent army department in 1913. Although Hawaii was not directly involved in World War I, many Islanders had volunteered for the French and German armies before the United States entered the conflict. The depression of the 1930s blew through the islands with the relative calm of a trade wind, compared with the hurricane-like disaster on the mainland. Business and industry were not yet too big or well developed.

But Hawaii felt the impact of World War II more than any U.S. state. The harbors and military installations that had been developed on the islands by the United States were prime targets for the Japanese. After the devastating bombing attack by Japan on December 7, 1941, Hawaii entered a period of martial law. Liquor consumption was regulated, curfews were imposed, and blackouts were common. Fortunately, residents of Japanese ancestry in Hawaii were not forcibly resettled as their counterparts in California were. In fact, a group of *nisei* volunteers served with exceptional distinction with the U.S. army in southern Europe. The 442nd Regimental Combat Team is one of the most decorated units in U.S. military history (and one of its members, Daniel K. Inouye, has been a longtime U.S. senator from Hawaii). Participation in the war did a great deal to break down the ethnic dividing lines in Hawaii. The G.I. Bill enabled thousands of Japanese veterans to be educated. Today, people of Japanese heritage make up the largest, and one of the most powerful, ethnic groups in the state.

After World War II, transportation expanded significantly between the U.S. mainland and Hawaii. Tourism became a major industry, and existing industries grew at phenomenal rates. Years of labor disputes in the 1940s, spearheaded by the militant ILGWU, raised the standard of living of Hawaiian workers to an all-time high. Finally, in 1959, after a 30-year struggle for statehood, which began with Hawaii's first representative to congress (Prince Jonah Kuhio Kalanianaole), delegate John A. Burns (later governor of the state) helped to enact legislation that made Hawaii the 50th U.S. state. Dancing in the streets celebrated a goal long promised and arduously won.

2 Hawaii & Oahu Today

AS THE FIFTIETH STATE   Since statehood, Hawaii has been catapulted into a new era. In politics, the longtime Republican stranglehold was finally broken. With a legislature and Congressional delegations controlled by Japanese-Americans, the state is now largely Democratic (with some Republican opposition and a few mavericks, like longtime Honolulu mayor Frank Fasi, who was a Democrat one term, a Republican another) and liberal in its outlook.

With the coming of the jumbo jet in the same year that statehood was achieved, the scope of tourism changed dramatically. No longer faced with a daunting nine-hour propeller plane trip from the West Coast, visitors could fly to Hawaii in five hours or less from Los Angeles and San Francisco; they came, first by the thousands, then by the millions (today there are almost six million visitors a year). Nowhere has their impact been felt more than on Oahu. Sleepy little Waikiki, the gracious village by the sea, became home to high-rises and freeways, to unbridled construction that threatened—before it was held in check—to almost destroy the paradise that visitors had come to experience. Japanese tourists discovered Hawaii, too, and began arriving in record numbers. By the 1980s, Japanese investments in Hawaii had reached the point where the Japanese had bought up a majority of the luxury hotels and resorts in the state—including every major beachfront hotel in Waikiki—as well as numerous other properties and private homes on Oahu. Real estate, always expensive because of the large amount of land owned by private trusts that can only be long-term leased and not rented, went sky high. Prices have leveled off somewhat, but the high cost of housing still makes Oahu one of the most expensive places to live, if not to visit.

In 1976, the year of the United States' bicentennial, a new birth of sorts—a Hawaiian Renaissance—took place in Hawaii. The *Hokule'a,* a 60-foot Polynesian sailing canoe, an exact replica of the one used by Hawaii's first settlers, took off for Tahiti, using only the ancient Hawaiian navigational tools—the stars, planets, and ocean. This living-history experiment proved that early Polynesians were master mariners long before the Vikings, not to mention the later Europeans.

Oahu is the economic leader in today's Hawaii. Of the $10.9 billion brought in yearly by the state's visitor industry, Oahu receives the lion's share. Of the more than $3 billion generated by the defense industry, Oahu—25% of which is owned by the military—is the greatest beneficiary. Sugarcane and pineapple are still big business on Oahu, but they are being cut back, even the Dole Pineapple Cannery has shut down and been converted into a factory outlet center. But other industries—particularly construction, steel, cement, garment makers—are making strides. Technology has made, as the mid-Pacific outpost of U.S. space efforts and oceanographic research. Oahu's University of Hawaii and the East West Center for Cultural and Technical Interchange have raised the state's education level remarkably and are attracting scholars from all over the world. The population of the state has reached some 1.08 million, and about 80% of the Islanders call Oahu home. Thus, despite economic uncertainty here as elsewhere, Hawaii—and especially Oahu—continues its remarkable economic growth.

THE HAWAIIAN RENAISSANCE   On my last trip to Hawaii, while sitting on an interisland plane, I overheard a young woman seated behind me speaking exquisite, lyrical Hawaiian. I was entranced. When I asked her about her ability, she replied, "We're studying it in school. Isn't it beautiful?"

The movement to bring back the language and culture of Hawaii, its art forms, dances, and musical expressions—not only to those of pure Hawaiian descent (only about 11,000 people, or approximately 1%, of the population) or those of mixed-Hawaiian descent (about 250,000 people, or 19% of the population), but to all those who have chosen to live in these islands, to share its aloha, and to call themselves "Islanders"—is in full bloom. On the Big Island of Hawaii, there is a program to teach Hawaiian in the elementary schools. People of many ethnic backgrounds join hula *halaus* (schools), which demand tremendous dedication and discipline from their students. The ancient Hawaiian arts of herbalism, of *lomi-lomi* massage, and the Hawaiian problem-solving practice of *ho'o'pono'pono* have adherents all over the Islands. Traditional wedding and first-birthday luaus are celebrated throughout the Islands.

Slowly, the visitor industry is beginning to catch the wave. Several major hotels have Hawaiian educational programs for their staffs and invite visitors to share a variety of Hawaiian experiences, from learning lauhala weaving and lei-making to visiting with respected *kapunas* (elders) who "talk story" about the old days. The serious art of hula *kahiko* is coming back; these ancient dances are presented at almost every floor show or luau these days. Of course, there's still plenty of prefabricated Hawaii being offered to the visitor: Many in the hospitality industry still have the idea that all the visitor to Hawaii wants is a nondescript resort, plastic souvenirs, and young beauties doing the Tahitian shimmy. But all that's changing. The visitor who wants to, can—with just a little effort—find authentic Hawaii on Oahu today.

None of this has happened easily, or without resistance. The Hawaiian Renaissance movement is only the tip of the iceberg, part of something much bigger. The activists' movement of indigenous peoples started in the 1970s. After a century of being dispossessed of their lands, of being made to feel like second-class citizens, after being forced to give their heritage a back seat (until the 1960s, Hawaiian parents could not even give their children Hawaiian first names), after being shunted into low-paying work or no work at all, the native population had simply had enough. Their leaders began pushing for land rights for Hawaiians, and for the preservation of their ancient lands. So successful were they on the island of Maui, for example, that the movement forced the builders of the Ritz-Carlton Hotel to choose another site, once it was discovered that a sacred burial ground would have to be disturbed in order to build the resort.

The Hawaiian Sovereignty movement began to emerge, and its goals are as varied as its many factions: They range from the restoration of native lands to turning back the clock and reestablishing independence. Some proponents want financial reparations, limited sovereignty under continued statehood, or some combination of the above. The movement is becoming so powerful that, in 1993, on the 100th anniversary of the defeat of the monarchy and the toppling of Queen Liliuokalani, protesters received a long-deserved formal apology for the forcible annexation of Hawaii on behalf of the American people from President Bill Clinton. Iolani Palace, where Liliuokalani was kept under house arrest, is treated by local people with something approaching awe and reverence. And a day does not go by when her statue on the grassy mall facing the State Capitol Building is not ringed with blossoms or leis, left by those who long for the days of royalty.

Culturally, Hawaii is both a melting pot and a tossed salad. Most of the younger people are part of the melting pot; some of the older people, who still remember the segregation their parents and grandparents went through in the plantation days, tend to stick to their own kind. But in a city like Honolulu, a place where traditional Hawaii meets modern America, where island life and international society most clearly intersect, it's difficult not to be a part of the modern global community. And in a state where no single ethnic group is larger than the rest of the population and where racial lines are blurring because of generations of intermarriage, it's not easy to stay isolated. The Japanese, Chinese, Koreans, Samoans, Portuguese, Puerto Ricans, the *haoles* from Europe or the mainland— all of them answer more readily to "Islander" than anything else.

3 The Languages of the Islands

by Lisa Legarde

Lisa Legarde graduated from Wellesley College with a degree in English and worked as an assistant editor at Macmillan Travel before embarking on her career as a travel writer. She has authored a number of Frommer's travel guides, including *Frommer's Maui.*

With such a diverse population, it should come as no surprise that Hawaii is a multitongued state. Of course, English is the dominant language spoken here, so you won't have any trouble communicating. Occasionally you'll hear some Chinese, Japanese, Portuguese, and Spanish, but there are two other Hawaiian languages that are the key to understanding the Hawaiian spirit and culture.

PIDGIN   In early Hawaii, when migrant plantation workers came to the islands from all over the world, all speaking different languages, communication was difficult. Over time they all learned to communicate with each other in a language now known as pidgin. Pidgin is a true reflection of Hawaii's ethnic mix and it is quite literally a combination of several different languages. Its base is Hawaiian, but it also has English, Japanese, Filipino, Chinese, and Samoan elements. The Portuguese had their own influence on pidgin—not in terms of vocabulary but intonation and musicality.

Some people consider pidgin low-class, nonsensical, and illiterate, and many have even tried to wipe it out, but to no avail. *Brah* (brother), *cockaroach* (steal), *geev um* (sock it to them), *hele on* ("right on" or "hip"), *lesgo* (let's go), and *tita* (short for sister, but used only with friendly, earthy types) are just a few of the words you might pick up during your trip. Today, pidgin is such a part of daily Hawaiian life that the Hawaiian House of Representatives has declared it one of Hawaii's official languages. If you'd like to learn more, try reading the very funny *Pidgin to Da Max* and *Fax to Da Max* (Bess Press, Honolulu), both of which are humorous "studies" of the language.

HAWAIIAN   The Hawaiian language has its roots in the languages of the Polynesians; however, the Hawaiian spoken today is probably very different from the Hawaiian of old. Over the years, as the oral tradition was changed to a written one, translations and transcriptions inadvertently changed the spellings and meanings of certain words and phrases. For a long while, after the introduction of English and pidgin, Hawaiian was a dying language. Fortunately, today it is experiencing a rebirth through courses of study and the Hawaiian people's general interest in their roots.

Two of the most commonly used Hawaiian words are *aloha* (hello or goodbye; an expression of love) and *mahalo* (thank you). A short list of words and phrases follows. If you're interested in learning more, virtually every bookstore stocks a Hawaiian dictionary or two. A good pocket version is *Instant Hawaiian*, which is available throughout the Islands.

AN EASY-REFERENCE HAWAIIAN GLOSSARY

There are just 12 letters in the Hawaiian alphabet: five vowels—*a, e, i, o, u*—and seven consonants—*h, k, l, m, n, p, w*. Every syllable ends in a vowel, every vowel is pronounced, and the accent is almost always on the next-to-the-last syllable, as it is in Spanish. Consonants receive their English sounds, but vowels get the Latin pronunciation: *a* as in farm, *e* as in they, *i* as in machine, *o* as in cold, and *u* as in tutor. Note, also, that when *w* comes before the final vowel in a word, it is given the "v" sound, as in Hawaii. Purists say Ha-VYE-ee for Hawaii, but most people call it Ha-WYE-ee.

The glossary will give you an idea of what the Hawaiian language sounds like. No one, of course, expects you to go around spouting phrases like "Holo ehia keia?" to ask what time it is, but a familiarity with the most important words is what distinguishes the kamaainas from the malihinis.

Words

English	Hawaiian	Pronunciation
Rough lava	**Aa**	**AH-ah**
Eat	**Ai**	**EYE**
Friends as in "Aloha, aikane"	**Aikane**	**eye-KAH-nay**
Smart	**Akamai**	**ah-kah-MY**
Road, as in Ala Moana (Ocean Road)	**Ala**	**AL-lah**
Noblemen, the old royalty of Hawaii	**Alii**	**ah-LEE-ee**
Welcome, farewell, love	**Aloha**	**ah-LOW-hah**
No	**Aole**	**Ah-OH-lay**
Alas! woe!	**Auwe**	**OW-way**

English	Hawaiian	Pronunciation
In the direction of Ewa, a town on Oahu ("Drive Ewa 5 blocks.")	Ewa	EH-vah
The pandanus tree, the leaves of which are used for weaving	Hala	HAH-lah
Pineapple	Halakahiki	hah-lah-kah-HEE-kee
School (as in hula halau)	Halau	HAH-lau
House	Hale	HAH-lay
To work	Hana	HAH-nah
Caucasian, white	Haole	HOW-lay
White man	Haolekane	how-lay-KAY-nay
White woman	Haolewahine	how-lay-wah-HEE-nay
A small part, a half	Hapa	HAH-pah
Pregnant (originally "to carry")	Hapai	hah-PIE
Happiness	Hauoli	how-OH-lee
Ancient temple	Heiau	hey-EE-au
To sleep	Hiamoe	hee-ah-MOW-ay
To go, to walk	Hele	HEY-lay
Ashamed	Hilahila	hee-lah-HEE-lah
To run	Holo	HO-low
To have fun, to relax	Holoholo	ho-low-HO-low
Formal dress with train	Holoku	ho-low-KOO
A cross between a holoku and a muumuu (long and without a train)	Holomuu	ho-low-MOO
To kiss, as in "Honikaua wikiwiki!" (Kiss me quick!)	Honi	HO-nee
To flatter	Hoomalimali	ho-oh-mah-lee-MAH-lee
Angry	Huhu	HOO-hoo
A club, an assembly	Hui	HOO-ee
A fishing festival	Hukilau	hoo-KEE-lau
A dance, to dance	Hula	HOO-lah
Underground oven lined with hot rocks, used for cooking the luau pig	Imu	EE-moo
Sweetheart	Ipo	EE-po
The	Ka	KAH
Ancient (as in hula kahiko)	Kahiko	kah-HEE-ko
Sea	Kai	KYE
Money	Kala	KAH-lah
To bake underground	Kalua	kah-loo-AH
Old-timer	Kamaaina	kah-mah-EYE-nah

English	Hawaiian	Pronunciation
Man	**Kane**	KAH-nay
Tapa, a bark cloth	**Kapa**	KAH-pah
Crooked	**Kapakahi**	kah-pah-KAH-hee
Forbidden, keep out	**Kapu**	kah-POO
Food	**Kaukau**	kow-KOW
Child	**Keiki**	kay-KEE
Help, cooperation	**Kokua**	ko-KOO-ah
South	**Kona**	KO-nah
Sun, light, day	**La**	LAH
Porch	**Lanai**	lah-NYE
Heaven, sky	**Lani**	lah-NEE
Leaf of the hala or pandanus tree	**Lauhala**	lau-HAH-lah
Garland	**Lei**	LAY
Stupid	**Lolo**	low-LOW
Massage	**Lomilomi**	low-mee-LOW-mee
Feast	**Luau**	LOO-au
Thank you	**Mahalo**	mah-HAH-low
Good, fine	**Ma'i ka'i**	mah-ee-KAH-ee
Toward the sea	**Makai**	mah-KEY
Stranger, newcomer	**Malihini**	mah-lee-HEE-nee
Free	**Manawahi**	mah-nah-WAH-hee
Heavenly, or heavenly powers	**Mana**	MAH-nah
Toward the mountains	**Mauka**	MAU-kah
Song, chant	**Mele**	MAY-lay
A mysterious race who inhabited the islands before the Polynesians (mythology claims they were pygmies)	**Menehune**	may-nay-HOO-nay
Loose dress (Hawaiian version of missionaries "Mother Hubbards")	**Muumuu**	moo-oo-MOO-oo
Lovely	**Nani**	NAN-nee
Coconut	**Niu**	nee-OO
Big, as in "mahalo nui" ("big thanks")	**Nui**	NOO-ee
Sweet taste, delicious	**Ono**	OH-no
Belly	**Opu**	OH-poo
Stubborn	**Paakiki**	pah-ah-KEE-kee
Precipice	**Pali**	PAH-lee
Hawaiian cowboy	**Paniolo**	pah-nee-OH-low
Finished	**Pau**	POW
Trouble	**Pilikia**	pee-lee-KEE-ah
Crushed taro root	**Poi**	POY
Hole	**Puka**	POO-kah

English	Hawaiian	Pronunciation
Couch	**Punee**	poo-NAY-ay
Hors d'oeuvre	**Pupu**	POO-poo
Crazy	**Pupule**	poo-POO-lay
Rain	**Ua**	OO-ah
Speech, mouth	**Waha**	wah-HAH
Female, woman, girl	**Wahine**	wah-HEE-nay
Fresh water	**Wai**	WHY
To hurry	**Wikiwiki**	wee-kee-wee-kee

Phrases

English	Hawaiian	Pronunciation
Be careful	**Malama pono**	mah-LAH-mah PO-no
Bottoms up	**Okole maluna**	oh-KO-lay mah-LOO-nah
Come and eat	**Hele mai ai**	HEY-lay MY-EYE
Come here	**Hele mai**	HEY-lay MY
Come in and sit down	**Komo mai e noho iho**	ko-MO my ay NO-ho EE-ho
For love	**No ke aloha**	no kay ah-LOW-hah
Go away	**Hele aku oe**	HEY-lay AH-koo OH-ay
Good evening	**Aloha ahiahi**	ah-LOW-hah AH-hee-AH-hee
Good morning	**Aloha kakahiaka**	ah-LOW-hah kah-kah-hee-AH-kah
Greatest love to you	**Aloha nui oe**	ah-LOW-hah NOO-ee OH-ay
Happy Birthday	**Hauoli la hanau**	hah-OO-oh-lee-lah hah-NAH-oo
Happy New Year	**Hauoli Makahiki Hou**	hah-OO-oh-lee man-kah-HEE-kee HO-oo
Here's to your happiness	**Hauoli Maoli oe**	hah-OO-oh-lee mah-OH-lee OH-ay
How are you?	**Pehea oe?**	pay-HAY-ah OH-ay
I am fine	**Ma'i ka'i**	mah-EE-kah-EE
I am sorry	**Ua kaumaha au**	OO-ah cow-mah-HAH OW
I have enough	**Ua lawa au**	OO-ah LAH-wah OW
I love you	**Aloha wauia oe**	ah-LOW-hah vow-EE-ah OH-ay
It isn't so	**Aole pela**	ah-OH-lay PAY-lah
Let's go	**E hele kaua**	au-HEY-lay COW-ah
Many thanks	**Mahalo nui loa**	mah-HAH-low NOO-ee LOW-ah
Merry Christmas	**Mele Kalikimaka**	may-LAY kah-lee-kee-MAH-kah
Much love	**Aloha nui loa**	ah-LOW-hah NOO-ee-LOW-ah
No trouble	**Aole pilikia**	ah-OH-lay pee-lee-KEE-ah
What is your name?	**Owai kau inoa?**	OH-why KAH-oo ee-NO-ah

4 The Natural World: An Environmental Guide to the Island of Oahu

by Jeanette Foster

The Oahu of today—with its crescent-shaped coves sloping gently down to azure water, thundering waterfalls exploding into cavernous pools, whispering palms bordering moonlit beaches, and vibrant rainbows arching through the early morning mist—differs dramatically from the island that came into being at the dawn of time.

Born of violent volcanic eruptions from deep beneath the ocean's surface, the first Hawaiian islands emerged about 70 million years ago—more than 200 million years after the major continental land masses had been formed. Two thousand miles from the nearest continent, Mother Nature's fury began to carve beauty from barren rock. Untiring volcanoes spewed forth curtains of fire that cooled into stone. Severe tropical storms, some with hurricane-force winds, battered and blasted the cooling lava rock into a series of shapes. Ferocious earthquakes flattened, shattered, and reshaped the islands into precipitous valleys, jagged cliffs, and recumbent flat lands. Monstrous surf and gigantic tidal waves rearranged and polished the lands above and below the reaches of the tide.

A geological youngster, Oahu itself was born only 3 to 5 million years ago, when the Waianae volcano spewed lava above the ocean's surface. It continued to erupt until 2.5 million years ago; after the volcano was done, erosion and the whims of Mother Nature worked at it until only a crescent-shaped piece on its eastern rim, now known as the Waianae Range, remained. Nearby, between 1 and 3 million years later, the Koolau volcano erupted. The new series of eruptions created the plateau between the two volcanoes, joining them together and forming the flat central part of the island of Oahu. Finally, about 1.1 million years ago, several cone-building eruptions began on the southeast end of the young island. The cones remaining after the eruptions (which ended around 31,000 years ago) can be seen today: Diamond Head, Koko Head, Koko Crater, and Hanauma Bay.

It took many more years to chisel the dramatic cliffs of the west and east ends of the island, to form the majestic peak of Mt. Kaala, to create the deeply cut waterfalls of the north side of the island, to form the reefs of Hanauma Bay, and to shape the coral sand beaches that ring Oahu. The result is an island like no other on the planet—a tropical dream rich in unique flora and fauna, surrounded by a vibrant underwater world, covered with a landscape that will haunt your memory forever.

THE LANDSCAPE

Oahu, the island where the major metropolis of Honolulu is located, is the third largest island in the Hawaiian archipelago (after the Big Island and Maui). It's also the most urban, with a resident population of nearly 900,000; in fact, nearly half of the population of the entire state of Hawaii resides in just one-quarter of Oahu, in Honolulu and Waikiki. Pearl Harbor, with its naturally deep waters, is the key to Oahu's dominant position in the state. Ancient Hawaiians using outrigger canoes could maneuver easily in fairly shallow waters, but European ships, with deep keels, needed a deep-draft harbor; Pearl Harbor was perfect. The harbor has three deep lochs, which are actually river valleys gouged out during the ice age when the sea level was lower.

The island, which is 40 miles long by 26 miles wide, is ringed by more than 130 sandy beaches and defined by two mountain ranges: the Waianae Ridge (Mt. Kaala, at 4,050 feet, is the highest point on the island) in the west and the jagged Koolaus in the east, which form a backdrop for the city of Honolulu. These two ranges divide the island into three different environments. The Koolaus, with their spectacular peaks, fluted columns, lone spires, and steep verdant valleys, keep the naturally rainy windward side of the island lush and beautiful with tropical vegetation and flowing waterfalls. Mist frequently forms around the peaks like an ethereal lei, rainbows pour from the sky, and continuous but gentle rain blesses the land. On the other side of the island, the area between the Waianae Range and the ocean (known as the leeward side) is drier; it's an arid landscape with little rainfall and sparse vegetation. Powdery sand beaches, one after another, line the shoreline. Perpetually sunny days and big, thundering surf mark the Waianae coastline.

In between the two mountain ranges lies the central valley, moderate in temperature and vibrant with tropical plants and verdant agricultural fields. As farming centers and military bases (which occupied this area for decades) begin to diminish, housing tracts are slowly moving in. Red dirt and dust have previously kept this area from becoming highly populated, but as the amount of available land on Oahu shrinks and real estate prices continue their astronomic climb, Oahu's central plain is becoming an increasingly attractive suburban alternative.

Oahu is not only surrounded by water; it permeates the landscape. Natural lakes and human-made reservoirs supply water not just for living purposes but also recreational opportunities, especially for fishing enthusiasts. Streams abound on the island, and many have waterfalls, from Sacred Falls' spectacular cascades to the gentle, meandering Nuuanu Stream, which feeds into the "Jackass Ginger" swimming hole.

Hawaii's most well-known area, Waikiki, which lies along the western end of the island's southern coast, hasn't always been home to the soft sand and swaying palms that are its trademark. In fact, its name, meaning "spouting water," came from the gushing springwaters that kept the area a perpetual swamp. Until the 1920s, Waikiki was populated by noisy ducks, enormous toads, and other water creatures that inhabited the area's fishponds, damp taro patches, and water-logged rice paddies. But in 1922, the swamps were drained to make way for the Waikiki reclamation project. Sand was imported to create the "Waikiki Beach" we see today. Anchoring one end of Waikiki Beach is Oahu's world-famous symbol, Diamond Head. The Hawaiians called this crater *lae'ahi,* which means brow (*lea*) of the *ahi* fish. Some years later, map makers shortened this name to *Leahi.* Today, we know the crater as Diamond Head because some British sailors in 1825, who had perhaps overindulged in liquid libations during shore leave, mistakenly thought that the glittering—but worthless—calcite crystals they found in the crater were diamonds. Despite their error, the name stuck.

THE FLORA OF OAHU

The Oahu of today radiates with sweet-smelling flowers, lush vegetation, and exotic plant life. Some of the more memorable plants and flowers on the islands include:

African Tulip Trees   Even at a long distance, you can see the flaming red flowers on these large trees, which can grow over 50 feet tall. Children love the trees because the buds hold water—they use them as water pistols.

Angel's Trumpet   This is a small tree that can grow up to 20 feet tall, with an abundance of large (up to 10 inches in diameter) pendants—white or pink flowers that resemble, well, trumpets. The Hawaiians call this *nana-honua,* which means "earth gazing." The flowers, which bloom continually from early spring to late fall, have a musky scent. However, beware: All parts of the plant are poisonous and all parts contain a strong narcotic.

Anthurium   One of Hawaii's most popular cut flowers, anthuriums originally came from the tropical Americas and the Caribbean islands. There are more than 550 species, but the most popular are the heart-shaped flowers (red, orange, pink, white, even purple) with a tail-like spath (green, orange, pink, red, white, purple, and in combinations thereof). Look for the heart-shaped green leaves in shaded areas. These exotic plants have no scent, but will last several weeks as cut flowers.

Birds of Paradise   This native of Africa has become something of a trademark of Hawaii. They're easily recognizable by the orange and blue flowers nestled in gray-green bracts, looking somewhat like birds in flight.

Bougainvillea   Originally from Brazil and named for the French navigator Louis A. de Bougainville, these colorful, tissue-thin bracts (ranging in color from majestic purple to fiery orange) hide tiny white flowers.

Bromeliads   The pineapple plant is the best known bromeliad; native to tropical South America and the Caribbean islands, there are more than 1,400 species. "Bromes," as they are affectionately called, are generally spiky plants ranging in size from a few inches to several feet in diameter. They're popular not only for their unusual foliage but also for their strange and wonderful flowers. The flowers range from colorful spikes to delicate blossoms resembling orchids. Bromeliads are widely used in landscaping and as interior decoration, particularly in resort areas like Waikiki.

FRUIT TREES

Banana   Edible bananas are among oldest of the world's food crops. By the time Europeans arrived in the islands, the Hawaiians had more than 40 different types of bananas planted. Most banana plants have long green leaves hanging from the tree, with the flower giving way to fruit in clusters.

Breadfruit   A large tree—over 60-feet tall—with broad, sculpted, dark-green leaves. The fruit is round and about 6 inches or more in diameter. The ripe fruit, a staple in the Hawaiian diet, is whitish-yellow.

Lychee   This evergreen tree, which can grow to well over 30 feet across, originated in China. Small flowers grow into panicles about a foot long in June and July. The round, red-skinned fruit appears shortly afterward.

Mango   From the Indo-Malaysian area comes the delicious mango, a fruit with peach-like flesh. Mango season usually begins in the spring and lasts through the summer, depending on the variety. The trees can grow to more than 100 feet tall. The tiny reddish-flowers give way to a green fruit that turns red-yellow when ripe. Some people enjoy unripe mangoes, sliced thin or in chutney as a traditional Indian preparation. The mango sap can cause a skin rash on some.

Papaya   Yellow pear-shaped fruit (when ripe) found at the base of the large, scalloped-shaped leaves on a pedestal-like, nonbranched tree. Papayas ripen year-round.

Gingers   Some of Hawaii's most fragrant flowers are white and yellow gingers (which the Hawaiians call 'awapuhi-ke'oke'o and 'awapuhi-melemele). Usually found in clumps, growing four to seven feet tall, in the areas blessed by rain, these sweet-smelling, 3-inch wide flowers are composed of three dainty petal-like stamen and three long, thin petals. White and yellow gingers are so prolific that many people assume they are native to Hawaii; actually, they were introduced in the 19th century from the Indo-Malaysia area. Look for yellow and white ginger from late spring to fall. If you see them on the side of the road, stop and pick a few blossoms—your car will be filled with a divine fragrance for the rest of the day. The only downside of white and yellow ginger is that, once picked, they'll live only briefly.

Other members of the ginger family frequently seen on Oahu (there are some 700 species) include red ginger, shell ginger, and torch ginger. Red ginger consists of tall, green stalks with foot-long red "flower heads." The red "petals" are actually bracts; inch-long white flowers are protected by the bracts and can be seen if you look down into the red head. Red ginger ('awapuhi-'ula'ula in Hawaiian), which unfortunately does not share the heavenly smell of white ginger, will last a week or longer when cut. Look for red ginger from spring through late fall. Cool, wet mountain forests are the ideal condition for shell ginger; Hawaiians called them 'awapuhi-luheluhe, which means "drooping" ginger. Natives of India and Burma, these plants, with their pearly white, clam shell–like blossoms, bloom from spring to fall.

Perhaps the most exotic gingers are the red or pink torch gingers. Cultivated in Malaysia as seasoning (the young flower shoots are used in curries), torch ginger rises directly out of the ground; the flower stalks (which are about five to eight inches in length) resemble the fire of a lighted torch. One of the few gingers that can bloom year-round, the Hawaiians call this plant 'awapuhi-ko'oko'o, or "walking-stick" ginger.

Heliconias   Some 80 species of the colorful heliconia family came to Hawaii from the Caribbean and Central and South America. The brightly colored bract (yellow, red, green, orange, etc.) overlap and appear to unfold like origami birds as they climb up (or down, as heliconias have both erect and pendant bracts). The most obvious heliconia to spot is the lobster claw, which resembles a string of boiled crustacean pincers—the brilliant crimson bracts alternate on the stem. Another prolific heliconia is the parrot's beak. Growing to about hip height, the parrot's beak is composed of bright-orange flower bracts with black tips, not unlike the beak of a parrot. Look for parrot's beak in the spring and summer, when they bloom in profusion.

Hibiscus   One variety of this year-round blossom is the official state flower: the yellow hibiscus. The four- to six-inch hibiscus flowers come in a range of colors, from lily-white to lipstick-red. The flowers resemble crepe paper, with stamens and pistils protruding spire-like from the center. Hibiscus hedges can grow up to 15 feet tall. Once plucked, the flowers wither quickly.

Jacaranda   Beginning about March and sometimes lasting until early May, these huge, lacy-leaved trees metamorphose into large clusters of spectacular lavender-blue sprays. The bell-shaped flowers drop quickly, leaving a majestic purple carpet beneath the tree.

Night-Blooming Cereus   Look along rock walls for this spectacular night-blooming cactus flower. Originally from Central America, this vine-like member of the cactus family has green scalloped edges and produces foot-long white flowers that open as darkness falls and wither as the sun rises. The plant also bears a red fruit that is edible.

Orchids   In many minds, nothing says Hawaii more than orchids. The orchid family is the largest in the entire plant kingdom; orchids are found in most parts of the world. There are some species that are native to Hawaii, but they're inconspicuous in most places, so most people overlook them. The most widely-grown orchid—and the major source of flowers for leis and garnish for tropical libations—are the vanda orchids. The vandas used in Hawaii's commercial flower industry are generally lavender or white, but they grow in a rainbow of colors, shapes, and sizes. The orchids used for corsages are the large, delicate cattleya; the ones used in floral arrangements—you'll probably see them in your hotel lobby—are usually dendrobiums.

Plumeria   Also known as frangipani, this sweet-smelling, five-petal flower, found in clusters on trees, is the most popular choice of lei makers. The Singapore plumeria has five creamy-white petals, with a touch of yellow in the center. Another popular variety, ruba—with flowers from soft pink to flaming red—is also used in making leis. When picking plumeria, be careful of the sap from the flower, as it is poisonous and can stain clothes.

Proteas   Originally from South Africa, this unusual plant comes in more than 40 different varieties. Proteas are shrubs that bloom into a range of flower types. Different species of proteas range from those resembling pincushions to a species that looks just like a bouquet of feathers. Proteas are long-lasting cut flowers; once dried, they will last will last for years.

Taro   Around pools, streams, and in neatly planted fields, you'll see the green heart-shaped leaves of taro. Taro was a staple to ancient Hawaiians, who pounded the root into poi. Originally from Sri Lanka, taro is not only a food crop, but also grown as an ornamental.

Other Trees & Plants   Banyans—among the world's largest trees—have branches that grow out and away from the trunk, forming descending roots that grow down to the ground to feed and form additional trunks, making the tree very stable during tropical storms.

Monkey-pod trees are among Hawaii's most majestic trees; they grow more than 80 feet tall and 100 feet across and are often seen near older homes and in parks. The leaves of the monkey pod drop in February and March. The wood from the tree is a favorite of wood-working artisans.

Another common plant is **marijuana,** or *pakalolo*—"crazy weed" as the Hawaiians call it—which is grown (usually illegally cultivated) throughout the islands. You probably won't see it as you drive along the roads, but if you go hiking you may glimpse the feathery green leaves with tight clusters of buds. Despite years of police effort to eradicate the plant, the illegal industry continues. Don't be tempted to pick a few buds, as the purveyors of this nefarious industry don't take kindly to poaching.

THE FAUNA OF OAHU

The inspiration for the first Polynesian voyages to Hawaii may have come from the **Kolea,** or Pacific golden plover—a homely speckled bird that migrates from Siberia and Alaska every year, traveling through Hawaii and down to the

Marquesas, Tahiti, and New Zealand. Historians wonder if the Marquesans, watching the bird arrive and depart, speculated where it came from and what that place was like. When the first Marquesans arrived in Hawaii between 500 and 800 A.D., scientists say they found 67 varieties of endemic Hawaiian birds, a third of which are now believed to be extinct, including the **koloa** (the Hawaiian duck) and **nene** (the Hawaiian goose). What's even more astonishing is what they didn't find—there were no reptiles, amphibians, mosquitoes, lice, no fleas, not even a cockroach.

When the Polynesians from the Society Islands arrived in Hawaii, around 1000 A.D., they found only two endemic mammals: the **hoary bat** and the **monk seal.** The Hawaiian monk seal, a relative of warm water seals previously found in the Caribbean and Mediterranean, was nearly slaughtered into extinction for its skin and oil during the 19th century. Recently these seals have experienced a minor population explosion in some of their haunts, forcing relocation of some males from their protected homes in the inlets north of the main Hawaiian Islands. Periodically, these endangered marine mammals turn up at various beaches throughout the state. They are protected under federal law by the Marine Mammals Protection Act. If you're fortunate enough to see a monk seal, just look; don't approach too close and disturb one of Hawaii's living treasures.

The first Polynesians brought a few animals from home: dogs, pigs, and chickens (all were for eating). A stowaway on board the Polynesian sailing canoes was the rat. All four animals are still found in the wilds of Oahu today.

HAWAIIAN BIRDS   In the last 200 years, more native species of birds have become extinct in the Hawaiian Islands than anywhere else on the planet. Of the 67 native Hawaiian species, 23 are extinct, 29 are endangered, and one is threatened (*'alala,* the Hawaiian crow). Two native birds that have managed to survive are the:

Nene   Endemic to Hawaii, the nene is Hawaii's state bird. It is being brought back from the brink of extinction through captive breeding and by strenuous protection laws. A relative of the Canadian goose, the nene stands about two feet high and has a black head and yellow cheek, a buff neck with deep furrows, a grayish-brown body, and clawed feet. It gets its name from its two syllable, high nasal call "nay-nay." Although they're not found on Oahu, the approximately 500 nenes alive today are being carefully bred in captivity and are thriving on nearby islands.

Pueo   The Hawaiian short-eared owl, which grows to about 12 to 17 inches in size, can be seen at dawn and dusk on Kauai, Maui, and the Big Island. The brown-and-white bird with a black bill goes hunting for rodents at night. Pueos were highly regarded by Hawaiians; according to legend, spotting a Pueo is a good omen.

SEABIRDS   On the east coast of Oahu, from Kahuku to Makapuu Point, are numerous small islands, islets, and rocks that are nesting areas for seabirds native to the region. Once part of the island of Oahu, these small land masses, some just a few hundred yards offshore, are environmentally necessary for the survival of these birds. The seabird population has suffered since the arrival of people to the Hawaiian Islands, as coastal areas have been altered for human use. Many seabirds are ground nesters, making them easy prey for introduced animals like dogs, cats, rats, and mongooses. Introduced plants, such as sea grape and lantana, have encroached upon the nesting grounds as well.

Because of their ecological importance, the offshore islands dotting Oahu's windward coast have been made part of the Hawaii State Seabird Sanctuary. Shearwaters, noddies, and petrels are among the birds that use the protected islands for roosting and nesting, and migratory birds like ruddy turnstones, wandering tattlers, and golden plovers forage along the shore. The islands also provide protected environments for native coastal vegetation. Because the nesting grounds are fragile environments, access to the offshore islands is limited; visitors should observe all posted signs. Many seabirds build their nests under dense vegetation or in shallow, sandy burrows that cannot be seen by unwary hikers and sightseers. Human disturbance can cause birds to abandon their nests, leaving eggs and chicks exposed.

The seabirds found on these offshore islands include the:

Great Frigatebird *('Iwa)*   The Hawaiian name, *iwa,* meaning thief, refers to the frigatebirds' habit of snatching food from other birds in mid-air. Frigate birds are superb flyers and so well adapted to life in the air that they can barely walk on land. They are often seen soaring above Waimanalo Bay on the island's windward side.

Wandering Tattler *('Ulili)*   Wandering tattlers are migrants who travel annually over 2,000 miles from Alaska to Canada to Hawaii, where they spend their winters foraging for insects and fish. They're usually solitary and can be seen hunting for food along rocky shorelines and tidal flats. Their Hawaiian name, *'ulili,* mimics their unique call.

Sooty Tern *('Ewa'ewa)*   These seabirds nest in large numbers on the offshore islands of Manana and Moku Manu. They lay single, camouflaged eggs directly on the ground, and are easily disturbed by curious humans.

Ruddy Turnstones *('Akekeke)*   These winter visitors, who fly from their Arctic nesting grounds to Hawaii in August and September, can be seen probing with their bills in search of insects and tiny crustaceans along Oahu's shorelines.

Bristle-thighed Curlew *(Kioea)*   In early August, the *kioea* leave their nesting grounds in the Alaskan tundra and fly to Hawaii (as well as to other islands in the Pacific). They prefer undisturbed sandy shorelines and secluded grassy meadows.

Wedge-tailed Shearwater *('Ua'u kani)*   The most common birds found on the offshore islands, these birds get their Hawaiian name from their eerie, drawn-out call.

Red-footed Booby *('A)*   These large white birds are often seen flying low over the water, far out to sea, in search of fish and squid. Fishermen love to spot these birds because *'a* often circle and feed directly over schools of tuna or mahimahi.

Red-tailed Tropicbird *(Koa'e'ula)*   Distinguished by their white plumage and long red tail feathers, these birds nest not only on the offshore islands but also on Oahu's cliffs.

Brown Noddy *(Nolo koha)*   These common birds nest in small colonies on the open ground and raise their single offspring on a diet of small fish and crustaceans.

Bulwer's Petrel *('Ou)*   These birds spend most of their life at sea, returning to land—usually back to the island where they were born—only to mate. They're nocturnal feeders, spending nights hunting for small surface-water fish.

Other Fauna   When the Polynesians arrived in the Hawaiian islands, there was no native wild game. However, descendants of the pigs they brought with them escaped into Oahu's hills, and the goats the Europeans carried to Hawaii followed.

Oahu still has feral goats and wild pigs, which generally make a nuisance of themselves by destroying the rain forest and eating native plants. Non-native game birds (ring-neck pheasants, green pheasants, Erkel's francolins, Japanese quail, spotted doves, and zebra doves) are also found on Oahu.

The Hawaiian islands have only one tiny earthworm-like snake. Strict measures are taken to keep other snakes out of Hawaii. On the island of Guam, the brown tree snake has obliterated most of the bird population. Officials in Hawaii are well aware of this danger to Hawaii and are vigilant to prevent snakes from entering the state.

Two non-native creatures that visitors to Oahu are likely to see are:

Geckos   These harmless, soft-skinned, insect-eating lizards come equipped with suction pads on their feet that enable them to climb walls and windows, so they can reach tasty insects like mosquitoes and cockroaches. You'll see them on windows outside a lighted room at night, or hear their cheerful chirp.

Mongooses   The mongoose is a mistake. It was brought here in the 19th century to counteract the evergrowing rat problem. But rats are nocturnal creatures, sleeping during the day and wandering at night. Mongooses are day creatures. Instead of getting rid of the rat problem, the mongooses eat bird eggs, enhancing the deterioration of the native bird population in Hawaii.

SEALIFE

Oahu has an extraordinarily unique world to explore offshore, beneath the sea. Approximately 680 species of fish are known to inhabit the underwater world around the Hawaiian islands. Of those, approximately 450 species stay close to the reef and inshore areas.

Coral   The reefs surrounding Hawaii are made up of various coral and algae. The living coral grow through sunlight that feeds a specialized algae, called zooxanthellae, which in turn allows the development of the coral's calcareous skeleton. It takes thousands of years for reefs to develop. The reef attracts and supports fish and crustaceans, which use the reef for food, habitat, mating, and raising their young. Mother Nature can cause the destruction of the reef with a strong storm or large waves, but humans—through a seemingly unimportant act such as touching the coral, or allowing surface runoff of dirt, silt, or chemicals to blanket the reef and cut off the life-giving light—have proven even more destructive to the fragile reefs.

The coral most frequently seen in Hawaii are hard, rock-like formations named for their familiar shapes: antler, cauliflower, finger, plate, and razor coral. Wire coral, looks just like its name—a randomly bent wire growing straight out of the reef. Some coral appear soft, such as tube coral; it can be found in the ceilings of caves. Black coral, which resemble winter-bare trees or shrubs, are found at depths of over 100 feet.

Reef Fish   Of the approximately 450 reef fish, about 27% are native to Hawaii and found nowhere else on the planet. This may seem surprising for a string of isolated islands, 2,000 miles from the nearest land mass. But over the millions of years of gestation of the Hawaiian islands, as they were born from the erupting volcanoes, ocean currents—mainly from the Indo-Malay Pacific region—carried the larvae of thousands of marine animals and plants to Hawaii's reef. Of those, approximately 100 species not only adapted, but thrived. Some species are much bigger and more plentiful than their Pacific cousins; many developed unique characteristics. Some, like the lemon or milletseed butterfly fish, are not only particular to Hawaii but also unique within their larger, worldwide family in their specialized schooling and feeding behaviors.

Another surprising thing about Hawaii endemics is how common some of the native fish are. You can see the saddleback wrasse on virtually any snorkeling excursion or dive in Hawaiian waters. Some of the reef fish you might encounter in the waters off Oahu are:

Angel Fish   Often mistaken for butterfly fish, angel fish can be distinguished by looking for the spine, located low on the gill plate. Angel fish are very shy; several species live in colonies close to coral for protection.

Blennys   Small, elongated fish, blennys range from 2 to 10 inches long, with the majority in the 3-to-4-inch range. Blennys are so small that they can live in tide pools. Because of their size, you might have a hard time spotting one.

Butterfly Fish   Some of the most colorful of the reef fish, butterfly fish are usually seen in pairs (scientists believe they mate for life) and appear to spend most of their day feeding. There are 22 species of butterfly fish, of which three (bluestripe, lemon or milletseed, and multiband or pebbled butterfly fish) are endemic. Most butterfly fish have a dark band through the eye and a spot near the tail resembling an eye in order to confuse their predators (the moray eel loves to lunch on butterfly fish).

Eels   Moray and conger eels are the common eels seen in Hawaii. Morays are usually docile unless provoked, or if there is food or an injured fish around. Unfortunately, some morays have been fed by divers and—being intelligent creatures—associate divers with food; thus, they can become aggressive. But most morays like to keep to themselves, hidden in their hole or crevice. While morays may look menacing, conger eels look downright happy, with big lips and pectoral fins (situated so that they look like big ears) that give them a perpetually smiling face. Conger eels have crushing teeth so they can feed on crustaceans; in fact, since they're sloppy eaters, they usually live with shrimp and crabs, who feed off the crumbs they leave.

Parrot Fish   One of the largest and most colorful of the reef fish, parrot fish can grow as large as 40 inches long. Parrot fish are easy to spot—their front teeth are fused together, protruding like buck teeth and resembling a parrot's beak. These unique teeth allow the parrot fish to feed by scraping algae from rocks and coral. The rocks and coral pass through the parrot fish's system, resulting in fine sand. In fact, most of the sand found in Hawaii is parrot fish waste; one large parrot fish can produce a ton of sand a year. Hawaiian native parrot fish species include yellowbar, regal, and spectacled.

Scorpion Fish   This is a family of what scientists call "ambush predators." These fish hide under camouflaged exteriors and ambush their prey when they come along. Several sport a venomous dorsal spine. These fish don't have a gas bladder, so when they stop swimming, they sink—that's why you usually find them "resting" on ledges and on the bottom. Although they are not aggressive, an inattentive snorkeler or diver could inadvertently touch one and feel the effects of those venomous spines—so be very careful where you put your hands and feet while you're in the water.

Surgeon Fish   Sometimes called tang, the surgeon fish get their name from the scalpel-like spines located on each side of their bodies near the base of their tails.

Some surgeon fish have a rigid spine; others have the ability to fold their spine against their body until it's needed for defense purposes. Some surgeon fish, like the brightly colored yellow tang, are boldly colored. Others are adorned in more conservative shades of gray, brown, or black. The only endemic surgeon fish—and the most abundant in Hawaiian waters—is the convict tang (*manini* in Hawaiian), a pale white fish with vertical black stripes (like a convict's uniform).

Wrasses   This is a very diverse family of fish, ranging in size from 2 to 15 inches. Several wrasses are brilliantly colored and change their colors through aging and sexual dimorphism (sex changing). Wrasses have the unique ability to change gender from female (when young) to male with maturation. There are several wrasses that are endemic to Hawaii: the Hawaiian cleaner, shortnose, belted, gray (or old woman), psychadelic, pearl, flame, and the most common Hawaiian reef fish, the saddleback.

Game Fish   Fishers have a huge variety to choose from in the waters off Oahu, from pan-sized snapper to nearly one-ton marlin. Hawaii is known around the globe as *the* place for big game fish—marlin, swordfish, and tuna—but its waters are also great for catching other offshore fish (like mahimahi, rainbow runner, and wahoo), coastal fish (barracuda, scad), bottom fish (snappers, sea bass, and amberjack), and inshore fish (trevally, bonefish, and others), as well as freshwater fish (bass, catfish, trout, bluegill, and oscar).

Billfish are caught year-round. There are six different kinds of billfish found in the offshore waters around the islands: Pacific blue marlin, black marlin, sailfish, broadbill swordfish, striped marlin, and shortbill spearfish. Hawaii billfish range in size from the 20-pound shortbill spearfish and striped marlin to an 1,805-pound Pacific blue marlin, the largest marlin ever caught on rod and reel anywhere in the world. **Tuna** ranges in size from small (a pound or less) mackerel tuna used as bait (Hawaiians call them *oioi*), to 250-pound yellowfin ahi tuna. Other species of tuna found in Hawaii are bigeye, albacore, kawakawa, and skipjack.

Some of the best eating fish are also found in offshore waters: **mahimahi** (also known as dolphin fish or dorado) in the 20- to 70-pound range, **rainbow runner** (*kamanu*) from 15 to 30 pounds, and **wahoo** (*ono*) from 15 to 80 pounds. Shoreline fishers are always on the lookout for **trevally** (the state record for giant trevally is 191 pounds), **bonefish, ladyfish, threadfin, leatherfish,** and **goatfish.** Bottom fishermen pursue a range of **snappers**—red, pink, gray, and others—as well as **sea bass** (the state record is a whopping 563 pounds) and **amberjack,** which weigh up to 100 pounds.

Reservoirs on Oahu are home to Hawaii's many freshwater fish: **bass** (large, smallmouth, and peacock), **catfish** (channel and Chinese), **rainbow trout, bluegill sunfish, pungee,** and **oscar.** The state record for freshwater fish is the 43-pound, 13-ounce channel catfish caught in Oahu's Lake Wilson.

WHALES Humpbacks   The most popular visitors to Hawaii come every year in the winter, around November, and stay until the springtime (April or so) when they return to their summer home in Alaska. Humpback whales—some as big as a city bus and weighing many tons—migrate to the warm, protected Hawaiian waters in the winter to mate and calve. You can take whale-watching cruises on every island that will let you observe these magnificent leviathans close up, or you can spot their signature spouts of water from shore as they expel water in the distance. Humpbacks grow to up to 45 feet long, so when they breach (propel their entire body out of the water) or even wave a fluke, you can see it for miles.

Other whales   Humpbacks are among the biggest whales found in Hawaiian waters, but other whales—like pilot, sperm, false killer, melon-headed, pygmy killer, and beaked whales—can be seen year round. These whales usually travel in pods of 20 to 40 animals and are very social, interacting with each other on the surface.

Sharks   Yes, Virginia there are sharks in Hawaii, but more than likely you won't see a shark unless you specifically go looking for one. About 40 different species of sharks inhabit the waters surrounding Hawaii; they range from the totally harmless whale shark—at 60 feet, the world's largest fish—which has no teeth and is so docile that it frequently lets divers ride on its back, to the not-so-docile, infamous—and extremely uncommon—great white shark. The ancient Hawaiians had great respect for sharks and believed that some sharks were reincarnated relatives who had returned to assist them. The most common sharks seen in Hawaii are white-tip reef sharks, gray reef sharks (about 5 feet long), and blacktip reef sharks (about 6 feet long). Since records have been kept, starting in 1779, there have been only about 100 shark attacks in Hawaii, of which 40% have been fatal. The biggest number of attacks occurred after someone fell into the ocean from the shore or from a boat. In these cases, the sharks probably attacked after the person was dead.

General rules for avoiding sharks are: Don't swim at sunrise, sunset, or where the water is murky due to stream runoff—sharks may mistake you for one of their usual meals. And don't swim where there are bloody fish in the water (sharks become aggressive around blood).

OAHU'S ECOSYSTEM PROBLEMS

Oahu may be paradise, but even paradise has its problems. The biggest threat Oahu's natural environment faces is human intrusion—simply put, too many people want to experience paradise firsthand. From the magnificent underwater world to the breathtaking rain forest, the presence of people isn't always benign, no matter how cautious or environmentally aware they might be.

MARINE LIFE   Hawaii's beautiful and abundant marine life has attracted so many visitors that they threaten to overwhelm it. A great example of this overenthusiasm is Oahu's Hanauma Bay, a marine preserve. Thousands of people flock to this beautiful bay, which features calm, protected swimming and snorkeling areas loaded with tropical reef fish. It was such a perfect spot that too many people flocked here, forcing government officials to limit the number of people entering the bay at any one time. Commercial tour operators have been restricted entirely in an effort to balance the people-to-fish ratio.

People who fall in love with the colorful tropical fish and want to see them all the time back home are also thought to be impacting the health of Hawaii's reefs. The growth in home, office, and decor aquariums has risen dramatically in the last 20 years. As a result, more and more reef fish collectors are taking a growing number of reef fish from Hawaiian waters.

The reefs themselves have faced increasing impacts over the years. Runoff of soil and chemicals from construction, agriculture, erosion, and even heavy storms can blanket and choke a reef, which needs sunlight to survive. In addition, the intrusion of foreign elements—like breaks in sewage lines—can cause problems to Hawaii's reef. Human contact with the reef can also upset the ecosystem. Coral, the basis of the reef system, is very fragile; snorkelers and divers grabbing on to coral can break off pieces that took decades to form. Feeding fish can also upset the balance of the ecosystem (not to mention upsetting the digestive system of the fish). One glass-bottom boat operator on the Big Island reported that they fed an eel for years, considering it their "pet" eel. One day the eel decided that he wanted more than just the food being offered and bit the diver's fingers. Divers and snorkelers report that in areas where the fish are fed the fish have become more aggressive; clouds of certain reef fish—normally shy—surround divers, demanding to be fed.

FLORA   One of Hawaii's most fragile environments is the rain forest. Any intrusion—from a hiker carrying seeds in on their shoes to the rooting of wild boars—can upset the delicate balance in these complete ecosystems. In recent years, development has moved closer and closer to the rainforest.

FAUNA   The biggest impact on the fauna in Hawaii is the decimation of native birds by feral animals, which have destroyed the bird's habitats, and by mongooses that have eaten the birds' eggs and young. Government officials are vigilant about snakes because of the potential damage tree snakes can do to the remaining birdlife.

VOG   When the tradewinds stop blowing for a few days, Oahu begins to feel the effects of the volcanic haze—caused by gases released by the continuous eruption of the volcano on the flank of Kilauea, on the Big Island, and the smoke from the fires set by the lava—that has been dubbed "vog." The hazy air, which looks like smog from urban pollution, limits viewing from scenic vistas and plays havoc with photographers trying to get clear panoramic photographs. Some people claim that the vog has even caused bronchial ailments.

CULTURE   Virtually since the arrival of the first Europeans, there has been a controversy over balancing the preservation of history and indigenous cultures and lifestyles with economic development. The question of what should be preserved—and in what fashion—is continually debated in Hawaii's rapidly growing economy. Some factions argue that the continuously developing tourism economy will one day destroy the very thing that visitors come to Hawaii to see; another sector argues that Hawaii's cost of living is so high that new development and industries are needed so residents can earn a living.

5 The Arts & Crafts of the Islands

by Lisa Legarde

Art has always been integral to Hawaiian life. The art of early Hawaii often took forms that were useful in everyday life. Kapa cloth was used as bedding and clothing. Beautiful featherwork capes, cloaks, helmets, and leis were worn by the Hawaiian ali'i to indicate rank; and beautifully carved wood bowls were designed specifically to hold poi, a staple of daily Hawaiian life. Ancient Hawaiians took great pride in their work and elevated its execution to an art form. Unfortunately, some of the traditional arts and crafts of Hawaii have died out. This is due, in part, to the commercialization of the islands, but also because the natural supply of craft materials has diminished.

Today, native Hawaiian art is highly prized and every effort is being made to revitalize traditional arts and crafts. Many hotels sponsor lei-making classes and some even hold quilt-making lectures and demonstrations. There are also arts-and-crafts shows every year that celebrate local artisans.

Below you will find descriptions of a variety of traditional Hawaiian arts and crafts, that will, I hope, lead you to a greater understanding of Hawaiian culture.

KAPA (TAPA) CLOTH Before woven fabrics made their way from Europe and the U.S. mainland to Hawaii, the women of Hawaii made cloth from the bark of a variety of trees and plants. The kapa-making process was long and somewhat tedious and it was so much a part of daily life that many households reserved a separate hut in which to work. Each day, village men would go out searching for wauke, mamake, ma'aloa, or poulu plants, the branches of which they would cut and take back to their wives. The women would peel the bark from the branches (not in strips, but whole), and then set the inner bark in a stream to soak until it reached the desired softness. After the bark had soaked long enough, the women would beat it on a log *(kua)* with a round club *(hohoa)* until it was flat and paper thin. The soaking and flattening process might take up to four days. The last step was to set the kapa in the sun to dry. Mamake bark was preferred above all others because its cloth was the most durable, but rather than being soaked first, mamake was steamed in an oven with a *pala'a* (a fern that gave out a dark red dye in the cooking process). After the steaming process was finished, mamake was soaked and beaten just like the other types of bark.

Most Hawaiian women dyed their kapa using the color of a variety of different plants. The mao plant would stain the cloth green, while the hoolei gave it a yellow tint. It was also customary for women to print patterns on the cloth. Almost every design was different and as individual as the artists who created them.

So old is the art of making kapa that it is even mentioned in the mythology of the demigod Maui. It is said that his mother complained that the sun moved too quickly across the sky and her kapa didn't have enough time to dry in the afternoon. Maui, sensitive to the needs of his mother, snared the sun by lassoing his legs (all 16 of them) and threatened to hold him there forever if he didn't slow his pace through the sky. The sun, like the rest of us, enjoyed a good night's sleep, so he agreed to slow down.

Hawaiian Quilts Not so ancient as the art of kapa, but equally as beautiful, the art of quilting has been in existence in Hawaii since the mid-19th century. In fact, the first quilting bee held in the Hawaiian islands took place on April 3, 1820. The basic techniques were introduced to the women of the islands by missionary women from New England; however, the appliqués and stitch patterns you'll see on original Hawaiian quilts are authentically Hawaiian. Early quilt patterns were similar to designs found on kapa cloth, and very often women were inspired to create original designs by dreams or major events in their lives.

Usually the quilt consisted of a single-colored appliqué on a white background. The material to be used for the appliqué could be cut freehand, or with a paper pattern. Interestingly, the paper pattern was often made of kapa. Usually the appliqué material would be folded four or eight times before it was cut so the pattern would be uniform in all sections of the quilt. Most often the designs were inspired by the leaves of various trees and plants, like the fig or breadfruit trees and ferns. Outlines of pineapples, the octopus, and the sea turtle were also popular design elements.

Many of the patterns were unique to a particular artist, and most of the women knew the designs of their fellow quilters. If a women invented a particular design it would forever be associated with her. Other women were not allowed to copy her design without crediting her. However, if a pattern were not carefully guarded before a quilt was completed it could be (and was often) stolen by someone else who might try to claim it as her own.

While the patterns and design elements of the appliqué were important, so were the stitches around the appliqué, because the stitching is actually what makes a quilt a quilt. Traditional New England–style stitch patterns used parallel lines and diagonals; Hawaiian women incorporated these patterns into their early work, but later they began inventing their own freehand stitch patterns that are much more elaborate and, in many ways, more beautiful than what we recognize as traditional stitching. This technique is referred to as "quilting following the pattern." The stitches flowed in free-form lines around the appliqué, in most cases following the pattern of the appliqué, but I've seen quilts with free-form stitching around the appliqué and cross-hatching superimposed on the appliqué. You can view antique quilts like the ones described above at some of the island's hotels.

FEATHERWORK   Unfortunately, little is known about the origins of Hawaiian featherwork because over the years its history has been lost, but David Malo recorded in his writings that "the feathers of birds were the most valued possessions of the ancient Hawaiians," and around 1778, Captain Cook, along with members of his crew, reported and marveled at Hawaiian featherwork in their writings. Some of the ali'i of Kauai who greeted Cook and his shipmates went aboard the ship wearing feather cloaks, leis, and helmets and presented Cook with half a dozen feather cloaks. He was awed by the brilliant colors and the intricacies of the work.

Because feathers were so sacred, a guild of professional bird catchers was established on the islands. They caught the birds by enticing them onto a branch or stick covered with a sticky substance, trapping them, or throwing stones at them until they fell to the ground. The most valued feathers were yellow, particularly those found under the tail and wings of the mamo. Red feathers, especially those of the i'iwi, were next in order of importance, and black feathers were the least well liked. Today many of the birds with the most prized plumage have fallen into extinction.

Lei Hulu   Adornments known as lei hulu were worn on the heads of Hawaiian women, as well as around the neck, and were constructed in several ways. Some are completely cylindrical (or *pauku*), like the more common flower leis you'll see today. Some pauku might have been made from the light yellow feathers of the o'o while others were made of green, red, black, and yellow feathers (some in a spiral pattern, others in blocks of color). Another style lei was known as *kamoe*. The feathers on these leis were laid flat and attached directly to the lei backing. Leis made solely of yellow feathers were the most highly prized, and any other leis made only of one color were more valuable than those made of two or more. The lei hulu *manu* was worn by women of the ali'i class to distinguish them from the Hawaiian commoners, and later, men wore the leis as hatbands.

Kahili   These plumed staffs of state resemble giant bottle brushes. Everywhere the king went the kahili (and kahili bearer) followed. In the evenings when the king slept the kahili were used to keep flies from settling on his highness's face. One report insists that rather than flies, the kahili were used to chase off bad *mana* (the Hawaiian equivalent of karma). No Hawaiians other than the ali'i could carry kahili. Because of their association with Hawaiian royalty, kahili were made with great care and came in an endless variety of shapes and sizes. The feathers from which they were formed were usually the tail and wing feathers of larger birds, such as the nene, the frigate bird, and even ducks and chickens. Handles were frequently made of tortoise shell or whale bone and the staffs might reach 10 to 25 feet in height.

Head Gear *Manihole,* or feathered head gear, were also mentioned in the journals of Captain Cook, who described these ornate head coverings as " . . . caps . . . made so as to fit very close to the head with a semicircular protuberance on the crown exactly like the helmets of old." He also comments that "the Ground-work of the Cap is Basket Work, made in a form to fit the Head, to which the Feathers are secured." It seems that Hawaiians believed the head to be the most important part of the body, and feathers were thought to have the power to ward off evil, so the helmet was as much a physical adornment as it was a form of protection for the wearer.

There were several different types of manihole, including the crescent-crested, low-crested, wide-crested, hair helmets, and ornamented helmets. No one really knows the significance of each style because these things were never documented, but it is safe to assume that all who wore them had some connection to Hawaiian royalty. Most of the helmets that survive today have lost the majority of their feathers and what you'll see is the "basket work" described by Captain Cook. There are a few, however, that have been well preserved over the years—for example, the helmet of Kaumuali'i, the last king of Kauai, covered with red feathers and trimmed (on the crest) with feathers of an exquisite gold, which can be seen at the Bishop Museum on Oahu.

If you have the good fortune to see a manihole helmet you'll no doubt be struck by the number of feathers used in its creation. It is unfortunate that there is no written record of the people who assembled these wonderful creations. I, for one, wonder just who would have the patience to sit for what must have been an endless number of hours, painstakingly weaving each feather into the underlying basketwork.

Capes Perhaps the most spectacular and beautiful pieces of Hawaiian featherwork are the capes and cloaks once worn by Hawaiian royalty. They are said to have been worn as a means of identification in battle. Each high chief or king had his own design. We do know, however, from Cook's writings that wartime was not the only time these capes were worn.

The majority of the capes (which reached to the feet of the wearer) were made with a background coloring of red or yellow, and design elements, like circles, triangles, or crescent shapes were most frequently made of the opposite color (if the background were red, the design elements would be yellow, and vice versa). Sometimes black feathers were introduced into the pattern as well. Some people believe that the geometrical designs were representational of gods or birds, but in truth, not much is known about the patterns. Unless you visit the Bishop Museum on Oahu, you probably won't get a look at a feather cape, but many bookstores carry books about Hawaiian featherwork.

LEIS Of all ancient Hawaiian art forms, traditional lei making is the only one that has survived intact throughout the ages and is still being practiced island-wide today. Past and present, leis of all shapes and sorts have special significance. They are presented at comings and goings of all varieties—births, deaths, weddings, graduations, departures to another land, as well as homecomings, and they represent and encompass the true spirit of aloha. During your trip you'll have no trouble finding flower and ti leaf leis, and if you're lucky you'll come across an even rarer lei to take home and share with your friends.

Perishable Leis   There are all sorts of perishable leis being made in the islands today, the most common of which is the flower lei. Leis made with fragrant plumeria blossoms are particularly popular with tourists. Easily strung, these flowers can be found almost everywhere on the island. My personal favorite flower lei is made with white ginger, which has a light but distinctive fragrance. The white ginger blossoms are typically gathered in the evening when they are about to open so they'll last longer, and if someone presents you with a white ginger lei you should be deeply flattered, for it is one of Hawaii's most special leis. Gardenia leis are also very fragrant, but are less common. Experienced Hawaiian lei makers can construct a lei with virtually any flower of any shape or size. I've even heard that some people have made leis of the very delicate bougainvillea blossom. The manner in which the flowers are strung depends entirely on the shape and size of the flowers being used.

Leis can also be made of ferns and garlands of almost any variety. Primitive-looking ti leaf leis can be extraordinarily beautiful because the ti leaf is pliable and easily manipulated. Primitive Hawaiians believed that the ti plant had special healing powers, and the kahuna of ancient Hawaii often used it to ward off evil spirits. If you buy a ti leaf lei to wear home, don't throw it out or hang it to dry when you get there—put it in the freezer where it will keep its shape and color until you feel like wearing it again.

Nonperishable Leis   While flower and ti leaf leis are most often purchased by visitors to the islands, there are several other types of nonperishable leis that you can take home and keep forever. Some of the most popular are *lei pupu* (shell leis) and *lei hua* (seed leis).

Shell leis can be both simple and extremely intricate. Early Hawaiians gathered shells from the beaches of Kauai and Niihau, and either filed them down to make holes for stringing or strung them using the shells' natural holes. The first lei pupu were typically made up of several separate strands, each holding up to 200 shells. Other lei pupu were fashioned out of shells that are flat, like buttons, after having been worn down by the constant wave action of the ocean. Ancient Hawaiians collected the shell fragments that had washed ashore, punched holes in them, and strung them together. Many of today's shell leis are made much the same way as they were in ancient Hawaii. Lei pupu might be sold for a few dollars or a few hundred dollars, depending on the quality and rarity of the shells. If you're interested in purchasing a really fine shell lei, try to find one that was made on Kauai.

The most common seed lei is the kukui nut lei. I say common, but even as I write, these leis are becoming less and less common. This is largely because the process of polishing the kukui nuts is so difficult and time-consuming that it is simply not cost-effective. The fruit of the candlenut tree, the kukui nut might be "blond," brown, or black. In old Hawaii, the leis made of black kukui nuts were the most coveted. The nuts would be gathered by lei makers after they'd fallen from the tree, and then sorted according to shape and size. The difficulty comes in polishing the nuts. In old Hawaii, all the polishing was done by hand. The outer layer of the shells in their raw form has a cloudy, whitish layer that must be removed. Then the grooves, which give the nut a walnut-like quality, have to be filed down, and finally, the shell is polished to a high shine. Ancient

Hawaiians utilized natural files, such as sea urchin spines, and natural sandpapers like shark skin. The final polish was done with a pumice stone. Old-time kukui nut lei makers had an interesting way of extracting the nutmeat from the shell—they would make a hole in the top and bottom of the nut and then they would bury it until the nutmeat was eaten out by insects. Today there are polishing machines available, but most kukui nut lei makers believe it's best to polish the shells by hand. Kukui leis are moderately expensive, depending on where you buy them, but they are uniquely Hawaiian, and they're quite beautiful.

Currently, other seeds in a variety of shapes and sizes are being used in lei making, but they're more difficult to find. On my last trip to Maui I also visited Molokai, where I found a rare kukui nut and ekoa seed lei.

WOOD CARVING   For ancient Hawaiians wood carving was a way of life. Primitive wood sculptures have been found all over the islands, and it seems that they were used for religious as well as practical purposes. Many religious figures were sculpted for the dedication of a heiau, or for a religious ceremony, and are thought to have been representational of particular Hawaiian gods. Ancient Hawaiians also carved food vessels (such as poi bowls), canoes, and furnishings out of wood. Some of the woods used by ancient woodcraftsmen included koa and ohi'a, both of which can be found on Maui today.

Koa wood is especially favored by current-day artists, but due to its extensive use in Hawaiian culture (both past and present), it is becoming more and more difficult to find. As a result, koa pieces you find in gift shops, from bracelets to bowls, are fairly costly. You'll probably end up buying a koa piece anyway—the wood is so rich and light that you'll have a difficult time passing it by. A word of advice: Be wary of carved figurines. Though they might appear to be Hawaiian, chances are they aren't even made in Hawaii.

6 The Cuisine of the Islands

The food of Hawaii, like its people, reflects a cultural diversity—a lot of American, quite a bit of Japanese, a little less of Chinese, a smattering of Hawaiian, Korean, Filipino, and you-name-it thrown in for good measure. You quickly get used to the fact that a delicatessen can be Japanese and to the fact that saimin (a Japanese-type noodle soup with a seaweed base) is just as popular as a hamburger and is often served at the same counter.

You soon learn that the exotic-sounding *mahimahi* is Hawaiian for dolphin, a pleasant-tasting fish—not to be confused with the intelligent mammal of the same name. You'll be introduced to poi (crushed taro root), the staff of life of the early Hawaiians, at your very first luau—you may develop a liking for this purple-gray goo thats one of the most nutritious foods known, so high in vitamin B and calcium that its fed to babies and invalids. Just ignore the old joke that it tastes like library paste; the Hawaiians, and quite a few malihinis, think it's delicious.

Hawaii's fruits are among the islands special glories. Pineapple, while not exactly invented here, might just as well have been. It's well priced in the markets, served everywhere, and as good as you'd imagine. Pineapple juice is a kind of national drink, something like tea for the English. If you hit the mango season in summer, when the local trees are bursting with this succulent fruit, you're in for a great treat. Guavas, coconuts, and papayas (one of the most common breakfast foods) are all superb, as are guava juice and passion-fruit juice, which you'll often see listed under its Hawaiian name, *lilikoi* (lilikoi sherbet is wonderful). In the supermarkets, you'll see a very popular drink called POG—that's short for passion-fruit juice, orange juice, and guava juice—very popular and very good. Macadamia-nut pancakes, as well as coconut ice cream and syrup, are special treats that taste better in Hawaii than anywhere else. We should warn you coffee addicts right here and now—the kind of coffee you'll get everywhere is Kona coffee, grown on the Big Island of Hawaii, and it's so good that you may find yourself drinking innumerable cups a day.

Don't miss the chance to try Hawaii's game fish, caught fresh in local waters and served up in fish houses under "catch of the day." If you're lucky, the catch that day will be ahi (a kind of tuna and a personal favorite), aki (another tuna), marlin, ulua, opakapaka, rock cod, or a special island delicacy called ono. That word has, in fact, slipped into local parlance as meaning "delicious"—or even "great"—as in "ono ono." At this writing, "catch of the day" was selling for about $16 to $20 in most restaurants.

LUAUS You'll probably first experience Hawaiian food at a luau, and then you'll find the same dishes in Hawaiian restaurants. You're already on speaking terms with poi. Other basic dishes are kalua pig (pig steamed in an underground oven, or *imu*), laulau (ti leaves stuffed with pork, salt fish, bananas, sweet potatoes, and taro shoots, and steamed), chicken luau (chicken cooked with coconut milk and taro or spinach leaves), sweet potatoes, pipikaula (jerked beef), and lomi-lomi salmon. The last is a triumph of linguistics: Lomi-lomi means massage, and this is salmon massaged with tomatoes and chopped onions, then marinated. Haupia (coconut pudding) and a piece of coconut cake are the usual desserts, along with fresh pineapple.

Most luaus are serve-yourself buffet affairs; food is usually eaten from paper plates, with plastic cutlery. The correct way to eat poi, by the way, is to dip one or two fingers in it (in the old days, you could actually order "one-" or "two-finger" poi, scoop it up quickly, and attack). But nobody expects that of a malihini.

LOCAL FOOD Local food does not really have deep roots in Hawaiian culture. What most people refer to as local food—and it's eaten in "plate lunches" popular everywhere in Hawaii—consists of dishes such as fried chicken, beef stew, teriyaki pork, breaded mahimahi, and the like; much of it is deep-fried. This is invariably accompanied by *two* carbohydrates, usually rice and a macaroni or potato-macaroni salad. A very popular local dish is called the loco moco—that's a hamburger patty over rice topped with a fried egg and brown gravy. Warning: Don't go local if you're counting calories or looking for "heart-healthy" food!

HAWAIIAN REGIONAL CUISINE A style called Hawaiian Regional or sometimes Pacific Rim cuisine is served more and more in better restaurants. This cuisine marries the remarkable fresh local produce of the islands, the freshly caught fish, the locally grown beef, and the like, with the best of European and Asian cooking traditions. Prime examples: Avalon Restaurant in Maui, A Pacific Café in Kauai, and Roy's in Honolulu and Maui.

KOREAN CUISINE The islands contain quite a few Korean restaurants, and they're good to know about for the budget traveler because of their modest prices and delicious food. Although Koreans make up a small part of the population, their culinary tradition has left its mark, especially in the ubiquitous kimchee—pickled cabbage seasoned with red-hot peppers. You'll find it in grocery stores, on menus everywhere in Honolulu, and even at beach stands along Waikiki serving kimchee dogs. Korean cuisine has much more to offer, including barbecued meat and chicken, hearty noodle soups, tasty meat dumplings, fish filets sautéed in spicy sauces, and daintily shredded vegetables. Some but not all dishes are served with fiery hot sauces; if you're not accustomed to that sort of thing, check with the serving staff before you order.

SHAVE ICE   A unique treat that's loved by just about all islanders is a phenomenon called shave ice. That's not "shaved" ice, or a snow cone or a slush. It's just wonderful Hawaiian shave ice. You can have a "plain" shave ice—that's just the incredibly fine ice particles bathed in syrup—and there are all kinds of syrups. Strawberry is the most popular, but there's also vanilla, guava, lemon, cherry, orange, root beer, coconut, and combinations of the above, known as "rainbow." Or you can have ice cream or adzuki beans (a sweet Japanese bean used in desserts) on the bottom, or throw caution to the winds and order ice cream *and* beans on the bottom. Shave ice is served in a cone-shaped paper cup, with both a straw and a spoon.

BEVERAGES   Generally, you need not worry about drinking tap water, except, alas, in some areas on Maui and upcountry on the Big Island. Because of acid rain pollution, it's best to drink bottled spring water here. Soft drinks and mineral waters are the same as you find back home. There's a potent local liquor called okolehao, distilled from the ti root. Wine is now produced on Maui: Tedeschi Vineyards offers a pineapple wine, a champagne, a blush, and a red table wine in the Beaujolais Nouveau tradition. Wine and liquor are sold in supermarkets.

A GLOSSARY OF ISLAND FOODS

Chinese, Japanese, Korean, Filipino, and Portuguese influences are all reflected on island menus—as well as American and Hawaiian, of course. Here are some helpful definitions:

Adobo   Filipino dish made with pork or chicken.

Bento   Japanese box lunch.

Chicken luau   Chicken cooked with coconut milk and taro or spinach leaves.

Crackseed   Chinese confection that's a cross between preserved fruit and candy. Kids go crazy for these sticky sweets.

Guava   Slightly tart tree fruit made into jams and juice. They grow wild on the mountainsides, and are under cultivation on Kauai, at Guava Kai Plantation.

Haupia   Coconut pudding, the traditional luau dessert.

Kimchee   Korea's contribution, pickled cabbage and red-hot peppers.

Kona coffee   The best! Grown on the Big Island in many small family plantations.

Laulau   Ti leaves stuffed with pork, salt fish, bananas, sweet potatoes, and taro shoots, then steamed.

Lilikoi   Passion fruit (named after the passion of Christ). A tart fruit that's turned into wonderful juice or sherbet.

Macadamia nuts   Delicious nuts grown on plantations on the Big Island. Chocolate-covered macadamias are one of the most delicious gifts you can bring the folks back home.

Malasadas   Deep-fried Portuguese doughnuts, served hot and sugared. They have no holes.

Manapuas   Steamed dumplings filled with pork, meat, or bean paste. The Chinese call them dim sum.

Maui onions   Mild, sweet onions, sometimes known as Kula onions.

Papayas   Grown on the Big Island, available everywhere: one of the favorite breakfast fruits in the islands. Highly nutritious and rich in vitamin C.

Pipikaula   Jerked beef.

Poha   Wild berry, used in jams.

Poi   Staple starch of the Hawaiian diet, made from cooked and mashed taro root. Very digestible and nutritious. To the ancient Hawaiians, the poi bowl had an almost spiritual significance.

Portuguese bean soup   Savory soup made from Portuguese sausages, beans, and vegetables, a veritable meal in a bowl.

Portuguese sweet bread   Very soft bread made with eggs, wonderful in french toast.

Saimin   Most popular soup in the islands, a thin noodle broth topped with bits of fish, shrimp, chicken, or pork, and vegetables.

Sashimi   Raw fish, a favorite Japanese delicacy.

Sushi   Vinegared rice topped with either raw fish or other toppings, and then rolled in seaweed, another great Japanese delicacy.

7 Recommended Reading

HISTORY, POLITICS & SOCIOLOGY   The definitive book on Hawaii is Gavan Daws's *Shoal of Time* (University Press of Hawaii), a history of Hawaii from 1778 until statehood (1959). It reads like a novel. Collaborating with George Cooper, Daws has also written *Land and Power in Hawaii* (University of Hawaii Press), a controversial, much-talked-about book on politics and personal financial interests in the state.

Frederick Simpich, Jr.'s book *Anatomy of Hawaii* (Coward, McCann & Geoghegan) is considered one of the most comprehensive historical and sociological studies. Also of note is *Hawaii, an Uncommon History* by Edward Joesting (Norton). *Hawaii* by Gerrit P. Judd (Macmillan) is another worthwhile study, from the point of view of the missionaries. Kristin Zambucka's book on Princess Kaiulani is considered a classic: *Kaiulani, The Last Hope of the Monarchy* (Mana Publishing Co.). *The Betrayal of Liliuokalani* (Mutual Publishing) is a definitive account of the overthrow of the queen. Liliuokalani's story is told in her own words in her autobiography, written in 1896 and recently republished: *Hawaii's Story by Hawaii's Queen* (Mutual Publishing). *The Real Hawaii, Its History and Present Condition, Including the True Story of the Revolution* (reprint edition published by Arno Press) by Lucien Young, USN, covers the author's personal observations of the political situation in 1892 and 1893 and later years.

FICTION   James Michener's *Hawaii* (Random House) is required reading before a trip to Hawaii. Michener has taken a leading figure from each of the groups who settled the islands—the Polynesians, the American missionaries, the Chinese, the Japanese—and through their stories, told the story of Hawaii.

Reading it will illuminate your trip as nothing else will. Also illuminating, beautifully written, and tremendously informative are the five historical novels written by O. A. Bushnell, a kamaaina with a touch of Hawaiian blood, and a reverence for Hawaii and his heritage. They are: *Molokai,* which tells the story of the leper colony (University Press of Hawaii); *The Return of Lono* (University of Hawaii Press), dealing with Captain Cook; *Kaaawa* (University Press of Hawaii), set in Hawaii in the 1850s; and his last two, *The Stones of Kannon* (University Press of Hawaii) and *The Water of Kane* (University Press of Hawaii), both of which are about the Japanese who came to the islands to work the sugar plantations. For another fictional account of the Japanese in Hawaii, read Kazuro Miyamoto's *Hawaii, End of the Rainbow* (Tuttle).

James Jones's *From Here to Eternity* (Scribner's), set at Schofield Barracks, was a big bestseller of the 1950s and is still worth reading for its portrayal of army life in Hawaii in the early 1940s. There is also a noted film adaptation.

Several collections of short stories make for absorbing reading. Among these are *A Hawaiian Reader,* edited by A. Grove Day (Appleton), and its companion volume, *The Spell of Hawaii* (Meredith), which include, among others, stories by Jack London, Robert Louis Stevenson, W. Somerset Maugham, Mark Twain, and James Michener. Jack London's *Stories of Hawaii* (Appleton) and Gerrit P. Judd's *A Hawaiian Anthology* (Macmillan) are also engaging.

NATURE   Sherwin Carlquist's *Hawaii: A Natural History* (Doubleday) is comprehensive and authoritative. George Munroe's *Birds of Hawaii* (Tuttle) is well illustrated and very helpful for bird-watchers. For a well-illustrated guide to Hawaii's seashells, with 380 full-color illustrations, read *Seashells of Hawaii* by Stephen Quirk and Charles Wolfe (W. W. Distributors). *Stars Over Hawaii,* originally written by E. H. Bryan, Jr., of the Bishop Museum and published by Petroglyph Press, is an illustrated paperback with monthly star charts of the Hawaiian skies.

PHOTOGRAPHY   Scores of photographers were given one-day assignments in Hawaii and the result was a fascinating tome: *A Day in the Life of Hawaii* (Workman Publishing). Robert Wenkham has produced five superb pictorial books with magnificent full-color photographs, all published by Rand McNally. They include *Honolulu Is an Island.* Jocelyn Fujii's *Under the Hula Moon* (Crown Publishers) contains beautiful photographs of Hawaiian homes and environments. *Architecture in Hawaii, A Chronological Survey,* by Rob Sandler and Julie Mehta (Mutual Publishing), provides more than 150 splendid photographs illustrating the history of architecture in the state from the days of early Hawaii and the missionary period up to the present. *Na Wahi Pana O Ko'olau Poko: Legendary Places of Ko'olau Poko,* by Anne Kapulani Landgraf (University of Hawaii Press), augments its dramatic black-and-white photos with a text discussing the traditional Hawaiian context of these sites. Long-time residents of Manoa Valley contributed old photographs and historical anecdotes to Malama O. Manoa's *Manoa: The Story of a Valley* (Mutual Publishing), an engaging work.

FOLKLORE, GHOST STORIES, LEGEND & PHILOSOPHY   Martha Beckwith's *Hawaiian Mythology* (University of Hawaii Press) is a reprint of a valuable scholarly text. David Kalakaua's *The Legends and Myths of Hawaii: The Fables and Folklore of a Strange People* (Tuttle) is an early source of folklore recorded by King Kalakaua. *Man, Gods and Nature,* by Michael Keone Dudley (Na Kane Oka Malo Press), outlines traditional Hawaiian spiritual practices.

Master storyteller Glen Grant has recorded his personal collection of local stories and comments in *Obake: Ghost Stories in Hawaii* (Mutual Publishing); reading them is almost as good as going on a walk with Grant himself (see Chapter 9, "What to See and Do in Honolulu").

The classic books on Huna, the ancient philosophy of Hawaiians passed down by secret oral tradition, were written by Max Freedom Long, beginning with *The Secret Science Behind Miracles* (Huna Research Publications). Leilani Melville's *Children of the Rainbow* (DeVorss Publishers) is another classic on Huna. A modern-day Hawaiian shaman, Serge Kahili King, has also written books on Huna, including *Kahuna Healing, Mastering Your Hidden Self* and *Imagineering for Health* (both published by Quest) and *Urban Shaman* (Simon & Schuster). All these books are available at Kauai Village Museum, 4-831 Kuhio Hwy. in Kauai (☎ 808/822-9272).

COOKBOOKS Hawaiian Regional Cuisine is fast evolving into world-class fare. Two new books reveal the secrets: *The New Cuisine of Hawaii: Recipes from the Twelve Celebrated Chefs of Hawaii Regional Cuisine* (Villard) and *Pacific Bounty: Hawaii Cooks with Roy Yamaguchi* (KQED, Inc.).

3

Planning a Trip to Oahu

This chapter is devoted to the when, where, and how of your trip—the advance planning required to get it together and take it on the road.

1 Visitor Information & Money

SOURCES OF INFORMATION

For information on traveling and living in Hawaii, contact the Hawaii Visitors Bureau (HVB), which has offices in the following cities:

Chicago: Suite 2210, 180 N. Michigan Ave., Chicago, IL 60601 (☎ 312/236-0632).

Los Angeles: Room 601, Central Plaza, 3440 Wilshire Blvd., Los Angeles, CA 90010 (☎ 213/385-5301).

New York: Suite 808, Empire State Building, 350 Fifth Ave., New York, NY 10018 (☎ 212/947-0717).

San Francisco: Suite 450, 50 California St., San Francisco, CA 94111 (☎ 415/392-8173).

On Oahu, HVB is located in Suite 801, Waikiki Business Plaza, 2270 Kalakaua Ave., Honolulu, HI 96815 (☎ 808/923-1811).

MONEY

People always ask, "Is Hawaii expensive?" The answer is yes and no: It all depends on you. Although Honolulu is one of the most costly of U.S. cities for those who live there, the visitor has such a wide range of options—princely resorts and budget bed-and-breakfasts, world-class restaurants and funky ethnic eateries, costly scuba diving and free swimming at the world's best beaches—that, all in all, Oahu has to be considered one of the best vacation values anywhere. You can pick where and how you want to splurge, as well as when and how you want to save. Despite its exotic flavor, Oahu, of course, is very much part of the U.S.A., so U.S. dollars are accepted everywhere, as are traveler's checks and major credit cards.

2 When to Go

THE CLIMATE

Oahu is one of those rare, blessed places on earth where the weather is always—well, *almost* always—wonderful. Any time of the year you

What Things Cost in Honolulu	U.S.$
Taxi from airport to Waikiki	20.00–25.00
Van from airport to Waikiki	7.00
Local telephone call	0.25
Local bus fare	0.85
Double at Halekulani (deluxe)	275.00–440.00
Double at Waikiki Joy (moderate)	125.00
Double at Royal Grove (budget)	36.00–55.00
Lunch at Oceanarium Restaurant (moderate)	7.00–12.00
Lunch at ScooZee's (budget)	5.00–7.00
Dinner without wine at The Secret (expensive)	50.00–65.00
Dinner without wine at Gordon Biersch (moderate)	18.00–25.00
Dinner without wine at The Old Spaghetti Factory (budget)	9.00
Bottle of beer (restaurant)	2.50
Cup of coffee (restaurant)	1.50–2.50
Roll of ASA 100 Kodacolor 36-exposure film	4.69
Admission to Bishop Museum	7.95
Movie ticket	5.50–6.00
Theater ticket, Manoa Valley Theater	19.00–27.00
Don Ho at the Waikiki Beachcomber Hotel	
dinner show	46.00
cocktail show	28.00

can go there is the right time to go. Most people go during the summer months of June, July, and August (usually mainland families and young people) or during winter (the Christmas-to-Easter "high season," with higher prices), when the crowd is older and as much Canadian as it is American. Winter in Hawaii feels like spring—or even summer—somewhere else. The average statewide temperature is in the low 70s; in summer it's usually in the high 70s. Leave your warm coats at home. Bring a sweater or light topper for some mountain areas at night; pack a light raincoat, too, just in case.

During summer, a Hawaiian "rain" will probably be a 10-minute light shower during which nobody bothers to go inside. During winter, there may be an occasional thunder-and-lightning storm, and sometimes it rains for several days in a row; the weather then can be cool and cloudy. However, some winters it hardly rains at all. The varying amounts of rainfall can be explained in terms of northeasterly winds bringing rain clouds that are subsequently blocked by the main mountain range on the northern side of each island. Oahu has its windward side (where rain falls) and leeward side (which storm clouds seldom reach). Honolulu is leeward and, consequently, usually dry and sunny. If you don't like the weather where you are, you can usually drive to better weather fairly quickly. Gentle trade winds keep the weather on a pretty even keel.

Average Monthly Temperatures

	Jan	Feb	Mar	Apr	May	June	July	Aug	Sept	Oct	Nov	Dec
Temp °F	72.2	71.9	72.2	73.2	74.9	76.8	77.7	78.4	78.3	77.4	75.4	73.3

CALENDAR OF EVENTS

For information on events other than those listed below, see "Spectator Sports" in Chapter 8.

January

⚙ **50th Annual Hula Bowl Game.** Celebrating "50 Years of Glory," the annual college all-star football classic will be the center of a week-long series of festivities, with former Hula Bowl participants. Many concerts and other events will be held. At Aloha Stadium on January 21. For ticket information, ☎ 808/947-4141. Prices range from $5 to $15.

• **Cherry Blossom Festival.** A festival championing Japanese culture on Oahu, complete with a Queen Pageant, a Coronation Ball at which the Governor crowns the new queen, culture and crafts fairs at Kapiolani Park, and the Red and White Song Festival at Blaisdell Concert Hall. From mid-January through April. For information, ☎ 808/955-2778.

February

• **NFL Pro Bowl.** The annual all-star football game involving the National and American conferences of the National Football League will be played at Aloha Stadium on February 4. For information, ☎ 808/486-9300.

• **Narcissus Festival.** February 19 marks the beginning of the Chinese New Year—The Year of the Rat. The weekend before, Chinatown celebrates with lion dances, live entertainment, arts and crafts demonstrations, and fireworks at the Chinese Cultural Plaza in Honolulu. For information, ☎ 808/533-3181.

⚙ **Punahou School Carnival.** One of the most popular family events in Honolulu, this yearly carnival features 23 rides, including a Ferris wheel and a merry-go-round, and 60 booths offering plants, foods, arts and crafts, and so forth. Best of all is the White Elephant tent at the end of the carnival, when leftovers—often clothing in good condition—sell for ridiculously low prices.

   At Punahou School, 1601 Punahou St., Honolulu, the first weekend in February. Admission is free. For information, ☎ 808/944-5753.

• **$50,000 Makaha World Surfing Championships.** This international longboard competition is one of the major surfing events of the year. Team members from Australia, Brazil, Costa Rica, Europe, Japan, Mexico, New Zealand, Puerto Rico, South Africa, California, and Hawaii will share their country's culture and traditions with spectators and other competitors. Activities include pageants, parades, hula and musical performances, and a re-creation of traditional Hawaiian Makahiki celebrations. The **Buffalo Big Board Surfing Classic,** in which old-timers compete on the kind of huge wood surfboards used in early Hawaii, is part of the event. The action takes place at world-famous Makaha Beach February 3 to 18. For information, ☎ 808/951-7877.

March

• **Second Annual Honolulu Festival.** This two-day U.S./Japanese Cultural Exchange Festival, March 8 to 10, includes kite workshops, U.S./Japan High

School Sumo Championships at Bishop Museum, and a finale festival at Aloha Tower Marketplace. For information, ☎ 808/922-0200.

- **Prince Kuhio Day.** On March 26, Hawaii's beloved "people's prince" and first delegate to the U.S. Congress is honored with impressive ceremonies at The Prince Kuhio Federal Building. At Kuhio Beach in Waikiki, the site of his home, a memorial tablet is decorated with leis, and Hawaiian societies hold special programs and events.
- **Outrigger Hotels Hawaiian Mountain Tour.** Four days, March 28 to 31, of fast, furious downhill bike riding by daredevils from near and far. For information, ☎ 808/521-4322.

April

- **Easter Sunrise Service** at Punchbowl Cemetery is a moving Honolulu tradition.

May

- ✪ **Lei Day.** May Day is Lei Day in Hawaii. Lei competitions are held throughout the state. Everybody wears a lei, a Lei Queen is crowned, and there's a Lei Day concert at the Waikiki Shell, usually with the beloved Brothers Cazimero in the evening. Oahu events are held in Kapiolani Park on May 1. Tickets are on sale at Waikiki Shell after 5pm (before that at Blaisdell Center and Sears outlets). The price is around $15 for general admission. Come early, bring a picnic supper and a blanket, and join Hawaii's people for a joyous event. Some visitors plan their entire trip around this event.
- **Buddha Day.** Flower festival pageants at island temples throughout the state celebrate the birth of Buddha on May 7.

June

- **Kamehameha Day.** A state holiday (many offices are closed) honoring Kamehameha the Great, Hawaii's first monarch. It's one of the biggest celebrations of all; there are parades and festivities all over the islands. In Honolulu, the annual King Kamehameha Celebrations Floral Parade includes floral floats, pageantry, Pa'u mounted riders, bands, and more, concluding with a cultural and arts festival at Kapiolani Park. June 11, with festivities starting a few days earlier. The parade may be cancelled because of budget cuts; call Keahl Allen at 808/586-0333 to see if it's on this year.
- **Taste of Honolulu.** Here's a way to sample the culinary creations of Hawaii's top restaurants and support a good cause at the same time. Hawaii's largest food event, Taste of Honolulu, draws some 100,000 residents and visitors to the grounds of Honolulu Hale (City Hall) each June for a festive three-day event. Scrip is sold for the tastings and all proceeds go to benefit the Easter Seal Society of Hawaii. In addition, there's continuous entertainment, cooking demonstrations, wine tasting, a gourmet marketplace, and children's festivities. What a blast! For information, ☎ 808/536-1015.
- **23rd Annual King Kamehameha Hula Competition.** This international competition features groups coming from as far away as California and Japan. Both modern and ancient (kahiko) hulas will be presented. Programs are held on June 22 at Blaisdell Center in Honolulu, with an admission charge of $7.25 to $15.25.
- **Annual Duke Kahanamoku Longboard Surfing Classic.** The Hawaii Longboard Surfing Association presents this event in the months of June and July at Kuhio Beach in Waikiki. Similar events are held at Sunset Beach in April and at Makaha Beach in December. For information, ☎ 808/593-9292.

July

- **Hale'iwa Bon Odori Festival.** This is one of the happiest and most colorful events in the islands, and includes traditional dances to welcome the arrival of departed souls in paradise. The dances are sponsored by Japanese Buddhist temples whose members practice for months. Usually held in mid-July.

- **Prince Lot Hula Festival.** Local hula halaus perform ancient and modern hulas in a festival that honors King Kamehameha V. At Moanalua Gardens in Honolulu, usually the third week in July.

- **6th Hawaii All-Collectors Show.** True collectors of Hawaiiana never miss this show. This is Hawaii's largest collectibles and antique show, with the largest selection of Hawaiiana for sale under one roof, from early historical artifacts to Boat Day memorabilia. Held at Blaisdell Exhibition Hall, in Honolulu, July 26, 27, and 28. Admission for adults is $3, for children ages 7 to 11, $2.

August

- **21st Annual Queen Liliuokalani Keiki Hula Competition.** The first week in August, children from the ages of 6 to 12, representing 25 hula *halaus* (schools) from around the state, compete in a delightful program at Blaisdell Center in Honolulu. For information, ☎ 808/521-6905.

- **14th Annual Ka Himeni'Ana.** Over $2,000 in cash prizes is awarded at this concert and contest of old-style Hawaiian singing without amplification; all songs are in the Hawaiian language and date to before World War II. The event takes place August 9 and 10 at Orvis Auditorium at the University of Hawaii in Honolulu. Tickets are $6, $8, and $10; for tickets, call Marge Hansen, 808/742-0421.

- **14th Annual Bankoh Ki'Hoalu Hawaiian Slack Key Guitar Festival.** Some 20 of Hawaii's best slack key artists get together for a five-hour free concert at Makoi Pavilion in Ala Moana Park on August 18. There will be solo instrumentalists as well as singers accompanied by slack key guitar. For information, ☎ 808/537-8610.

- **Toro Nagashi Floating Lantern Ceremony.** Each year, on August 15, the anniversary of the end of World War II, local Buddhist groups float 2,000 colorful paper lanterns bearing the names of departed souls from the Waikiki-Kapahulu Public Library to McCully Bridge. The ceremony begins with a Bon Dance at Ala Wai Park, followed by an Obon ceremony, all part of the annual Bon season.

September

- **Aloha Festival.** Take the celebrations of all the ethnic groups, roll them into one, and you'll get some idea of Aloha Festivals. The Asian, Polynesian, and Western groups all get together for this *hoolaulea* (gathering for a celebration), each vying to demonstrate the warmth and beauty of the wonderful Hawaiian aloha. Music and dance events, demonstrations of ancient arts and crafts, a beautiful orchid show, water sports, an enormous flower parade, pageants, the crowning of both a king and a queen, are featured. Check with the Hawaii Visitors Bureau for the exact dates of the Aloha Festivals. They usually begin on Oahu at the end of August. For information, ☎ 808/944-8857.

- **Molokai-to-Oahu Canoe Race.** This is the most important event in the sport of outrigger canoeing. Participants paddle from Molokai to Fort DeRussy Beach in Honolulu in traditional Hawaiian canoes, going over some very choppy water. The women's race takes place in September, the men's race in October.

- **7th Annual Outrigger Hotels Hawaiian Oceanfest.** A 10-day celebration of sports and entertainment, much of it nationally televised. The Waimea Open Ocean Challenge on the 4th, the Outrigger's Waikiki King's Race on the 8th, and the Diamond Head Biathlon on the 14th are all open to the public; the Hawaiian International Ocean Challenge on the 6th and 7th are for professional international lifeguard teams only; the Diamond Head Wahine Windsurfing Classic on the 8th is for professional women boardsailors only. For information, ☎ 808/521-4322.

- **Parade of Homes.** Here's a chance to see what's behind the closed doors of Hawaii's homes, town houses, and high-rise apartments. The major annual event of Hawaii's building and real estate industries, the Parade of Homes showcases the latest trends in homebuilding, remodeling, interior design, and landscaping, with entrants competing for a variety of awards. Realtors host open houses from 10am to 5pm on the third and fourth weekends in September. For information, ☎ 808/847-4666.

October

- ✪ **Waimea Falls Park Makahiki Festival.** Hawaiian games, music, and food are featured in this festival, whose highlight is the Hula Kahiko Competition, in which ancient dances of Hawaii are performed. Held at Waimea Falls Park, usually the first week in October. Events are included in general admission to the park. For information, ☎ 808/638-8511.

- **Compadres South Pacific Chili Cookoff.** A hundred teams—from community organizations, restaurants, hotels, businesses, and the military—compete to create Hawaii's best chili. The gigantic block party, held out on the street at Ward Centre, features chili tasting and continuous entertainment. Usually held in October with admission charges of about $10 (all proceeds go to local charities). For information, ☎ 808/591-8300.

- **Tour O' Hawaii.** This world-class bicycle competition held October 31 to November 3, brings top amateur cyclists from around the world to Oahu. Oahu Cycle Classic, a preliminary competition open to the public, is October 26 to 27. For information, ☎ 808/521-4322.

November

- **Kamehameha Schools Ho'olaule'.** This old-time Hawaiian festival, held November 9th, features continuous hula, Hawaiian and contemporary entertainment, arts and crafts, Hawaiian children's games, and food. Alumni groups from five islands take part. For information, ☎ 808/842-8412.

- **World Invitational Hula Festival.** Moanalua Gardens Foundation sponsors an annual international hula festival called "E Ho'i Mai I Piko Hula," which usually takes place at the Blaisdell Arena the second week in November. Competing hula halua have come from many mainland states, Europe, and Japan to compete. For information, ☎ 808/839-5334.

- **Mission Houses Museum Christmas Fair.** This popular Honolulu Thanksgiving weekend event features many specialty gift items for Christmas and food. Craftspeople from all over the islands show their wares. Free admission. For information, ☎ 808/531-0481.

December

- **Bodhi Day.** The enlightenment of Buddha is commemorated with religious observances in the Buddhist temples and with Japanese dance programs and ceremonies elsewhere on the nearest Sunday to December 7.

✪ **Honolulu Marathon.** Held on December 10, this is one of the most popular—and scenic—U.S. marathons. It draws some 30,000 entrants, about 20,000 from Japan, but many from the U.S. mainland, Europe, Canada, Mexico, and Australia. The marathon starts at Ala Moana Beach Park and ends at Kapiolani Park. Spectators line the route; there are no admission fees. For runners: To obtain entry forms, send a stamped, self-addressed business-size envelope to Honolulu Marathon Association, 3435 Waialae Ave., Room 200, Honolulu HI 96816.

• **Princess Bernice Pauahi Bishop's Birthday.** Societies and schools remember the beloved princess at the Royal Mausoleum on December 19.

• **Christmas.** What could be nicer than a Polynesian Christmas? There aren't any chimneys, so Santa might arrive in an outrigger canoe or on a surfboard. He might—it's not as bad as it sounds—be wearing a hula skirt. Carols are sung to ukulele accompaniment. Christmas lights are hung on everything from evergreens to bamboo; the decorations in downtown Honolulu are enchanting. There are special programs for children at the Honolulu Academy of Arts. The stores are jammed, just as they are on the mainland—a view of the bustling crowds (thronging the mall at Ala Moana Shopping Center, for example) is one of the prettiest of holiday pictures. The Christmas greeting: "Mele Kalikimaka!"

• **Jeep Eagle Aloha Bowl Football Classic.** The 15th annual NCAA-sanctioned post-season football game featuring two top-ranked college football teams will be held at Aloha Stadium on Christmas Day. The event will benefit local Hawaiian charities. For ticket information, ☎ 808/947-4141. Prices range from $10 to $25.

• **New Year's Eve.** "First Night," a moveable feast of theater, music and dance performances, art exhibits, and cultural demonstrations is held on sidewalks, street corners, and in lobbies and store windows all over town. Otherwise, celebrations are much like those on the mainland, except that the firecrackers are noisier (Asian style), costume balls are held at the leading hotels, and purification ceremonies are performed at the Buddhist temples (visitors welcome). January 1 is open house among island Japanese families.

3 Health & Insurance

STAYING HEALTHY

Inoculations are not necessary for a visit to Hawaii. Standards of sanitation are very high, so you needn't worry about unsanitary food or polluted drinking water.

SUN SAFETY Unless you take sensible precautions when you're out in the sun, you're playing with fire. Because of the angle at which it strikes the earth, the Hawaiian sun is especially fierce. Limit your suntanning times, try to avoid the beach between the hours of 11am and 3pm, and wear either a sunscreen with a protection factor of at least 15 or, if you're extremely fair, use sunblock. Wear sunglasses and a hat on the beach.

OCEAN SAFETY Ocean conditions can be very tricky on Oahu; sadly, there are many drownings and accidents each year. All of them probably could have been avoided if people took simple safety precautions. Never swim at an unknown beach where there is no lifeguard or beach attendant; it's important to ask someone who knows if the water is safe, if there is an undertow or rocks or riptides. Never swim alone. Avoid any area where there are huge waves unless you are an experienced surfer or bodysurfer. Beaches like Waikiki and Ala Moana Beach Park and Hanauma Bay are popular because they are safe and waves are gentle; many other beaches can be treacherous, especially those on the North Shore and the Waianae Coast in winter months (October through March), when storm swells from the northwest produce high surf and strong currents; in winter, the waves can be as high as 30 or 40 feet; in summer, the beaches are usually safe and swimmable. For further details on Oahu's beaches, see "Beaches" in Chapter 8.

A most important precaution: Never, never, turn your back on the sea, even if you are simply *walking* along a wild and beautiful shoreline. Waves have been known to suddenly come out from the sea, sweep over the land, and take whomever or whatever is in their path back into the ocean with them!

As for dangers *in* the water, there are some, but not many. You might encounter a pesky Portuguese man-of-war occasionally (usually there will be a warning sign posted). If you should be unfortunate enough to get stung, immediately apply some alcohol or MSG. Do be careful of coral, as a cut can easily get infected, since coral contains many living organisms (treat any coral cut with antiseptic and watch it carefully). It's best to wear protective water shoes around coral and avoid touching it entirely, as you could damage it much more easily than it can harm you. Also wear underwater shoes if you're exploring tidepools to avoid stepping on poisonous sea urchins, whose spines can break off and enter your foot. Vinegar and wine, applied topically, are the prescribed antidotes for pain. Lifeguards at state beach parks have remedies for all of these maladies—another reason to stay close to civilization when you enter the water.

As for sharks, they rarely swim close to shore. You really don't have to be concerned about them.

INSURANCE

It probably won't be necessary for you to take out any insurance for your trip to Hawaii if you already have adequate coverage at home. Take a look at your current insurance policies first. Many plans cover doctor and hospital visits you may need while traveling. Your homeowner's insurance policy may cover stolen luggage. Your automobile insurance may be sufficient for Hawaii. If you are not adequately covered, you might contact the following organizations to get supplemental insurance:

Access America, 6600 W. Broad St., P.O. Box 11188, Richmond, VA 23230 (☎ 804/285-3300 or 800/284-8300), offers travel insurance and 24-hour emergency travel, medical, and legal assistance. One call to their hotline center, staffed by multilingual coordinators, connects travelers to a worldwide network of professionals able to offer specialized help in reaching the nearest physician, hospital, or legal advisor and in obtaining emergency cash or the replacement of lost travel documents. Varying coverage levels are available.

Carefree Travel Insurance, P.O. Box 9366, Garden City, NY 11530 (☎ 800/ 323-3149), offers comprehensive plans that include trip cancellation, interruption, bankruptcy, and trip delay; accident and sickness medical expenses; accidental death and dismemberment, emergency evacuation, baggage loss, and baggage delay. A telephone hotline offers worldwide assistance for medical, travel, and legal problems before and during your trip.

Travel Guard International, 1145 Clark St., Stevens Point, WI 54481 (☎ 800/826-1300), features comprehensive insurance programs starting as low as $44. The program covers basically everything: trip cancellation and interruption—

including bankruptcy and financial default, lost luggage, medical coverage abroad, emergency assistance, accidental death, and 24-hour worldwide emergency hotline. A special "cancel for any reason" feature is available.

4 Tips for Special Travelers

FOR TRAVELERS WITH DISABILITIES   Disabled people are made to feel very welcome in Hawaii. There are more than 2,000 ramped curbs on Oahu alone, hotels provide special facilities, and tour companies provide many services. In fact, the Society for the Advancement of Travel for the Handicapped considers it the country's most accessible place. Helpful brochures are available for each island, listing the accessibility features of Hawaii's major hotels, shopping malls, beach parks, and sightseeing and visitor attractions. Write the **Commission on Persons with Disabilities,** 919 Ala Moana Blvd., Honolulu, HI 96814 (☎ 808/586-8121), or the **Hawaii Center for Independent Living,** 677 Ala Moana Blvd., Suite 118, Honolulu, HI 96813 (☎ 808/537-1941). Enclose a check or money order for $3 payable to *Aloha Guide to Accessibility.*

Handi-Cabs of the Pacific, P.O. Box 22428, Honolulu, HI 96823 (☎ 808/ 524-3866), provides wheelchair taxi service and a variety of tours, including luaus, cruises, and sightseeing journeys.

FOR SENIORS   For information on activities for senior citizens, contact the Department of Parks and Recreation at 808/973-7262 (or 808/973-7258) and be sure to check the local papers for special events, sightseeing tours, picnics, and other activities.

Puuwai Opio Pio (Young at Heart), a senior citizens' club, meets on Mondays at 9:30am at the Ala Wai Recreation Center, 2015 Kapiolani Blvd. For information on activities, phone **808-973-7266.**

Discounts for seniors are available at almost all major attractions in the islands and occasionally at hotels and restaurants. When making a hotel reservation, always ask. Members of the American Association of Retired Persons (AARP), 601 E St. NW, Washington, DC 20049 (☎ 202/434-2277), are usually eligible for such discounts.

In Honolulu, seniors 65 and older can ride TheBUS at reduced rates after getting a pass at 811 Middle St. (☎ 808/848-4444).

If you're visiting some of the national parks on the neighboring islands, such as Hawaii Volcanoes National Park on the Big Island, you can obtain a Golden Age Passport free. It can be picked up at the park and is available to anyone over age 62 who can show proof of age.

FOR FAMILIES   Hawaii is a very easy place to travel with children. Airlines provide a discount for children under 12, and most hotels allow children to stay free in their parents' rooms if they use existing bedding (there is usually a fee for a crib or a rollaway bed). Strollers can easily be rented. Many restaurants offer special menus for the *keikis,* as they're called. And you'll have no trouble amusing children—in addition to numerous attractions suitable for them, they have the best playground in the world right at their doorstep: the beach.

FOR STUDENTS   Get in touch with the people at the University of Hawaii to find out about all sorts of activities open to students, even those not enrolled at the university. Inquire at Campus Center, Room 212, at the Manoa Campus.

5 Getting There

MAJOR AIRLINES

The largest carrier with the most frequent service to Hawaii is **United Airlines** (☎ 800/241-6522 or 808/547-2211), closely followed by **Continental Airlines** (800/525-0280 or 808/523-0000). To get into the mood of your Hawaiian vacation the minute you leave the West Coast, you might consider flying Hawaiian Airlines, the largest airline based in the Hawaiian Islands, and the only one offering service to the mainland. Hawaiian offers two flights a day from Los Angeles, one from San Francisco, one from Seattle, four flights a week from Portland, and four from Las Vegas, all on wide-bodied DC10s. Fares are very competitive—from $300 to $350 roundtrip—and special promotional fares are often available: For several weeks last winter, for example, they were offering midweek fares of $258, weekend fares of $278, for a roundtrip from the West Coast. You can also save a bundle by booking one of their package deals: In 1995, for instance, a five-night stay in Waikiki was available starting at $460 per person, including roundtrip airfare from the West Coast and an economy-sized Hertz Rent A Car for the entire stay. Note that fares vary and restrictions apply, but overall, this is one of the best travel bargains we know. Hawaiian works with Fly Away Vacations, the tour operations unit of American Airlines. For information, phone **Hawaiian Airlines Vacations** at 800/353-5393, or ask your travel agent.

Other airlines that fly into Honolulu are as follows: Toll-free numbers are given first, when applicable, and then the local (808) numbers, when applicable. **American Airlines,** ☎ 800/433-7300 or 808/526-0044; **Canadian Airlines International,** ☎ 800/426-7000 or 808/922-0533; **China Airlines,** ☎ 800/227-5118 or 808/955-0088; **Delta Airlines,** ☎ 800/221-1212; **Garuda Indonesian,** ☎ 800/826-2829 or 808/945-3791; **Japan Airlines,** ☎ 800/525-3663 or 808/521-1441; **Korean Air,** ☎ 800/223-1155 (East Coast), 800/421-8200(West Coast), ☎ 808/923-7302; **Northwest Airlines,** ☎ 800/225-2525 or 808/955-2255; **Philippine Airlines,** ☎ 800/435-9725 or 808/536-1928; **Qantas,** ☎ 800/227-4500, or 808/836-2461; **Singapore Airlines,** ☎ 800/742-3333 or 808/524-6063; **Trans World Airlines,** ☎ 800/221-2000.

REGULAR AIRFARES

The most reasonable way to fly to Hawaii is to ask for an **Economy** or **APEX** (Advance Purchase Excursion) fare. Typically, you are required to reserve and pay for the ticket 14 or 21 days in advance, stay for a minimum and maximum number of days, and possibly meet some other requirements (such as flying before a specific date). In spring 1995, Hawaiian's APEX fares, Los Angeles to Honolulu, ranged from $300-$350 round trip, depending on the days of the week you traveled and how far in advance you purchased your ticket. Hawaiian's first-class ticket from Los Angeles to Honolulu in spring 1995 was $799 roundtrip. *Note:* Airfares were changing dramatically during mid-1995 and may be quite different when you read this guide.

OTHER OPTIONS

BUCKET SHOPS   These discount travel agencies can sometimes offer flights to Hawaii at discounts ranging anywhere from 20% to 40%, depending on season and availability. You may do as well on your own or with your regular travel agent, but it's worth a call. Remember that it's very difficult to return these tickets, and many restrictions apply. So once you've bought them, for good or bad, they're all yours. One bucket shop that you might try is **Community Travel Service,** 5299 College Ave., Oakland, CA 94618 (☎ 510/653-0990).

PACKAGE TOURS In addition to the fly/drive packages offered by the airlines (see above), excellent values are sometimes available with group tours, which usually last one to two weeks. Group packages are occasionally offered by airlines in conjunction with flights. A number of travel companies in Honolulu offer tours of Oahu and to the neighboring islands:

   American Express Travel Related Services, 2222 Kalakaua Ave., Honolulu, HI 96815 (☎ 808/946-7741 or toll-free 800/241-1700). They will refer you to the closest American Express Tours and Activities office on the island.

   Pleasant Island Holidays, 270 Lewers St., Lobby Level, Honolulu, HI 96815 (☎ 808/922-1515).

   Roberts Hawaii Tours, 680 Iwilei Rd., 7th floor, Honolulu, HI 96817 (☎ 808/523-7750).

INTERISLAND FLIGHTS

It will cost you roughly $74 to fly from Oahu to another island on the jets of either **Hawaiian Airlines** (☎ 800/367-5320) or **Aloha Airlines** (☎ 800/367-5250). Island-hoppers might want to take advantage of Hawaiian's Island Pass, which allows you to take an unlimited number of interisland flights for one flat fee: $169 for five days, $189 for eight days, $229 for ten days, $269 for two weeks. There is a $10 discount for seniors 60+ and children 2 to 11. Special deals on car rentals are available from Alamo Rent A Car.

   Mahalo Airlines (☎ 800/277-8333) offers $54 flights for out-of-staters (local residents pay only $35) to and from Honolulu and Kauai, Maui, and Kona on the Big Island, on propeller aircraft. Check with them, though; they sometimes offer specials for visitors.

For Foreign Visitors 4

Although American fads and fashions have spread across Europe and other parts of the world so that America may seem like familiar territory before your arrival, there are still many peculiarities and uniquely American situations that any foreign visitor will encounter.

1 Preparing for Your Trip

ENTRY REQUIREMENTS

DOCUMENT REGULATIONS   Canadian citizens may enter the United States without visas; they need only proof of residence.

Citizens of the United Kingdom, New Zealand, Japan, and most western European countries traveling on valid passports may not need a visa for fewer than 90 days of holiday or business travel to the United States, providing they hold a roundtrip or return ticket and enter the United States on an airline or cruise line participating in the visa waiver program.

(Note that citizens of these visa-exempt countries who first enter the United States may then visit Mexico, Canada, Bermuda, and/or the Caribbean islands and then reenter the United States, by any mode of transportation, without needing a visa. Further information is available from any U.S. embassy or consulate.)

Citizens of countries other than those stipulated above, including citizens of Australia, must have two documents:

- a valid **passport,** with an expiration date at least six months later than the scheduled end of the visit to the United States; and
- a **tourist visa,** available without charge from the nearest U.S. consulate. To obtain a visa, the traveler must submit a completed application form (either in person or by mail) with a $1\frac{1}{2}$-inch-square photo and demonstrate binding ties to a residence abroad.

Usually you can obtain a visa at once or within 24 hours, but it may take longer during the summer rush from June to August. If you cannot go in person, contact the nearest U.S. embassy or consulate for directions on applying by mail. Your travel agent or airline office may also be able to provide you with visa applications and instructions. The U.S. consulate or embassy that issues your visa will determine whether you will be issued a multiple-or-single-entry visa and any restrictions regarding the length of your stay.

MEDICAL REQUIREMENTS   No inoculations are needed to enter the United States unless you are coming from, or have stopped over in, areas known to be suffering from epidemics, particularly cholera or yellow fever.

If you have a disease requiring treatment with medications containing narcotics or drugs requiring a syringe, carry a valid signed prescription from your physician to allay any suspicions that you are smuggling drugs.

CUSTOMS REQUIREMENTS   Every adult visitor may bring in free of duty: one liter of wine or hard liquor; 200 cigarettes or 100 cigars (but no cigars from Cuba) or three pounds of smoking tobacco; $100 worth of gifts. These exemptions are offered to travelers who spend at least 72 hours in the United States and who have not claimed them within the preceding six months. It is altogether forbidden to bring into the country foodstuffs (particularly cheese, fruit, cooked meats, and canned goods) and plants (vegetables, seeds, tropical plants, and so on). Foreign tourists may bring in or take out up to $10,000 in U.S. or foreign currency with no formalities; larger sums must be declared to Customs on entering or leaving.

INSURANCE

There is no health system in the United States. Because the cost of medical care is extremely high, we strongly advise every traveler to secure health coverage before setting out.

You may want to take out a comprehensive travel policy that covers (for a relatively low premium) sickness or injury costs (medical, surgical, and hospital); loss or theft of your baggage; trip-cancellation costs; guarantee of bail in case you are arrested; costs of accident, repatriation, or death. Such packages (for example, "Europe Assistance" in Europe) are sold by automobile clubs at attractive rates, as well as by insurance companies and travel agencies.

MONEY

CURRENCY & EXCHANGE   The U.S. monetary system has a decimal base: one American **dollar** ($1) = 100 **cents** (100¢).

Dollar bills commonly come in $1 ("a buck"), $5, $10, $20, $50, and $100 denominations (the last two are not welcome when paying for small purchases and are not accepted in taxis or at subway ticket booths). There are also $2 bills (seldom encountered).

There are six denominations of coins: 1¢ (one cent or "penny"), 5¢ (five cents or a "nickel"), 10¢ (ten cents or a "dime"), 25¢ (twenty-five cents or a "quarter"), 50¢ (fifty cents or a "half-dollar"), and the rare $1 piece.

The "foreign exchange bureaus" so common in Europe are rare even at airports in the United States, and nonexistent outside major cities. Try to avoid having to change foreign money, or traveler's checks denominated other than in U.S. dollars, at a small-town bank, or even a branch in a big city; in fact, leave any currency other than U.S. dollars at home—it may prove more nuisance to you than it's worth.

TRAVELER'S CHECKS   Traveler's checks denominated in U.S. dollars are readily accepted at most hotels, motels, restaurants, and large stores. But the best place to change traveler's checks is at a bank. Do not bring traveler's checks denominated in other currencies.

CREDIT CARDS   The method of payment most widely used is the credit card: VISA (BarclayCard in Britain), MasterCard (EuroCard in Europe, Access in Britain, Chargex in Canada), American Express, Diners Club, Discover, and Carte Blanche. You can save yourself trouble by using "plastic money" rather than cash or traveler's checks in most hotels, motels, restaurants, and retail stores (a growing number of food and liquor stores now accept credit cards). You must have a credit card to rent a car. It can also be used as proof of identity (often carrying more weight than a passport), or as a "cash card," enabling you to draw money from banks that accept them.

SAFETY

GENERAL   While tourist areas are generally safe, crime is on the increase everywhere, and U.S. urban areas tend to be less safe than those in Europe or Japan. Visitors should always stay alert. This is particularly true of large U.S. cities. It is wise to ask the city's or area's tourist office if you're in doubt about which neighborhoods are safe. Avoid deserted areas, especially at night. Don't go into any city park at night unless there is an event that attracts crowds—for example, the Waikiki Shell concerts in Kapiolani Park. Generally speaking, you can feel safe in areas where there are many people and many open establishments.

Avoid carrying valuables with you on the street, and don't display expensive cameras or electronic equipment. Hold on to your pocketbook, and place your billfold in an inside pocket. In theaters, restaurants, and other public places, keep your possessions in sight.

Remember also that hotels are open to the public, and in a large hotel, security may not be able to screen everyone entering. Always lock your room door—don't assume that once inside your hotel you are automatically safe and no longer need to be aware of your surroundings.

DRIVING   Safety while driving is particularly important. Question your rental agency about personal safety, or ask for a brochure of traveler safety tips when you pick up your car. Obtain written directions, or a map with the route marked in red, from the agency showing how to get to your destination.

Recently more and more crime has involved cars and drivers. If you drive off a highway into a doubtful neighborhood, leave the area as quickly as possible. If you have an accident, even on the highway, stay in your car with the doors locked until you assess the situation or until the police arrive. If you are bumped from behind on the street or are involved in a minor accident with no injuries and the situation appears to be suspicious, motion to the other driver to follow you. *Never* get out of your car in such situations. You can also keep a pre-made sign in your car which reads: PLEASE FOLLOW THIS VEHICLE TO REPORT THE ACCIDENT. Show the sign to the other driver, and go directly to the nearest police precinct, well-lighted service station, or all-night store.

If you see someone on the road who indicates a need for help, do *not* stop. Take note of the location, drive on to a well-lighted area, and telephone the police by dialing 911.

Park in well-lighted, well-traveled areas if possible. Always keep your car doors locked, whether attended or unattended. Look around you before you get out of your car, and never leave any packages or valuables in sight. If someone attempts to rob you or steal your car, do *not* try to resist the thief/carjacker—report the incident to the police department immediately.

2 Getting To & Around the U.S.

Travelers from overseas can take advantage of the **APEX (Advance Purchase Excursion)** fares offered by all major U.S. and European carriers. Aside from these, attractive values are offered by **Icelandair** on flights from Luxembourg to New York and by **Virgin Atlantic Airways** from London to New York/Newark. You can then catch a connecting domestic flight to Honolulu. Advance purchase fares are available to travelers from Australia via **Qantas Airways,** which runs daily flights from Sydney to Honolulu (plus additional flights four days a week); they are also available for travelers from New Zealand via **Air New Zealand,** which runs 40 flights per week from Auckland.

Some large American airlines (for example, TWA, American Airlines, Northwest, United, and Delta) offer travelers on their transatlantic or transpacific flights special discount tickets under the name **Visit USA,** allowing travel between any U.S. destinations at minimum rates. They are not on sale in the United States, and must, therefore, be purchased before you leave your foreign point of departure. This system is the best, easiest, and fastest way to see the United States at low cost. You should obtain information well in advance from your travel agent or the office of the airline concerned, since the conditions attached to these discount tickets can be changed without advance notice.

The visitor arriving by air should cultivate patience and resignation before setting foot on U.S. soil. Getting through Immigration control may take as long as two hours on some days, especially summer weekends. Add the time it takes to clear Customs and you'll see that you should make very generous allowance for delay in planning connections between international and domestic flights—an average of two to three hours at least.

For further information about travel to Hawaii, see "Getting There" in Chapter 3.

FAST FACTS: For the Foreign Traveler

Automobile Organizations   Auto clubs will supply maps, suggested routes, guidebooks, accident and bail-bond insurance, and emergency road service. The major auto club in the United States, with 955 offices nationwide, is the **American Automobile Association (AAA; often called "triple A").** Members of some foreign auto clubs have reciprocal arrangements with the AAA and enjoy its services at no charge. If you belong to an auto club, inquire about AAA reciprocity before you leave. The AAA can provide you with an **International Driving Permit** validating your foreign license. You may be able to join the AAA even if you are not a member of a reciprocal club. To inquire, call **800/336-4357.** In addition, some automobile rental agencies now provide these services, so you should inquire about their availability when you rent your car.

Automobile Rentals   To rent a car you need a major credit card and a valid driver's license. You usually need to be at least 25. Some companies do rent to younger people but add a daily surcharge.

Business Hours   Banks are open weekdays from 9am to 3 or 4pm, although there's 24-hour access to the automatic tellers (ATMs) at most banks and other outlets. Generally, offices are open weekdays from 8am to 4 or 5pm. Stores are open six days a week, with many open on Sunday, too; department stores usually stay open until 9pm at least one day a week.

Climate   See "When to Go" in Chapter 3.

Currency   See "Preparing for Your Trip," above.

Currency Exchange   You will find currency exchange services in major airports with international service. Most major banks on Oahu provide currency exchange. In addition, in Honolulu, the capital city, you can get reliable currency service at Thomas Cook Currency, 830 Fort Street Mall (☎ 808/523-1321); A1 Foreign Exchange, Royal Hawaiian Shopping Center (☎ 808/922-3327); and Monyx International, 307 Royal Hawaiian Ave. (☎ 808/923-6626).

Electricity   The United States uses 110–120 volts, 60 cycles, compared to 220–240 volts, 50 cycles, as in most of Europe and in other areas of the world. In addition to a 100-volt transformer, small appliances of non-American manufacture, such as hair dryers or shavers, will require a plug adapter, with two flat, parallel pins.

Embassies and Consulates   All embassies are located in the national capital, Washington, D.C.; some consulates are located in major cities, and most nations have a mission to the United Nations in New York City.

Listed here are the embassies and some consulates of the major English-speaking countries. Travelers from other countries can obtain telephone numbers for their embassies and consulates by calling "Information" in Washington, D.C. (☎ 202/555-1212).

The embassy of **Australia** is at 1601 Massachusetts Ave. NW, Washington, D.C. 20036 (☎ 202/797-3000). There is also an Australian consulate in Hawaii at 1000 Bishop St., Honolulu, HI 96813 (☎ 808/524-5050).

The embassy of **Canada** is at 501 Pennsylvania Ave. NW, Washington, D.C. 20001 (☎ 202/682-1740). Canadian consulates are also at 1251 Ave. of the Americas, New York, NY 10020 (☎ 212/768-2400), and in Los Angeles, San Francisco, and Seattle.

The embassy of the **Republic of Ireland** is at 2234 Massachusetts Ave. NW, Washington, D.C. 20008 (☎ 202/462-3939). Irish consulates are in Boston, New York, and San Francisco.

The embassy of **New Zealand** is at 37 Observatory Circle NW, Washington, D.C. 20008 (☎ 202/328-4800). The only New Zealand consulate in the U.S. is in Los Angeles.

The embassy of the **United Kingdom** is at 3100 Massachusetts Ave. NW, Washington, D.C. 20008 (☎ 202/462-1340). British consulates are at 845 Third Ave., New York, NY 10022 (☎ 212/745-0200), and in Los Angeles.

The embassy of **Japan** is at 2520 Massachusetts Ave. NW, Washington, D.C. 20008 (☎ 202/939-6700). The consulate general of Japan is located at 1742 Nuuanu Ave., Honolulu, HI 96817 (☎ 808/536-2226). There are several other consulates, including one in New York at 299 Park Ave., New York, NY 10171 (☎ 212/371-8222).

Emergencies   Call **911** to report a fire, call the police, or get an ambulance. If you encounter traveler's problems, check the local directory to find an office of the **Traveler's Aid Society,** a nationwide, nonprofit, social-service organization geared to helping travelers in difficult straits. Their services might include re-uniting families separated while traveling, providing food and/or shelter to people stranded without cash, or even emotional counseling. If you're in trouble seek them out.

Gasoline (Petrol)   One U.S. gallon equals 3.8 liters, while 1.2 U.S. gallons equal one Imperial gallon. You'll notice there are several grades (and price levels) of gasoline available at most gas stations. And you'll also notice that their names change from company to company. The unleaded ones with the highest octane are the most expensive (most rental cars take the least expensive "regular" unleaded) and leaded gas is the least expensive, but only older cars can take this, so check if you're not sure.

Holidays   On the following legal national holidays, banks, government offices, post offices, and many stores, restaurants, and museums are closed: January 1 (New Year's Day); Third Monday in January (Martin Luther King Day); Third Monday in February (Presidents Day, Washington's Birthday); Last Monday in May (Memorial Day); July 4 (Independence Day); First Monday in September (Labor Day); Second Monday in October (Columbus Day); November 11 (Veteran's Day); Fourth Thursday in November (Thanksgiving Day); December 25 (Christmas).

Finally, the Tuesday following the first Monday in November is Election Day, and is a legal holiday in presidential-election years.

Languages   Major hotels may have multilingual employees. Unless your language is very obscure, they can usually supply a translator on request.

Legal Aid   The ordinary tourist will probably never become involved with the American legal system. If your are pulled up for a minor infraction (for example, of the highway code, such as speeding), never attempt to pay the fine directly to a police officer; you may wind up arrested on the much more serious charge of attempted bribery. Pay fines by mail, or directly into the hands of the clerk of the court. If accused of a more serious offense, it's wise to say and do nothing before consulting a lawyer. Under U.S. law, an arrested person is allowed one telephone call to a party of his or her choice. Call your embassy or consulate.

Mail   If you want your mail to follow you on your vacation and you aren't sure of your address, your mail can be sent to you, in your name, c/o **General Delivery** at the main post office of the city or region where you expect to be. The addressee must pick it up in person and produce proof of identity (driver's license, credit card, passport, etc.).

Generally to be found at intersections, mailboxes are blue with a red-and-white stripe and carry the inscription U.S. MAIL. If your mail is addressed to a U.S. destination, don't forget to add the five-figure postal code, or Zip Code, after the two-letter abbreviation of the state to which the mail is addressed (HI for Hawaii, FL for Florida, NY for New York, and so on).

Newspapers/Magazines   National newspapers include the *New York Times, USA Today,* and the *Wall Street Journal.* National news weeklies include *Newsweek, Time,* and *U.S. News and World Report. The Honolulu Advertiser* and the *Honolulu Star-Bulletin* are the major local newspapers.

Radio and Television   Audiovisual media, with four coast-to-coast networks—ABC, CBS, NBC, and FOX—joined in recent years by the Public Broadcasting System (PBS), the cable network CNN, and two new networks, WBN and UPN, play a major part in American life. In big cities, televiewers have a choice of about a dozen channels (including the UHF channels), most of them transmitting 24 hours a day, without counting the pay-TV channels showing recent movies or sports events. All options are usually indicated on your hotel TV set. You'll also find a wide choice of local radio stations, each broadcasting particular kinds of talk shows and/or music—classical, country, jazz, pop, gospel—punctuated by news broadcasts and frequent commercials.

Safety See "Safety" in "Preparing for Your Trip," above.

Taxes In the United States there is no VAT (Value-Added Tax) or other indirect tax at a national level. Every state, and each city in it, has the right to levy its own local tax on all purchases, including hotel and restaurant checks, airline tickets, and so on. (In Hawaii, sales tax is 4%.)

Telephone and Fax The telephone system in the United States is run by private corporations, so rates, particularly for long-distance service and operator-assisted calls, can vary widely—especially on calls made from public telephones. Local calls in the United States usually cost 25¢.

Generally, hotel surcharges on long-distance and local calls are astronomical. You are usually better off using a **public pay telephone,** which you will find clearly marked in most public buildings and private establishments as well as on the street. Outside metropolitan areas, public telephones are more difficult to find. Stores and gas stations are your best bet.

Most **long-distance and international calls** can be dialed directly from any phone. For calls to Canada and other parts of the United States, dial 1 followed by the area code and the seven-digit number. For international calls, dial 011 followed by the country code, city code, and the telephone number of the person you wish to call.

For **reversed-charge or collect calls,** and for **person-to-person calls,** dial 0 (zero, *not* the letter "O") followed by the area code and number you want; an operator will then come on the line, and you should specify that you are calling collect, or person-to-person, or both. If your operator-assisted call is international, ask for the overseas operator.

Note that all phone numbers with the area code 800 are toll-free.

For local **directory assistance** ("information"), dial 411; for **long-distance information,** dial 1, then the appropriate area code and 555-1212.

Fax facilities are widely available, and can be found in most hotels and many other establishments. Try Mailboxes Etc. or any photocopying shop.

Telephone Directory There are two kinds of telephone directories available to you. The general directory is the so-called **White Pages,** in which private and business subscribers are listed in alphabetical order. The inside front cover lists the emergency number for police, fire, and ambulance, and other vital numbers (like the Coast Guard, poison-control center, crime-victims hotline, and so on). The first few pages are devoted to community-service numbers, including a guide to long-distance and international calling, complete with country codes and area codes.

The second directory, printed on yellow paper (hence its name, *Yellow Pages*), lists all local services, businesses, and industries by type of activity, with an index at the back. The listings cover not only such obvious items as automobile repairs by make of car, or drugstores (pharmacies), often by geographical location, but also restaurants by type of cuisine and geographical location, bookstores by special subject and/or language, places of worship by religious denomination, and other information that the tourist might otherwise not readily find. The *Yellow Pages* also include city plans or detailed maps, often showing postal Zip Codes and public transportation routes.

Time   The United States is divided into six **time zones,** including Alaska and Hawaii. From east to west, these are: eastern standard time (EST), central standard time (CST), mountain standard time (MST), Pacific standard time (PST), Alaska standard time (AST), and Hawaii standard time (HST). Always keep changing time zones in mind if you are traveling (or even telephoning) long distances in the United States. For example, noon in New York City (EST) is 11am in Chicago (CST), 10am in Denver (MST), 9am in Los Angeles (PST), 8am in Anchorage (AST), and 7am in Honolulu (HST).

Daylight saving time is in effect from the last Sunday in April through the last Saturday in October (actually, the change is made at 2am on Sunday) except in Arizona, Hawaii, part of Indiana, and Puerto Rico. Daylight saving time moves the clock one hour ahead of standard time, but this is something you won't encounter on Oahu.

Tipping   This is part of the American way of life, on the principle that you must expect to pay for any service you get (many personnel receive little direct salary and must depend on tips for their income). Here are some rules of thumb:

In **hotels,** tip bellhops at least $1 per piece ($2 to $3 if you have a lot of luggage) and tip the chamber staff $1 per day. Tip the doorman or concierge only if he or she has provided you with some specific service (for example, calling a cab for you or obtaining difficult-to-get theater tickets).

In **restaurants, bars, and nightclubs,** tip service staff 15% to 20% of the check, tip bartenders 10% to 15%, tip checkroom attendants $1 per garment, and tip valet-parking attendants $1 per vehicle. Tip the doorman only if he has provided you with some specific service (such as calling a cab for you). Tipping is not expected in cafeterias and fast-food restaurants.

Tip **cab drivers** 15% of the fare.

As for **other service personnel,** tip redcaps at airports or railroad stations at least 50¢ per piece ($2 to $3 if you have a lot of luggage) and tip hairdressers and barbers 15% to 20%.

Tipping ushers in movies and theaters and gas-station attendants is not expected.

Toilets   Foreign visitors often complain that public toilets are hard to find in most U.S. cities. True, there are none on the streets, but the visitor can usually find one in a bar, restaurant, hotel, museum, department store, or service station—and it will probably be clean (although the last-mentioned sometimes leaves much to be desired). Note, however, a growing practice in some restaurants and bars of displaying a notice that "toilets are for the use of patrons only." You can ignore this sign, or better yet, avoid arguments by paying for a cup of coffee or soft drink, which will qualify you as a patron. The cleanliness of toilets at railroad stations and bus depots may be more open to question, and some public places are equipped with pay toilets, which require you to insert one or more coins into a slot on the door before it will open.

Getting to Know Oahu

5

Oahu means "the gathering place" in Hawaiian, and no other name could be so apt. Although it's merely the third largest of the islands in the Hawaiian chain in size (40 miles long, 26 miles wide), it is the most populous (850,000 people, and more arriving all the time). It also has the most skyscrapers, schools, hospitals, radio and television stations—and the most visitors. It's also a tremendous military stronghold; approximately one-quarter of the island is owned by the military and defense is a major industry.

Honolulu, the bustling capital city plunked in the middle of the Pacific, is the center of island life, the metropolis youngsters from the other islands dream of. Just 10 minutes away from Honolulu is Waikiki Beach, a favorite resort of Hawaiian royalty long before the word "tourist" came into being. For the visitor, this is an ideal geographical situation; it's as if Mexico City were just 10 minutes away from Acapulco, Paris a short bus ride from the Riviera. You can, with such an arrangement, have the best of both worlds—as much beach or city life, relaxation or excitement, as you choose.

The island is dominated by two mountain ranges: the 4,000 feet high Waianae, along the leeward (western) coast, and the Koolaus, whose verdant cliffs rise more than 3,000 feet, forming the spectacular green backdrop to the city of Honolulu. Ringing the island is a breathtaking succession of emerald beaches. Inland, you'll find rural Oahu: tiny plantation villages, miles of red earth planted with sugarcane, gorgeous trails for riding and hiking, a vast natural wonderland where there's plenty of room to explore and enjoy, on or off the beaten path.

1 The Regions in Brief

HONOLULU   The capital city, the business and financial center, an area rich in historical and cultural attractions, from Iolani Palace to Kawaiahao Church, from the Mission Houses Museum to the Honolulu Academy of Art. Chinatown is part of downtown Honolulu.

WAIKIKI   One of the world's most famous beaches, Hawaii's favorite resort. It's technically part of the city of Honolulu, but it's a distinct region with its own distinct personality, along the island's southern coast west of Pearl Harbor and downtown.

What's Special About Honolulu and Oahu

Natural Wonders
- Diamond Head Crater, the sleeping volcano that has become the symbol of Honolulu and Waikiki.
- Hanauma Bay, an idyllic beach cove created centuries ago when one side of Koko Head Crater washed into the sea, now a marine reserve that's popular with snorkelers.
- The Blow Hole, a natural geyser where water surges up through an under-water vent in the lava rock, sometimes as high as 60 feet.

Beaches
- World-famous Waikiki Beach, great for swimming, surfing, people-watching.
- Lanikai Beach in Kailua on Windward Oahu—gentle surf, no crowds—as Waikiki was before the world discovered it.
- Superb sandy swimming beaches all over Oahu, especially Sunset Beach and Waimea Bay during the mild summer months, when the world-famous surfing waves are calm.

Outdoor Activities
- Great snorkeling, notably at Hanauma Bay.
- Surfing, all around Oahu, particularly the mighty winter waves at Sunset Beach and Waimea Bay on the North Shore.
- Hiking the mountains and valleys, with many opportunities to go out with local groups.
- Sailing, day and night, including recreational and dinner cruises out of Honolulu Harbor.
- Golf and tennis at fabulous public and private facilities.

Museums and Historic Sites
- Bishop Museum, a prime resource center and lively showcase for Pacific culture.
- Hawaii Maritime Center, which traces Hawaiian maritime history from ancient times to the present.
- Mission Houses Museum, for a look back at the days when the New England missionaries transformed Hawaii forever.
- Pearl Harbor, where history was made on Dec. 7, 1941.
- National Memorial Cemetery of the Pacific at Punchbowl Crater, final resting place for thousands of American war dead.
- Iolani Palace, the only royal palace on U.S. soil, where Hawaii's embattled monarchy made its ill-fated last stand.

Botanical Gardens
- Foster Botanic Gardens, 15 splendid acres of rare trees, flowers, and plants.
- Lyon Arboretum, a research and educational center prized as a beautiful nature spot.

Shopping
- Ala Moana Shopping Center, one of the world's best malls, with products ranging from downhome to upscale.
- International Market Place and Kuhio Mall, giant outdoor bazaars.

Oahu's Regions in Brief

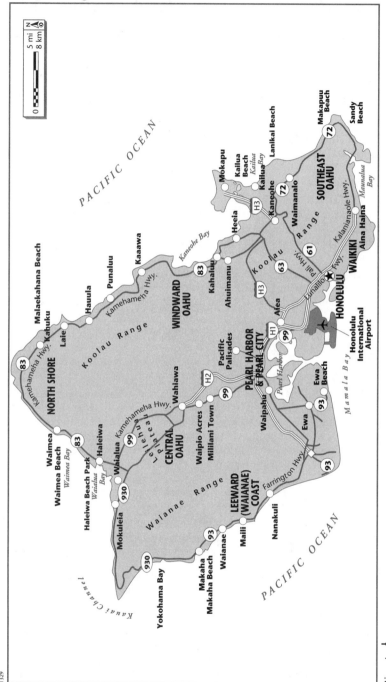

Airport

SOUTHEAST OAHU   The suburban area east of Waikiki, past Diamond Head, is home to some of Hawaii's loveliest (and wealthiest) suburbs. But that doesn't mean that it doesn't hold any interest for the visitor—you'll find the natural wonders of Koko Head and the Halona Blowhole, Sea Life Park, and more, including some of Hawaii's best snorkeling at Hanauma Bay. And, if nothing else, you'll have to trek out this way to dine at one of Hawaii's finest restaurants, Roy's.

WINDWARD OAHU   The pretty little towns of Kailua and Kaneohe are among Oahu's favorite suburban communities. Tunnels bored through the Koolaus take commuters back and forth from all the windward suburbs to downtown Honolulu. A string of beautiful beaches and parks dot the entire eastern coast-line, leading to the northern most point of Oahu at Kahuku Point. The world-famous Polynesian Cultural Center and the Mormon Temple at Laie are high points here.

NORTH SHORE   This is where you'll find Hawaii's biggest beach-bum/surf community. Some of the world's biggest waves hit the shores at Sunset Beach and Waimea Bay. World-class surfing championships held here during the winter months draw thousands of spectators. Haleiwa is a charming arts-and-crafts community.

CENTRAL OAHU   From Haleiwa to Honolulu, the interior is given over to sugarcane and pineapple fields, with one exception: Schofield Barracks Military Reservation, a major army base (you've seen it in *From Here to Eternity*) with its own Schofield Museum.

PEARL HARBOR AND PEARL CITY   Pearl Harbor, along Hawaii's southern shore, is the U.S. Naval Reservation where the Japanese sneak attack on December 7, 1941, catapulted the United States into World War II. The USS *Arizona* Memorial is a major attraction for both American and Japanese visitors.

LEEWARD (WAIANAE) COAST   Hawaii's population is moving west. This side of the island is home to the new subdivision of Kapolei, where hundreds of new homes are being built. Nearby, Ko Olina, the first planned resort destination outside Waikiki, is already open for business with a golf course and a major resort hotel. Yet on the rugged Waianae Coast, further west, there is very little tourist development, and local working people are not overly thrilled to welcome tourists into their domain. The area is dotted with world-class surfing beaches, Makaha Beach, in particular, is the home of international surfing events. The coast ends at rugged Kaena Point, the westernmost tip of Oahu, where, according to legend, souls of deceased Hawaiians depart for the other world.

2 Honolulu Orientation

ARRIVING BY PLANE

You're off the plane and standing in the Hawaiian sunshine. If you're lucky, some doting friend—maybe even a representative from your hotel—has greeted you with an aloha kiss and draped a fragrant lei around your neck. If not, don't worry; there are lei stands all over the island, and you'll have worn dozens by the time you're ready to go home. Your biggest problem right now is traveling the 10 miles from the airport to Waikiki, where you'll most likely be staying. If you've reserved a **rental car** in advance, it's easy; just pick it up and you're on your way. Or you could grab a **taxi** (they're always waiting at the airport); the tab to Waikiki will run about $20 to $22. It makes more sense for the individual traveler to take the Airport Waikiki Express shuttle bus (☎ 808/735-7797), which makes pickups outside the airline baggage-claim area every 20 to 30 minutes (depending on the time of day) and operates 24 hours a day. The fare is $7 each way (or $12 roundtrip ticket) for adults, $4 for children (those 2 years and under are free).

Although we are great believers in public transportation, the local bus system (TheBUS) is not ideal for baggage-laden tourists. Buses nos. 19 and 20 operate from the terminal into Waikiki, but make no provisions for luggage. If, however, you can hold all your bags on your lap, the price is certainly right—85¢ a ride. And you'll get a head start at meeting the local population.

DIRECTIONAL TERMS

In order to navigate your way around the city, by foot, bus, or car, you should know something about where you are.

Honolulu is, of course, the state capital, and it's the only major city on the island of Oahu. But before we get you oriented, we must tell you that people here have little use for such terms as *north, south, east,* or *west*—not even *uptown* or *downtown* are much help. The Hawaiian Islands sit in a kind of slantwise position on the map, and the reference points used most are either place names or directional signals meaning "toward the mountains" or "toward the sea."

Here's how it works. Suppose you are standing on Waikiki Beach, looking at Diamond Head crater; this means you are facing in a Diamond Head direction. You are, of course, at the beach area. But just a few miles away from this Pacific Riviera, the water is deep enough for oceangoing vessels to dock in Honolulu Harbor, which fronts on the downtown business district. (It was, in fact, that harbor's depth that made Honolulu a logical center for international commerce.) The downtown area is in an *Ewa* (EH-vah) direction (toward the village of Ewa) from Waikiki, and farther out in this section of the island, low plains of rich, red volcanic earth give birth to uncountable tons of sugar and pineapple. Anything toward the ocean is *makai.* To your left from the beach area, in a *mauka* (toward the mountains) direction, are the striking Koolau Mountains, which form the dramatic backdrop for the city. On the other side of the Koolaus is Windward Oahu, miles of verdant countryside bordering the water. This area is fast being transformed into the suburbs, from which Honolulu's commuters speed to the city's offices every day via tunnels bored through the mountains.

THE NEIGHBORHOODS IN BRIEF

Waikiki   This area runs from Ala Moana Boulevard in an Ewa direction, up to Kapahulu Avenue in a Diamond Head direction, and from the Ala Wai Canal on the mountain side to the ocean. Within Waikiki, Kalakaua Avenue is the main thoroughfare, bordering the ocean; parallel to it is Kuhio Avenue; and parallel to that is the Ala Wai Boulevard. Along these avenues and their side streets are concentrated the main hotels, restaurants, shops, and sights of the tourist area.

Kapahulu   This area is centered around Kapahulu Avenue, going one or two blocks on either side of Interstate H-1, otherwise known as the Expressway. Many stores, businesses, and restaurants are located here.

University   This district runs from McCully to South King Street, until South King becomes Waialae Avenue, then mauka up into Manoa Valley. It includes the University of Hawaii.

Honolulu's Neighborhoods in Brief

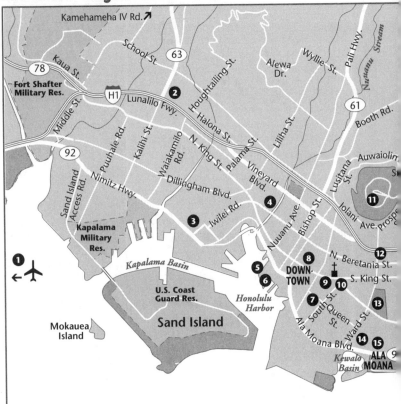

Kamehameha IV Rd.

School St.

63

Kaua St.

78

Fort Shafter
Military Res.

H1

Lunalilo Fwy.

2

Houghtailing St.

Halona St.

Alewa
Dr.

Wyllie St.

Pali Hwy.

Nuuanu Stream

61

Booth Rd.

Middle St.

92

Puuhale Rd.

Kalihi St.

Waiakamilo Rd.

N. King St.

Palama St.

Liliha St.

Lusitana St.

Auwaiolin

Nimitz Hwy.

Dillingham Blvd.

Vineyard Blvd.

Iolani Ave.

Prosp

Sand Island Access Rd.

Kapalama
Military
Res.

Iwilei Rd.

4

3

Bishop St.

Nuuanu Ave.

11

Kapalama Basin

U.S. Coast
Guard Res.

Honolulu
Harbor

5

6

DOWN-
TOWN

8

9

10

S. King St.

N. Beretania St.

12

13

Mokauea
Island

Sand Island

7

South St.

Queen St.

Ward St.

Ala Moana Blvd.

14

15

Kewalo
Basin

ALA
MOANA

9

M a m a l a   B a y

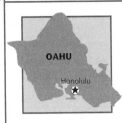

OAHU

Honolulu

Ala Moana Park **16**
Ala Moana Shopping
   Center **17**
Aloha Tower Marketplace **5**
Bishop Museum **2**
Diamond Head State
   Monument **26**
Dole Cannery Square **3**

Foster Botanic Garden
Hawaii Maritime Center
Hawaii Visitor's Bureau **6**
Honolulu Academy of
   Arts **12**
Honolulu International
   Airport **1**
Ilikai Marina **18**

1330

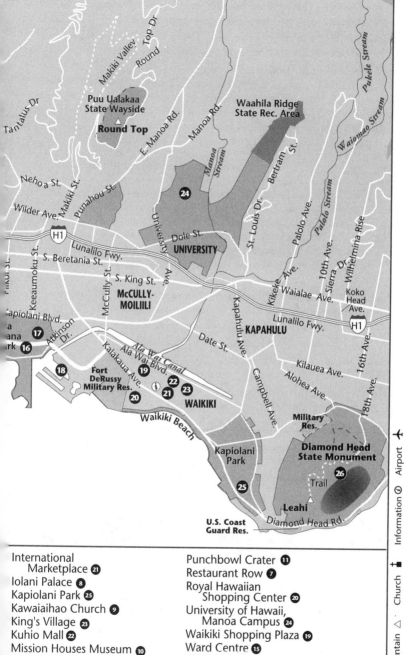

International
   Marketplace 21
Iolani Palace 8
Kapiolani Park 25
Kawaiaihao Church 9
King's Village 23
Kuhio Mall 22
Mission Houses Museum 10
Neal S. Blaisdell Center 13

Punchbowl Crater 11
Restaurant Row 7
Royal Hawaiian
   Shopping Center 20
University of Hawaii,
   Manoa Campus 24
Waikiki Shopping Plaza 19
Ward Centre 15
Ward Warehouse 14

Mountain △   Church ✝   Information ⓘ   Airport ✈

McCully-Moiliili   This is the area running from Kapiolani Boulevard to South King Street. There are stores, businesses, and Asian restaurants.

Ala Moana   This district extends mauka of Ala Moana Boulevard, between Waikiki and Restaurant Row. The Ala Moana Shopping Center is here.

Downtown Honolulu   Downtown includes everything from Restaurant Row to the Historical Chinatown District. The latter is bordered by Beretania Street on the mountain side, Nuuanu Avenue on the Diamond Head side, Nimitz Highway on the harbor side, and River Street on the Ewa/airport side. The city's major business and financial district is here.

MAIN STREETS & HIGHWAYS

To help you get your bearings in Waikiki, you should know that there are three major parallel arteries. Fronting the beach is **Kalakaua Avenue,** Waikiki's main street and its choicest location, full of big hotels, shops, restaurants, and thousands of tourists. About three short blocks mauka is **Kuhio Avenue,** a bit (but just a bit) quieter and less crowded. A few more blocks mauka is **Ala Wai Boulevard,** next to Ala Wai Canal and close to the mountains. This peaceful waterway was created in 1920 when a brilliant entrepreneur got the idea of draining the swampland that was Waikiki. It is adjacent to the inexpensive, public Ala Wai Golf Course, and joggers love it.

Nimitz Highway/Ala Moana Boulevard   This two-way divided highway runs from the airport to Waikiki.

King Street   This goes one-way from downtown Honolulu to the University of Hawaii, passing Iolani Palace and downtown historical sights.

Beretania Street   This is one-way going in the opposite direction; it starts at University Avenue and goes through Chinatown.

The H-1 Freeway   This goes from Pearl Harbor/Airport to the Kahala Mall, then continues as a divided express highway, Kalanianaole, which goes around the island.

STREET MAPS

Locals consider the best Oahu maps to be Bryan's *Sectional Maps of Oahu* and the *Oahu Reference Maps* by James A. Bier, Cartographer. Both can be obtained in many bookstores, or from Hawaii Geographic Maps and Books, 49 South Hotel St., Suite 218, P.O. Box 1698, Honolulu, HI 96808 (☎ 808/532-3952). Also very useful is H. M. Gousha's *FastMap*™ for Honolulu/Oahu.

3 Getting Around

The most efficient and enjoyable way to travel around the island is by rental car. But if you are unable or don't want to rent a car for some reason or another, or if you just would prefer to avoid the hassle and expense, Oahu has some great public transportation alternatives for you. They will take you almost anywhere you want to go on the island, but they're particularly viable if you're trying to make your way around the city.

BY PUBLIC BUS

Your best form of transportation in Honolulu is owned and operated by the city and county of Honolulu: TheBUS. Buses run all over town and maintain frequent schedules between Waikiki and downtown Honolulu. It operates daily from 5am to 12:30am on main routes. If you need assistance, call TheBUS information department at 808/848-5555 between 5:30am and 10pm. The fare is 85¢; have exact change ready. Students age 6 through high school are charged 25¢. If you want a free transfer to a connecting bus, ask for it as you board. Senior citizens can ride the buses at a savings by showing a bus pass (call 808/848-4444 for information).

Bus schedules are not, unfortunately, available on the buses themselves, but if you have any questions about how to get where, simply call TheBUS information number (☎ 808/848-5555). Keep in mind that the buses you will take from Waikiki to Ala Moana Shopping Center or to downtown Honolulu must be boarded on Kuhio Avenue.

If you're at Ala Moana Shopping Center, you can use the no-cost direct telephones to TheBUS information, located at the bus stops on the north and south sides of the center. You should also note that traffic on Kalakaua Avenue, Waikiki's main thoroughfare, goes Diamond Head most of the way.

It's also possible to visit most parts of Oahu, and even to circle the entire island, by public transportation. TheBUS no. 55, "Circle Island," which leaves Ala Moana Shopping Center daily at 5 and 35 minutes after the hour from 6:05am on, will enable you to see many island points of interest: the big surf at Haleiwa, Sunset Beach, the North Shore, and the Polynesian Cultural Center, to name a few. The cost is $1.70, with no transfers; you'll have to pay 85¢ every time you reboard the bus.

However, this is not the most efficient and enjoyable way to travel around the island; you'll do better in a rented car. Frequent tours leave Waikiki to major destination points as well.

BY SIGHTSEEING TROLLEY

More expensive than TheBUS, but in some instances cheaper than a cab, the Waikiki Trolley offers another means of transportation. Old-fashioned motorized trolleys that recall turn-of-the-century streetcars travel between the Royal Hawaiian Shopping Center and Dole Cannery Square daily, making stops en route at Ala Moana Shopping Center, the Hilton Hawaiian Village, the Honolulu Academy of the Arts, Ward Warehouse and Fisherman's Wharf, Ward Centre, the state capitol and Iolani Palace, the Mission Houses Museum and the King Kamehameha Statue, Chinatown, the Hawaii Maritime Center, Restaurant Row, and the Hilo Hattie Factory. The cost is $15 per day for adults, $5 for children. Stay on for the entire two-hour narrated trip, or jump on and off whenever you like and continue on another trolley. Phone 808/591-2651 for exact routes and schedules, or check the local tourist papers.

BY TAXI

Taxis cruise the main streets of Waikiki, so you should have no trouble flagging one. You can also ask your hotel desk to get one for you, or phone for one yourself. Some reliable companies are Charley's Taxi (☎ 808/531-1333), City Taxi (☎ 808/524-2121), Aloha State Cab (☎ 808/847-3566), and Sida of Hawaii (☎ 808/836-0011). The first flip of the meter will cost $1.50. Taxis are not inexpensive, but they might be cheaper than renting a car if you're only doing a limited amount of traveling.

TheBUS

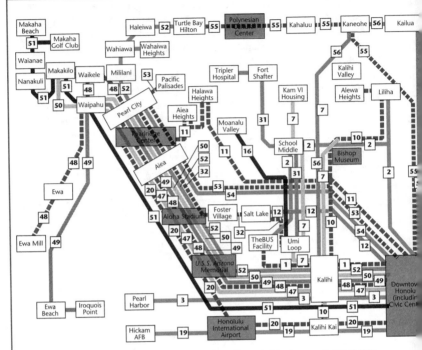

Common Bus Routes (all routes originate from Kuhio Avenue in Waikiki):

Ala Moana Shopping Center: Take bus #8 & #58 ALA MOANA CENTER, #19 & #20 AIRPORT or #47 WAIPAHU. Return #8 WAIKIKI or #19 WAIKIKI, or across Ala Moana Blvd. #20 & #47.

Bishop Museum: Take #2 SCHOOL STREET get off at Kapalama St., cross School St., walk down Bernice St. Return to School St. and take #2 WAIKIKI.

Byodo-In Temple: Take bus #2 to Hotel-Alakea St. (TRF) to #55 KANEOHE-KAHALUU. Get off at Valley of the Temple cemetery. Also #19 & #20 AIRPORT to King-Alakea St., (TRF) on Alakea St. to #55 KANEOHE-KAHALUU.

Circle Island: Take a Bus to ALA MOANA CENTER (TRF) to #52 WAHIAWA CIRCLE ISLAND or #55 KENEOHE CIRCLE ISLAND. This is a four-hour bus ride.

Chinatown or Downtown: Take any #2 bus going out of Waikiki, to Hotel St. Return take #2 WAIKIKI on Hotel St., or #19, #20, #47 WAIKIKI on King St.

Contemporary Museum & Punchbowl (National Cemetery of the Pacific): Take #2 bus (TRF) at Alapai St. to #15 MAKIKI-PACIFIC HGTS. Return, take #15 and get off at King St., area (TRF) #2 WAIKIKI.

Diamond Head Crater: #22 or #58 HAWAII KAI-SEA LIFE PARK to the crater. Take a flashlight. Return to the same area and take #22 WAIKIKI or #58 ALA MOANA.

Dole Plantation: Take bus to ALA MOANA CENTER (TRF) to #52 WAHIAWA CIRCLE ISLAND.

Foster Botanic Gardens: Take #2 bus to Hotel-Riviera St. Walk to Vineyard Blvd. Return to Hotel St. Take #2 WAIKIKI, or take #4 NUUANU and get off at Nuuanu-Vineyard. Cross Nuuanu Ave. and walk one block to the gardens.

Hawaii Maritime Center: Take #19-#20 AIRPORT, #47 WAIPAHU and get off at Alakea–Ala Moana. Cross the Street to the Aloha Tower.

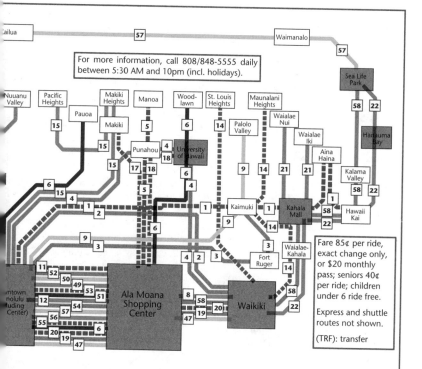

Honolulu Zoo: Take any bus on Kuhio Ave. going DIAMOND HEAD direction to Kapahulu Ave.

Iolani Palace, also **State Capitol, Kawaihao Church, Mission Houses, King Kamehameha Statue, State Judiciary Bldg:** take any #2 bus and get off at Punchbowl and Beretania St. Walk to King St. Return #2 WAIKIKI on King St.

Kodak Hula Show: (Tues-Thurs 10AM.) Free. Take #8, #19, #20, #47 WAIKIKI or #2 KAPIOLANI PARK to Kapiolani Park. Walk to the Waikiki Shell.

Pearl Harbor (USS *Arizona* Memorial): Open Daily 8AM to 3PM. Free. Take #20 AIRPORT or #47 WAIPAHU. Get off across from Memorial, or take a bus to Ala Moana Center (TRF) to #49, #50 or #52.

Polynesian Cultural Center: Take a bus to ALA MOANA CENTER (TRF) to #55 KANEOHE CIRCLE ISLAND. Bus ride takes two hours one way. PCC opens at 12:30PM. Closed on Sundays.

Queen Emma's Summer Palace: Take #4 NUUANU and it will take you there, or board a bus to ALA MOANA CENTER (TRF) to #55 KANEOHE, #56-#57 KAILUA.

Sea Life Park: #22-#58 HAWAII KAI-SEA LIFE PARK. #22 will stop at Hanauma Bay enroute to the park.

University of Hawaii: Take #4 NUUANU. The bus will go to the University enroute to Nuuanu.

Waimea Falls Park: Take a bus to ALA MOANA CENTER (TRF) to #52 WAHIAWA CIRCLE ISLAND or #55 KANEOHE CIRCLE ISLAND.

BY CAR

RENTALS   At some time during your Hawaiian stay, you may want to slip behind the wheel of a car, maybe to tour the entire island of Oahu or just to take a sightseeing excursion on the windward side. The car-rental business is one of the most competitive in the state. The best idea is to check out the companies on the scene, since prices change so quickly; the tourist newspapers will give you leads. If, however, you know in advance that you're going to do a great deal of driving (and especially if you're going to the neighbor islands, where your own set of wheels is a must), reserve your car in advance from one of the reputable national companies. All offer "flat rates," which means that mileage is included. They usually turn out to be less expensive for extensive driving than the regular rates plus mileage. **Alamo Rent A Car** (☎ 800/327-9633), **Avis Rent A Car** (☎ 800/331-1212), **Budget Rent A Car** (☎ 800/527-0700), **Dollar Rent A Car of Hawaii** (☎ 800/367-7006), **Hertz Rent A Car** (☎ 800/654-3131), and **National Interrent** (☎ 800/227-7368) are all reputable firms.

Depending on the car, the company, and whatever special deals are available at the time you're there (be sure to inquire about "all-island" specials), expect to pay from $25 to $40 per day for your car. Many hotels, especially those belonging to the Outrigger chain, often have room-and-car packages that provide considerable savings; inquire when you make hotel reservations.

PARKING   Parking is extremely difficult in Waikiki. You'll probably have to put your car in a lot overnight, which can run anywhere from $4 to $10. As for street parking, Ala Wai Boulevard, along the canal, is less crowded than other main thoroughfares. Street meters sometimes limit parking to 12 to 24 minutes. Read each meter carefully.

DRIVING RULES   A few words about driving in Honolulu. Many major thoroughfares are now one-way streets, which helps the flow of traffic but often makes it seem that you are driving miles out of your way to reach a specific destination. Downtown Honolulu is an especially confusing place for driving. You may want to keep in mind that in this area Beretania Street is Ewa, King Street is Diamond Head, Pensacola traffic now heads makai, and Piikoi cars go in a mauka direction. In Waikiki, Kalakaua traffic is Diamond Head most of the way, with a short stretch downtown running in both directions; Kuhio Avenue is two-way and the Ala Wai Boulevard is Ewa.

Those painted white arrows on the various lanes are not to be ignored. They indicate in what directions you are permitted to drive from each lane: right only, left only, left and straight ahead, or right and straight ahead. It's legal to make right turns when the light is red at most intersections—but not all—so read the signs first. And if you come across a sign reading "We appreciate your kokua," it's not an invitation to pay a toll. Kokua means "cooperation" in Hawaiian.

BY BICYCLE

Honolulu, like big cities everywhere, has become very cycle conscious. Bicycles used to be available for rental at a number of locations, but lately most of the hotels and rental agencies (like Hertz) have stopped renting them because of the high equipment mortality rate. "We kept finding them in the ocean," said one supplier. But we discovered *one* place where they can still be rented: **Blue Sky Rentals,** 1920 Ala Moana Blvd. (☎ 808/947-0101) at a rate of $25 for 24 hours ($50 deposit).

FAST FACTS: Honolulu & Oahu

AAA Hawaii   The local office of the **American Automobile Association** is at 590 Queen St. (☎ 808/528-2600; road service, 808/537-5544).

Area Code   The entire state of Hawaii has one telephone area code: 808.

Babysitters   Check first at your hotel desk. You can also try **Aloha Babysitting Service** (☎ 808/732-2029), **Available Sitters** (☎ 808/951-6118), and **Sitters Unlimited** (☎ 808/262-5728).

Business Hours   Most offices are open from 8am to 4 or 5pm Monday through Friday. Normal bank hours are 8:30am to 3 or 3:30pm Monday through Thursday, to 6pm on Friday. Most shopping malls are open from 9 or 10am to 9pm Monday through Friday, to 5:30pm on Saturday, and usually to 4pm on Sunday.

Car Rentals   Names and telephone numbers of major car-rental companies, which rent automobiles on Oahu can be found in "Getting Around" in this chapter.

Dentists   The Dental Care Centers of Hawaii offer 24-hour emergency service. There are many locations around the island; addresses can be found in the telephone book. The after-hours number to call is 808/488-5200. Hawaii Family Dental Center (☎ 808/944-0011), conveniently located at Sears at the Ala Moana Shopping Center, has a number of dentists on hand who can provide speedy treatment at a reasonable cost.

Doctors   We hope it won't happen, but if you should need medical assistance while you're in Honolulu, there are several good possibilities. The Queen's Medical Center has a Waikiki affiliate: Queen's Health Care Center, 1778 Ala Moana Blvd. (☎ 808/943-1111). The clinic is open Monday through Friday from 8am to 8pm, Saturday and Sunday from 8am to 4pm; they also have 24-hour emergency care available. On the windward side, 24-hour emergency care is available at Castle Medical Center, 640 Ulikahiki, Kailua (☎ 808/263-5500).

Kuhio Walk-In Medical Clinics has a very convenient location at 2310 Kuhio Ave., no. 223 (second floor), across from the International Market Place (☎ **808/924-6688**). They are open Monday through Saturday from 9am to 5pm; no appointment is required. They also make house/hotel calls.

Should you require a house call—or hotel call—contact Doctors on Call (DOC). They're on duty every day, 24 hours a day, and a phone call to **808/971-8000** will bring them to your hotel room promptly; the charge is a hefty $170! DOC also maintains 24-hour walk-in clinics: Phone the central number and you will be directed to the one closest to your hotel.

Emergencies   Dial 911 for fire, ambulance, or police; if you cannot reach 911, dial 0 and the operator will assist you. For Poisoning emergencies, call the Poison Center, ☎ 808/941-4411.

Newspapers/Magazines   There are two newspapers, both published by the Hawaii Newspaper Agency. During the week, the *Honolulu Advertiser* is the morning paper; the *Honolulu Star-Bulletin* is the evening paper with the bigger circulation. On Sunday, it's the *Honolulu Advertiser*.

Aloha magazine (published bimonthly) and *Honolulu* magazine (published monthly) make for interesting reading.

Police   Dial 911; if that doesn't work, dial 0 for the operator.

Post Office   In Waikiki, it's at 330 Saratoga Rd., next to Fort DeRussy (☎ 808/423-3990). Open Monday, Tuesday, Thursday, and Friday 8am to 4:30pm, Saturday 9 to noon.

Radio/TV   **Radio:** For all-Hawaiian music, tune in to KCNN, 1420 AM; for island music, contemporary Hawaiian to reggae, it's KCCN, 100.3 FM. KHPR, 88.1 FM, is Hawaii Public Radio for classical music and news; KIPO, 1380 AM and 89.3 FM, is Hawaii Public Radio for news, jazz, classical, and folk music. Station KTUH, 90.3 FM, presents jazz, classical, rock, and Hawaiian music. Try KHVH, 990 AM, for news, sports, and talk.

TV: Most hotels have cable TV, as cable is necessary virtually everywhere on Oahu; 95% of the island is served by Oceanic Cablevision, whose major offerings are Channel 3, KHON (NBC); Channel 6, KITV (ABC); Channel 7, KGMB (CBS); Channel 10, PBS; Channel 14, CNN; Channel 24, HBO; Channel 25, Cinemax; Channel 26, AMC; Channel 28, A & E; Channel 29, TNT; Channel 31, MTV; Channel 32, TMC; Channel 33, Showtime; Channel 34, Disney; Channel 44, JMC.

Taxis   See "Getting Around" in this chapter.

Telegrams/Fax   Fax services are available at many copy centers and at all Phone Mart locations. The ones closest to Waikiki are at Ward Warehouse (☎ 808/521-3373; fax 808/538-0361) and downtown Honolulu (☎ 808/521-2722; fax 808/523-6418). Also, some hotels will let you use their fax machines; inquire at the desk.

Telephone Calls   Five dollars doesn't buy a great deal in Hawaii these days, but it can buy you an eight-minute phone call back to the mainland or a series of phone calls for up to eight minutes. Here's how it works: You go to one of the Phone Line Hawaii's Waikiki telecom centers at either the International Market Place, 2330 Kalakaua, or the Discovery Bay Center, 1778 Ala Moana Blvd., where the cards are on sale every day 8:30am to 11pm. Then you use your card from any telephone, either in a phone booth or your hotel room, and you eliminate the charges that hotels levy on operator-assisted calls. Cards calling Canada cost $5, and cards for other countries are also available at $10 to $20.

Transit Info   For information on TheBUS, call MTL at 808/848-5555.

Useful Telephone Numbers   For time, call 808/983-3211. For a surf report, call 808/836-1952.

Weather   In the Honolulu area, call 808/833-2849; for the rest of Oahu, call 808/836-0121; For the Hawaiian waters, call 808/836-3921.

Visitors Bureau   The Hawaii Visitors Bureau (☎ 808/923-1811) is at 2270 Kalakaua Ave., 7th floor.

Accommodations 6

Somewhere on Oahu there's a hotel that's exactly right for you—whether you want to swim, play, and party in world-famous Waikiki; relax in the peaceful surroundings of a windward Oahu bed-and-breakfast, close to uncrowded beaches; or do business in bustling, cosmopolitan downtown Honolulu. Should you want to hang out with the surfing set on Oahu's North Shore or venture out to the Leeward Coast's fabulous new resort mecca, we've got the place for you. While the majority of Oahu's accommodations are in Waikiki, there are enough scattered around the island to allow you to explore beyond the confines of the city, even a bit off the regularly beaten path, if you so desire.

Unfortunately, Oahu's zoning laws regarding bed-and-breakfasts are very strict—much more so than those on the neighbor islands—so their numbers are limited. Nevertheless, we've included a good list for you to choose from, as well as a selection of reliable bed-and-breakfast reservation services (see below).

As for Waikiki itself, there's much to like—and a lot to dislike. On the negative side, Waikiki has become a victim of its own success: It *is* crowded, noisy, and overbuilt. On the other hand, one of the world's greatest beaches is within walking distance of any hotel; there's no need to have a car here. Restaurants in every price range are a short walk from wherever you are. It has vast possibilities for recreation, sightseeing, shopping—much of it free or at little cost. Waikiki offers easy bus access to downtown Honolulu and, via public bus and organized tour, to all the adventures around the island. And Waikiki has been much improved in recent years, thanks to a beautification program that widened the sidewalks and improved traffic conditions. As for people watching, it can't be beat: It sometimes seems that half of Japan, Australia, Canada, and the United States are all here—and they're all having a great time.

There are two general categories of hotel in Waikiki; the big, lively, resort-type hotels that may be perfect for active singles and unencumbered couples; and the usually smaller, apartment-type hotels that are better suited for families with children or for anyone who wants to stay in the islands more than the usual week or two. These smaller apartment hotels (most of which are condos) all have a money-saving (and child-pleasing) advantage—a kitchenette, which is ideal for making coffee, storing Junior's chocolate milk, and

Finding Yourself a Home Away from Home: Bed & Breakfast Reservations Services

If you would like to stay in a private home or cottage, the following bed-and-breakfast services can help you.

✪ **Bed & Breakfast Hawaii,** P.O. Box 449, Kapaa, HI 96746 (☎ 808/822-7711 or 800/733-1632; fax 808/822-2723), offers accommodations in private homes, apartments, condos, and small inns, on all islands, for rates ranging from $40 to $125 single, $50 to $108 double. Send $12.95 for a directory.

Bed & Breakfast Honolulu (Statewide), 3242 Kaohinani Dr., Honolulu, HI 96817 (☎ 808/595-7533 or 800/288-4666; fax 808/595-2030), offers more than 400 "homestays" and studios on the major islands.

Pacific-Hawaii Bed & Breakfast, 99-442 Kekoa Pl., Aiea, Oahu, HI 96701 (☎ 808/487-1228 or 800/999-6026; fax 808/261-6573), focuses mostly on Oahu, with a few offerings on other islands as well. Rates begin at $45 a day.

✪ **Hawaii's Best Bed & Breakfasts,** P.O. Box 563, Kamuela, HI 96743 (☎ 808/855-4550 or 800/262-9912; fax 808/855-0559), lives up to its name with high-quality lodgings throughout the state. Daily rates go from $75 to $175. Write for a brochure.

Go Native Hawaii, 65 Halaulani Place, P.O. Box 11418, Hilo, HI 96721 (☎ 808/935-4178 or 800/662-8483), has 250 locations on all islands except Lanai, at rates beginning at $40 single, $65 double, and luxury properties from $100 to $150 double.

fixing a quick meal when you don't want to eat out. (Most large hotels do not have kitchenettes, but some will furnish a small refrigerator at your request.) The condo hotels tend to be on side streets between the three major thoroughfares, Kalakaua and Kuhio avenues and Ala Wai Boulevard. Remember, all hotels are within easy walking or bus distance of one another, and all are near the important attractions of Waikiki.

How much is it going to cost? Because there's such an incredible variety of accommodations—everything from rundown bohemian haunts to hotels with ballroom-sized bedrooms where presidents, movie stars, Arabian princes, and Japanese business moguls are right at home—the price range is, accordingly, enormous. You can rent a cute little kitchenette apartment a few blocks from the beach for about $70 a night, an oceanfront suite for $2,000 a night at a beachfront palace, or anything in between.

We've picked out the best accommodations in each price category. If you can spring for $185 and (way) up for a double, make your selection from the **Very Expensive** category. If you'd prefer to spend about $135 to $185 per night, stick to the **Expensive** category. If a price tag between $100 and $135 a night suits you better, consult our **Moderate** category. And if you're really watching your dollars, turn to the **Budget** category. Here we've described some clean, comfortable, and sometimes surprisingly lovely accommodations where the nightly tab is under $100—sometimes way under—for two. Please note that these categories are only general, since there is a wide variety of rates in each hotel, and that rates are usually much higher in winter than in summer.

Most hotels in Hawaii have different rates for high season (usually mid-December to April 1) and low season (the rest of the year).

High-season rates add at least $10 to $20 to your bill per day. During slack periods, rates may come down considerably, especially in the smaller establishments. Many hotels offer special incentives for weekly and monthly stays. Hawaii's hotel tax is now a whopping 10.17%. The tax is not included in rates given in this book. (Tax rates are subject to change.) Parking rates given in the listings below are per day.

Please note that the landmark Kahala Hilton Hotel has closed its doors. Oahu's most popular luxury celebrity haven will reopen sometime this year as the Kahala Mandarin Oriental, Hawaii: The Mandarin Oriental folks have several hotels in the Far East, one in Thailand, and one in San Francisco. As of press time, there were few details available. The fine dining restaurant (formerly known as The Maile) will be relocated, perhaps overlooking the water, and will have a new name. Another restaurant will be open all day and will be suitable for families with children. There will be a business center, and, possibly, a fitness center. All rooms will be redecorated. And yes, the playful dolphins will be much in evidence. Danny Kaleikini, the entertainer who became synonymous with the Kahala over the years, has, alas, retired. Call the Hawaii Visitors Bureau for an update.

1 Diamond Head Waikiki

VERY EXPENSIVE

✪ Hyatt Regency Waikiki

2424 Kalakaua Ave., Honolulu, HI 96815. ☎ **808/923-1234,** or 800/233-1234. Fax 808/923-7839. 1,230 rms, 21 suites. A/C MINIBAR TV TEL. $190–$305 double, $320 Regency Club, $380 Regency Club ocean, $475–$600 suite, $1,100–$1,400 penthouse, $1,500–$2,000 Ambassador or Presidential two-bedroom suite. AE, CB, DC, DISC, JCB, MC, V. Valet parking $10, self-parking $8.

This $100-million caravansary by the sea occupies an entire city block, and accomplishes the seemingly impossible: creating an oasis of tranquility and lush tropical beauty in the midst of the most bustling, heavily trafficked area in town. All the public areas have been placed around a huge, lushly landscaped atrium, or Great Hall, above which the guest rooms rise in twin 40-story towers that afford maximum views of ocean and mountains, as well as substantial privacy and peace. The Great Hall, one of the most beautiful spots in Honolulu—replete with tumbling waterfalls, fountains, cascades of greenery, flowers, magnificent sculptures, and dotted with art, antiques, and intimate conversation areas—is also one of the most popular shopping, restaurant, and promenade areas.

The guest rooms are among the largest in town, and each has a furnished lanai, a sofa, huge closets, wall-to-wall carpeting, and king-size and double beds. The natural pastel tones complement whitewashed oak, ash, light marble, and rattan furnishings. Regency Club guests enjoy more elaborate rooms and special amenities, including complimentary breakfast and cocktails and daily newspapers from around the world.

The beach is directly across the street, but guests can also swim and sun at the third-floor pool and enjoy poolside drinks at the Elegant Dive. Regency Club guests enjoy rooftop sun decks with a cool-water Jacuzzi.

Dining/Entertainment: The hotel has four restaurants and five cocktail lounges, including the Terrace Grille, an indoor-outdoor restaurant overlooking the ocean; Musashi, a stunning Japanese restaurant; Harry's Bar; Ciao Mein for creative Chinese and Italian cuisine; and the Colony for steaks, fresh seafood, salad, and dessert bars. Kento's is a Japanese dance club featuring 1950s and '60s music.

Services: Concierge, business services (including typing, personal computer rental, stock news, notary public), Camp Hyatt for kids, room service, daily maid service.

Facilities: Beach across street, swimming pool, and Hyatt's Hawaii, a historical center.

✪ Sheraton Moana Surfrider Hotel

2365 Kalakaua Ave., Honolulu, HI 96815. ☎ **808/922-3111**, or 800/325-3535. Fax 808/923-0308. 793 rms and suites. A/C MINIBAR TV TEL. $210 city view, $240 large city view, $295 ocean view in Banyan Wing, $305 partial ocean view in Tower Wing, $350 deluxe ocean view in Tower and Diamond Wings. Extra person $25. Rollaway bed $25. Children under 18 free in parents' room with existing bedding. AE, CB, DC, MC, V. Parking $10.

Perhaps the most significant historical renovation in Hawaii since that of Iolani Palace, the $50-million restoration of the venerable Moana Hotel has created a world-class hotel that recalls the charms of turn-of-the-century Waikiki while combining them with every modern comfort and luxury. Built in 1901, the Moana Surfrider was for generations the classic South Seas hostelry on the beach at Waikiki. The restoration has preserved the colonial architecture of the handsome white building, restoring its original porte-cochère and the Kalakaua Avenue verandas, so popular in the early years of the century. Outdoors, the Banyan Court, original home of the famed "Hawaii Calls" radio show, offers a freshwater pool and a recreation deck.

Guest rooms combine the best of old-world traditions with modern convenience. New additions include, in the Banyan Wing, colonial reproduction armoires and luxurious bathrooms with such amenities as hair dryers, lighted makeup mirrors, and plush bathrobes.

Dining/Entertainment: The Beachside Café, overlooking the ocean, is great for casual dining, as is W. C. Peacock and Co., Ltd., also at ocean's edge in a tropical garden setting. The Banyan Veranda is the setting for breakfast, Sunday brunch, high tea, and afternoon cocktails. The Moana's fine dining restaurant, the Ship's Tavern, features steak and seafood. The Beach Bar and a poolside snack bar are outdoors.

Services: Free, supervised children's program in the summer months for ages 5 to 12; "Golden Guests" program for those 55 and older which includes room upgrades and discounts. Daily guest activities feature Hawaiian arts and crafts such as coconut-palm weaving and Hawaiian quilting.

Facilities: Beach, freshwater swimming pool.

EXPENSIVE

Aston Waikiki Beachside Hotel

2452 Kalakaua Ave., Honolulu, HI 96815. ☎ **808/931-2100**, or 800/922-7866 from U.S. mainland, 800/445-6633 from Canada. Fax 808/922-8785. 79 rms. A/C TV TEL. $99–$160 standard room, $120–$180 superior room, $135–$195 partial ocean view, $250–$290

Waikiki Accommodations

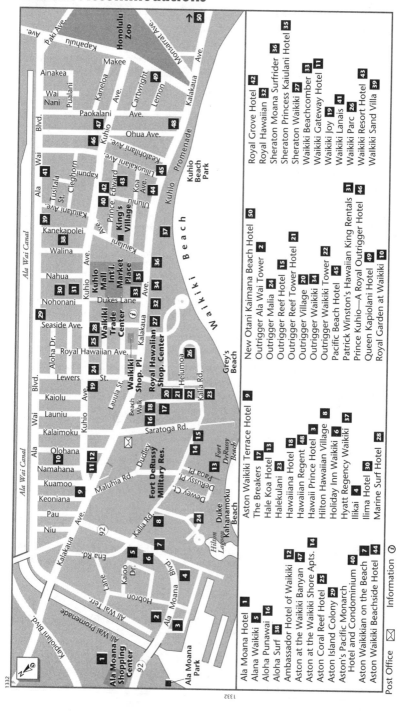

Ala Moana Hotel **1**
Alana Waikiki **5**
Aloha Punawai **16**
Aloha Surf **38**
Ambassador Hotel of Waikiki **12**
Aston at the Waikiki Banyan **47**
Aston at the Waikiki Shore Apts. **14**
Aston Coral Reef Hotel **25**
Aston Island Colony **29**
Aston's Pacific Monarch
Hotel and Condominium **40**
Aston Waikikian on the Beach **7**
Aston Waikiki Beachside Hotel **44**

Aston Waikiki Terrace Hotel **9**
The Breakers **17**
Hale Koa Hotel **13**
Halekulani **38**
Hawaiiana Hotel **18**
Hawaiian Regent **48**
Hawaii Prince Hotel **3**
Hilton Hawaiian Village **8**
Holiday Inn Waikiki **6**
Hyatt Regency Waikiki **37**
Ilikai **4**
Ilima Hotel **30**
Marine Surf Hotel **28**

New Otani Kaimana Beach Hotel **50**
Outrigger Ala Wai Tower **2**
Outrigger Malia **24**
Outrigger Reef Hotel **15**
Outrigger Reef Tower Hotel **21**
Outrigger Village **20**
Outrigger Waikiki **34**
Outrigger Waikiki Tower **22**
Pacific Beach Hotel **45**
Patrick Winston's Hawaiian King Rentals **31**
Prince Kuhio—A Royal Outrigger Hotel **46**
Queen Kapiolani Hotel **49**
Royal Garden at Waikiki **10**

Royal Grove Hotel **42**
Royal Hawaiian **32**
Sheraton Moana Surfrider **36**
Sheraton Princess Kaiulani Hotel **35**
Sheraton Waikiki **27**
Waikiki Beachcomber **33**
Waikiki Gateway Hotel **11**
Waikiki Joy **19**
Waikiki Lanais **41**
Waikiki Parc **26**
Waikiki Resort Hotel **43**
Waikiki Sand Villa **39**

Post Office ⊠   Information ⓘ

oceanfront. Maximum occupancy two adults per room. Rates subject to change. AE, CB, DC, DISC, JCB, MC, V. Parking $9.50 at nearby hotel.

World-class luxury on a small, intimate scale—this lovely hotel has a lot going for it. First, it's directly across the road from one of the best stretches of Waikiki Beach; second, it enjoys the ministrations of an extremely cordial and helpful staff; and third, it's exquisitely furnished, from lobby to guest rooms, with a superb collection of arts and antiques, much of them 18th-century European. Guests can relax downstairs in the Palm Court (where continental breakfast is served), with its handsome Italian stone fountain, or upstairs in their lovely rooms (there are no more than eight on each floor). The rooms are beautifully decorated in peach, gold, and black; the fanciful bathrooms have every amenity, and you'll find exquisite details like yukata robes, hand-painted Oriental screens, flowers, and plants. Each room has its own mini-refrigerator, in-room safe, a PC-compatible phone line with two phones and voicemail, and VCR (tapes can be rented at the front desk). The hotel has no restaurant of its own, but guests have full billing privileges for all the entertainment and dining facilities of the Hyatt Regency Waikiki, just next door.

Services: European concierge service, twice-daily maid service, morning newspaper, same-day laundry, and dry cleaning.

✪ Colony Surf

2895 Kalakaua Ave., Honolulu, HI 96815. ☎ **808/923-5751,** or 800/252-7873 from U.S. mainland, 800/423-7781 from Canada. Fax 808/922-8433. 90 suites. A/C TV TEL. Main building, $180–$200 limited view, $285 partial Diamond Head view, $285–$315 direct oceanfront view one-bedroom suite; East Building, $125–$150 limited view, $170 partial ocean and Diamond Head view studio. Extra person $15. AE, DC, MC, V. Free parking.

If what you crave is elegant living, glorious views of the ocean, and room to stretch out, then this all-suite boutique hotel is for you. It's located in the quieter Diamond Head section of town, across from Kapiolani Park, and right on one of the best swimming beaches in town. The heart of Waikiki is a 10-minute stroll or short bus ride. And the size of the rooms matches the splendor of the vistas—many of the rooms have 25-foot windows providing spectacular ocean views.

There are two buildings: The Colony Surf, whose elegant and immense one-bedroom suites each have a fully equipped kitchen, two double beds, and every nicety; and the Colony Surf East, where the studio suites are luxuriously appointed, with kitchenettes. Two double beds, plenty of closet space, and large bath vanities. You can't go wrong in either building.

Dining/Entertainment: Michel's is an award-winning, seaside French/European restaurant reviewed in Chapter 7.

Services: Full concierge, daily maid service with nightly turn down, morning newspaper, full beach service including food and beverages, room service from Michel's.

✪ Hawaiian Regent

2552 Kalakaua Ave., Honolulu, HI 96815. ☎ **808/922-6611,** or 800/367-5370. Fax 808/921-5255. 1,346 rms, 6 deluxe suites. A/C TV TEL $140–$250 double, $250 junior suite, $430 one-bedroom suite, $570 two-bedroom suite, $700–$875 deluxe suite. Extra person $20. Children under 18 free in parents' room with existing bedding. Attractive honeymoon packages are available. AE, CB, DC, DISC, JCB, MC, V. Parking $7.

Although it's in the midst of the Waikiki madness, the Hawaiian Regent has the ambience of a retreat. It's wrapped around a cool, lush inner courtyard, and the architectural details are striking. The third-floor swimming pool and sitting area, with glorious views of Waikiki beach just across the street, is a stunner.

The good looks continue in the rooms, which are large and exquisitely furnished in teak and rattan. The spacious private lanais have breathtaking views of sea, mountains, or Diamond Head.

Dining/Entertainment: You can dine at the attractive Summery Restaurant, on fine continental cuisine or at the award-winning Secret. For Japanese cuisine, try the Regent Hatsuhana or the Kobe Fugetsudo, a Japanese coffee shop. Have a drink at the Library, a contemporary bar, or a coffee and croissant at the Café Regent, a Parisian-style café. The Ocean Terrace offers casual lunches and poolside cocktails. The Lobby Bar hosts Hawaiian entertainment nightly in the midst of all the activity in the main lobby.

Services: Concierge desk, room service, summer programs for children, complimentary aloha activities in the Garden Courtyard Monday, Wednesday, and Friday mornings, hospitality rooms for guests with early arrivals or late departures. **Facilities:** Two swimming pools, tennis court, shopping arcade.

The New Otani Kaimana Beach Hotel

2863 Kalakaua Ave., Honolulu, HI 96815. ☎ **808/923-1555,** or 800/35-OTANI from U.S. mainland and Canada. Fax 808/922-9404. 94 rms, 30 suites. A/C MINIBAR TV TEL. $104–$240 double, $180–$225 junior suite, $278–$600 suite; $10 higher in all categories Dec 20–Mar 31. Extra person $15. AE, CB, DC, DISC, JCB, MC, V. Parking $6.

This is the kind of hotel that regular guests prefer to keep secret. It's small and charming, with a staff that is attentive to even the slightest detail. Located at the foot of Diamond Head, it's somewhat removed from the hustle and bustle of Waikiki, yet close enough for you to enjoy all the activities of the city. (You really need a car here; buses are on infrequent schedules, and the walk to Waikiki is a long one.) Best of all, it's situated on our favorite beach area in Waikiki— Sans Souci, which, with its uncrowded sands and gentle surf, is a wonderful place to relax quietly in the sun.

A recent renovation has made the hotel more attractive than ever. It's now lighter and brighter from top to bottom, and the graceful, open-air lobby is furnished in wicker. Refurbished rooms and luxury suites are spacious and well appointed. Amenities include tables for two, vanity rooms, massage showers, hair dryers, and other luxuries. The corner rooms have lanais on two sides, offering stunning views. Rooms in the Diamond Head wing have refrigerators, coffee makers, and microwave ovens.

Since the hotel overlooks Kapiolani Park, guests have easy access to such activities as golf, tennis, kite flying, jogging, and bicycling. Kayaking and snorkeling are available at the beach. The hotel also arranges for visitors to climb to the top of Diamond Head Crater and welcomes them to the Diamond Head Climbers' Hui when they've completed their hike.

Dining/Entertainment: The Hau Tree Lanai is a delightful beachfront restaurant, one of the most romantic spots in Hawaii (see review in Chapter 7). Miyako Restaurant offers gourmet Japanese dining with an ocean view. The beachfront Sunset Lanai Lounge is great for cocktails.

Pacific Beach Hotel

2490 Kalakaua Ave., Honolulu, HI 96815. ☎ **808/922-1233,** or 800/367-6060. Fax 808/922-8061. 830 rms. A/C TV TEL. $155–$255 single or double; $10–$20 less Apr 1–Dec 19. Extra person $20. AE, CB, DC, DISC, JCB, MC, V. Parking $7.

A striking 37-story, 495-room tower has made the popular Pacific Beach Hotel, right across from the beach, more exciting than ever—especially since the tower boasts the fantastic three-story, 280,000-gallon saltwater oceanarium, which allows lobby and restaurant patrons to observe the marine life of the Hawaiian coral reefs without ever having to take snorkel in hand.

All of the large, luxurious rooms have great views, whether they face ocean, mountain, or Diamond Head, and all have such conveniences as coffee makers, refrigerators, and double-double or king-size beds. The decor is cool pastels, the furniture contemporary. You can rent a standard single or double, or a special room in front that offers the ocean—and spectacular sunsets—just outside.

Dining/Entertainment: The hotel has three restaurants and lounges: the Oceanarium Restaurant (see review in Chapter 7) for casual, family dining; Neptune, for continental fare; and Shogun, a Japanese steak and seafood restaurant.

Services: Room service.

Facilities: Two professionally designed tennis courts, swimming pool, 24-hour medical clinic, 24-hour health club, whirlpool spa, 17 shops.

MODERATE

Aston at the Waikiki Banyan

201 Ohua Ave., Honolulu, HI 96815. ☎ **808/922-0555,** or 800/922-7866 from U.S. mainland and Canada. Fax 808/922-8785. 330 one-bedroom apts. A/C TV TEL. $129–$175 one-bedroom. Seniors 55 and older get 25% off regular rates, depending on availability. Extra person $15. AE, DC, JCB, MC, V. Parking $4.

The 38-story-high Aston at the Waikiki Banyan is perfect for those who want the at-home comforts of a condominium apartment combined with the attentions of a full hotel—daily maid service, bell service, a 24-hour front desk, and much more, including an enormous sixth-floor recreation deck complete with pool, tennis court, sauna, barbecue areas, snack bar, and a children's play area—a great boon for families—all with glorious mountain views. Note the stunning laquer wall mural in the lobby, hand-carved and hand-painted in Hong Kong. Apartments are nicely if not elaborately decorated, and very comfortable; each has a large living-dining area, a well-equipped kitchen, a sofa bed in the living room, and two twins in the bedroom. You're well set up for vacation living here.

Aston's Pacific Monarch Hotel and Condominium

142 Uluniu Ave., Honolulu, HI 96815. ☎ **808/923-9805,** or 800/922-7866 from U.S. mainland and Canada. Fax 808/922-8785. 166 apts. A/C TV TEL. Apr 1–Dec 22, $100–$110 studio suite; $150 one-bedroom apt. Dec. 23–Mar 31, $120–$130 studio suite; $150–$170 one-bedroom apt. Extra person $15. Children under 17 free in parents' room with existing bedding. AE, DC, MC, V. Parking $7.

This Aston resort is choicely located just a block from Kuhio Beach, right behind the Hyatt Regency Waikiki. It's a handsome modern skyscraper at a convenient Waikiki address. Studios and one-bedroom apartments are large, pleasant, and nicely decorated, with all the amenities. Studios, for one or two people, have coffeemaker, refrigerator, and hot plate. One-bedroom apartments, for one to four people, boast full kitchens. All rates include daily maid service. Many of the lanais are quite large and offer views (depending on the floor and angle) of Diamond Head, the ocean, or the lights and sights of Waikiki. Facilities are excellent: a secured building, sky-top pool, sun deck, Jacuzzi, and even a sauna with a picture-perfect view of Diamond Head. Tops for comfort, convenience, and easy living.

The Prince Kuhio, A Royal Outrigger Hotel

2500 Kuhio Ave., Honolulu, HI 96815. ☎ **808/922-0811,** or 800/822-4282 from U.S. mainland and Canada, 0014/800/124-171 from Australia. Fax 800/622-4852. 625 rms. A/C MINIBAR TV TEL. $120–$180 double, $375–$500 suite. Extra person $20. Children under 18 free in parents' room, with existing bedding. Maximum of four persons per room. AE, CB, DC, DISC, JCB, MC, V. Parking $7.

For luxury accommodations at reasonable prices, this is the place. Everything about the Prince Kuhio is a delight, from the gracious doormen to the spacious and beautiful lobby to the luxuriously appointed rooms. There's a business center with state-of-the-art equipment, plus the assistance of a full-time secretary. No-smoking and wheelchair-accesible rooms are available. The 10th floor recreation area has a sun deck, swimming pool, and Jacuzzi whirlpool spa, as well as a snack and cocktail bar. Breakfast, lunch, and dinner are served daily in Trellisses (see review in Chapter 7), which overlooks the hotel gardens. Hawaiian entertainment is featured nightly in Cupid's Lobby Bar.

Each room has either a king-size bed or two doubles, a small refrigerator, and a bathroom done in Italian marble. Each has its own private lanai, with either ocean or mountain view; from the latter, you can see wonderful sunsets and, at night, the lights on the hills.

Prices go up as you move from the lowest floors up to the 20s and 30s. On the top floors, with access by key only, is the splendid Kuhio Club, whose guests receive special niceties, like complimentary breakfast, free newspapers delivered to their doors, hors d'oeurves and beverages in the evening, plus the services of charming and helpful concierges.

Queen Kapiolani Hotel

150 Kapahulu Ave., Honolulu, HI 96815. ☎ **808/922-1941,** or 800/367-5004 from U.S. mainland and Canada. Fax 800/477-2329. 308 rms, 11 suites. A/C TV TEL. Apr 1–Dec 23, $100–$125 double, $135–$140 kitchenette, $225 family suite, $265 one-bedroom kitchenette apt., $340 one-bedroom ocean-view kitchenette apt.; add $10 rest of year. Extra person $15. AE, CB, DC, DISC, ER, JCB, MC, V. Parking $7.

Walking into the lobby of this regal hotel is like walking back in time to the Hawaii of a century ago, when royalty was in full bloom. This towering hotel overlooking Kapiolani Park, less than a block from the beach, represents the elegance that Queen Kapiolani, the consort of Kalakaua, Hawaii's last reigning king, represented to her people. Tropical plants line the path to the lobby, which is accented by magnificent chandeliers.

The Kalakaua Dynasty decor carries over to the rooms, too. The door to each room, in fact, has a full-color reproduction of the Hawaii state seal over it. The views, are splendid, with unimpeded vistas to Diamond Head or the ocean. The rooms offer such modern comforts as in-room movies and safes. Most have lanais, and some have kitchenettes. All rooms have refrigerators and coffee makers.

Dining facilities include the Queen's Garden Lanai—scene of some of the most popular buffet meals in Waikiki—and the handsome Peacock Room. There's a swimming pool and sun deck on the third floor.

Waikiki Lanais

2452 Tusitala St., Honolulu, HI 96815. ☎ **808/923-0994,** or 800/535-0085. Fax 808/923-4708. 120 units. A/C TV TEL. $115–$135 one-bedroom apt. for up to four persons, $135–$165 two-bedroom apt. for up to six persons. Extra person $10. Children under 12 free in parents' room. Minimum stay three nights. MC, V. Free parking.

Most centrally located hotels in Waikiki have more than their share of street noise. But the half-hidden location of this Marc Resort's property, on a secluded street, blocks out street noises and traffic. But it's still only a block away on one side from the Ala Wai Canal and a few short blocks on the other side from the sands of Waikiki. This 23-story condominium hotel has plenty of good things going for it: attractive, spacious one- and two-bedroom apartments with thoroughly equipped kitchens and private lanais. The rooftop recreation deck, with its panoramic view of mountains and ocean, is great for parties and cookouts. The sixth-floor recreation deck boasts a small pool, Jacuzzi, sauna, and exercise room. There is a coin-operated laundry on the premises.

Waikiki Resort Hotel

2460 Koa Ave., Honolulu, HI 96815. ☎ **808/922-4911,** or 800/367-5116 from U.S. mainland. Fax 808/922-9468. 296 rms, 5 suites. A/C TV TEL. Mar 1–Jul 7, Sept 1–Dec 19, $95–$125 double, $135 kitchenette, $290–$450 penthouse suite; Dec 20–Feb 28, Aug 1–Aug 31, $105–$135 double, $145 kitchenette, $290–$450 penthouse suite. Extra person $15. Children under 17 free in parents' room with existing bedding. AE, DISC, JCB, MC, V. Parking $5.

Half a block from Kuhio Beach is Korean Air's lovely hotel. The results of its recent $4-million renovation and redecorating program are evident everywhere: in the spacious lobby with its sparkling chandeliers, very cozy for relaxing; in the karaoke bar off the lobby, with its small dance floor and etched mirrors; in the improved pool area on the second floor; and in the new Orchid Lounge, the charming Camellia restaurant for gourmet Korean cuisine, and the Ilima Café. Desk clerks speak English, Korean, and Japanese.

The rooms are attractive, and all have refrigerators and alarm clock radios. The more expensive rooms are on higher floors and face the ocean; the lower-priced ones are below the eighth floor and face the mountains. Some 30 ocean-view rooms have new kitchenettes (as opposed to just refrigerators). All rooms have lanais, and the one- and two-bedroom suites are luxurious.

BUDGET

Aloha Surf

444 Kanekapolei St., Honolulu, HI 96815. ☎ **808/923-0222,** or 800/423-4514 from U.S. mainland and Canada. Fax 808/924-7160. 200 rms. A/C TV TEL. Apr 1–Dec 22, $70–$95 double, $115 junior suite, $145 one-bedroom suite; Dec 23–Mar 31, $79–$104 double, $120 junior suite, $150 one-bedroom suite. Suite rates for four persons. Extra person $15. AE, DISC, MC, V. Parking $6.

For those who like the feeling of a big, efficient hotel, the 15-story Aloha Surf is an excellent choice, offering friendly service and good value. The hotel looks out on the Ala Wai Canal and is about a 10-minute walk from the beach. A gift shop and pool adjoin the open lobby, where complimentary tea and coffee are available in the morning. Rooms have bright but tasteful color schemes, wall-to-wall carpeting, and either two twins or a queen-size bed; most have lanais, and about half have kitchenettes. A few floors above street level, rooms offer views of the Koolau Mountains and a tiny bit of ocean. The Yokohama Restaurant, specializing in Chinese seafood, offers lunch and dinner daily.

✪ Royal Grove Hotel

151 Uluniu Ave., Honolulu, HI 96815. ☎ **808/923-7691.** 85 units. A/C TV TEL. $36–$55 double, $75–$85 one-bedroom suite, $85–$95 condo apt. at Colony's Pacific Monarch, across the street. Extra person $10. AE, DC, DISC, MC, V. Parking $8.

There's a friendly feeling about this modest little hotel, where the hospitable Fong family is in charge. Just a block away from Kuhio Beach, the six-story pink hotel has a small pool right on the premises, a grocery, a health-food store, a Korean restaurant off the lobby, an attentive staff, some nicely put-together rooms, and comfortable kitchenette units. The one-bedroom apartments are good buys, too. This is a one-of-a-kind place, and the faithful fans who come back year after year practically consider it a second home.

Waikiki Sand Villa

2375 Ala Wai Blvd., Honolulu, HI 96815. ☎ **808/922-4744,** or 800/247-1903 from U.S. mainland and Canada, 0014/800/127-756 from Australia. Fax 808/923-2541. 220 rms, 12 apts. A/C TV TEL. Mar 1–Dec 22, $64–$89 double, $125 kitchenette studios; Dec 23–Feb 28, $77–$120 double, $125 kitchenette studio. Extra person $10. Children under 8 free in parents' room with existing bedding. AE, CB, DC, DISC, JCB, MC, V. Parking $4.

This hotel, sand colored and with turrets, looks like a sandcastle. The lobby and dining room have a Hawaiian plantation style reminiscent of the 1930s, with ceiling cornices, a pink Chinese slate floor, and tapestry-upholstered couches. A 70-foot kidney-shaped swimming pool boasts its own island, a Jacuzzi, and a poolside bar. There's a game room with Ping-Pong tables, a dart board, and an assortment of video games. Continental breakfast is served free in the lobby, and the Lobster Bay Restaurant features pound-and-a-half stuffed lobsters.

The good-sized rooms are newly renovated and attractively decorated. All have spacious lanais, refrigerators, and in-room safes. There's a convenience store on the premises, with souvenirs, sundries, liquor, snacks, and food. Another big plus: a comfortable hospitality room, with TV and plenty of books, where guests who have late planes but early checkouts can shower and change when they come back from the beach.

2 Central Waikiki

VERY EXPENSIVE

✪ Royal Hawaiian

2259 Kalakaua Ave., Honolulu, HI 96815. ☎ **808/923-7311,** or 800/325-3535 from U.S. mainland and Canada, 1/800/073-535 from Australia. Fax 808/924-7098. 526 rms and suites. A/C MINIBAR TV TEL. $260 Historic Wing double, $325 Historic Garden Wing double, $409 Historic Ocean Wing double, $430 tower oceanfront double, $415 luxury ocean double, $425 junior garden suite, $650 garden suite, $1100 Historic Ocean/tower suite. Extra person $35. Inquire about Sheraton's "Sure Saver" rates, available at different times of the year, which could mean as much as 25% in savings. AE, MC, V. Valet parking $18; self-park at Sheraton Waikiki $7.

A landmark on the Waikiki skyline, this pink stucco, Moorish-style palace stands on the site of King Kamehameha I's home by the sea. It was Hawaii's original luxury hotel and has been the favorite resort for royalty and discriminating travelers alike— as well as the scene of scores of television shows and movies—since it opened in 1927. Now under the Sheraton banner and with all its rooms, suites, and public areas redecorated and refurbished, the Royal Hawaiian wears its regal heritage like a proud mantle. You can't help saying, "They don't build hotels like this anymore."

Surrounded by acres of lush tropical gardens (note the splendid monkeypod tree) and fronting a handsome stretch of beach, the hotel exudes that unmistakable aura of regality—it's in the black terrazzo marble of its lobby floors; the coral-toned, hand-loomed rugs; and the high-ceilinged splendor everywhere.

The guest rooms are beautiful, immense, and in the old style. Views are superb, and service is immediate and gracious. As you would expect, suites are splendid. You can stay in either the original six-story hotel building or the new 17-story tower, where all rooms overlook the pool and the Pacific.

Dining/Entertainment: The famed Monarch Room, overlooking the ocean, is Waikiki's premier dinner showroom. The Surf Room, also oceanfront, offers all three meals and is known for its elaborate seafood buffets. The Mai Tai Bar is one of the most popular places in Waikiki for the namesake drink reputed to have originated here. The Royal Hawaiian Luau, done in the grand style, is held on Monday nights.

Services: Multilingual concierge desk, 24-hour room service, 24-hour medical service, babysitting, preferential tee-off times at Makaha Golf Club. Using the "Dine-Around" plan, guests can use the food, beverage, and shopping facilities of the other Sheraton resorts in Waikiki—Sheraton Moana Surfrider, Sheraton Waikiki, and Princess Kaiulani—as well as the Makaha Golf Club, and charge them to their bill.

Facilities: Freshwater swimming pool, one of the best stretches of Waikiki Beach.

EXPENSIVE

✪ Outrigger Waikiki

2335 Kalakaua Ave., Honolulu, HI 96815. ☎ **808/923-0711,** or 800/688-7444 from U.S. mainland and Canada, 1/800/124-171 from Australia. Fax 800/622-4852. 477 rms, 53 suites. A/C TV TEL. $160–$305 double, $425–$690 suite. AE, CB, DC, DISC, JCB, MC, V. Parking $7.

The undisputed jewel in the crown of the Outrigger hotel chain is this flagship property, the recently renovated ($35 million) Outrigger Waikiki. Located right on the beach, it truly has everything. The lobby is impressive, with huge white columns; comfortable island-style furniture; abundant palms, bromeliads, and orchids; and extraordinary artwork, especially Carol Bennett's outstanding painting of outrigger canoe paddlers, located over the front desk, and "Groundswell," Laddie John Dill's unique multimedia mural located at the top of the marble staircase to the lower lobby.

The guest accommodations are something special. Rooms feature queen-size or twin beds covered in beautiful Hawaiian quilt-pattern spreads, and cane and blond-wood furniture. Each room has its own refrigerator, coffee maker (amply stocked), clock radio, and small safe. Bathrooms have both tub and shower. The one-bedroom suites have two lanais and are furnished with queen sleeper sofas, as well as twin beds or a king- or queen-size bed. Corner suites may be combined to make a two-bedroom, two-bath suite. Suites have huge console TVs in addition to smaller ones in the bedrooms. Kuhio Club rooms, on the 14th and 17th floors, are individually and handsomely decorated. Guests there have use of the Kuhio Club—with its oceanfront lanai where breakfast is served in the morning and hot pupus in the evening—and its spacious lounge area where guests can read (there's a small library), socialize, or play board games.

Dining/Entertainment: Duke's Canoe Club is right on the beach; Monterey Bay Canners and Chuck's Steakhouse are both popular places for seafood and steaks; Rigger specializes in family dining; Brass Rail is a "Cheers"-like pub and deli.

Services: Beach services pavilion, surfing lessons, room service, concierge desk, beauty salon. Shopping galleria with many shops.

Facilities: An 800-square-foot fitness center, beautifully landscaped pool area with adjacent Jacuzzi, easy access to prime stretch of Waikiki Beach.

Sheraton Waikiki

2255 Kalakaua Ave., Honolulu, HI 96815. ☎ **808/922-4422,** or 800/325-3535. Fax 808/923-8785. 1,852 rms, 130 suites. A/C MINIBAR TV TEL. $195–$335 double, $500–$1,650 suite. Extra person $25. Inquire about Sheraton's "Sure Saver" rates, available at different times of the year, which could mean as much as 25% in savings. AE, DC, JCB, MC, V. Parking $8.

Blessed with a location directly on the beach, the Sheraton Waikiki is a light, vibrant place where everybody seems to be having a good time. The lobby has a wonderfully open feeling about it, and the breezy summer-house mood extends into all public rooms and the bedrooms as well.

The "standard mountain view" rooms are charming and quite large as hotel rooms go. Soft pastels dominate the color scheme and bathrooms and closets are roomy, as are the private lanais. The ocean-view rooms are dazzlers: Most nearby hotels only have views of the Sheraton, but Sheraton guests have panoramic views of the blue Pacific, the sun dancing on the waves in daytime, and the lights from Diamond Head to downtown Honolulu glistening under the night sky. Some of the suites boast a vast, 20-foot living room with an outdoor lanai, and can easily accommodate four people. The best values here are the doubles in the adjoining Manor Wing, all nicely decorated.

Dining/Entertainment: There's the open-air Ocean Terrace for casual buffet meals, the glamorous Hanohano Room for gourmet dining in a spectacular setting 30 stories up (take the glass elevator just for the view), as well as Ciao! (Italian cuisine), and Esprit nightclub for dancing, drinks, and entertainment.

Services: If you decide to leave "home," you can, of course, "play and charge" at the other Sheraton hotels in Waikiki as well as at the Makaha Golf Club's golf and tennis facilities.

Facilities: You'll probably spend a lot of time right at the hotel, what with all those great little shops in the lobby, that vast expanse of beach at your doorstep, and one of the biggest and sunniest pools in Waikiki on the beachfront.

MODERATE

Sheraton Princess Kaiulani Hotel

2342 Kalakaua Ave., Honolulu, HI 96815. ☎ **808/922-5811,** or 800/325-3535. Fax 808/923-9912. 1,150 rms. A/C TV TEL. $133 Princess Wing double (no balcony), $154 Kaiulani Wing double, $164 Princess Wing pool view, $175 Tower city view, $191 Ainahau Wing ocean view; $371 suites. Extra person $25. Children free in parents' room with existing bedding. Inquire about Sheraton's "Sure Saver" rates, available at different times of the year, which could mean as much as 25% in savings. AE, CB, DC, JCB, MC, V. Parking is $1.50 each exit.

Named in memory of Hawaii's beloved Princess Kaiulani, heir to the throne who died in 1899 at the age of 24, the hotel is located at Ainahau, near the site of the former royal estate that was her home. It's directly across the road from Sheraton's oceanfront Waikiki hotels—the Royal Hawaiian, the Sheraton Moana Surfrider, and the Sheraton Waikiki—and in the midst of the busy restaurant/shopping scene of Waikiki. The giant hotel has been popular with families and tour groups ever since the first of its buildings, the 11-story Princess Wing, opened in 1955 and became Waikiki's first skycraper. Then followed the Kaiulani Wing, and the 29-story Ainahau Wing in 1960. The three buildings are connected by graceful open-air lobbies and lovely gardens; out front there's a large pool, waterfall, and terrace. A recent $6-million renovation has upgraded all the public areas, making them regal indeed; original artworks and mementoes of Princess Kaiulani's era can be found throughout the hotel.

As for the guest rooms, the older ones are on the small side and have twin beds and limited views; rooms in the newer wings, however, have been redone and feature double-double beds. Most rooms have a private lanai, and many have connecting doorways to accommodate families.

Dining facilities are plentiful, including the Momoyama for Japanese food prepared at the table; the Lotus Moon for Mandarin and Szechuan-style delicacies; the Pikake Terrace, where a sumptuous breakfast is served every day in a tropical garden atmosphere; and fast food at the Minute Chef. One of Hawaii's best shows, the spectacular Polynesian Revue, is presented nightly in the lavish Ainahau Showroom. Poolside entertainment is also featured nightly from 5:45pm.

Waikiki Beachcomber

2300 Kalakaua Ave., Honolulu, HI 96815. ☎ **808/922-4646,** or 800/622-4646 from U.S. mainland, 800/338-6233 from Canada. Fax 808/923-4889. 500 rms and suites. A/C TV TEL. Apr 1–Dec 25 $115 city-view double, $130 partial ocean-view double. $145 ocean-view double, $225 suite; Dec 26–Mar 31, add $10–$30. Extra person $15. Children under 12 free in parents' room with existing bedding. Inquire about special packages: a $99 room-and-car or room-and-breakfast-buffet is sometimes available. AE, CB, DC, MC, V. Parking $6.

Located between Seaside Avenue and the International Market Place, the Beachcomber sits astride Waikiki's heartland. It's an attractive hotel, across the road from the beach, with smart Polynesian lobby and dining rooms, plus a pool and terrace looking over the avenue.

I like the spacious rooms here, especially the grass-textured wallpaper with its floral designs. Every room has a refrigerator, a safe, and a furnished lanai. Best views are from the ocean-view and deluxe ocean-view rooms on the higher floors; but beware, ocean views may be somewhat blocked by the Royal Hawaiian Hotel across the street.

The casual Beachcomber Restaurant features fresh fish, island cuisine, a nightly prime-rib buffet, and a nifty breakfast buffet as well. There's also live entertainment every night at the Surfboard Lounge. Every night except Monday it's the scene of the Don Ho show.

✪ Waikiki Joy

320 Lewers St., Honolulu, HI 96815. ☎ **808/923-2300,** or 800/733-5569. Fax 808/924-4010. 52 rms, 42 suites. A/C TV TEL. (including continental breakfast): $125 hotel rm, $155 club suite, $190 executive suite. Rates are often lower at certain periods of the year; call to inquire about property specials. AE, DC, MC, V. Valet Parking $10.

This is one hotel that truly deserves its name. It's a hidden jewel, an oasis right in the heart of busy Waikiki, offering not only outstanding personal service but a Bose entertainment system and a Jacuzzi in every accommodation. The Italian marble–accented open-air lobby and the tropical veranda, with swimming pool, sauna, and furnished deck, set the scene for the beautifully decorated guest rooms.

Rooms are located either in the hotel tower or in the all-suite tower. The hotel rooms, decorated in soft pastels, have a marble entry, a refrigerator, a safe, and a lanai wide enough for you to sit and enjoy the views. The suites are even more luxurious: Club suites have either a king-size bed or two double beds, a refrigerator, microwave, coffee maker, and a wet bar. Executive suites have two double beds and a kitchen with microwave and full refrigerator. The more expensive executive king suites add a separate living room and bedroom.

Cappuccino's, the hotel's Mediterranian-style café restaurant, features specialty coffees, petite sandwiches, and desserts. Guests can also enjoy a free hour of private karaoke fun (for up to nine people) in the hotel's state-of-the-art GS Studio. And there's a free continental breakfast at the Tropical Veranda every morning.

State-of-the-art voice mail is available, as well as fax and modern hookups in each room.

BUDGET

Aston Coral Reef Hotel

2299 Kuhio Ave., Honolulu, HI 96815. ☎ **808/922-1262,** or 800/922-7866 from U.S. mainland and Canada. Fax 808/922-5048. 247 rms and suites. A/C TV TEL. Apr 1–Dec 22, $79–$90 hotel room double, $95–$115 Junior studio, $130–$165 one-bedroom suite; Dec 23–Mar 31, $99–$110 hotel room double, $95–$115 Junior studio, $150–$185 one-bedroom suite. Extra person $12. AE, DC, JCB, MC, V. Parking $7.

It would be hard to ask for a more central location in Waikiki than the handsome Coral Reef, next door to the bustling International Market Place. The mood here is one of excitement and fun, with shops and restaurants on the main floor. Ferdinand's serves American cuisine, and Szechuan-style China Gardens specializes in seafood.

The good-sized guest rooms are nicely furnished in island style, with private lanai, carpeting, and a desk. Rooms have either two double beds or one double and one single. The hotel also has moderately priced suites, eminently suitable for families.

✪ Aston Island Colony

445 Seaside Ave., Honolulu, HI 96815. ☎ **808/923-2345,** 800/922-7866 from U.S. mainland, 800/445-6633 from Canada. Fax 808/921-7109. 400 rms and suites. A/C TV TEL. Apr 1–Dec 22, $77–$90 double, $87–$100 studio with kitchenette, $130–$165 one-bedroom suite with kitchen; Dec 23–Mar 31, $93–$110 double, $107–$120 studio with kitchenette. $150–$185 one-bedroom suite with kitchen (suites for up to four). Extra person $12. AE, DC, JCB, MC, V. Parking $7.

This stylish and comfortable Three-Diamond hotel has a spacious, airy lobby, a pool and sun deck on the sixth floor, a shiatsu clinic, and convenience store. Each of the rooms has a lanai; some of the views are breathtaking. You have your choice here of several types of accommodation: If you want a refrigerator, take one of the hotel rooms, which have one or two double beds. Or you can have a studio with kitchenette. Then there are one-bedroom suites with full kitchen that can accommodate up to four guests. Island Colony is truly a beautiful place, abounding in aloha.

Ilima Hotel

445 Nohonani St., Honolulu, HI 96815. ☎ **808/923-1877.** Fax 808/924-8371. 74 studios, 25 suites. A/C TV TEL. $72–$88 single, $77–$99 double, $105 executive suite for three, $129 one-bedroom for three. $149–$159 two-bedroom suite for four, $220 three-bedroom penthouse for six. Extra person $8. Crib or rollaway $6. AE, DC, JCB, MC, V. Free parking.

If you'd like the graciousness and charm that a small hotel can offer, then you'll be as happy as we were to discover the Ilima, tucked away on a quiet street near the Ala Wai Canal. Comfort and convenience are the keys here: Every unit in this attractive condominium hotel has a modern, fully equipped kitchen, private lanai, radio, and double long-boy beds. Sun-worshipers will love the two sun decks on the 10th floor, as well as the ground-level pool area with its ample sunning space on one side and shade tree on the other. Fitness fans will appreciate the exercise room and sauna off the pool area. Business travelers will make good use of the fully equiped conference room. And everyone will welcome the free local phone calls.

As for the units, they are impeccably clean and attractively furnished, with Polynesian-style rattan furniture and plush carpeting. The studios have two double beds and can easily accommodate four. Rates get progressively higher as you go up and the views get better. The deluxe executive suite has a king-size waveless waterbed. The penthouse units can be used as one-, two-, or three-bedroom suites.

Sergio's, one of Honolulu's finest Italian restaurants, is on the premises.

Marine Surf

364 Seaside Ave., Honolulu, HI 96815. ☎ **808/923-0277,** or 800/367-5176. Fax 808/926-5915. 115 studios, 1 penthouse one-bedroom suite. A/C TV TEL. Apr 1–Dec 20, $75–$85 single or double studios, $135 one-bedroom penthouse suite. Dec 21–Mar 31, $85–$95 single or double studio, $150 penthouse suite. Children under 18 free in parents' room with existing bedding. Crib $10. Extra person $10. CB, DC, DISC, MC, V. Parking $4.

The Marine Surf boasts a central location just a block from bustling Kalakaua Avenue and two blocks from the beach. And that's not all it boasts: You get a spacious studio apartment, not just a hotel room—this means a fully equipped electric kitchen and a dining area. Give them points too, for sliding glass doors to a furnished lanai and two extra-length double beds. The views get better as you go up, and the rates go up accordingly. The swimming pool in this 23-story building is on the fourth floor. You'll find a bright new lobby with a "plantation home" feeling and bright, colorful apartments. Inside the building is Matteo's, a longtime favorite for superb Italian food.

Outrigger Malia

2211 Kuhio Ave., Honolulu, HI 96815. ☎ **808/923-7621,** or 800/688-7444 from U.S. mainland and Canada, 1/800/124-171 from Australia. Fax 800/622-4852. 328 rms and suites. A/C TV TEL. $90–$100 double, $105–$115 suite. Extra person $15. AE, CB, DC, DISC, JCB, MC, V. Parking $7.

The attractive Outrigger Malia has a lot going for it, including a rooftop tennis court, a therapeutic spa, and a wonderfully central location. And right off the colorful, breezy lobby is Wailana Malia, one of the best coffee shops in town, open 24 hours a day.

Guest rooms, cheerfully decorated with cane furniture and crimson carpeting, have two double beds, a refrigerator, and a private lanai. One entire floor features rooms designed especially for physically disabled guests, with wide doors to accommodate wheelchairs and grab-bars in the bathrooms. The junior suites consist of a sitting room with two daybeds (or punees, as they are called in Hawaii) plus a bedroom, and can accommodate up to four people.

Outrigger Reef Tower Hotel

227 Lewers St., Honolulu, HI 96815. ☎ **808/924-8844,** or 800/688-7444 from U.S. mainland and Canada, 1/800/124-171 from Australia. Fax 800/622-4852. 385 rms,

94 suites. A/C TV TEL. $85–$135 double. Extra person $15. AE, CB, DC, DISC, JCB, MC, V. Parking: $7.

Located a half-block from the beach in one direction and a half-block from busy Kalakaua Avenue in the other, this hotel is right in the midst of everything. The Islander Coffee Shop and Lewers Street Fish Company are on the premises as is the Irish Rose Saloon, a jolly gathering spot. Accommodations here lean toward the living-room-by-day, bedroom-by-night feeling; most rooms are equipped with a refrigerator, and some higher-priced suites also have a kitchenette. Nonsmoking and handicapped rooms are available. Don't expect much in the way of view here, since the property is really socked in by big hotels. Be satisfied with a glimpse of the ocean, the mountains, or a view of the pool or a nearby hotel.

Outrigger Village

240 Lewers St., Honolulu, HI 96815. ☎ **808/923-3881,** or 800/688-7444 from U.S. mainland and Canada, 1/800/124-171 from Australia. 440 rms and suites. A/C TV TEL. $85–$110 double, $125–$135 suite. Extra person $15. AE, CB, DC, DISC, JCB, MC, V. Parking $7.

The Outrigger Village enjoys a great location in the midst of all the Waikiki action, and one of the prettiest stretches of Waikiki Beach awaits just across Kalia Road. The enormous lobby boasts several shops, and a swimming pool is just behind the reservations desk. The guest rooms are attractively furnished, modern with a Polynesian flair, and most have lanais. The kitchenette units have a sink, half-size refrigerator, cupboards, counter space, and hot plates—perfectly adequate for light meals. There's also an attractive coffee shop and a cocktail lounge.

Outrigger Waikiki Tower

200 Lewers St., Honolulu, HI 96815. ☎ **806/922-6424,** or 800/688-7444 from U.S. mainland and Canada, 1/800/124-171 from Australia. Fax 800/622-4582. 439 rms, 20 suites. A/C TV TEL. $85–$110 double, $125–$140 studio with kitchen. Extra person $15. AE, CB, DC, DISC, JCB, MC, V. Parking $7.

Another very popular part of this chain is the Outrigger Waikiki Tower, and very pleasant it is. The back of the attractive open lobby looks onto the pool area that it shares with the Outrigger Edgewater, and the beach is a very short walk away. Just off the lobby is the attractive and moderately priced Waikiki Broiler Restaurant, not just the usual hotel coffee shop. The bright, smartly decorated rooms have refrigerators and in-room safes. Most rooms have lanais, and corner rooms have two; two corner rooms can be opened up to create a suite with three lanais and two TVs. Only the corner rooms have kitchenettes.

✪ Patrick Winston's Hawaiian King Rentals

417 Nohonani St., Honolulu, HI 96815. ☎ **808/924-3332,** or 800/545-1948. 11 units in 66-unit hotel-condominium. A/C TV TEL. Apr 15–Dec 15, $59–$89; Dec 16–Apr 14, $75–$109. Extra person $10. Airline employees' discounts. AE, DC, MC, V. Parking $7.

This five-story condominium apartment building is centered around a lovely garden and pool area—a great place to chat with fellow guests. Patrick Winston's accommodations are definitely superior to many in Waikiki. Each unit—designed with families in mind—has a beautifully decorated large living room, separate bedroom, and full kitchenette, which is separated from the living room by a rattan bar. All of the apartments are as quiet as they are attractive. The new corporate suites are spacious renovated one-bedroom apartments furnished with a washer/dryer, microwave oven, VCR, answering machine, and typewriter. There's a cocktail lounge, minimart, and laundry nearby.

3 Ewa Waikiki

VERY EXPENSIVE

✪ Halekulani

2199 Kalia Rd., Honolulu, HI 96815. ☎ **808/923-2311,** or 800/367-2343. Fax 808/926-8004. 456 rms and suites. A/C MINIBAR TV TEL. $275–$440 double, depending on location and view, $595–$3,500 suite. Extra person $75. Children under 14 free in parents' room. Maximum three persons per room. AE, CB, DC, DISC, JCB, MC, V. Validated parking.

Old Hawaii has been born again in the brilliant new interpretation of the classic Hawaiian seaside hotel, the Halekulani. Understated elegance might best describe the style of this new "House Befitting Heaven." The resort, right on the beach at Waikiki, is a reincarnation of the famed hotel that dates from the 1930s. One of the original buildings has been incorporated into the new design—five interconnecting buildings of stepped heights surrounding courtyards and gardens overlooking the ocean.

Arriving guests are escorted directly to their rooms, where registration is completed in private and a porter is available to unpack the luggage. Guests like this kind of pampering so much that the hotel continues to win award after award: It's Oahu's only AAA Five-Diamond property, and the Number One Hotel in Hawaii, according to a recent Zagat U.S. Travel Survey.

Guest rooms, most of which face the ocean, are very large and have separate sitting areas, no fewer than three telephones, plus a small refrigerator stocked with bottled water and ice. A number of rooms are equipped for the disabled. Decor is in tones of white, beige, and gray, with blue accents. The tiled lanais, with their chaise longues, tables, and chairs, are large and comfortable, and many have views of the ocean beach and the magnificent pool, its huge cattleya orchid mosaic made of a million imported South African tiles sparkling at its base. (The pool and its orchid have become the symbol of the new Halekulani.)

Dining/Entertainment: Dining facilities are superb: there's Orchids, the oceanside main dining room, which serves all three meals and highlights locally grown produce; the award-winning French restaurant, La Mer, where dinner is a three-hour haute-cuisine experience, at $68, $78, or $98 per person; and the famous House Without a Key, an oceanside restaurant under a century-old kiawe tree, surely one of the world's most romantic spots for sunset cocktails, light meals, and entertainment. (See Chapter 7 for reviews of La Mer and Orchids.)

Services: Concierge desk, business and secretarial services, free daily newspapers, twice-daily maid and turndown service, free local telephone calls.

Facilities: Fitness room, running sessions and aerobic workouts, in-room massage by professional therapists, magnificent oceanside swimming pool, easy access to superb stretch of Waikiki Beach.

Hawaii Prince Hotel

100 Holomoana St., Honolulu, HI 96815. ☎ **808/965-1111,** or 800/321-OAHU. Fax 808/946-0811. 464 rms, 57 suites. A/C TV TEL. $200–$330 double, $450–$2,500 suite. Extra person $35. Children 17 or younger free in parents' room with existing bedding. Valet and self-parking.

With its two rose-colored glass-and-stone towers rising 32 stories at the gateway to Waikiki, this architecturally striking contemporary $150-million hotel is one of Hawaii's newer world-class hostelries. Facing the Ala Wai Marina and the sea, it offers its guests spectacular views and comforts. The high-ceilinged lobby, with its

Italian marble walls highlighted with English slate, suggests not just luxury but splendor. Tea is served here every afternoon. On the fifth-floor deck, a pool, a poolside grill, and stepped terraces offer guests swimming, sunning, sunset watching, entertainment, and refreshments along with spectacular ocean views.

Each room and suite has a waterfront view. The Diamond Head Tower offers rooms with two double beds; the Ala Moana Tower has suites and king-size beds. Other rooms have either two double beds or kings and are done in warm tones of sand and sunset, cool ocean blues, and greens. Each has separate shower and tub in a large compartmentalized bathroom, VCR, safe, refrigerator with complimentary fruit juices, and lovely furnishings. There are no lanais, but floor-to-ceiling windows open to the marina and ocean views.

Since Waikiki Beach is a 10-minute walk away, shuttle buses take guests there and to the Ala Moana Shopping Center every 15 minutes. And shuttle buses also run on a scheduled basis between the hotel and the 27-hole Hawaii Prince Golf Club at Ewa Beach.

Dining/Entertainment: The Prince Court, with breathtaking nautical views, offers a sophisticated bistro menu. The Hakone Japanese Restaurant offers traditional cuisine prepared by master chefs; casual Japanese dining is available at the Takanawa Sushi Bar and Restaurant. The outdoor Promenade Deck is the place for café-style dining and tropical drinks.

Services: Concierge desk, 24-hour room service, complimentary newspaper, amenity basket, and hot towels (oshibori) upon arrival.

Facilities: Business center, fitness room, full-service beauty shop.

✪ Hilton Hawaiian Village

2005 Kalia Rd., Honolulu, HI 96815. ☎ **808/949-4321,** or 800-HILTONS. Fax 808/947-7898. 2,540 rms, 365 suites. A/C MINIBAR TV TEL. $165–$305 double, $195–$330 Ali'i Tower, $525–$3,100 suite. Extra person $25. Children of any age free in parents' room. AE, CB, DISC, ER, JCB, MC, V. Valet parking $12; self-parking $9.

To use the word *hotel* to describe this grand Hilton is really an understatement: With 20 acres of lush tropical greenery, three swimming pools, a secluded lagoon, a supper-club theater, acres of upscale shops, more than a dozen places for wining, dining, and catching the celebrities, even its own U.S. Post Office, it's a wonderful world of its own. Henry Kaiser built it, Hilton bought it, and visitors love it. If you're a guest here, you may not find it necessary to leave the village during your entire stay. You can surf, take catamaran cruises and submarine dives, or just swim at what many consider one of the finest stretches of beach in Waikiki, with acres of white sand even at high tide.

There is also a wide choice of accommodations, ranging from simply lovely to absolutely breathtaking. Rooms in the Rainbow Tower, the Tapa Tower, and the Diamond Head Tower are all large and beautifully furnished, and they offer views that range from court and garden to yacht harbor and ocean. The newly created Rainbow Tower Executive Club rooms and suites are designed to recall the grace and elegance of an old-fashioned countryside manor. Specialty rooms and penthouse suites are also available; 34 rooms are equipped for the disabled. Even more splendor and services are available to guests in the Ali'i Tower, a concierge tower offering 348 ultra-deluxe guest rooms and suites on the ocean. Guests receive the royal treatment the name implies, including in-room registration, their own health club and swimming pool, and the attentions of a multilingual concierge staff. Each room has a fully stocked refreshment center, in-room coffee services, no fewer than three phones (one of which is PC-compatible), and even a mini-TV on the bathroom vanity.

Dining/Entertainment: Both the Cantonese Golden Dragon and the romantic Bali-by-the-Sea for continental fare are named among Honolulu's best restaurants year after year by readers of *Aloha* magazine. Illusionist John Hirokawa and "The Magic of Polynesia" is at the Hilton Dome. The beachfront Tropica Bar, the Paradise Lounge, the Shell Bar, and the Tapa Bar are all favorite nightspots.

Services: Multilingual concierge staff; in-room fax and computer hookups in many rooms; daily bilingual activities for kids 4 to 12; walking tours for adults; classes in lei making, hula, and the ukulele; room service.

Facilities: Business center, fitness center, three swimming pools, scores of shops (including those in the Rainbow Bazaar), and easy access to a superb stretch of Waikiki Beach.

EXPENSIVE

Alana Waikiki

1956 Ala Moana Blvd., Honolulu, HI 96815. ☎ **808/941-7275,** or 800/367-6070 from U.S. mainland and Canada. Fax 808/949-0996. 268 rms, 45 suites. TV TEL. $120–$160 double guest rm; $200–$240 Alana Suite; $400–$500 Luxury Suite; $2,000 Royal Amethyst Suite, including boardroom. Children 18 or younger free in parents' room (rollaways and cribs complimentary). Extra person $25. AE, CB, DC, DISC, JCB, MC, V. Parking $7.

Located halfway between the heart of Waikiki and the Ala Moana Beach Park and Shopping Center, Alana Waikiki considers itself "More than a hotel—a work of art." And indeed it is. Contemporary works—highlighted by a collection of original Picasso ceramics—grace the entire hotel. Guest rooms, most with queen-size beds, are subtly decorated and provide many amenities helpful to business or vacation travelers: two-line telephones, voice mail, computer-fax outlets, flashlights, and coffee/tea makers. The bathrooms have phones. The Alana Suites are handsome, and the Luxury Suites on the penthouse floor are like privately designed apartments with original artwork. Each suite is decorated with a motif centered around such gems as crystal, jasper, and amethyst. Twenty-four-hour butler service is available for these suites.

Dining/Entertainment: Harlequin and Café Picasso, are works of art, too, offering superb Pacific Rim cuisine.

Services: Concierge, room service.

Facilities: Business center, with secretarial and translation services, computers, fax, and more; fitness center with Universal equipment, cedar sauna, and massage rooms (massage service in guest rooms is also available); Art Gallery, 24-hour reading room with major international newspapers and magazines; and heated swimming pool.

Ilikai

1777 Ala Moana Blvd., Honolulu, HI 96815. ☎ **808/949-3811,** or 800/367-8434 from U.S. mainland and Canada. Fax 808/947-0892. 800 rms, 52 suites. A/C TV TEL. $165–$245 double, $400–$1,200 suite. Extra person $25. AE, CB, DC, DISC, JCB, MC, V. Parking $7.

The Ilikai is a self-contained resort community that provides enough glamorous diversion for weeks of Hawaiian living. This has been one of Waikiki's best hotels for over 30 years; with a recent $50-million renovation, it's better than ever. Inside this unique island-within-an-island you can choose from more than 800 of Waikiki's largest luxury accommodations housed in two buildings overlooking both the Ala Wai Yacht Harbor and Ala Moana Beach Park, with its acres of green lawns shaded by huge monkeypods, banyans, and coconut palms. Your vacation here can be as lazy or as lively as you wish. In addition to sun and sports activities, you can shop until you run out of traveler's checks, eat your way through a variety of restaurants, watch top island entertainment under the stars, and stay in some of the nicest hotel rooms in town.

Rooms at the Ilikai are extraordinarily spacious. Many have full electric kitchens, all have wall-mounted hair dryers, in-room safes, and large lanais overlooking the ocean and the mountains. All rooms have either a king-size bed or two twin beds, and most have queen-size sofa beds. At the Yacht Harbor Tower, rooms have king-size, double-double, or twin beds, wall-mounted hair dryers, coffee makers, and in-room safes; most rooms have lanais.

Dining/Entertainment: Much of Ilikai's excitement is in its restaurants and nightclubs. Its casual restaurant, Canoes, looks out over the Ala Wai Yacht Harbor, and is perfect for moderately priced open-air, family-style dining, it also offers a fabulous Sunday brunch. Nightfall signifies the start of the hotel's traditional torchlighting ceremony. Then you must choose between the Honolulu Comedy Club and Sarento's for regional Italian cuisine.

Services: Sterling Club for business travelers, express checkouts, voice mail, shopping arcade.

Facilities: Waikiki's most complete tennis resort with six newly resurfaced Plexipave courts overlooking Waikiki and the yacht marina, full-time tennis staff, pro services, tennis clinics; a sports and fitness center; swimming in two pools and a nearby blue lagoon; plus sailing, surfing, and scuba diving.

Outrigger Reef Hotel

2169 Kalia Rd., Honolulu, HI 96815. ☎ **808/923-3111,** or 800/688-7444 from U.S. mainland and Canada. 1/800/124-171 from Australia. Fax 800/622-4852. 838 rms, 47 suites. A/C TV TEL. Rates: $135–$395 double, $270–$475 suite. Extra person $20. Children under 18 free in parents' room with existing bedding. AE, CB, DC, DISC, JCB, MC, V. Parking $7.

One of the first high-rise hotels to be built in Waikiki and still one of the largest, the Outrigger Reef boasts a top beachfront location, plenty of activities, warm hospitality, and nicely furnished rooms. Now that a $30-million renovation has been completed, it's truly up to date. The new entrance, a wide stone esplanade with a flowered porte-cochère, leads to an attractive lobby and to rooms that are prettier than ever. Each has a refrigerator and an in-room safe. Nonsmoking and handicapped-accessible rooms are also available.

Dining/Entertainment: At poolside is the Chief's Hut for casual, family dining. At oceanside is The Shorebird Beach Broiler, an immensely popular spot offering broil-your-own dinners. The Aloha Lobby features Hawaiian entertainment, the Shorebird Beach Bar offers karaoke, and the Pool Terrace is a poolside sports bar.

Services: Many beach services, including catamaran sailing, canoe rides, and surfboard lessons; room service; and concierge desk.

Facilities: One of the largest freshwater swimming pools in Waikiki, and a business center with state-of-the-art equipment and the assistance of a full-time secretary.

✪ Waikiki Parc

2233 Helumoa Rd., Honolulu, HI 96815. ☎ **808/921-7272,** or 800/422-0450. Fax 808/923-1336. 298 rms. A/C MINIBAR TV TEL. $150–$235 double, $165–$225 deluxe.

Extra person $30. Children 14 and under free in parents' room. Inquire about room-and-car packages. AE, CB, DC, DISC, JCB, MC, V. Valet parking $7.

Just when you thought there wasn't space in Waikiki for one more room—let alone an entire hotel—Waikiki Parc has gone and done it. They've conjured up some space and opened a 22-story luxury hotel 100 yards from the beach at Waikiki and directly across from the Halekulani Hotel. In fact, this hotel has been dubbed the "Halekulani, Jr.," since it is managed by the same corporation and is similar to its parent hotel in its elegant simplicity, personalized service, and sophisticated style.

But the big difference here is in the prices: This hotel was designed to combine luxury with affordability, and prices are considerably lower than those at the Halekulani. Rooms are all the same, beautifully done in blue and white, with ceramic tile floors and plush inlaid carpeting, conversation areas, armoires, custom rattan furniture, adjustable white shutter doors on the lanai or view balcony, business desks in most rooms, and either a king-size or two twin beds. There are two phones in each room, an AM/FM radio, and an in-room safe. Eight rooms are equipped for the disabled.

Dining/Entertainment: Waikiki Parc has two excellent restaurants. Parc Café, with its garden-terrace atmosphere, serves fabulous buffet-style meals, featuring island specialties. Kacho, one of Hawaii's few Kyoto-style restaurants, is a charming oasis for true devotees of sushi and Japanese seafood dishes.

Services: Concierge desk, twice-daily maid service, secretarial and other business services, wheelchair accessibility to all public areas, room service.

Facilities: Freshwater pool on the eighth-floor recreation deck, a great stretch of Waikiki beach nearby.

MODERATE

Aston at the Waikiki Shore Apartments

2161 Kalia Rd., Honolulu, HI 96815. ☎ **808/926-4733,** or 800/367-2353. Fax 808/922-2902. 76 apts. A/C TV TEL. Apr 1–Dec 22, $115–$130 studio apt.; $150–$185 one-bedroom apt.; $240 two-bedroom apt.; $295–$350 two-bedroom, two-bath, ocean-view apt. Dec 23–Mar 31, $165 studio apt.; $220 one-bedroom apt.; $295–$475 two-bedroom, two-bath ocean-view apt. AE, DC, JCB, MC, V. Parking $7.

Here you'll find private apartment living right on the beach at Waikiki. Many of the condo owners have purchased their apartments as investments and make them available year round for short-term rentals. The rooms are spacious. Each apartment has its own full-width lanai, so you have views of the sea, mountains, and the green, spacious lawns of Fort DeRussy, next door. Each apartment is furnished and decorated differently, of course, but all are attractive, and all have a complete kitchen with garbage disposal and laundry facilities.

The beach is one of the loveliest around, and dozens of restaurants and shops are just a few steps from the front door of the cool, inviting lobby. This is genuine apartment living, not a tourist hotel.

Aston Waikiki Terrace Hotel

2045 Kalakaua Ave., Honolulu, HI 96815. ☎ **808/955-6000,** or 800/445-8811 from U.S. mainland and Canada. Fax 808/943-8555. 241 rms. A/C MINIBAR TV TEL. Mar 31–Dec 20, $115–$145 double, $295 suite; Dec 21–Apr 1, $125–$155 double, $295 suite. Extra person $15. Children under 17 free in parents' room with existing bedding. AE, CB, DC, DISC, MC, V. Parking $7.

One of the most popular small hotels on the Waikiki scene, the Waikiki Terrace has a lot going for it, it's a four-star property at affordable prices. The good-sized guest rooms are handsomely furnished with light woods, Berber carpeting, and splendid marble-and-granite bathrooms. Each room has a refrigerator, a dry bar with a hot-water dispenser, and a complimentary basket of coffees and Japanese and herbal teas. Views from private lanais are of ocean or mountains, sometimes a bit of both; sunrise views are especially lovely. There's a fully equipped pool deck on the second floor with whirlpool, spa, and fitness center. And there's a wonderful restaurant, the Mezzanine, offering light contemporary cuisine.

The Waikiki Terrace is located at the entrance to Waikiki, about a seven-minute walk (through Fort DeRussy Park) from a splendid stretch of Waikiki Beach.

✪ The Royal Garden at Waikiki

440 Olohana St., Honolulu, HI 96815. ☎ **808/943-0202.** 808/946-8777, or 800/367-5666 from U.S. and Canada. Fax 808/946-8177. 235 rms, 17 deluxe suites, 2 Royal suites. A/C TV TEL. $95–$180 double, $295–$500 suite. Each additional person $15. Children 17 and under free in parents' room using existing bedding. AE, CB, DC, JCB, MC, V. Valet parking $7.

Lush tropical gardens, abloom with Royal Palm trees, flowers, and shrubs, surround the stunning Royal Garden, a newer hotel offering beauty, luxury, and great service at very affordable prices. The lobby is right out of a movie set: marble, crystal chandeliers, ornate gilded mirrors—smashing! There are two swimming pools in the huge garden at the rear of the lobby; the larger one is a vision in marble with a huge Roman-inspired bath house in the middle and a waterfall crashing from the inside and cascading into the pool. Upstairs are the guest rooms, which are also very special. Every room has a lanai, attractive rattan furniture, in-room safe, voice mail, refrigerator. Many of the rooms are wheelchair accessible. All rooms are good sized and have either a queen-size bed or twins; rates vary according to floor. Guests staying on Executive floors have extra amenities, including use of the Royal Lounge. All guests receive daily complimentary continental breakfast and regular shuttle service to various points in Waikiki and to the Ala Moana Shopping Center.

The beach is about a 10-minute walk, but there are two swimming pools, two whirlpools, sauna, and fitness center with state-of-the-art equipment on the premises. Business travelers can take advantage of an array of special services in the Royal Business Center, including full secretarial services and access to computers and fax machines. Concierge service is available and the entire staff is most accommodating. Also at hand are two splendid and very popular restaurants: Cascada for Euro-Island cuisine and Shizu for classic Japanese cookery.

BUDGET

Aloha Punawai

305 Saratoga Rd., Honolulu, HI 96815. ☎ **808/923-5211.** 19 apts. A/C TV. $47–$52 studio for one without air conditioning; $52–$57 studio for one with air conditioning; $57–$62 bedroom for one with air conditioning; $62–$67 large bedroom for one with air conditioning. Extra person $8. Children under 12 free. Minimum stay three days; weekly and monthly discounts available. No credit cards. Parking $5.

The owners of this place try hard to keep a low profile, but we're revealing their secret: There are not many places in Waikiki that are this reasonable. Here you get a clean, comfortable apartment with a furnished kitchen, bath with shower, and a lanai. There are no telephones, although phones can be installed for those on long stays. Stay a month and the rate goes down to $32 and $52 a day. There are both small and large one-bedroom apartments available. Towels and linens are provided and there is cleaning service twice a week. Aloha Punawai has been family-owned and -operated since 1959. Saratoga Road is near Fort DeRussy, and the hotel is only a block from the beach.

Ambassador Hotel of Waikiki

2040 Kuhio Ave., Honolulu, HI 96815. ☎ **808/941-7777**. Fax 808/941-4717. 315 rms and suites. A/C TV TEL. $80–$104 double, $140–$175 one-bedroom suite with kitchen. Extra person $15. AE, CB, DC, JCB. Parking $4.

There's a very comfortable feeling about the Ambassador Hotel. This older hotel, neither too large nor too small, has a good location near the entrance to Waikiki, and the rooms are comfortable and attractive. All are done up in studio style and have a sliding glass door opening onto a private lanai. The views are bigger and better in certain locations, which carry higher price tags. We especially like the one-bedroom suites, which include full electric kitchen, and the corner suites with their great views of the ocean and Diamond Head. You can dine at the Café Ambassador, or have drinks at the Embassy Bar. And if you're too lazy to walk the Pacific, there's a large pool and sun deck lanai one floor above the bustle of Waikiki, where drinks and snacks are available.

Aston Waikikian on the Beach

1881 Ala Moana Blvd., Honolulu, HI 96815. ☎ **808/949-5331**, or 800/922-7866. Fax 808/922-8785. 132 rms and suites. A/C TEL. Apr 1–Dec 22, $63–$97 double, $115 family suite with kitchenette, $160 penthouse with kitchen; Dec 23–Mar 31, $77–$100 double, $135 family suite with kitchenette, $180 penthouse with kitchen. Kitchenettes in hotel rooms available upon request. Children under 18 free in parents' room using existing bedding. Extra person $12. AE, CB, DC, JCB, MC, V. Parking $4.

Built in 1956, this Polynesian-style hotel, with a cave-like lobby and the roof of an ancient spirit house, set in lush tropical gardens that lead to a lagoon fronting the ocean, still maintains that feeling of the beachside bungalow hotels of days gone by.

The Waikikian has had many illustrious guests, among them Prince Charles, who stayed here when he played in the British-Hawaii polo matches in 1974. James Michener spent time here when writing *Hawaii*, and the symphony suite has hosted such musical greats as Leonard Bernstein and Arthur Fiedler. Rudy Vallee and Dolores Del Rio were among the early guests.

The hotel has two wings: The original Garden Wing has older rooms done in simple island decor, with phone and refrigerator (no TVs here). The newer, seven-story Banyan Wing is more modern, has air conditioning and color TV, and is decorated in brighter colors. These rooms face the mountains or the ocean, but with limited ocean views over the tops of the coconut trees. The average room has one double and one single bed. The family suite accommodates up to four and the penthouse up to six. Kitchenettes are available on request.

At night, the torches are lit in the garden and strolling musicians wander along the paths to serenade the guests underneath their lanais. On Tuesday nights (5:45 to 6:45 pm), guests are treated to a party with all the fresh pineapple they can eat and all the mai tais they can drink. (Believe it or not, anybody can come to these parties—you don't have to be a hotel guest. This must be the best-kept secret in Waikiki!) Any day of the week, guests can dine in thatched huts or around the palm-fringed pool at the lovely Tahitian Lanai Restaurant, or have tropical drinks at the Papeete Bar, where a lively local crowd gathers for late-evening sing-alongs.

And there's plenty of activity, too, out on the lagoon: windsurfing lessons, water bikes, and wonderful swimming.

The Breakers

250 Beach Walk, Honolulu, HI 96815. ☎ **808/923-3181,** or 800/426-0494. Fax 808/923-7174. 64 rms, 15 suites. A/C TV TEL. $93–$100 double; $134 for two-person, $145 for three-person, $150 for four-person garden suite. Extra person $8. AE, DC, MC, V. Free parking for only 9 cars.

Just a half-block from one of the best stretches of Waikiki Beach, The Breakers offers its guests plenty of comfort and charm; it has that relaxed Hawaiian-garden feeling of years gone by. There are six ranch-style buildings surrounding the large freshwater swimming pool and a garden where guests are so comfortable they may never even get to the beach. The rooms are nicely appointed, with completely equipped electric kitchens and modern Asian-style decor; many have lanais. The Café Terrace snack bar and lounge is a comfortable spot. Guests enjoy complimentary coffee in the mornings, leis on departure, beach facilities down the road, and many extras.

Hawaiiana Hotel

260 Beach Walk, Honolulu, HI 96815. ☎ **808/923-3811,** or 800/367-5122 from U.S. mainland and Canada. Fax 808/926-5728. 95 rms, 7 one-bedroom units. A/C TV TEL. $85–$95 double, $165–$190 Alii studios, $135–$145 one-bedroom units. Extra person $8. AE, DC, JCB, MC, V. Parking $6 (spaces limited).

In this era of high-rise Hawaii, it comes as a shock to find a low-slung, two-story hotel cozily nestled in a tropical garden, complete with pools, greenery, and that old-time Hawaiian ambience you weren't sure still existed. That's the kind of pleasant feeling you'll get when you walk into the courtyard of this hotel. Located on a side street, a half-block from the beach on one side and Kalakaua Avenue on the other, the Hawaiiana is not well known among tourists, since it doesn't go about blowing its horn; but those who know it treasure it and wouldn't go anywhere else.

The rooms are rustic but attractive, furnished as studio rooms or suites, with tropical rattan furniture, complete electric kitchen, and electronic safes. There are 15 Alii ultra-deluxe rooms. All units catch the trade winds, and most have lanais overlooking the gardens or one of the two swimming pools.

But the comfort and charm of the rooms are just the beginning of the story here. The hotel believes in doing extra things for its guests, such as serving them free coffee and pineapple juice by the pool in the morning, placing a pineapple in their rooms when they arrive, giving the women leis on departure, presenting two free Hawaiian shows a week, and leaving a morning or evening paper at the door. The Hawaiiana is the kind of place where you get to know your neighbors, and many couples who have met here now plan their vacations together and reunite at the Hawaiiana every year.

Waikiki Gateway Hotel

2070 Kalakaua Ave., Honolulu, HI 96815. ☎ **808/955-3741,** 800/633-8799 from U.S. mainland and Canada, 1/800/125-921 from Australia. Fax 808/955-1313. 190 rms and suites. A/C TV TEL. Apr 1–Dec 20. $64–$112 double, $112 penthouse suite; Dec 21–Mar 31, $74–$112 double, $112 penthouse suite. Extra person $10. AE, DC, JCB, MC, V. Parking $7.

Waikiki Gateway is a small charmer. The muraled lobby is beautifully complemented by cane furniture and a deep red-and-blue color scheme. Each room has an under-the-counter refrigerator, an in-room safe, a beautiful bathroom, and a lanai—some even have two. One of the island's finest restaurants, Nick's

🕑 Family-Friendly Hotels

Hyatt Regency Waikiki *(p. 83)* Hyatt makes Camp Hyatt available to kids between 3 and 15 at a cost of $5 per hour. Members receive room discounts, special keiki menus, birthday recognition, and Camp Hyatt merchandise. Adult-supervised evening activities include games, arts and crafts, movies, cartoons, and a mid-evening snack.

Hawaiian Regent *(p. 86)* This hotel offers the KidQuest program during the summer months: Each child receives an age-appropriate gift, which includes valuable discount coupons to family-oriented visitor attractions. A free "Children's Guide to Fun Under the Sun" is also available to guests.

Halekulani *(p. 98)* Halekulani has its Junior Program for ages 6 to 13. Daily programs include crafts, games, sightseeing, and excursions. This is a complimentary service for hotel guests; the only charges are for lunch and admission to excursions. The program runs from late June to late August.

Ihilani Resort & Spa *(p. 116)* The Keiki Beachcomber Club, available every day of the year, has its own facility for children from toddlers to teenagers, with everything from a built-in sandbox to a Computer Center to its own pool. Cultural sharing of games, crafts, foods, and international experiences is the hallmark of the program, which includes both indoor and outdoor activities. Fees are $55 per day; half-day rates are available.

Fishmarket, is right in the lobby. There are laundry facilities on the fourth floor, adjacent to the sun deck and the delicious blue pool, which is backed by a wall of lava rock. The Waikiki Gateway is about a 10-minute walk to the beach, but TheBUS, which stops out front, will get you there promptly.

A HOTEL FOR THE MILITARY

Hale Koa Hotel

Armed Forces Recreation Center, Fort DeRussy, 2055 Kalia Rd., Honolulu, HI 96815-1998. ☎ **808/955-0555**, or 800/367-6027. Fax 800/833-6060. 419 rms. A/C TV TEL. (depending on rank): $47–$75 standard, $56–$87 superior, $62–$89 park view. $70–$106 ocean view, $82–$114 oceanfront. Single occupancy deduct $2; more than two persons, add $10 per person. Children under 12 free in parent's room using existing bedding. Cribs $4. AE, CB, DC, MC, V. Parking $3.

This hotel has a select guest list: It's available only to active-duty and retired military of all services, including Reserve and National Guard members, and their families. What a deal! Fronting a superb stretch of Waikiki Beach next door to the posh Hilton Hawaiian Village, it's comparable to many first-class beachfront hotels in Waikiki, and prices, depending on one's rank, are far less than what one pays in regular hotels. Reservations can be hard to come by; they can be made up to a year in advance, and are often honored within a much shorter time period. Rooms are of good size and nicely furnished, and most have two double beds. There's a pool, fitness center with sauna, volleyball and racquetball courts, and many services on the premises, including a Post Exchange, a military discount travel office, laundry facilities, and car-rental desk.

One needn't, however, be a guest at Hale Koa to use many of its facilities. In addition, military club members and DOD civilian employees are also welcome to enjoy many of the dining and recreational facilities, including a Sunday Champagne Brunch and shows that include a delicious dinner or buffet: Tama's Polynesian Revue on Wednesday, Hale Koa Luau on Thursday, and a Tuesday-night Magic Show.

4 Ala Moana Area

MODERATE

Ala Moana Hotel

410 Atkinson Dr., Honolulu, HI 96815. ☎ **808/955-4811** or 800/367-6025. Fax 808/944-2974. 1,113 rms and 59 suites. A/C TV TEL. Feb 28–Dec 19, $110–$165 double, $175 concierge floor double; Dec 20–Feb 27, $120–$175 double, $185 concierge floor double; year round, $215–$2,000 suite. Extra person $20. Children 18 and under free in parents' room. AE, MC, V. Parking $6.

Thanks to a $30-million renovation, the Ala Moana Hotel is nicer than ever, from its elegant porte-cochère and magnificent lobby to its guest rooms and suites. There are eight restaurants and lounges in the building, including the famous rooftop supper club Nicholas Nickolas, and the equally noted Rumours disco. The Ginger Terrace serves tropical drinks and snacks at the pool and sun deck, and the Plantation Café offers affordable family dining. There's also Tsukasa for Japanese dining and Royal Garden for Chinese fare.

The good-sized rooms are attractively furnished and have AM-FM radios, mini-refrigerators, and safes. The rooms in the Waikiki Tower have lanais. Rooms on the concierge floors have extra amenities.

The hotel overlooks Ala Wai Yacht Harbor and is adjacent to Honolulu's largest public beach park, Ala Moana Beach Park, with tennis courts, expansive beach, and surfing. The hotel is connected to Ala Moana Shopping Center by a private pedestrian bridge. The main action, Waikiki Beach, is about a 10-minute bus ride away.

Holiday Inn Waikiki

1830 Ala Moana Blvd., Honolulu, HI 96815. ☎ **808/955-1111,** or 800/HOLIDAY. Fax 808/947-1799. 199 rms, 2 suites. A/C TV TEL. $100–$120 double, $300 suite. Extra person $20. Children under 18 free in parents' room. AE, DC, DISC, JCB, MC, V. Parking $5.

Across Ala Moana Boulevard from the Ilikai, and equaling it in proximity to both the beach and the Ala Moana Shopping Center, is the Holiday Inn Waikiki. Rising 17 stories, this resort is set well back from traffic noise. There's a large pool, sun deck, and a round-the-clock Chinese restaurant on the premises. The rooms are regular size, but the bed sizes are deluxe: When you ask for twins, you get double beds. The closets, too, are big, and a smart vanitorium extends the whole length of the bathroom. The nicely decorated rooms all have compact refrigerators, and most provide peeks at the ocean; some feature lanais.

BUDGET

✪ Outrigger Ala Wai Tower

1700 Ala Moana Blvd., Honolulu, HI 96815. ☎ **808/942-7722,** or 800/688-7444 from U.S. mainland and Canada, 1/800/124-171 from Australia. Fax 800/622-4852. 120 studio rms and suites. A/C TV TEL. $85–$120 double. 20% discount for senior citizens. Extra person $15. (Rates include continental breakfast.) AE, CB, DC, DISC, JCB, MC, V. Parking $7.

Located at the entrance to Waikiki, a block from the Ala Moana Shopping Center and the Hilton Hawaiian Village, this hotel has wonderful views from almost every floor and amenities galore, including a lighted tennis court, pool, sauna, and whirlpool spa, and complimentary continental breakfast, as well as cocktails on the roof in the evening. All rooms are identical, four rooms to a floor, and on one side of the building two rooms can be joined to make a suite. They are furnished with wicker or cane furniture; have either twin beds or a queen-size bed; and a kitchen equipped with refrigerator, dishwasher, microwave oven, two-burner stove, and everything necessary in the way of dishes and utensils. The floors and bathroom counters are Italian marble. Riding in the glass elevators here is quite spectacular.

5 University Area

MODERATE

✪ Manoa Valley Inn

2001 Vancouver Dr., Honolulu, HI 96822. ☎ **808/947-6019,** or 800/634-5115. Fax 808/946-6188. 7 rms (4 with bath), 1 cottage (with bath). A/C. $110–$120 double with shared bath, $140 double with private bath, $165 cottage with private bath, $190 double in suite (all rates include continental breakfast). AE, DC, JCB, MC, V. No children under 14. Free parking.

It would take an entire book to detail the charms of this three-story gingerbread house, one of the grand old mansions of Honolulu (it's listed in both Hawaii and the National Registers of Historic Places). The inn has been authentically restored to the resplendence of the 1920s and now functions as Honolulu's most glamorous bed-and-breakfast inn.

Furnished with period antiques, each of the guest rooms (and the intimate cottage) has its own personality; each is named in honor of a well-known person who lived in Hawaii. From the Dole Room on the third floor, furnished with a double bed, on up to the John Guild Suite, with a private sitting room and bath, they all resemble a wonderful movie set. All rates include a generous continental breakfast complete with island fruits, juices, Kona coffee, and freshly baked goodies; fruits, wine, and cheese are served in the evening; and juice, tea, and coffee are available at all times. Sherry and port wine are left out for a nightcap.

The living room offers an antique piano and nickelodeon. The reading room has a TV. There's also a billiard room and a lanai with a hypnotic view of Waikiki's city lights. Board games, books, and magazines are everywhere, and a croquet set is available, too. This is a haven for incurable romantics.

BUDGET

Hostelling International Honolulu

2323 Seaview Ave., Honolulu, HI 96822. ☎ **808/946-0591.** Fax 808/946-5904. 38 beds. $12 members; $15 nonmembers. JCB, MC, V. Free parking.

In lovely Manoa Valley, this hostel facility has developed a reputation over the past 25 years as a safe, clean, friendly environment for world travelers. Nonmembers are accepted. There are beds for 18 women and 20 men. Common rooms, a kitchen, a ping-pong table, games, and a patio under the stars create a relaxed mood here. House parents Thelma and Susan Akau are helpful sources of information. Waikiki is a 10-minute bus ride away. Walking, hiking, and restaurant tours are available. Many restaurants are available within a quarter-mile. Facilities are locked between 10am and 5pm daily.

6 Downtown Honolulu

✪ Executive Centre Hotel

1088 Bishop St., Honolulu, HI 96813. ☎ **808/539-3000**, or 800/949-EXEC (U.S. only). Fax 808/523-1088. 114 all-suite rms. A/C MINIBAR TV TEL. $95 city/mountain view suite; $120 ocean-view suite; $135 city/mountain view Executive Suite; $150 ocean-view Executive Suite. (All rates include continental breakfast.) AE, CB, DC, DISC, JCB, MC, V. Parking $10.

Here's exactly what the business traveler to Honolulu has dreamed of—a handsome, all-suite hotel smack in the middle of the downtown business and financial district, with every conceivable amenity and comfort, enough to make conducting business in Hawaii almost as pleasurable as, well . . . going to the beach. About a 15-minute drive from Honolulu International Airport, Executive Centre is very close to the new Aloha Tower Marketplace's many dining, shopping, and entertainment possibilities, and it's a short drive to Waikiki Beach.

The new hotel occupies the top 10 floors of a 40-story mixed-use, glass-walled tower so that each room boasts unobstructed views of the city, the mountains, or the Honolulu harbor waterfront. Best of all, every room is a suite; even the most inexpensive accommodation has a sitting area with remote-control TV; a kitchenette complete with wet bar, coffee maker, and refrigerator stocked with juice and cold beverages; whirlpool bathtub. Smartly done in contemporary furnishings, each suite has three telephones, voice mail, complimentary in-room safes, hair dryers, and many luxury bath amenities. Executive suites, at the higher end of the price scale, are larger and make ideal little homes-away-from-home with their spacious living room with TV and writing desk, a separate bedroom with another TV, a fully stocked kitchen with oven, a washer and dryer, and a luxurious bathroom with whirpool tub and a separate shower.

Dining/Entertainment: The contemporary Centre Court features the work of an innovative chef (see review in Chapter 7). A separate room, with seating for up to 25 guests, is available for private functions.

Services: The Business Services Center provides a full range of office and secretarial services: personal and laptop computers with a variety of word processing programs, printers, copy machines, typewriters, and more; free daily newspaper and local phone calls; concierge service.

Facilities: A 20-meter outdoor swimming pool and Jacuzzi with sun deck; fitness center with free weights, aerobic equipment, men's and women's saunas. Small- to medium-sized rooms for business meetings and gatherings are available, as well as two corporate-style board rooms.

7 Hawaii Kai

Hawaii Kai is suburban, easygoing, and just about eight miles from the hustle-bustle of Waikiki, but it's a different world altogether. One of its big pluses is Roy's Restaurant. Here's a B&B that exemplifies the Hawaii Kai lifestyle:

Joan Webb and Barbara Abe

P.O. Box 25907, Honolulu, HI 96825. ☎ **808/396-9462.** 2 rms (1 with bath). TV. $55–$65 double (rates include breakfast). No credit cards. Free parking.

If you'd like a bed-and-breakfast accommodation close to Hanauma Bay and Sea Life Park (and about a 25-minute drive from Waikiki), contact Mrs. Joan Webb, or her daughter, Barbara Abe—two Englishwomen who have a beautiful home, with garden and swimming pool, in Hawaii Kai. The larger room, with access to the pool area, has a queen-size bed, a small refrigerator, and a private bath. The smaller room, also cozy, has a double bed and shares a bath with the hosts. Joan and Barbara prepare full island breakfasts for their guests, who join them at the dining table for fresh fruits, juices, homemade breads, English muffins, cereals, and beverages. They are generous with sightseeing advice and tips and also provide beach mats and towels.

8 Windward Oahu

Windward Oahu is on the other side of the mighty Koolau Mountain range that serves as a backdrop to Honolulu. Here you'll find suburban Kailua and, about a 10-minute drive from it around the bay and the Kaneohe Marine Corps Air Station, Kaneohe. What makes these towns ideal as vacation headquarters is Kailua Beach and Lanikai Beach—both have white sand, gentle waves, and much smaller crowds than you see in Waikiki. There are major shopping centers here and restaurants galore. And should you crave that Waikiki madness, it's just about 25 minutes away, through tunnels scooped into the mountains, via car or public bus. There is no major resort development here—just one older hotel dedicated to promoting marine recreation, a handful of bed-and-breakfasts, and realtors who can help you find a house or cottage close to—or right on—those big, beautiful beaches.

Pat O'Malley of **Pat's Kailua Beach Properties,** 204 S. Kalaheo Ave., Kailua, HI 96734 (☎ 808/261-1653 or 808/262-4128; fax 808/262-8275 or 808/261-0893), is a good man to know. Pat offers more than 25 fully-furnished houses and cottages on or near Kailua Beach, from a million-dollar beachfront estate to "beachy" cottages on or close to the water. Some of the cottages were former staff quarters for beach estates—of these, studio or one-bedroom cottages will go from about $60 to $100. He also has two-bedroom cottages that range from around $80 to $100, and some superb beach homes that can go as high as $325. Many of these are homes that have been bought by people from the mainland for their retirement years in the future; they pay off the mortgage by putting them up for rental now. Each of Pat's units is different, but all are fully furnished and provide cooking and dining utensils, bedding and towels, telephone and TV. Some are duplexes. The interiors of the cottage we saw were well maintained; some have been recently renovated. The exteriors of some are weather-beaten, which gives them a rustic look. Settings and views are lovely, and many have delightful yards and gardens. For example, a one-bedroom/one-bath beachfront cottage is priced at $90 a day and can sleep two adults and two children. Overlooking Kailua Beach Park, less than 100 yards from the surf, are one-bedroom/one-bath units for $65 to $85 that can sleep three to four people, and two-bedroom units for $100 to $125 that can sleep five people. Call Pat O'Malley for information and reservations: Be sure to ask about the deposit requirements.

✪ Schrader's Windward Marine Resort

47-039 Lihikai Dr., Kaneohe, HI 96744. ☎ **808/239-5711,** or 800/735-5711. Fax 808/239-6658. 53 units. A/C TV TEL. $49–$146 one-bedroom: $110–$190 two-bedroom,

$170–$320 two-bedroom with den (for up to six persons). Extra person $7.50. AE, CB, DC, DISC, JCB, MC, V. Free parking.

On the shores of Kaneohe Bay, this older, rural hotel, about a half-hour drive from both Waikiki and downtown Honolulu, is something special for those who like a country setting. It's a world unto itself, dedicated to introducing the field of marine recreation to its guests. It has its own pier services, the North Bay Boat Club and Sailing School; daily boat trips are available and a variety of sailboats; windsurfers, kayaks, and jet boats are also on hand. Beginners can learn how, and experts can just take off.

Five buildings here share a compound bordered by a stream on one side and Kaneohe Bay on the other. There's a swimming pool and a therapy pool (a Jacuzzi with unheated water). Picnic tables and barbecues abound.

Each unit has a living room, bathroom, lanais, and full-size refrigerator; some have kitchen facilities as well. Furnishings are modest but comfortable; you might have an old-fashioned tub instead of a shower. Rooms with waterfront views are more expensive. Daily cleaning service is provided. Three-bedroom suites are also available.

BED & BREAKFASTS
IN KAILUA

Akamai Bed and Breakfast

172 Kuumeie Place, Kailua, HI 96734. ☎ **808/261-2227,** or 800/642-5366. 2 studios (with bath). TV. $65 double. Extra person $10, to a maximum of four. Minimum stay three nights. No credit cards. Free parking.

Three blocks and an eight-minute walk from the beautiful white-sand beaches of Kailua is this charming home. A separate wing from the main house has two spacious studios, each with its own kitchen, including a refrigerator and microwave oven. The refrigerator is stocked with breakfast foods, and guests are free to do light cooking. Guests enjoy the convenience of the pool and lanai in a lovely tropical setting. Diane Van Ryzin and her husband, Joe, are cordial hosts.

Fairway View Bed & Breakfast

515 Paumamua Place, Kailua, HI 96734. ☎ **808/263-6439,** or 808/262-0485. 2 rms, shared bath. $40–$50 double, including breakfast, depending on length of stay. No credit cards. Free parking.

Louise (Weezie) and Neal Wooden's charming home is located at the end of a quiet cul-de-sac and has the Mid Pacific Golf Course—perhaps the most beautifully landscaped course on the island—right in its backyard. Weezie is a delightful hostess and a veritable treasure trove of Hawaiiana who has endless resource material and ideas about fun and intriguing things to do and places to go. There are two guest rooms: One has a queen-sized bed and the same dusty rose and seafoam green color scheme of the living room and family room, where breakfast is served by the big picture window overlooking the golf course and the Koolau Mountains. The other room has twin beds with cream-and-black bedspreads and, like the queen room, Pegge Hopper prints framed in koa and beautiful etched glass mirrors. The two guest accomodations share a big bath across the hall. The queen room has its own TV, and there's a big TV in the family room. Two of the most glorious beaches on the island are just down the hill. In addition to Louise and Neal, the Wooden family includes Krista, an adorable bright-eyed champion West Highland Terrier.

⑤ Lanikai Bed & Breakfast

1277 Mokulua Dr., Kailua, HI 96734. ☎ **808/261-1059.** 1 studio, 1 apt (with bath). TV
TEL. $60 garden studio, $85 one-bedroom apt. MC, V. Free parking.

If you love being right on the beach, you can't beat this one. Mahina and Homer
Maxey's large, comfortable home is just across the street from idyllic Lanikai Beach,
with its soft white sand and inviting, always-calm water. There's a large covered
lanai in front, with banana trees, lawa'e ferns, and plenty of tables and chairs. The
studio, which has a private entrance, is at the back of the house overlooking the
garden, with a stunning view of what many consider the most beautiful mountains
in the islands—the Windward Koolaus. There's a queen-size bed, a sitting room/
TV area, and a kitchen/dining area, complete with microwave, refrigerator, and
coffee maker. Upstairs is a spacious apartment with a living room/dining area, a
den, one bedroom with a king-size bed, another with a queen-size bed, refrigerator, coffee maker, toaster, and a small appliances for light meal preparation.
Every few days Mahina will bring homemade bread, muffins, juice, and coffee for
your continental breakfast. There are ceiling fans, lots of beautiful plants, and, of
course, that heavenly beach just across the street. By the way, both Maxeys are from
old kamaaina families; ask Mahina about the family photos.

Papaya Paradise

195 Auwinala Rd., Kailua, HI 96734. ☎ and fax **808/261-0316.** 2 units. $70 single/double.
(Rates include breakfast.) Extra person $15. Three-day minimum stay. No credit cards.
Free parking.

Very popular with a number of German-speaking guests who return year after
year, Jeanette and Bob Martz's cozy home is located on a residential street in the
Enchanted Lake section of Kailua, a short walk from Kailua Beach. There's a
separate entrance to the bed-and-breakfast units through the garage, which leads
to the lanai, a pool with Jacuzzi, and an enormous backyard. Papayas were just
taking hold at this writing and there are plenty of shade trees, flowers, and a delightful dinosaur rock garden created by the Martz grandkids. The two units, each
with private bath, air conditioning, and ceiling fans, are decorated Polynesian style
in rattan and wicker with colorful upholstery. There's a well-stocked library of
books in both English and German. Breakfast is served on the lanai by the pool
overlooking that big backyard; it's a great place for birdwatching.

Sharon's Serenity

127 Kakahiaka St., Kailua, HI 96734. ☎ **808/263-3634,** or 808/262-5621. 2 rms with
private baths. TV TEL. $55–$65 double. No credit cards. Free parking.

Sharon and Bob Price's lovely home is located on a quiet residential street a
short walk from Kailua Beach. The house is decorated in an elegant Oriental
and contemporary style, enhanced by Sharon's striking floral arrangements. The
two-room suite has a sitting room with a comfortable daybed, ceiling fans, small
refrigerator, a queen-size bed, and a full bath with tub and shower and a door
opening to the pool area. The Blue Room also has a queen-size bed, ceiling fan,
and a small refrigerator. The Yellow Room has a twin bed and TV; it is used only
with the suite, and shares the same bathroom. Each room has its own color TV,
but guests are welcome to join the Prices in the spacious living room, with its three
huge comfy counches, big TV, plants, and plenty of books. The setting is gorgeous, with a pool, beautiful flowers, Kaelepulu Stream running by, and views of
a private golf course and the mountains. A cuddly Bichon Frise named Trouble

(a misnomer if we've ever heard one) completes the Price ménage. A good breakfast is served. A washer and dryer are available at a small fee.

Sheffield House Bed & Breakfast

131 Kuulei Rd., Kailua, HI 96734. ☎ **808/262-0721.** 1 rm, 1 one-bedroom suite (both with bath). $40 double, $60 one-bedroom suite, $95 two-bedroom suite. Minimum stay three days; monthly rates on request. No credit cards. Free parking.

Architects Paul and Rachel Sheffield and three Sheffield children, along with a cat named Hillary, comprise the household here. Their house is in an ongoing process of renovation, but the cozy guest accommodations are all finished. Each has a private entrance, Mexican tile floors, bright tropical-print bedspreads and accessories, and a kitchen area with a refrigerator, microwave, toaster oven, and coffee maker. The suite has its own sitting room, a small dining area, a queen-size bed, and a view of its own private garden. The room, which is wheelchair-accessible, has a queen-size bed. The two units may be combined as a two-bedroom/two-bath suite. There's no pool, but who needs one when you're just a hop, skip, and a jump from beautiful Kailua Beach? Complimentary continental breakfast is provided on the first day only.

In Kaneohe

A 5-Star Bed and Breakfast-BJG's

44-491 Kaneohe Bay Dr., Kaneohe, HI 96744. ☎ **808/235-8235,** or 800/235-5214. 3 rms (1 with private bath). $75–$85 double. No credit cards. Free parking.

Next door to the posh Kaneohe Bay Yacht Club is the movie set–style home of Bonnie and Richard Green. We were entranced by the magnificent Italian tile pool nestled in a tropical garden and guarded by two stone lions; at night, the area is illuminated by tiki torches. The house is decorated in an Asian motif with some extraordinary antiques and art work. The living room has a great collection of books and magazines, which guests are invited to peruse. Two rooms share a bathroom; one has twin beds, the other a queen-size bed. The master bedroom, which has a king-size bed, overlooks the pool area. Both bathrooms are gracefully appointed, with makeup lights and private garden views. Breakfast is served in the dining room or by the pool. The entire home, which comfortably sleeps six adults and four children, can be rented for $300 daily, with a seven-day minimum. There is a 20% discount for one month or more.

Ali'i Bluffs Bed & Breakfast

46-251 Ikiiki St., Kaneohe, HI 96744. ☎ **808/235-1124,** or 800/235-1151. 2 rms (with bath). $55 Circus Room; $60 Victorian Room. No credit cards. Free parking.

Set in a lush tropical garden with a pool, this charming home is filled to the brim with Victorian antiques—toys, posters, teddy bears, ornaments—and fine paintings, reminders of the days when hosts L. De Chambs and Donald Munro ran an art gallery in New York. Now they're here in Hawaii, in a gracious home overlooking Kaneohe Bay. Their guest wing consists of the Victorian Room, with a wonderful old china doll on its double bed, and an attached private bath. The Circus Room has antique teddy bears on each of the twin beds, circus posters from all over the world on the walls, and a private bath across the corridor. The hosts are delightfully warm people who enjoy having their guests in for late-afternoon tea in the living room and library. And they serve breakfast—fruits, cereal, juices, toast, and coffee—out on the pool lanai whenever guests wish.

Hula Kai Hale

44-002 Hulakai Place, Kaneohe, HI 96744. ☎ **808/235-6754.** 2 rms (with bath). $65 King Room; with den for extra person, $25; $55 Queen Room.

Hula Kai Hale (House of the Dancing Waters) is located right on Kaneohe Bay, with panoramic ocean and mountain views. Tom and Ditty Pico, longtime Hawaii residents, thoroughly enjoy having guests. They provide an ample breakfast served poolside or on the huge waterfront dock. There are two nicely furnished guest rooms, each with color TV, bar-refrigerator, coffee makers, microwave, and toaster oven. The King Room has an adjacent den with a twin daybed, ideal for a teen family member. Each room has its own private full bath and a private exit. Nearby you'll find a shopping center, restaurants, and movie theaters; it's about a 10-minute drive to Kailua and Lanikai beaches.

9 The North Shore

About an hour's drive from Waikiki is Oahu's North Shore, another world altogether. This is the land of the mighty waves, the scene of major surfing competitions at Sunset Beach and Waimea Bay. Staying here puts you close to swimming, surfing, windsurfing, diving, horseback riding, and championship golf and tennis activity. But remember, if you want ocean swimming, come here only in the summer months, when the ocean waters are as gentle as lakes; in winter, the waves can be as high as 30 feet, and the ocean is for very experienced swimmers and surfers only.

There are not too many accommodations in this neck of the woods—one major resort hotel, some vacation rentals, and a place for the backpacking set. The quaint town of Haleiwa offers delightful restaurants, shops, and galleries. A car is a definite advantage.

Marilyn and Lucky Cole, who run **North Shore Vacation Homes,** 59-229 C Ke Nui Rd., Haleiwa, HI 96712 (☎ 808/638-7289, or 800/678-5263; fax 808/638-8736), have four lovely vacation homes for rent in this area, just 1¹/₂ miles west of the Turtle Bay Hilton Resort. All oceanfront, these are two- and three-bedroom beachfront cottages and homes with large, covered redwood decks, plentiful indoor space, and a sleeping capacity of from 4 to 10 persons. During the off-season—after Labor Day to Thanksgiving and after Easter to the first of June—the rates are $105, $150, and $160 per day; from Thanksgiving through Easter and from June through Labor Day weekend, rates are $125, $165, and $175 per day; during the week before and after Christmas, rates are $150, $185, and $200. A minimum stay of one week is required, except during Christmas, when the minimum stay is two weeks.

⊛ Backpackers, Vacation Inn/Plantation Village

59-788 Kamehameha Hwy., Haleiwa, HI 96712. ☎ **808/638-7838.** Hostel bunks, rms, apts. cabins. At Vacation Inn, $14 hostel bunk across from the beach, $16 hostel bunk oceanfront, $40–$45 room across from the beach; $70–$85 oceanfront studio apt. At Plantation Village, $16 hostel bunk; $100–$120 cabin for four to six. $105–$120 large cabin for six, $110–$120 deluxe ocean-view cabin for six. $120 large ocean-view cabin for eight. Weekly rates available. MC, V. Free parking.

This place is definitely not for the perfectionist, as buildings and furniture have seen wear and tear, but management is always fixing and upgrading as much as possible. Backpackers caters to young and young-at-heart travelers from around the world. There are several possibilities here for casual country living. At Vacation

Inn, one can find basic accommodations overlooking Waimea Bay. Backpackers like the inexpensive hostel facilities, which consist of several rooms furnished with four bunks each. There's a common living room with TV, a bathroom, and a kitchen. The quarters are cleaned each morning. Moving one step up, you can rent a single or double room with a common bath, kitchen, and TV room. Studio apartments can sleep four to six and are comfortably furnished, with TV and kitchenette; all have good views of surf and beach. Some of these units are right on Three Tables Beach, which is next to Waimea Bay; others are higher up in a building on the mountain side of the road and command great ocean vistas.

Plantation Village consists of nine restored plantation cabins located across from Three Tables Beach Park, on an acre of gardens; bananas, papayas, ginger, and mangoes grow in the yard. Each cabin has its own kitchen and bath, cable TV, linens and dishes; a common area offers pay telephone, picnic and barbecue areas, and laundry facilities. The Circle Island bus no. 52 stops out front every half hour; all facilities are a short walk to Waimea Bay, Waimea Falls Park, and a good supermarket, so one could conceivably get by without a car here. A protected area is safe for children's swimming. Boogie boards and snorkels are part of the North Shore lifestyle, so they are supplied free to guests, as are tennis racquets and balls. Chaz Wagner and Sharlyn Foo are warm hosts, who provide inexpensive sailboat and hiking trips and island tours. Scuba-diving instruction is available in summer. They also rent many vacation homes and condos "in all shapes, sizes, and locations" (rates on request). Again, remember that Waimea Bay is perfect for summer swimming and snorkeling, but the water is extremely rough in winter; it's the scene of world-famous surfing events.

Ke Iki Hale

59-579 Ke Iki Rd., Haleiwa, HI 96712. ☎ **808/638-8229.** 12 units. $85–$125 one-bedroom unit; $145 one-bedroom cottage; $150–$165 two-bedroom cottage. AE, MC, V. Free parking.

Here's a place for those who long to be right on the beach, or just a few steps away from it. Alice Tracy's rental cottages on the North Shore are on 1½ acres of palm-fringed land near Waimea Bay. They are nicely furnished, with full kitchens; some have large picture windows overlooking the ocean. Guests can enjoy the barbecue facilities, the picnic tables at water's edge, and a small volleyball court. There's a public telephone on the premises, but not a TV in sight. Waimea Bay is ideal for swimming in the summer months, but during the winter its sky-high waves are for experienced surfers only.

Rodeway Inn Hukilau Resort

55-109 Laniloa St., Laie, HI 96762. ☎ **808/293-9282,** or 800/LANILOA (526-4562). 48 rms. A/C TV TEL. $79 double, $89 triple or quad. Children under 8 free in parent's room. AE, DC, DISC, MC, V. Parking $7.

A comfortable, motel-like hotel located next door to the Polynesian Cultural Center, Rodeway Inn boasts a sandy ocean beach and a pool. Rooms have refrigerators, microwave ovens (on request), and private lanais. The inn is also within walking distance of the Brigham Young University–Hawaii campus and the Mormon Temple. Temple-patron rates are available upon request.

Turtle Bay Hilton Golf and Tennis Resort

P.O. Box 187, Kahuku, HI 96731. ☎ **808/293-8811,** or 800/HILTONS. Fax 808/293-9147. 485 rms, cottages, and suites. A/C TV TEL. $180–$220 double, $330 cabana. $400–$1,500 suite. Extra person $25. Children of any age free in parents' room. AE, CB, DC, DISC, ER, JCB, MC, V. Parking $3.

If you're not going to the neighbor islands but seek a resort vacation in a glamorous country setting, then you can't do better than this self-contained resort on the North Shore, not far from Sunset Beach. Set amid five miles of white-sand beach and rugged shoreline, this gorgeously landscaped hotel, with its own golf course and tennis courts, affords a vacation as active or relaxed as one would wish.

Guest rooms, located in either the low-rise main building or in cottages, are beautifully furnished in Polynesian decor. Each room has a private lanai, tub or shower, all the amenities—and a great view of the ocean.

Dining/Entertainment: The Palm Terrace, overlooking the pool and Turtle Bay, is known for fabulous buffets. Sunday champagne brunch at the Sea Tide Room is a favorite. For fine dining overlooking Turtle Bay, there's the Cove, featuring continental and local cuisine and an excellent wine list. There's live entertainment nightly, plus drinks and dancing, at the Bay View Lounge. The "Hang Ten Lounge" is the place for poolside or sunset cocktails.

Services: Room service, concierge desk, many shops (including a branch of Liberty House), craft demonstrations daily.

Facilities: Ocean-view, championship 27-hole golf course designed by Arnold Palmer Management Company, 10 Plexipave-court tennis complex, horseback riding, idyllic beach, two swimming pools, snorkeling, scuba diving, and windsurfing.

10 Leeward Oahu

✪ Ihilani Resort & Spa

At Ko Olina Resort, 92-1001 Olani St., Kapolei, HI 96707. ☎ **808/679-0070,** or 800/626-4446 mainland U.S. and Canada. Fax 808/679-0080. 387 rms, 42 suites. A/C TV TEL MINIBAR. $275 garden-view single or double; $295 terrace room; $365 ocean view; $395 oceanfront; $425 deluxe oceanfront; $550 deluxe spa; $700–$5,000 suite. Extra person $35. Children under 14 free in parents' room using existing bedding. AE, CB, DC, JCB, MC, V. Free parking.

Seventeen miles and 25 minutes west of Honolulu International Airport—and worlds away from the tourist scene of Waikiki—lies an unparalleled resort hotel, the first to open in the 640-acre Ko Olina Resort community. Overlooking a pristine white-sand beach and positioned on the first of four lagoons, Ihilani (which means "heavenly splendor") is already living up to its name. There's little need to travel to a neighbor island when at Ihilani one can experience superb water sports, world-championship golf and tennis, and a state-of-the-art European health spa, all in an atmosphere of rarefied beauty and exquisite taste. From the superb modern art collection (with original Henry Moores and Robert Motherwells) in the lobby to its circular seaside pool with a glass mosaic on the bottom to the superbly-appointed guest rooms, everything here is top of the line.

Most guest rooms enjoy lagoon or ocean views. They are larger than most (680 square feet), and all boast extremely comfortable cushioned teak furniture, spacious lanais, ceiling fans, three telephones, and an in-room safe. Luxurious marble bathrooms have deep-soaking tubs, separate glass-enclosed showers, and many amenities. Spa rooms have their own whirlpool baths.

Dining/Entertainment: Extraordinary cuisine, using the freshest ingredients from neighboring farms and waters, is found in all four Ihilani restaurants. At Azul, the dinner-only restaurant, guests are seated on an intimate terrace overlooking the ocean and dine on Mediterranean-inspired cuisine. There's open-air dining on light tropical fare all day long at the informal poolside Naupaka Restaurant. A low-fat, low-calorie menu is served at The Spa Café. Traditional Japanese fare is served at Kyu-an's sushi counter, in private tatami rooms, or in the main dining room overlooking lagoon and ocean. Talented island artists provide entertainment and music to dance by in the resort's two lounges.

Services: Full-service concierge, 24-hour room service, daily newspaper, business services, transportation to Waikiki and Ala Moana Shopping Center. Keiki Beachcomber Club is a year-round program for toddlers to teens, housed in its own ground-floor facility, with a wide variety of outdoor adventures and indoor learning activities. It has its own Computer Learning Center, a 125-gallon fish tank, an outdoor performance space, an evening lounge for teen-themed parties, and more. Special meals are served and children can spend the day or half-day.

Facilities: Championship 18-hole Ko Olina Golf Course, designed by Ted Robinson and recognized as Hawaii's premier golf course; a tennis club with pro shop; shopping arcade; three-mile coastal fitness trail; two pools and a super-stretch of white-sand beach for ocean activities.

The world-class Ihilani Spa offers just about everything to enhance one's health, fitness, and well-being, including hydrotherapies such as Thalasso treatments with sea water and seaweeds, Swiss showers, Grand Jets, Vichy showers, and Roman pools. Shiatsu, Swedish, and Hawaiian Lomi Lomi massages are offered, as well as herbal bodywraps. Complete fitness and relaxation programs can be designed for each guest. For us, the Spa alone would be reason enough to leave home and come to Hawaii.

11 Oahu's Campgrounds & Wilderness Cabins

by Jeanette Foster

Camping is a year-round experience on Oahu thanks to the balmy weather. There is, however, a wet (winter) and dry (summer) season. You should be prepared for rain year round. You also need to be ready for insects (have a good repellent for mosquitoes), water purification (boiling, filtration, or iodine crystals), and sun protection (sunscreen, a hat, and a long sleeve shirt).

If you don't plan to bring your own camping equipment, you can rent equipment at **Omar the Tent Man,** 650A Kakoi St. (☎ 808/836-8785), or **The Bike Shop,** at 1149 S. King St. (☎ 808/595-0588) and the Windward City Shopping Center (☎ 808/235-8722). Both also have equipment for sale.

Oahu is the only Hawaiian island with a public transportation system that serves the entire Island (see "Getting Around" in Chapter 5 for details). However, one problem with getting to a camping site on TheBUS is that luggage larger than you can hold on your lap, or place under your seat, is forbidden. Metal-frame packs are not permitted on TheBUS. Drivers do use discretion, but be forewarned.

The best places to camp on Oahu are listed below. You can locate them on the map entitled "Outdoor Activities on Oahu" on page 179.

KEAIWA HEIAU STATE RECREATION AREA

Located at the southern end of central Oahu, above Halawa Heights, this 385-acre wooded park offers a cool mountain camp with hiking trails and picnic facilities. This area, in the foothills of the Koolaus, is filled with eucalyptus, ironwood, and Norfolk pines. The remains of the *heiau ho'ola* (temple of treating the sick) are on the grounds, and specimens of Hawaiian medicinal plants are on display. An excellent 5-mile hiking trail, the Aiea loop, offers magnificent Pearl Harbor and mountain views. There's tent camping only; campers have the choice of flat, open grassy areas or slightly sloping areas with shade trees. Facilities include picnic tables, restrooms with cold showers, outdoor grills, a dishwashing area, a covered pavilion, drinking water, and a public phone. Supplies are available in Aiea, 2 miles away.

You'll need a permit; applications are accepted no earlier than 30 days in advance. Write to the Department of Land and Natural Resources, State Parks Division, P.O. Box 621, Honolulu, HI 96809 (☎ 808/587-0300). Permits are limited to a 5-day stay in every 30-day period. The park is closed on Wednesdays and Thursdays for maintenance. The gates close at 6:45pm and do not open until 7am the next morning; cars cannot enter or leave during that period.

To get here from Waikiki, take the H-1 Freeway to Highway 78 and exit at Aiea (Exit 13A). Follow Moanalua Road to Aiea Heights Drive and turn right; the park entrance is at the end of the road. There is no bus service to this area.

HOOMALUHIA BOTANICAL GARDENS

This relatively unknown windward-side camping area, outside of Kaneohe, is a find. Hoomaluhia means "peace and tranquility," an apt description of this 400-acre botanical garden. In this lush garden setting with rare plants and craggy cliffs in the background, it's hard to believe that you're just a half-hour from downtown Honolulu. The gardens are laid out in areas devoted to the plants specific to tropical America, native Hawaii, Polynesia, India-Sri Lanka, and Africa. A 32-acre lake sits in the middle of the scenic park (no swimming or boating is allowed, though), and there are numerous hiking trails. The Visitor's Center can suggest a host of activities, ranging from guided walks to demonstrations of ancient Hawaiian plant use. The facilities for this tent-camp area include restrooms, cold showers, dishwashing stations, picnic tables, grills, and water. A public phone is available at the visitor center, and shopping and gas are available in Kaneohe, 1 mile away.

Permits are free, but stays are limited to 5 nights (the park is closed on Tuesdays and Wednesdays). For information, contact Hoomaluhia Botanical Gardens, 45-680 Luluku Road, Kaneohe, HI 96744 (☎ 808/233-7323). The gate is locked at 4 pm and does not open again until 9am, so you're locked in for the night from 4pm. TheBUS no. 55 (Circle Island) stops 4 miles from the park entrance.

KUALOA REGIONAL PARK

Located on a peninsula on Kaneohe Bay, this park has a spectacular setting—the quiet waters of the bay surround it on three sides, and there's a view of Mokolii Island (Chinaman's Hat) offshore. The white-sand beach is excellent for swimming and snorkeling, and the fishing can be productive. There are two campgrounds: One is in a wooded area with palm trees, ironwoods, kamani, monkeypods, and a sandy beach that is mainly reserved for groups but has a few sites for families. The other campground is on the main beach; it has fewer shade trees, but there's a great view of Mokolii Island. Facilities at both sites are nearly the same: restroom, showers, picnic tables, drinking fountains, and a public telephone. The group campground also has dishwashing sinks, a volleyball court, and a kitchen building. Gas and groceries are available in Kaaawa, 2¹/₂ miles away.

In the summer, the group site is nearly always filled, frequently by groups with young children, so you might want to consider this when requesting an area. Permits are free, but limited to five days (there's no camping on Wednesday and

Thursdays); they can be obtained from the Honolulu Department of Parks and Recreation, 650 South King St., Honolulu, HI 96713 (☎ 808/523-4525), or at any satellite city hall. The two closest to the campgrounds are in Hauula at 54-316 Kamehameha Hwy. (☎ 808/293-8551), or in Kaneohe at 46-018 Kamehameha Hwy., (☎ 808/235-4571). To get to the park, take TheBUS no. 55 (Circle Island).

KAHANA BAY BEACH PARK

A beautiful, white-sand, crescent-shaped beach, with dramatic mountains framing the valley, is the breathtaking setting of Kahana Bay Beach Park. Opportunities to enjoy the ocean, from safe swimming to bodysurfing and fishing, abound. You can hike, picnic, and even pick fruit in the nearby vegetated forest.

Tent and vehicle camping only is allowed at this oceanside paradise. Facilities include restrooms, picnic tables, drinking water, public phones, and a boat-launching ramp. Do note that the restrooms are located at the north end of the beach, far away from the camping area, and there are no showers. There's no fee for camping, but you must get a permit. Reservations for permits are taken no earlier than two Fridays before the date requested. Applicants must appear in person to get a permit at any satellite city hall or at the City and County of Honolulu Department of Parks and Recreation, 650 South King St., Honolulu 96813 (☎ 808/523-4525). Permits are limited to 5 days; no camping is allowed on Wednesdays and Thursdays.

To get there from Waikiki, take the H-1 west to the Likelike Highway (Hi. 63). Continue north on the Likelike, through the Wilson Tunnel, turning left on Highway. 83; Kahana Bay is 13 miles down the road on the right. Or, take TheBUS no. 55 (Circle Island).

MALAEKAHANA STATE RECREATION AREA

This windward park is one of the most beautiful beach camping areas in the state. A gorgeous sandy beach backs up into a grove of ironwoods, kamani, and hao trees. Offshore lie several small islands; the largest one is Moku'auia (Goat Island), a bird sanctuary. Most of the long, white-sand beach is excellent for swimming. On calm days at low tide, you can wade through the waist-high water to Moku'auia. Snorkeling, surfing, and fishing are also available when conditions are right. Beachcombing, walks, and hikes are just a few of the activities available here. If you are lucky, you may even find a glass ball, the coveted Japanese fishing floats that occasionally drift ashore.

There are two areas for tent camping. Facilities include: picnic tables and small table to hold a portable stove with each camp site, restrooms, showers, dishwashing sinks, drinking water, and a phone.

Permits, which are free but limited to 5 nights (no camping is allowed on Wednesdays and Thursdays), can be obtained at any state parks office, including the State Parks Division, P.O. Box 621, Honolulu, HI 96809 (☎ 808/548-7455). Note that the park gate is closed between 6:45pm and 7am; vehicles cannot enter or exit during that time. Groceries and gas are available in Laie and Kahuku, less than a mile away. To get to the park, take TheBUS no. 55 (Circle Island).

CAMP MOKULEIA

This quiet, isolated beach is the site of a 9-acre camp. Camping is available both on the beach and in a grassy, wooded area. Activities include swimming, surfing, shore fishing, and beachcombing. The entire area is far from the maddening crowds—it's a great place to get away from it all. Kaena Point is just 4 miles away, and groceries are available in Waialua, also 4 miles away.

The facilities here include tent, cabins, and lodge camping. The tent camping site has portable chemical toilets, a water spigot, and outdoor showers. It doesn't have picnic tables or barbecue grills, so come prepared. The cabins have bunk beds and can sleep up to 18 people. The lodge facilities include rooms with and without a private bath. The cabins are $125 per night for the 14-bed cabin and $160 per night for the 18-bed cabin. The rooms at the lodge are $45–$50 for a shared bath and $55–$60 for a private bath. Many groups use the camp, but it's still a very peaceful place. The tent area is separated from the buildings—but you can use all the facilities if you opt for it—and there's a real sense of privacy. Tent camping is $5 per person, per night. Reservations for permits are needed; contact **Camp Mokuleia,** 68-729 Farrington Hwy., Waialua, HI 96791 (☎ 808/637-6241).

To get there from Waikiki, take the H-1 to the H-2 exit. Stay on H-2 until the end. Where the road forks, bear left to Waialua (Hwy. 803), which turns into Hwy. 930 to Kaena Point. Look for the green fence on the right, where a small sign at the driveway reads: "Camp Mokuleia, Episcopal Church of Hawaii." The Bus will get you within 4 miles: Take TheBUS no. 52 (Circle Island) to Haleiwa, then transfer to TheBUS no. 76 (Waialua Shuttle). From Waialua, you'll have to walk the remainder of the distance.

Dining

Do tourists spend more time eating than doing anything else? Statistics could never prove it, of course, but it has always seemed to us that dining out is one of the most popular pastimes under the Hawaiian sun. And with good reason: Although Hawaii is not one of the true gourmet capitals of the world, it embraces a wealth of cultural traditions from all over, and dining here can be more fun—and more adventurous—than almost anyplace else. And the cuisine that is unique to the Islands, Hawaiian Regional cuisine—and the chefs who created it, like Oahu's Roy Yamaguchi—is gaining worldwide recognition for its innovation, both in its blending of influences and its use of Hawaiian foodstuffs. Honolulu itself has perhaps a dozen great restaurants, even a few that are considered world-class; scores of unusual and interesting ones; and many where the food is hearty, well priced, and just what you would expect from a good restaurant back home. Because there are so many restaurants in Honolulu, however, and in so many price categories, some guidance is in order. You're not going to spend every evening dining out with wine and candlelight on Hawaiian Regional cuisine; neither are you going to eat all your meals at beachside saimin stands or in the coffee shop of your hotel. What we've done here, then, is to track down several dozen of what we consider the best restaurants on Oahu no matter how much or how little you want to pay or what kind of dining experience you're after. And we've divided these restaurants into the following three categories.

- **Expensive.** Here we'll give you details on restaurants at the top of our list, where the cuisine, service, ambience, and view—or any combination thereof—make for a memorable experience. Expect to pay at least $35 (plus drinks, tax, and tip), maybe a good deal more, for an evening meal at an expensive restaurant. At these places, reservations are a must. And when you phone, inquire about dress; although most Honolulu restaurants are eminently casual, a few prefer that men wear jackets and ties.
- **Moderate.** The bulk of the moderate restaurants we'll describe cover the range from about $20 to $35 for dinner. Many of these offer excellent table d'hôte dinners for reasonable prices. Here you'll continue to sample some of the international cuisines that have found a home in the islands—Japanese, Chinese, Mexican, Indonesian, Thai, French, Hawaiian, Italian, and continental.

And there'll be no shortage of the old Hawaiian favorite, the steak house. (This is the 50th American state, remember?)

- **Budget.** These are casual, come-as-you-are places, a few of them coffeehouses. You can expect to get dinner for under $20. Some budget restaurants are open around the clock, in case that hungry feeling should strike at an unexpected hour.

1 Diamond Head Waikiki

EXPENSIVE

Colony Steak and Seafood Restaurant

In the Hyatt Regency Waikiki, 2424 Kalakaua Ave. ☎ **808/923-1234.** Reservations recommended. Main courses (including salad bar) $19–$43. AE, DC, JCB, MC, V. Daily 6–10pm. STEAK/SEAFOOD.

Rudyard Kipling would have felt right at home here. It's a bit of the British Colonial past in India come to life, with rattan furniture, palm trees, revolving ceiling fans, gazebo-like tables in the center of the room, and the brilliant use of live greenery creating a warm ambience. Choose your meat from the unique deli case: It could be New York teriyaki, New York strip, prime rib, or double-cut lamb chops. Then proceed to the glorious salad bar, included in the price of your main course, while your selection is being cooked over a combination of charcoal and Hawaiian kiawe wood. If you prefer fish and seafood, there's fresh mainland and Hawaiian catch, broiled or sautéed, plus broiled Maine lobster. And if cuisine naturelle is more your thing, try the steamed filet of Norwegian salmon with balsamic pepper relish or the basted breast of chicken with fresh honeycomb. Treat yourself to one of the side dishes, too, like the oven-roasted Maui onions with bacon chips.

Hy's Steak House

In the Waikiki Park Heights Hotel, 2440 Kuhio Ave. ☎ **808/922-5555.** Reservations recommended. Main courses $15.50–$32.50. AE, DC, JCB, MC, V. Sun–Thurs 6–10pm, Fri–Sat 6–11pm. STEAK.

After 18 years of being one of Waikiki's most popular steak houses, Hy's is still going strong. It was recently voted the city's "Best Steak House" by readers of *Honolulu* magazine and Zagat's has named it one of Honolulu's Top Five Restaurants. It preserves a tradition of old-world elegance unusual for Hawaii; the Main Room and Broiler Room boast Victorian decor: a lighted Tiffany ceiling, paneled walls, bookshelves, family portraits, turn-of-the-century chandeliers. Tuxedoed waiters offer gracious service and prepare Caesar salad and flaming desserts at tableside. All of this is a backdrop for the superb beef: dry-aged, boned, and trimmed on the premises and then charcoal-broiled on Hawaiian kiawe wood under intense heat to bring out its natural flavor. Steaks, done to your specifications, are served on wooden planks with potatoes of your choice. All main courses come with soup or salad, a starch, a vegetable, and delicious fresh garlic-cheese bread.

For dessert, there's a variety of gourmet cheesecakes as well as spectacular flambé desserts. There is also, of course, an expansive wine list. The *Wine Spectator* has given Hy's its Award of Excellence. From 8pm, there's live entertainment in the Library Lounge, usually the award-winning guitarist-singer Audy Kimura. Valet parking is available. And "dressy attire" is preferred.

Waikiki Dining

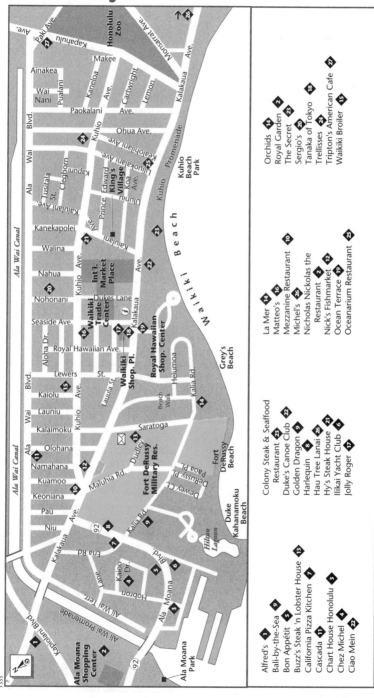

Orchids 14
Royal Garden 2
The Secret 23
Sergio's 20
Tanaka of Tokyo 18
Trellisses 24
Tripton's American Cafe 27
Waikiki Broiler 15

La Mer 14
Matteo's 16
Mezzanine Restaurant 22
Michel's 26
Nicholas Nickolas the Restaurant 10
Nick's Fishmarket 2
Ocean Terrace 19
Oceanarium Restaurant 25

Colony Steak & Seafood Restaurant 23
Duke's Canoe Club 22
Golden Dragon 9
Harlequin 8
Hau Tree Lanai 25
Hy's Steak House 21
Ilikai Yacht Club 6
Jolly Roger 47

Alfred's 4
Bali-by-the-Sea 9
Bon Appétit 5
Buzz's Steak 'n Lobster House 7
California Pizza Kitchen 11
Cascada 3
Chart House Honolulu 4
Chez Michel 22
Ciao Mein

Post Office ⌧   Information ⓘ

☉ Michel's

In the Colony Surf, 2895 Kalakaua Ave. ☎ **808/923-6552.** Reservations required. Main courses $22.50–$25 ($48 for beef and lobster combination). AE, DC, JCB, MC, V. Mon–Fri 11:30am–2pm; 5:30–10pm; Sun brunch 11am–2pm. HAWAIIAN REGIONAL.

Hidden away in the far reaches of Waikiki, down steps, around corridors, and behind doors, is a restaurant to which the cognoscenti of Honolulu and sophisticated visitors alike have beaten a path for many years. This is Michel's, which undoubtedly enjoys one of the best settings in Hawaii. The view from your table can rival anything on the Riviera—you're next to the incredibly blue-green Pacific, and you can watch the boats and bathers of the Outrigger Canoe Club as you dine.

After many years of serving a traditional French menu to a devoted local clientele, Michel's now boasts a Hawaiian Regional menu. Executive chef Bobby Masters has been trained by the new owner of Michel's, Jean-Marie Josselin, the acclaimed *wunderkind* chef known for his imaginative fare at A Pacific Café on Kauai and Maui. What's more, prices have come down dramatically. The new menu has been designed so that guests can create their own meals—perhaps choosing a variety of appetizers instead of a traditional three-course dinner. So, then, consider such "first tastes" as a spicy crabcake with papaya basil sauce, or tuna carpaccio with white truffle vinaigrette, or perhaps salmon-scallop gyoza with Thai peanut sauce. Soup and salad choices might include baked potato soup with smoked marlin and sour cream and chives, or southwest-style Ceasar salad with Margarita chicken breast and polenta croutons. Main courses include such offerings as seared peppered ahi with Wasabi soy black-pepper sauce, spinach fettucine with sea scallops and basil Alfredo sauce, or grilled Hawaiian swordfish with Tuscan beans, tapenade, and fried leeks. Lunch is similar, but with more pasta and risotto choices (in a $14 to $17 range), and a few elegant sandwiches. Unfortunately, Michel's no longer serves breakfast, but the Sunday brunch more than makes up for it: Dining here on a brilliant morning, overlooking the beach, is one of the special treats of Honolulu. The $18.75 to $24.50 brunch prices include champagne or juice, appetizer, and dessert.

☉ The Secret

In the Hawaiian Regent Hotel, 2552 Kalakaua Ave. ☎ **808/922-6611.** Reservations highly recommended. Main courses $18.50–$27. AE, CB, DC, DISC, MC, V. Tues–Sun 6:30pm–closing. CONTINENTAL.

The Secret has long held a reputation as one of Honolulu's most splendid restaurants. The decor is extraordinary, the service excellent, and the fine continental cuisine replete with unexpected touches. You dine beneath open-beam ceilings, magnificent copper chandeliers, and multicolored Camelot banners, against a romantic background of rippling fountains and koa wall mosaics. And the menu of chefs Klaus Saballus and Wolfgang Horndlein lives up to every expectation.

Little things make a difference here. You're served Indian naan bread, baked in an imported clay charcoal-heated oven, and it's accompanied by a duck liver pâté as well as butter. A tray of relishes (miniature baby corn, mild cherry peppers, olives) is yours to nibble on while you study the wine list (the house has an excellent cellar) and the menu. You could start your meal with hot appetizers (like the Thai-style sautéed tiger prawns) or cold ones (like the seafood medley served with linguini and a basil vinaigrette); then go on to such main courses as the fresh island fish, abalone steak sautéed with lemon and capers, free-range chicken, or fresh Maine lobster. Main course salads make for a satisfying light meal. For a nice island touch, the rack of lamb is served with an ohelo berry sauce, roast duckling with guava sauce nestled on fried wonton skins. For dessert, it's hard to resist the hot Grand Marnier—or chocolate, lemon, or macadamia—soufflés. But do save room for the surprise of the evening, as your server presents you with a frosted dish of chocolate-covered ice-cream bonbons, courtesy of the house. There's piano music to dine by, too, by one of Honolulu's best, Paul Conrad.

MODERATE

✪ Ciao Mein

In the Hyatt Regency Waikiki Hotel, 2424 Kalakaua Ave. ☎ **808/923-CIAO** or 808/ 923-2426. Reservations recommended. Main courses $10.25–$19.75. Sunday brunch $22.95 adults, $8.95 children 6–12, under 6 free. AE, CB, DC, DISC, JCB, MC, V. Daily 6–10pm, Sun brunch 10am–2pm. CHINESE/ITALIAN.

Can't decide whether you want to eat Italian or Chinese? Don't! Enjoy the best of both worlds at Ciao Mein, where gourmet Chinese and Italian delicacies are superbly prepared, presented with élan, and served in a casually elegant, bistro-style, indoor-outdoor setting. No wonder this has quickly become one of Honolulu's most popular restaurants and continues to garner award after award. At a recent "Taste of Honolulu" competition, Ciao Mein was voted tops in five categories, including "Best of Show." Everything is served family style, so come with friends and enjoy.

Sit down, nibble on the basil or sun-dried tomato rolls and garlic Romano cheese breadsticks, have a drink, order a wine, and peruse the menu. Both Ciao Mein's Chinese chef and its Italian chef keep today's health-conscious lifestyles very much in mind by eliminating fats, heavy cream, rich sauces, and cholesteral-laden foods whenever possible. The results are simply delicious: the Szechuan eggplant, the chicken broth with lobster wontons, and the classic Caesar salad with giant garlic croutons all offer great ways to start a meal on the mix-and-match menu. Then continue on: I'm always hard put to choose between the risotto and the outstanding cake noodle with chicken, lobster, and vegetables. Roast duck served on daikon, carrots, and cucumbers, gamberoni (broiled prawns with a tomato-butter sauce), and beef sirloin presented on a sizzling platter with mushroom sauce are all worthy main courses.

Desserts are extravagant treats: The house's tiramisù has won an award as the best in town, but there's also a cappuccino crème brûlée to consider, and more. Sunday brunch is another knockout, featuring both Chinese and Italian stations, omelets cooked to order, and a floating dessert station.

✪ Hau Tree Lanai

In the New Otani Kaimana Beach Hotel, 2863 Kalakaua Ave. ☎ **808/923-1555.** Reservations recommended. Main courses $18.50–$22.50. Complete meals $29.50–$32.50. AE, CB, DC, JCB, MC, V. Daily 6:30–11am, 11:30am–1pm, 5–9pm. NOUVELLE CONTINENTAL.

Hau Tree Lanai has long enjoyed one of the best locations in Waikiki—right on the Sans Souci Beach at Diamond Head. And the menu is a match for the alfresco setting. Seated under the same hau tree where Robert Louis Stevenson once whiled away the hours, diners can enjoy sunny breakfasts and lunches and watch spectacular sunsets at dinner time. Having breakfast here has long been one of our favorite things to do in Honolulu; they prepare excellent eggs Benedict, Belgian waffles, and French toast with fresh fruit. The Aloha Friday lunch, with music by Arthur Lyman, is a special treat: There's a Hawaiian platter for $12.50, as well as a shrimp curry and a smoked fish salad at the same price. The dinner menu is even more extensive. Complete dinners, which include soup or salad, sautéed fresh vegetables, a selection from the dessert tray, and beverage, are good buys.

Oceanarium Restaurant

In the Pacific Beach Hotel, 2490 Kalakaua Ave., corner of Liliukalani Ave. ☎ **808/922-1233.** Reservations recommended. Complete dinners $14.95–$25.95; Sunday brunch $19.95 adults, $9.95 children 5–10. AE, CB, DISC, JCB, MC, V. Daily 6:30am–10pm. Sun brunch 10am–2:30pm. AMERICAN.

I'd call the food here pretty good American family fare, but the real attraction is something else: a 280,000 gallon, three-story glass aquarium brimming with tropical fish. If you have kids with you, bring them at fish-feeding times; they'll love the show. From Monday to Saturday, there are dives at 6, 7, and 8:30pm; on Sundays, it's 10:45am and 12:30 and 1:45pm.

Dinner here is an especially good bargain, since main courses such as New York steak, island bouillabaisse, stuffed jumbo prawns, and live Maine lobster are accompanied by New England clam chowder or Caesar salad; roasted potatoes or white rice; vegetables; and Hawaiian sweet rolls. Lunch features burgers and sandwiches on the order of mahimahi, grilled ahi or Pacific crab, salads like Thai chicken, and lunch courses such as mahimahi. There's a plentiful breakfast buffet at $11.95 for adults, $5.95 for children. Local specialties are featured at Sunday brunch.

Tripton's American Cafe

449 Kapahulu Ave. ☎ **808/737-3819.** Reservations recommended. Main courses $14.75–$22. AE, DC, MC, V. Daily 5:30–10pm, cocktails from 4pm. AMERICAN.

Tripton's just keeps getting better year after year. Readers of *Honolulu* magazine have chosen it as "Best Value Restaurant" and as one of their 20 favorite restaurants for the past two years. It's a cool, attractive place with uncluttered, modern decor. The menu here does not go on for pages, but what Tripton's does, it does expertly. Appetizers include a marvelous Cajun shrimp cocktail, salmon mousse, sashimi, a beautiful cheese platter garnished with fresh fruits, and our favorite—caviar pie. Main courses include steaks, roast prime rib, homemade pasta, and seafood, all prepared superbly. There are several keiki dinners as well, from $6.95 to $12.75. And don't forget to consult Susie's Dessert Board for daily selections of homemade pies, mousses, and crisps.

BUDGET

Trellisses

In the Outrigger Prince Kuhio Hotel, 2500 Kuhio Ave. ☎ **808/922-0811,** ext. 5151. Reservations recommended. Breakfast buffet $8.95; buffet dinner $14.95, $17.95 and $18.95; main courses $10.95–$21.95; Sun brunch $17.95 adults, half-price ages 3–10. AE, DISC, JCB, MC, V. Daily 6am–9pm; buffet until 10am Mon–Sat, until 9:30am Sun; Sun brunch 10:30am–2:30pm. AMERICAN.

One of the prettiest budget restaurants in town is in the beautiful Outrigger Prince Kuhio Hotel. Artfully decorated and overlooking a waterfall and gardens, Trellisses serves all three meals plus a bevy of evening buffets: It's Southern style on Monday, Italian on Tuesday, an international mix on Wednesday, Asian on Thursday, seafood on Friday, and family style (prime rib, turkey, fish) on Sunday. If you're eating lightly, soup, salad, and dessert bar is just $11.95, and soup and salad bar only $8.95. The Sunday champagne brunch is fun, and there's a daily breakfast buffet. On the regular menu, Trellisses offers a plentiful array of salads, sandwiches, burgers, and American and island standbys.

2 Central Waikiki

MODERATE

Buzz's Steak 'n Lobster House

In the Reef Lanais Hotel, 225 Saratoga Rd. ☎ **808/923-6762.** Reservations not accepted. Main courses $7.95–$38.95. AE, DC, MC, V. Daily noon–4pm and 5–11pm. STEAK/ SEAFOOD.

Can't choose between steak and lobster? You don't have to. Buzz's makes a specialty of both, and does a terrific job. Enjoy your candlelit dinner surrounded by antiques, Polynesian artifacts, and South Pacific artwork. Buzz's prices are more than reasonable. Come between 5 and 6:30pm for the Early Bird Special, and you can have unlimited salad bar, plus fish and fries for just $7.95. After that time, prices are still $7.95 for the fish and fries or the ground beefsteak, but they go up for the likes of prime rib, New York–cut steak, Alaskan king crab, sautéed shrimp, and many other varieties of fresh fish and seafood. The bar opens at noon, so you can relax on your way back from the beach or shopping with specially priced happy hour drinks until 5pm. A limited luncheon menu includes soups and sandwiches. Free parking is available beneath the restaurant.

Matteo's

In the Marine Surf Hotel, 364 Seaside Ave., at Kuhio Avenue. ☎ **808/922-5551.** Reservations recommended. Main courses $14.95–$29.95; complete dinners $24.95–$33.45. AE, CB, DC, DISC, JCB, MC, V. Daily 6–11pm. ITALIAN.

Matteo's is a longtime Italian favorite that just keeps winning kudos year after year; it's always among the "Top 20" favorite restaurants chosen by readers of *Honolulu* magazine. It's romantic and luxurious, done in lush earth tones, with deep booths and soft lighting. The dining room is artfully divided to give the feeling of intimacy and privacy. Service is gracious, and the wine list is extensive. The food is excellent and need not be expensive: The complete dinners are served with a fresh green salad or soup, pasta, vegetable, and coffee or tea—and the price includes such main courses as the classic sal timbocca or osso buco, filet mignon, and fresh fish of the day prepared with a Mediterranean-style crust with olives and capers. From the à la carte menu, you can start with a traditional antipasto platter for two, proceed to such main courses as chicken breast with eggplant parmigiana, scampi, Maine lobster, and Molokai rack of lamb. Whatever you choose, save some room for dessert: The award-winning pastry chef turns out marvels each night—perhaps a chocolate marble cheesecake topped with a raspberry sauce or chilled zabaglione. Finish your meal with dark espresso or the special house cappuccino.

Ocean Terrace

In the Sheraton Waikiki Hotel, 2255 Kalakaua Ave. ☎ **808/922-4422.** Reservations recommended. Breakfast buffet $16.95; lunch buffet $17.25; dinner buffet $25.95. AE, DC, JCB, MC, V. Daily 6am–3pm and 5:30–9:30pm. INTERNATIONAL.

If you love having a view of the ocean—and if you love buffet dining too—make a note of this poolside terrace at the Sheraton Waikiki Hotel. Prices are on the high side, but the value is excellent. The buffet table really shines at night: juicy prime ribs, mahimahi, fried chicken, plus a hot surprise or two. And there are always plenty of salads, vegetables, desserts, and beverages. There's a buffet lunch too— roast beef, stews, chop suey, cold cuts, salads, desserts (we counted some 20 choices recently). The breakfast buffet is recommended for the big morning eaters; all you

---

Great Places to Start Your Day:
Honolulu's Best Breakfast & Brunch Spots

Honolulu boasts some marvelous breakfast and brunch places. You'll think you're sipping your morning coffee on the Riviera from the seaside tables at **Michel's** *(p. 124)* at the Colony Surf and the **Hau Tree Lanai** *(p. 125)* at the New Otani Kaimana Beach Hotel. Both Italian and Chinese delicacies are featured at Sunday brunch at **Ciao Mein** *(p. 125)* at the Hyatt Regency Waikiki. Another glory of Honolulu is the Sunday brunch at **Orchids** *(p. 133)*, in the Halekulani Hotel, also oceanside. **Crêpe Fever** *(p. 141)* at Ward Centre is more down-to-earth, with great breakfast choices of crêpes, stuffed croissants, omelets, and waffles. And you'll get the chance to sample sushi, sashimi, breakfast dishes, and many of the other culinary sensations at the Sunday brunch at **Hanatei Bistro** *(p. 152)*, in Hawaii Kai.

---

want of fruits, cereals, eggs, breakfast meats, pastry, and pancakes. Like all of the Sheraton Waikiki, this is a strikingly vibrant spot.

Sergio's

In the Ilima Hotel, 445 Nohonani St. ☎ **808/926-3388.** Reservations recommended. Main courses $11.50–$27. AE, CB, DC, DISC, JCB, MC, V. Daily 5:30–10:30pm. ITALIAN.

Sergio's was the first fine-dining Italian restaurant to open in Honolulu, some 21 years ago, and it just keeps improving with age. And it's also one of the most romantic restaurants in town, with lilting background music serenading the diners. The room is lovely, with low lights, paneled walls, candles, and semiprivate booths. Wine bottles, casks, and foliage create a warm atmosphere. The favorites are such house specialties as the superb osso buco Milanese, chicken piccata, and the zesty cioppino Livornese (a kind of Italian bouillabaisse). In keeping with the new culinary spirit of the times, some of the heavier dishes have been removed from the menu, and some lighter ones added: There are now something like 18 pasta and vegetarian dishes—the bigolli alla puttanesca is a favorite. Dessert is a special treat, especially the *Biancaneve e i sette nani* (literal translation: "Snow White and the Seven Dwarfs")—seven fresh strawberries on a bed of lemon sherbet, topped with a shot of Stolichnaya vodka—it is well worth the effort. The dress code is "dressy casual"—no shorts, slippers, T-shirts, or tank tops.

Tanaka of Tokyo

In the Waikiki Shopping Plaza, at the corner of Seaside and Kalakaua avenues. ☎ **808/922-4702.** Reservations recommended. Main courses $13.50–$39.50. AE, DC, JCB, MC, V. Mon–Fri 11:30am–2pm; Mon–Sat 5:30–10:30pm; Sun 5:30–10pm JAPANESE.

So popular has this restaurant become that there are now three Tanaka of Tokyos in Waikiki: The original is on the fourth floor of the Waikiki Shopping Plaza, and the others are Tanaka of Tokyo East at King's Village, 131 Kaiulani Ave. (☎ 808/922-4233) and Tanaka of Tokyo West at the Ilikai Hotel Nikko Waikiki (☎ 808/945-3443). All are much the same except that Tanaka West serves a traditional Japanese breakfast daily from 5:30 to 10:30am and is open for lunch seven days a week. All have charming traditional settings and an excellent steak and seafood menu with portions big enough for hearty appetites. You'll be seated at a table for eight, centered around a table-range.

BUDGET

✪ Duke's Canoe Club

At the Outrigger Waikiki Hotel, 2335 Kalakaua Ave. ☎ **808/922-2268.** Reservations recommended. Main courses $7.95–$19.95. Breakfast daily 7–10:30am; Barefoot Bar Menu daily 11am–midnight; dinner daily 5–10pm; cocktails daily 11:30–1am. AMERICAN.

Duke's is exactly the kind of restaurant you hoped you would find in Hawaii. It's right out there on the beach, romantic in the old Hawaiian style, with thatched umbrellas, teak chairs, and photographs and other memorabilia recalling the legend of Duke Kahanamoku, the great surfer and Olympic swimming champion, long known as Hawaii's "Ambassador of Aloha," to whom the restaurant is dedicated. Duke would have loved it; so do we.

If you're watching your budget or just want a light meal, order from the Barefoot Bar Menu, which is served from 11am to midnight. Hawaiian local plates—stir-fry chicken cashew, fresh fish and the like—go from $8.95 to $9.95. Sandwiches like roast beef and Cheddar or teriyaki chicken breast, burgers, pizza, and pasta, range from $6.45 to $6.95. Ordering from the regular menu is still reasonable: fresh fish of the day, Pacific seafood fettuccine, Koloa pork ribs, and Polynesian chicken are all well priced, and all include a trip to the fabulous salad bar, which includes fresh papayas and pineapple, handmade Caesar salad, freshly baked muffins, sourdough rolls, and steamed rice. Keiki dinners are priced from $4.50 to $5.95, so bring the whole family. Now for desserts: Of course you'll have to have Kimo's original hula pie ("this is what the sailors swam to shore for"), and some fabulous tropical drinks from the bar. And if you hang around for the local Hawaiian entertainment, which takes place from 4 to 6pm and again from 10pm to midnight, you could easily while away the better part of your vacation here.

The Jolly Roger

150 Kaiulani Ave. ☎ **808/923-2172.** Reservations not accepted. Main courses $8.25–$14.45. AE, DC, JCB, MC, V. Daily 7am–midnight. AMERICAN.

While the venerable Jolly Roger on Kalakaua Avenue recently shut its doors, its newer sister restaurant, at the corner of Kuhio and Kalakaua, is still going strong. It's a big, bright space with its own cocktail lounge, Blue Kangaroo, entertainment Tuesday through Saturday night, and a popular happy hour from 4 to 8pm. As for the food, it's American coffeehouse style, quite tasty, and at good prices. Breakfast has always been my favorite meal at Jolly Roger; that's when you can get the MacWaple, a waffle covered in sliced, spiced hot apples topped with macadamia nuts. The cocktail lounge is open until 2am.

Waikiki Broiler

200 Lewers St. ☎ **808/923-8836.** Reservations not accepted. Main courses $9.75–$19.50. AE, DC, JCB, MC, V. Daily 6am–2am. AMERICAN.

Waikiki Broiler provides both indoor and outdoor tables for those who don't want to lose one moment of sunshine. Start soaking it up at breakfast with a $2.49 special of pancakes, bacon, and egg (breakfast is served until 2pm). Lunch consists of salads, burgers, sandwiches, and such specialties as mahimahi, teriyaki steak, and chicken piccata. Dinner offers good value, since the price of the main course includes steamed vegetables, San Francisco–style sourdough bread, and a choice of fries, pasta, or rice; for an additional $1.25 you can have salad or soup. Good choices include the teriyaki chicken breast, the shrimp dinner, and the smothered chicken. And there's always a "two for $15.95" dinner special—two complete teriyaki steak dinners. There's a really long happy hour from 6am to 9pm, when

Mai Tais go for just $1.75. There are also nightly lounge specials and entertainment every night, with karaoke on Sunday and Monday and Billy Chapman and the Edge Tuesday through Sunday. Children have their own menu ($2.75–$4.25).

3 Ewa Waikiki

EXPENSIVE

✪ Bali-by-the-Sea

In the Hilton Hawaiian Village, 2005 Kalia Rd. ☎ **808/949-4321.** Reservations required. Main courses $24.75–$28; Chef's menu $39.50. AE, CB, DC, DISC, JCB, MC, V. Mon–Fri 7–10am, 11am–2pm, and 6–10pm; Sat 6–10pm. CONTINENTAL.

This restaurant, overlooking the ocean, could be in the Mediterranean; it's done in whites, pinks, and greens, with beautiful watercolors gracing the white walls, handsome Chinese porcelain on display, bleached-wood furniture, and orchids abounding. Everything about this place—from the complimentary valet parking to the excellent wine list to the deft service—suggests an experience of gracious, exemplary dining, and that's just what you'll get here. Sit down, study the menu, and if you want an incredible soufflé for dessert—chocolate, vanilla, or Grand Marnier—place your order now. For an appetizer, it's hard to choose among the coquille of shrimp and scallops, the blackened ahi sashimi, or the strudel of escargots. The shrimp bisque is outstanding, as is the Manoa lettuce salad with avocado, papaya, and shrimp in a champagne dressing. Your main course choice is difficult, too: local friends advise that the Kaiwi Channel opakapaka with fresh basil sauce is the best in Hawaii.

Also superb are the filet of Pacific Northwest salmon baked in rice paper, the Dover sole, the Bali pepper steak, and the breast of duck with black currants and oranges. At lunch, the macadamia-nut-crusted lamb with mint mustard sauce is outstanding. If you like game, then you'll love the médaillons of venison, with pear, cranberry, and poivrade sauce. For dessert the pastry chef creates new marvels each day, but we'll vote for the house's signature dessert, the Bali Hai—three different local fruit sorbets served on a thin bed of fresh raspberry purée with a sprig of mint. Perfection!

✪ Cascada

In the Royal Garden Hotel, 444 Olohana St. ☎ **808/943-0202.** Reservations recommended. Main courses $14.50–$26. AE, CB, DC, JCB. Daily 11am–2pm and 6–10pm. EURO-ASIAN.

A cascading waterfall is visible through the wall of windows at this wonderfully romantic, enchanting restaurant. Along with a hand-painted trompe-l'oeil ceiling and French-country ceramic wall panels, it makes a striking background for the extraordinary cooking of Chef Nick Sayada, one of the most highly acclaimed of Hawaii's culinary gurus. If you prefer dining alfresco, savor Chef Nick's creations out on the marble terrace, covered by its peach-and-white-striped awning, the scene recalling the dining terraces found in villas in the south of France.

Chef Nick's dedication to the finest and freshest of ingredients, to light and healthful cooking in which the natural flavors are allowed to speak for themselves, is evident in his imaginative dishes, which combine the best of traditional classical cuisine (there are even some touches of his Russian-Asyrian heritage) with the fresh flavors, spices, and bounty of lighter California and Pacific Rim cooking. We like to come here with a small group so we can sample. Black and blue ahi, with sweet soy and hot mustard sauce, is Sayada's signature starter; equally good are the eggplant and zucchini soufflé on a bed of fresh tomato sauce, the chicken and sun-dried tomato spring rolls with spicy peanut sauce, and the crabcakes with panache of pepper, drizzled with aioli and rouille. The main courses are special, too: Sea scallops, our favorite, are lightly grilled, then topped with an orange and pomegranate butter sauce; Mongolian lamb chops are grilled and served with a red wine sauce that's drizzled with pomegranate oil and served with ratatouille; roasted duck breast comes with a sweet-and-sour cherry sauce.

Dinner at Cascada can be a bit pricey; if you're watching your budget, you might want consider lunch, when main courses go from $8.25 for a Royal Burger to a ceviche of salmon and scallops for $11 and main course salads—a personal favorite—such as the excellent salad niçoise with pan-seared ahi for $13.95. But no matter when you come, save room for dessert: Chef Nick's version of the classical peach melba or his tiramisu with vanilla and coffee creme anglàise are worth every last calorie.

✪ Golden Dragon

In the Hilton Hawaiian Village, 2005 Kalia Rd. ☎ **808/949-4321,** ext. 42. Reservations recommended. Main courses $10.95–$27.75; six-course Dragon Dinner $56 for two. AE, DC, DISC, JCB, MC, V. Tues–Sun 6–9:30pm. CHINESE.

For Chinese dining in the Imperial style, there's no grander place in Honolulu than the Golden Dragon. The setting is pure Asian drama, the vast room decorated with Chinese screens and sculptures, paintings and vases; black lacquer chairs surround white linen-clothed tables topped with red-and-gold china; and the room fronts the beach and lagoon, with three gazebos for indoor/outdoor seating. Wherever you sit, you're sure to enjoy the cuisine—and if you've been clever enough to phone 24 hours in advance, you may savor the Imperial Beggar's Chicken, wrapped in lotus leaves, encased in clay, and baked, or the Imperial Peking Duck, with plum sauce and mandarin pancakes. Ready without advance notice are tasty dishes such as crisp lemon chicken, superb braised lobster tail with black-bean sauce, and stir-fried baby eggplant. From the smoke oven (you can watch the chefs at work in the Exhibition Smoke Pavilion), you can have baby pork ribs, smoked tender duck, or smoked boneless chicken. Desserts here put those in other Chinese restaurants to shame: Consider the chocolate ginger mousse cake with swirls of chocolate shavings on the top, or the unforgettable Chinaman's Hat—that's chocolate sponge cake topped with thick layers of raspberry purée and chestnut mousse and chocolate icing. At the end of your meal, a "tea lady" visits your table to serve exotic Chinese teas and to tell fortunes. Jazz is offered nightly in the adjoining Paradise Lounge.

✪ La Mer

In the Halekulani hotel, 2199 Kalia Rd. ☎ **808/923-2311.** Reservations required. Main courses $29–$47; table d'hôte $67, $68, and $98. AE, CB, DC, JCB, MC, V. Daily 6–10pm. FRENCH.

Gone are the days when one had to travel all the way to France to experience the finest in French cooking. Now one need travel only to—Hawaii. La Mer would surely deserve a couple of Michelin stars if it were in France instead of Honolulu. Indeed, its extraordinary chef, George Mavrothalassitis, is doing something quite wonderful, creating a unique French cuisine with an island flair. He prefers to let the flavors of juices and herbs highlight the natural flavor of the ingredients—fish from local waters, vegetables and fruits grown on local farms, and imported products from Europe and the mainland. He is a stickler for detail; when fish is smoked, for example, it is smoked for that day only. His desserts are unforgettable. Combine this with a setting of subdued elegance—plush carpeting, rich Asian-inspired murals, tables set far apart and looking out over the moonlight on the ocean—and a meal at award-winning La Mer becomes a feast for the palate and senses, certainly one of the great dining experiences of Honolulu.

Although there is an à la carte menu, the best plan is to opt for one of the three different five-course, fixed-price menus, which change three times a year. As soon as you sit down, you're offered a complimentary glass of French champagne and an appetizer. You can order from a distinguished wine list. A typical $98 meal might begin with an appetizer salad of lobster followed by roasted squab on canabe. Then on to a fish course, such as charbroiled opakapaka with ginger, followed by a veal roast crusted with paprika. A magnificent assortment of French cheeses—at least 15 of them the last time we were there—follows, accompanied by tasty walnut bread. And then, the pièce de résistance—the dessert cart; you're welcome to two or three. Dessert may be the warm pineapple tart or the tatin tart with mango, both served with licorice ice cream; or Hawaiian Vintage Chocolate Suprise—chocolate crust filled with warm chocolate sauce. Just when you're convinced you couldn't touch another thing, along comes a tray of friandises (tiny cookies and pastries) along with homemade chocolate truffles. Magnifique! Jackets are required for gentlemen; ties are optional.

Nick's Fishmarket

In the Waikiki Gateway Hotel, 2070 Kalakaua Ave. ☎ **808/955-6333.** Reservations required. Main courses $18.99–$54.99; complete dinners $28.99. AE, DC, DISC, MC, V. Sun–Thurs 5:30–10pm, Fri–Sat 5:30pm–midnight; café lounge 5:30pm–1am. SEAFOOD.

For more than 23 years, Nick's Fishmarket, tucked away in the Waikiki Gateway Hotel, has been one of Honolulu's premier restaurants and the winner of numerous awards. Co-owners Randy Shock and Patrick Bowlen attract a fashionable celebrity and sports crowd who clamor for reservations when they're in town. And no wonder. Everyone appreciates the super service and the cheerful red-carpet and dark-leather ambience. The executive chef Mariano Lalica is acclaimed for his creative presentations of scrupulously fresh and delicious fish from Hawaiian waters, purchased each morning at the Honolulu Auction Block, as well as mainland catches; Maine lobster, flown in fresh every day, is a specialty. Any fish can be teamed with one of the special sauces—roasted garlic and sun-dried tomato balsamic vinaigrette, rock shrimp and stone-ground mustard sauce, cilantro–macadamia nut pesto, Thai peanut sauce, wasabe scallion sauce, or Chinese black bean sauce. It's hard to choose—they're all delicious.

It's fun to begin with a few drinks at the animated bar and then move on to a table for the main event. Fixed-price dinners include Fishmarket chowder, soup du jour, or Nick's special salad with its creamy spinach dressing; vegetable; beverage; and main courses such as fresh island ono, tiger prawns, Pacific sea scallops, or top sirloin. Or go à la carte with great "first plates" such as mozzarella marinara, blackened sashimi, oysters Rockefeller, calamari fritto, and more. Main-course specialties include roasted chicken, filet mignon with sauce béarnaise, and seafood linguine. Nick's also offers some wonderful desserts; favorites include a chocolate mousse cake, mocha-marbled cheesecake, and the house dessert, Vanbana's Pie—ice cream, bananas, and hot caramel sauce; by no means should you miss this! There's live entertainment in the lounge from 9:30pm, perfect for after-dinner dancing. If you're lucky, you may catch some vacationing performers who just might get up and do a turn or two. Stevie Wonder, Dolly Parton, Dionne Warwick, and the Beach Boys have all been known to do so.

Orchids

In the Halekulani hotel, 2199 Kalia Rd. ☎ **808/923-2311.** Reservations required. Main courses $18–$38; Pacific Edge $45; table d'hote grill and rotisserie $47; Sun brunch $28.50. AE, CB, DC, JCB, MC, V. Daily 7–11am and 11:30am–2pm; Mon–Sat 6–10pm; Sun brunch 9:30am–2:30pm. PACIFIC RIM (HAWAIIAN REGIONAL) ROTISSERIE.

Just as La Mer at the Halekulani raises French dining to an art form, Orchids does the same for Pacific Edge cuisine with its exciting new menu. In a beautiful, open-air, oceanside setting with a glorious view of Diamond Head, one can feast on Executive Chef George Mavrothalassitis' delightful innovations, combining the best local produce with culinary techniques of the East and West. Start your meal with such tantalizing appetizers as the seared ahi with a mustard shoyu sauce or charbroiled marinated shrimp and watercress with a Siam peanut sauce. Then on to such seafood choices as steamed onaga, Oriental style, or roasted duckling with a mango-and-lime glaze. Desserts are other-worldly: Coconut cake with raspberry coulis is the house signature dessert, but equally irresistible is the warm apple tart with vanilla ice cream, not to mention the tropical fruit poached in an almond-and-mint syrup with lychee sorbet. There's a similar menu, offered at lower prices, at lunch. Many people believe that Orchids has the finest Sunday brunch in Honolulu. There's sushi, sashimi, and dim sum aplenty; offerings from pasta and carving stations; and an incredible array of desserts from the hotel's own pastry kitchen. A harpist and flautist accompany the feast. It's a treat not to be missed. Dress code: evening resort attire (no shorts or T-shirts at dinner).

MODERATE

Chez Michel

444 Hobron Lane. ☎ **808/955-7866.** Reservations recommended. Main courses $18–$35. AE, CB, DC, DISC, JCB, MC, V. Daily 5:30–10pm. FRENCH.

Here's a bit of the Riviera in Waikiki. Chez Michel, in a gardenlike setting on Eaton Square, has long been one of Waikiki's best French restaurants. The restaurant is roofed and walled in by lattices hung with tropical plants, furnished with highbacked and comfortably cushioned wicker chairs, and graced with splashing fountains that create a cool, romantic atmosphere. Michel himself may greet you, if he's not on his annual wine-buying trip to Paris.

At dinner, the French onion soup is a must. Michel's sauces and gravies are exquisite, so that even chicken livers are transformed into a dining experience. Desserts are quite special: You can choose from chilled cherries jubilee or orange Grand Marnier soufflé. (Remember to order your soufflé when ordering dinner.)

Harlequin

In the Alana Waikiki Hotel, 1956 Ala Moana Blvd. ☎ **808/941-7275.** Reservations recommended. Main courses $21–$29. AE, CB, DC, DISC, JCB, MC, V. Daily 6:30am–noon and 6–9:30pm. PACIFIC RIM.

Chef Susan Richmond is one of the small band of women chefs in Honolulu, and her new menu at Harlequin proves she knows her way around the kitchen. The dining room is charming, an elegantly casual room filled with flowers and attractive artwork. Susan's talents start showing up right at breakfast; her eggs Benedict Hawaiiana is a new variation on an old theme—poached eggs atop Dungeness crabcakes and grilled herb sourdough bread, with a dill Hollandaise sauce. Her signature dinner starters include duck potstickers and spicy fried oysters remoulade, with a marinated Maui onion salad. Among the favorite main courses are pan-seared, scallion-studded ahi with a warm spicy jicama salad; roasted breast of duck with sautéed leeks and a sun-dried berry demi glace; and a roasted rack of lamb with Madras curry sauce. Desserts change nightly.

If you don't get to Harlequin for dinner, then be sure to sample Chef Richmond's works at the hotel's Cafe Picasso (yes, those ceramics you see everywhere are real Picassos) where a moderately priced ($7.50 to $10.50) all-day menu is served from 10:30am to 10pm, including appetizers like chicken satay with a fried tofu and cucumber-onion salad, sandwiches and burgers, pastas and ramen, and an Oriental chicken salad and Japanese-style beef curry. Picasso's dinner menu includes dishes like potato-crusted salmon with shiitake mushrooms, seafood risotto, and filet of beef tenderloin with a wild mushroom sauce.

BUDGET

○ California Pizza Kitchen

1910 Ala Moana Blvd., at Ena Rd., across from the Hilton Hawaiian Village. ☎ **808/ 955-5161.** Reservations not necessary. Pizzas and calzones $6.95–$9.95; pastas $7.95–$10.50. AE, CB, MC, V. Sun–Thurs 11am–10:30pm, Fri–Sat 11am–11pm. PIZZA.

Honolulu is known for a wide variety of international foods, but nowhere have we seen so many different cuisines represented under one roof as at California Pizza Kitchen, with two locations in town; the original is at Kahala Mall (☎ 808/ 737-9446). Don't let the "California" mislead you—we looked in vain for an avocado-and-alfalfa-sprouts pizza. However, we found the following: Peking-duck pizza (breast of duck, mushrooms, hoisin sauce), tostada pizza (with black bean, cheddar, and diced, grilled lime chicken), and teriyaki pizza (grilled chicken or shrimp marinated in orange teriyaki sauce). Other exotic pizza creations include Thai chicken (with spicy peanut-ginger sauce), goat cheese (with bacon, red onions, and fresh tomatoes), and shrimp pesto (with fresh tomatoes, Greek olives, and sun-dried tomatoes). All of the above are made with mozzarella, but there are also cheeseless pizzas, as well as calzones. A variety of pastas, freshly made on the premises are available as well. And not only are these pizzas and pastas unusual, but they are good! The California Pizza Kitchens are big, stylish places, done in black and white, with both counter and table service.

○ Mezzanine Restaurant

In the Waikiki Terrace Hotel, 2045 Kalakaua Ave. ☎ **808/955-6000.** Reservations recommended. Main courses $9.95–$21; breakfast buffet $9.25; dinner buffet $16.95. AE, CB, DC, DISC, JCB, MC, V. Daily 6:30–10:30am; Mon–Fri 11:30am–1:30pm; Mon–Sat 5:30–10pm, Sun 6–10pm. CONTEMPORARY AMERICAN.

Sophisticated contemporary American cuisine in a casually elegant indoor-outdoor setting—these are the ingredients that have made the Mezzanine a big hit since its opening a few years ago. The center of attention is the kiawe wood-burning oven and grill, which turns out fabulous breads and pizzas; every night the chef dreams up a new pie. Pasta platters are imaginative; salads are big enough to share; and North Shore prawns and roast chicken are succulent, done on the kiawe-wood broiler. Every night there's a big list of new and tantalizing specials, so you might want to eat here more than once during your stay. Desserts vary every day as well.

4 Ala Moana Area

WEST ALA MOANA
EXPENSIVE

Nicholas Nickolas The Restaurant
In the Ala Moana Hotel, 410 Atkinson Dr. ☎ **808/955-4466.** Reservations required. Main courses $20.95–$42.95. AE, CB, DC, JCB, MC, V. Daily 5:30–2 or 3am. AMERICAN.

Certainly one of Hawaii's most beautiful restaurants, Nicholas Nickolas occupies the top floor of the Ala Moana Hotel, the tallest building in the state of Hawaii. The view, as one can well imagine, is spectacular, as is the restaurant. The interior has been designed so that every table has a view of the city. There are booths so private that the occupants control their own lighting. Only dinner and late suppers are served here. The appetizers are special and include blackened sashimi. Complete dinners include a choice of Nick's classic salad or clam chowder, vegetable, starch, and beverage, plus main course such as ahi steak, fresh vegetable pasta, and filet mignon. On the à la carte menu, you could have salmon, scallops, veal piccata, lamb chops, or porterhouse steak; all steaks and fish are broiled over kiawe wood. Wonderful salads and the "famous" hash-brown potatoes, grilled and topped with sour cream, chives, and bacon bits, are good extras.

Dance music is provided by various entertainers, usually from 9:30pm until 2 or 3am. The late-night menu offers some of the dinner appetizers and side dishes.

MODERATE

✪ Alfred's
In Century Center, 1750 Kalakaua Ave., corner of Kapiolani Blvd. ☎ **808/955-5353.** Reservations recommended. Main courses $17–$28. CB, DC, MC, V. Tues–Fri 11am–2pm, Tues–Sat 6–10pm. CONTINENTAL.

The sophistication of a fine meal in a great European capital is what awaits you at Alfred's. The cozy, romantic restaurant is a celebration of the Swiss chef/proprietor Alfred Vollenweider, who serves his gourmet fare in a serene ambience. Today, after 15 years, Alfred's is one of Oahu's culinary landmarks, with a huge following among a knowledgeable local clientele.

With your dinner comes freshly prepared soup, a combination of salads—the last time we were there these included cucumbers in sour cream, shrimp-and-apple salad, marinated beets, and tomatoes with dill—and fresh vegetables. Fresh island fish is served every day and done remarkably well. Other good choices include veal médaillons with wild mushrooms, chateaubriand, and more continental favorites. Desserts are too good to miss, so ignore the calories and find some room for, the soufflé glacé Grand Marnier, strawberries Romanoff, or the Black Forest cake. Then again, there are tropical fruit sorbets and German cheesecake with pineapple to tempt you. To top off your meal, try a special coffee and one of seven different cordials from Alfred's well-stocked bar.

Weekday lunches offer good value. Salads, pastas, steak tartare, and fresh fish go from $9 to $15, and a daily lunch special for $10 to $15.50 includes soup or salad. Validated parking is available.

Byron II
At Ala Moana Shopping Center. ☎ **808/949-8655.** Reservations recommended. Main courses $15.45–$27.75; complete dinners $21.45–$33.75. Sun–Thurs 11am–10pm; Fri–Sat 11am–11pm. STEAKS/SEAFOOD.

Honolulu Area Dining

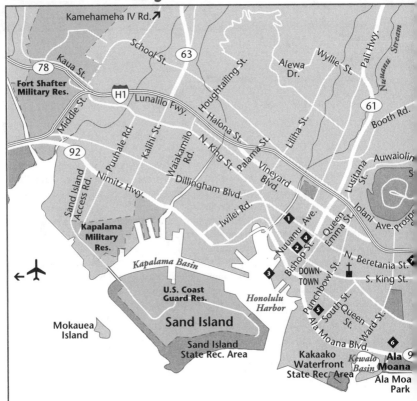

Kamehameha IV Rd.↗
School St.
63
Kaua St.
78
H1
Fort Shafter
Military Res.
Lunalilo Fwy.
Middle St.
92
Puuhale Rd.
Kalihi St.
Waiakamilo Rd.
Dillingham Blvd.
Houghtailing St.
Halona St.
N. King St.
Palama St.
Liliha St.
Vineyard Blvd.
Alewa Dr.
Wyllie St.
Pali Hwy.
Nuuanu Stream
Booth Rd.
61
Lusitana St.
Auwaiolin
Iolani Ave.
Prospe
Iwilei Rd.
Nuuanu Ave.
Queen Emma St.
N. Beretania St.
Sand Island Access Rd.
Nimitz Hwy.
Sand Island
Kapalama Military Res.
Kapalama Basin
U.S. Coast Guard Res.
Sand Island
Sand Island State Rec. Area
Mokauea Island
← ✈
Honolulu Harbor
DOWN-TOWN
Bishop St.
Punchbowl St.
South St.
Queen St.
Ward St.
S. King St.
Ala Moana Blvd.
Kakaako Waterfront State Rec. Area
Kewalo Basin
Ala Moana
Ala Moa Park
Mamala   Bay

① ④ ② ③ ⑤ ⑥ ⑨

OAHU

Honolulu ★

1334

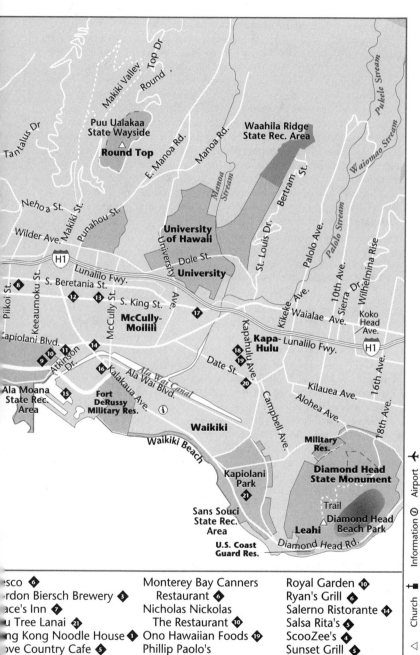

...esco 🕕
...rdon Biersch Brewery 🕄
...ace's Inn 🕖
...u Tree Lanai 🟤21
...ng Kong Noodle House 🕧1
...ove Country Cafe 🟤5
...igo 🕋2
...o's Thai Cuisine 🟤20

Monterey Bay Canners
  Restaurant 🕕6
Nicholas Nickolas
  The Restaurant 🟤10
Ono Hawaiian Foods 🟤19
Phillip Paolo's
  Seafood-Pasta House 🟤13
Rama Thai Restaurant 🟤18

Royal Garden 🟤10
Ryan's Grill 🕕6
Salerno Ristorante 🟤14
Salsa Rita's 🕔5
ScooZee's 🔷4
Sunset Grill 🕔5
Won Kee Sea Food 🔷1

Mountain △   Church ✚   Information ⓘ   Airport ✈

This is your old-fashioned steak house, with comfy booths, top quality food, solicitous service, and a cozy atmosphere that makes it the perfect place for a meal, or just a drink while shopping at Ala Moana Shopping Center. Celebrity guests are often spotted here. (It's located on the ground floor of the shopping center, Diamond Head end of Ala Moana, near Liberty House.) Chef James "Masa" Masuda's cooking continues to take local and national awards. You could start your meal here with something trendy, like black-and-blue ahi (the appetizer craze of the moment, and very good, too) or the baked brie with lingonberry sauce, or with something classic like nicely done oysters Rockefeller. Order à la carte or, for about $6 more, have a complete dinner, which includes salad or soup, dessert, and tea or coffee. Perfectly grilled steaks, like the top sirloin and steak teriyaki, or the double rib lamb chops and roast prime rib, are all fine choices; so, too, are the fresh fish and seafood dishes, the full-meal salads, a wide variety of pastas, and panini (Italian sandwiches). Byron II's signature dessert is grasshopper pie. There's a good wine list, with monthly selections.

✪ The Chart House Honolulu

In the Ilikai Marina, 1765 Ala Moana Blvd. ☎ **808/941-6669.** Reservations recommended. Main courses $14.95–$42.50. AE, DC, MC, V. Mon–Thurs 5:30–9:30pm; Fri–Sun 5:30–10pm; lounge Mon–Sat 4pm–2am, Sun 5pm–2am. STEAK/SEAFOOD.

The Chart House has everything a seafood house in Honolulu should have—a glamorous nautical setting overlooking the boats of the Ala Wai Yacht Harbor, a festive air, warm and friendly service, a menu that offers the freshest of fish and seafood—and all at prices that are refreshingly realistic. No wonder it's been popular for more than 20 years! Prepare yourself for a wonderful evening. Start with some drinks, select a wine, perhaps order one of the appetizers like oysters Rockefeller or Maryland soft-shell crabs. Your main course could be one of the several catches of the day; we recently sampled their opakapaka, flavorfully steamed Chinese style with cilantro and ginger. The house specialty is Hawaiian spiny and slipper lobster, so delicate they're kept swimming in the tank until you place your order. Shellfish specialties include an excellent bouillabaisse. And there's teriyaki chicken, prime rib, and filet mignon from the grill. All dinners are served with a tossed green salad or a cup of hearty chowder; new potatoes, pasta, or rice; squaw bread; and a vegetable, so there's really no need to order anything more. But you'll probably find the dessert tray hard to overlook, as we always do; chocolate macadamia-nut cream pie and Chart House mud pie (triple layers of chocolate, Kona coffee, and macadamia-nut ice cream with fudge and whipped cream on an Oreo cookie crust) are the main temptations.

Fishmonger's Wife

On the Mauka Walk at Ala Moana Shopping Center. ☎ **808/941-3377.** Reservations recommended. Main courses $9.95–$24.95. AE, DISC, MC, V. Sun–Thurs 10:30am–10pm, Fri–Sat 10:30am–11pm. AMERICAN.

This is a cozy place with big, comfy club chairs, soft lights, and lots of fish and lobster tanks. One could have a marvelous lunch or dinner here just grazing on the hot and cold appetizers, notably the sashimi, smoked salmon, cracked Dungeness crab, shrimp lumpia, or steamed clams. Then there's delicious Oriental duck salad, avocado stuffed with chicken, or jumbo shrimp Louis to tempt you, as well as wonderful chowders and gumbos. House specialties include wonderful crabcakes and a variety of stir-fried wok dishes, including scallops, prawns, shrimp, Dungeness crab, and lobster, prepared with your choice of black-bean or garlic sauce—we like them both! Desserts like strawberries with brown sugar and sour cream or saboyan are just heavenly.

The Royal Garden

In the Ala Moana Hotel, 410 Atkinson Drive. ☎ **808/942-7788.** Reservations recommended. Main courses $9.50–$29.95. AE, CB, DC, JCB, MC, V. Daily 11am–2pm and 5:30pm–2am. CHINESE.

This is surely one of the most beautiful restaurants in Honolulu—or anywhere. Its handsome restoration recently took overall honors at the 9th annual Building Industry Association of Hawaii Renaissance Competition, and rightly so. The oak wood walls, intricately carved chairs with green velvet cushions, exquisitely framed tile art on the walls, sparkling chandeliers accentuating gold columns, and dozens of potted orchids create an elegant yet inviting ambience. The clever use of mirrors, which reflect images of the chandeliers and the Chinese porcelains arranged on the display tables, make the place seem bigger than it is. What's more, there's an extensive menu. I recently dined here with a party of eight Chinese friends; our seven-course meal was served family style. We began with a mixed cold plate and a cold jellyfish platter, followed by a tantalizing crabmeat and diced melon soup. Next came fried scallops stuffed with minced shrimp, followed by stewed beef brisket, lettuce with oyster sauce, and baked crab with ginger and green onion (seasonally priced). Most of us chose almond float with fruit cocktail for dessert, but we were tempted by a combination of honeydew melon, tapioca, and coconut milk. There are also five complete dinners available, beginning at $21.50 per person. Service is deft and unobtrusive and the presentations are beautiful. A meal here is definitely memorable.

BUDGET

Eggs 'n Things

1911 B Kalakaua Ave. ☎ **808/949-0820.** Reservations not accepted. $4.25–$10. No credit cards. Daily 11pm–2pm. BREAKFAST.

If you love omelets, pancakes, waffles, crêpes—in other words, eggs 'n' things—then you're going to be thrilled to discover this neat and trim restaurant, which, since 1974, has been Honolulu's most unique breakfast shop. Unique not only in the quality of the food, but in the fact that it serves breakfast from 11pm on into the wee hours of the morning and up through 2pm. From the kitchen range come eggs any style, plus any side meats, from Vienna sausage at $6 to steak at $7.25, all accompanied by three of the lightest buttermilk pancakes we've tasted.

More than a dozen three-egg omelets are available, plus crêpes Suzettes with lemon, blueberry, strawberry, or fresh banana fillings; pancakes and waffles; and even fish of the day. There are Early Riser (5 to 9am) and Late Riser (1 to 2pm) specials, of three pancakes and two eggs, for just $2.75.

WARD CENTRE
MODERATE

✪ Fresco

At Ward Centre, 1200 Ala Moana Blvd. ☎ **808/591-8992.** Reservations recommended. Main courses $12.95–$17.95; light diner $7.95–$17.95. AE, DC, JCB, MC, V. Mon–Fri 11:30am–11pm, Sat 6–10pm, Sun 6–9pm. CONTEMPORARY ITALIAN.

One of the first places in Honolulu to serve contemporary Italian food, Fresco continues strong after 11 years. The restaurant features a kiawe grill and wood-burning red-brick oven totally visible to diners; it's fun, in fact, to sit at the bar and watch the food going into the oven. The decor is modern, almost minimalist, with nothing to detract from the splendor of the food. A long list of daily specials (a pizza dish, several pastas, several fish dishes, steak) complements the regular menu, but you can almost always count on such wonderful appetizers as shrimp summer rolls with a spicy peanut sauce, and grilled Japanese eggplant with an extraordinary chili goat cheese. Among main courses, the fresh clam pasta and Hawaiian wood-grilled fresh fish, with either a fresh salsa or black-bean sauce, is special. Everything is cooked to order and served precisely when ready. Enjoy a glass of wine while you're waiting; the large wine list includes many selections that go for close-to-retail prices. Desserts are fun, notably the chocolate decadence cake with fresh raspberry sauce, the hot fresh berry pie with whipped cream, and the best Irish creamy cheesecake in town. Weekdays there's a "Wiki Wiki Picnic Park Special" to go for just $4.95 (lunchtime only).

Monterey Bay Canners Restaurant

At Ward Centre, 1200 Ala Moana Blvd. ☎ **808/536-6197.** Reservations not required. Main courses $9.95–$26.95. AE, DC, DISC, JCB, MC, V. Mon–Thurs 11am–11pm, Fri 11am–midnight, Sat 4pm–midnight, Sun 4–11pm. SEAFOOD.

You'll feel as if you're back at the turn of the century, stepping into a Barbary Coast saloon when you enter Monterey Bay Canners. Ceiling fans, brass-ringed curtains, and hanging plants subdue the noise in this big, busy place, tremendously popular for fresh fish and seafood at refreshing prices. A large blackboard announces the fresh catch of the day, which is usually a tropical fish—ono, wahoo, mahimahi, and opakapaka. Your choice can be topped with either black-bean, creole-cream, lemon-garlic butter, ginger, or dill sauce. San Francisco–style sourdough bread, fresh steamed vegetables, and a choice of starch are included; add another $1.50 and you get chowder or salad as well. There are also steaks and pastas. The oyster bar features such delicacies as sashimi, mushrooms stuffed with crabmeat, steamed clams, and the like. And for dessert, try the frozen chocolate mousse (sinful), or the watermelon sherbet (safe). A similar lunch menu offers smaller portions at lower prices. There's live music and entertainment Tuesday through Saturday nights from 9pm to 1:30am.

Another Monterey Bay Canners is at the Outrigger Waikiki Hotel, 2335 Kalakaua Ave. (☎ 808/922-5761).

BUDGET

⑤ Compadres Mexican Bar and Grill

At Ward Centre, 1200 Ala Moana Blvd. ☎ **808/591-8307.** Reservations not required. Main courses $7.45–$16.95. AE, MC, V. Mon–Thurs 11am–11pm, Fri–Sat 11am–midnight, Sun 9am–10pm. MEXICAN.

The mood, the food, the drinks, the lights, and the festive feeling all add up to a resounding cheer for this restaurant. Prices are modest and the food is expertly prepared—so much so that readers of *Honolulu* magazine consistently name Compadres among Honolulu's "Top 20" restaurants year after year. Visiting celebrities can often be found enjoying the scene. Among the house specialties are classic arroz con pollo and chicken mole; avocado stuffed with crabmeat and topped with green chili and cheeses; huajolote, marinated and charbroiled turkey breast; a vegetarian Santa Fe tamale; and steak and chicken fajitas, served up with frijoles and salsa fresca. Delicioso! Nifty appetizers, good salads and sandwiches, oven-smoked baby back ribs and chicken, and a large selection of egg dishes and combination plates offer plentiful choices. The Quesadillas Internacionales menu offers such creative options as Baja, Thai, and Japanese quesadillas. There are many good possibilities for vegetarians. For dessert, try the Paradiso Tropic or the fresh fruit chimichanga. Of course, there are terrific margaritas, daiquiris, sangría by the glass and pitcher, Mexican and other imported beers, and other potions that mix well with these Tex-Mex treats.

☺ Crêpe Fever

At Ward Centre, 1200 Ala Moana Blvd. ☎ **808/521-9023.** Reservations not accepted. Main courses $4.25–$8.25. MC, V. Mon–Thurs 8am–10pm, Fri–Sat 8am–11pm, Sun 8am–4pm. VEGETARIAN/NATURAL.

Interested in natural, delicious, gourmet vegetarian food? This charming, open restaurant—so pretty with its inviting counter, oak tables on red tile floors, and a few tables in the garden outside—offers delicious food at very reasonable prices and caters to the health concious. Main course crêpes, served with brown rice and green salad, include Mexican chicken (it's not vegetarian only), ham melt, lemon spinach, and veggie burger; dessert crêpes are on the order of strawberries and cream or cheese-and-fruit blintzes. Stuffed croissants are good too, and so are the excellent breakfast specialties—omelets, crêpes, waffles, and French toast, served all day. There's a special vegetarian menu and daily specials in the evening.

Owner Sandee Norris runs a delightful espresso bar right next door called **Mocha Java,** which features a full bar menu and a full exotic coffee menu—which means you can finish, or start, your meal with a strawberry smoothie with rum, an espresso milk shake with brandy, Irish coffee, or a fabulous flambéed sundae. Mocha Java is open from 9am to 10pm Monday through Thursday, until 11pm Friday and Saturday, until 4pm Sunday. Phone number is **808/537-3611** for Mocha Java.

Ryan's Grill

At Ward Centre, 1200 Ala Moana Blvd. ☎ **808/523-9132.** Reservations recommended for dinner. Main courses $8.95–$17.95. AE, MC, V. Mon–Fri 11am–11pm. AMERICAN.

Ryan's is a standout among the many good restaurants at Ward Centre. Their draft beers are temperature-controlled, and their huge stock of liquors and liqueurs lines a whole wall behind the long bar from floor to ceiling. With that kind of look,

---

Dining with a View: Honolulu's Top Spots

Honolulu boasts a plethora of restaurants where the view's the thing. For beachfront views, you can't beat the **Hau Tree Lanai** at the New Otani Kaimana Beach Hotel *(p. 125)*. Elegant dining with an ocean view is yours in the Hilton Hawaiian Village at **Bali-by-the-Sea** *(p. 130)* and at the Halekulani Hotel at **La Mer** *(p. 131)* and **Orchids** *(p. 133)*. For a look at the Ala Wai Yacht Harbor and its boats bobbing at anchor, **The Chart House Honolulu** *(p. 138)* is wonderful. From your perch at any of the restaurants at Aloha Tower Marketplace you can check out all the busy goings-on of Honolulu Harbor. A giant three-story aquarium and its denizens greet the diner's eye at the **Oceanarium Restaurant** *(p. 126)*. Out in Kaneohe, in Windward Oahu, **Chart House** *(p. 158)* is located in one of the oldest and loveliest gardens on the island.

would you expect them to be concerned about heart-healthy dining and to offer a variety of low-saturated-fat and low-cholesterol preparations? It just proves that there's more here than meets the eye. Many different appetites can be satisfied, all in an attractive setting—wood and brass, high ceilings, slowly revolving fans, plants everywhere. Service is excellent; tell them you're in a hurry and they'll make sure you finish lunch in 40 minutes. Even the soups are special—fresh broccoli, borscht, Moroccan lentil, among others. Large main course salads are available at both lunch and dinner, as are sandwiches and burgers, along with meat, chicken, and fish broiled with kiawe-wood charcoal; fish fresh from Hawaiian waters; pasta made fresh daily; and nifty desserts. Go see for yourself.

◉ ScooZee's

At Ward Centre, 1200 Ala Moana Blvd. ☎ **808/597-1777.** Reservations taken only for 8 or more. Main courses $5.50–$10. AE, DC, DISC, MC, V. Mon–Thurs 11am–10pm, Fri–Sat 11am–11pm. ITALIAN.

If the prospect of great food served in generous portions, reasonable prices, and a fun and friendly atmosphere excites you make tracks to ScooZee's. "Pizza, Pasta and Pizzaz" is the house motto. Everything is made from scratch, and the presentation and style belie the tiny prices (nothing on the menu is over $10). Standouts on the menu include Italian pea soup with smoked ham and Italian sausage; grilled chicken Caesar salad; ahi with rigatoni; eggplant parmigiana, the mussels broiled in marsala wine and garlic. Watching the budget? For a mere $6.50, you can feast on a Peasant's Dinner: imported cheese, fresh fruit, Italian prosciutto, a chunk of fresh baked peasant bread, and a glass of Chianti. And desserts are the best: the "Tita I Miss Su" (an original rendition—and spelling—of tiramisù), the ricotta cheesecake, and the Grand Marnier chocolate fudge cake are too good to pass up. Ice-cream and liqueur smoothies, and a nice selection of beers and wines complement the meal. ScooZee's is an altogether pleasant place to be, whether seated indoors in the greenhouse-like dining room or outdoors on the umbrellaed lanai. Service is fast and friendly. As you travel around the island, you'll find branches of ScooZee's at Hawaii Kai in East Oahu and at Kapolei in West Oahu.

RESTAURANT ROW

At 500 Ala Moana Blvd., not far from downtown Honolulu, Restaurant Row is one of Honolulu's most happening dining scenes, with just about everything in the way of restaurants, from posh to budget. In addition to the places listed below, popular Restaurant Row establishments include **Ruth's Chris Steak House** (☎ 808/599-3860) for top-of-the-line beef (plan on spending $30 to $40 for a meal here); **C.J.'s Seafood Restaurant,** (☎ 808/526-0800) with wonderfully fresh fish and seafood, and main courses running from about $10.95 to $26.95. **Pizza Bob's** (☎ 808/532-4600) has super pies, plus generous salads and hot and cold sandwiches. **Trattoria Manzo** (☎ 808/522-1711) is a stylish Italian trattoria with pleasing prices: Pastas run $8.25 to $11.95, and most house specialties are under $10. And then, of course, there's **Studebaker's** (☎ 808/526-9888), a scene right out of the '50s, whose theme is "bop till you drop." The loud music, the neon, the wild-haired DJ, and the ebullient young staff who break out into song and dance every hour, make it easy to do so. From 4 to 8pm, an amazing free buffet, with several hot meals, salads, brown breads, and veggies with dip, is served along with your drinks. *Note:* No one under 21 is allowed in after 4pm.

MODERATE

✪ Sunset Grill

500 Ala Moana Blvd., in Restaurant Row. ☎ **808/521-4409.** Reservations recommended. Main courses $12.95–$23.95. AE, DC, MC, V. Mon–Thurs 11:30am–11pm, Fri–Sat 11am–midnight, Sun 10:30am–10pm; Sun brunch 10:30am–2pm. CONTEMPORARY AMERICAN.

Our favorite Restaurant Row dining place—indeed, one of our favorites in all of Honolulu—is this handsome 200-seat restaurant featuring grilled, rotisserie, wood-fire, and oven-roasted foods in a sophisticated indoor-outdoor setting. Blond woods, glass walls, and a large grill in the center of the restaurant set the mood for dining that's casual in style but elegant where it counts, in every detail of food preparation and service. Have a drink—they're known for terrific martinis—and doodle on the placemats (crayons are provided) while you're waiting for your meal; the best placemat art is displayed on the walls up front, along with autographs of famous visitors.

If you want a light meal, come for just a sandwich. Their grilled marinated chicken breast, with honey Dijon glaze, American cheddar, and grilled red peppers on a cracked whole-wheat roll, is a wonder at $9.95. Or graze on a few appetizers, like the oven-roasted garlic and herbed goat cheese or the Dungeness crabcakes with smoked papaya sauce and tamarind citrus vinaigrette. Make your main course the smoke-infused marinated salmon with shiitake mushroom salsa, or perhaps the fettucine with Florida rock shrimp; or choose one of the excellent rotisserie dishes, which comes with fresh vegetables. From the charcoal grill comes the nifty 10 oz. lean New York steak served with Tuscan mashed potatoes and grilled vine-ripened tomatoes. Desserts are always splendid here, especially the vanilla bean cheesecake with macadamia-nut crust and warm caramel sauce.

Sunset Grill is also a great spot for Sunday brunch; brunchgoers get complimentary copies of the major weekend papers. Remember it, too, on a Friday or Saturday night after the theater or a concert for a late-night bite or just dessert.

BUDGET

ⓢ Cafe Athena

One Waterfront Plaza, in Restaurant Row. ☎ **808/526-0071.** Reservations not required. Main courses $8.95–$11.55. AE, CB, DC, MC, V. Mon–Sat 11am–11pm, Sun 5–10pm. GREEK.

Authentic Mediterranean cuisine, low prices, and a cozy setting—just 10 tables with cane chairs, soft lighting, and a tidy bar in the corner—make this place a winner. Only one menu is served all day, and everything on it is delicious: All dishes and sauces are made from "mom's authentic recipes." We like to start with the tasty taramosalata among the appetizers, then move on to one of the platters served with Greek salad and either rice or pita bread: perhaps the lamb kebab, the delicately spiced and marinated chicken Athena, or beef-and-lamb gyros, right off the grill. Terrific sandwiches ($3.95 to $4.55) and salads ($4.50 to $5.85) are also good possibilities. Don't skip dessert—the Martinica, a blend of ice-cream cake and brandied rum chocolate, is nifty and just $2.95.

Chiu Chau Bistro

500 Ala Moana Blvd., in Restaurant Row. ☎ **808/524-8188.** Reservations not required. Main courses $5–$10. AE, DC, DISC, JCB. Daily 11am–2:30pm, Sun–Thurs 5:30–10:30pm, Fri–Sat 5:30pm–midnight. CHINESE SEAFOOD.

Besides being one of the most striking establishments in Restaurant Row, a study in red and black from the dramatic facade to the lacquer tables and red walls, Chiu Chau also offers some of the best values in the complex. The menu concentrates on seafood with a Chinese flair, and the most expensive item—the chef's special Fresh Maine lobster—is all of $10! Most of the other delicious seafood preparations—baked clams, steamed fresh oysters with spicy garlic sauce, Dungeness crab with black-bean sauce, and the like—are $8.50 or $9.50. The hot pot shabu-shabu is another favorite.

I Love Country Café

500 Ala Moana Blvd., in Restaurant Row. ☎ **808/537-1112.** Reservations not required. Plate lunches $5.45–$7.25; main courses $5.25–$7.50. No credit cards. Mon–Fri 6am–9pm, Sat 9am–3pm. AMERICAN/LOCAL.

The best bet for stylish budget dining here is this cute little café with pink papier-mâché pigs guarding the entrance and whimsical paintings of cows—some of them flying—on the walls. Miniature juke boxes at each table play popular oldies, and the food is homemade, country style—lots of vegetarian and local favorites, many dishes low in salt and with no preservatives. For those reducing their intake of fats, cholesterol, and sodium, there are house specialties like grilled chicken breast with fresh papaya salsa, fresh roast turkey, a vegetarian stir-fry, and a tofu burger plate. For those who want to eat local style, there are the traditional plate lunches (with both rice and macaroni), including such island favorites as chicken katsu, pork adobo, and beef lasagna. There's also deli sandwiches, salads, burgers, and more—a bit of something for everybody here.

Salsa Rita's

500 Ala Moana Blvd., in Restaurant Row. ☎ **808/536-4826.** Reservations not required. Main courses $5.55–$14.99. AE, CB, DC, MC, V. Daily 11am. MEXICAN.

There's good food and good fun here. The bar, outside on the mall, is always filled with a noisy, friendly crowd. The tiny dining room, done in brilliant yellow and hung with pictures of chili peppers and Mexican scenes, is the place for flavorful quesadillas, enchiladas, tacos, and the like. The light eater's and children's dishes—charbroiled chicken with tortillas ($5.99), quesadillas ($7.99), and vegetarian burrito ($4.99)—are good values. And huevos rancheros are a special treat.

ALOHA TOWER MARKETPLACE

The hottest, most "happening" scene at the moment in Honolulu is Aloha Tower Marketplace, a dining-shopping-festival complex right smack out on Honolulu's waterfront. Each of its half-dozen or so major theme restaurants offers a spectacular view. The local business crowd jams it at lunchtime (reservations are not taken), and tourists and residents alike keep it hopping until the wee hours. You can reach it from Waikiki via the Aloha Tower Express Trolley, which makes pickups at many hotels (phone **808/528-5700** for details).

In addition to the establishments listed below, there's the rather pricey San Francisco-based **Scott's Seafood** for local and mainland fish and seafood; **Big Island Steak House,** a handsomely decorated Hawaiian-style restaurant for steaks and seafood; **Rodeo Cantina,** for Tex-Mex fare in a Texas Roadhouse atmosphere; and **Sloppy Joe's,** a Hemingwayesque Key West–style bar that does manage to have a few decent sandwiches.

MODERATE

✪ Gordon Biersch Brewery Restaurant

At Aloha Tower Marketplace, 101 Ala Moana Blvd. ☎ **808/599-4877.** Reservations not accepted. Main courses $12.95–$18.95. AE, DC, MC, V. Mon 11am–5pm, Tues–Sat 11am–11pm, Sat–Sun 11am–10pm. PACIFIC RIM.

The world's largest microbrewery restaurant-cum-beergarden, Gordon Biersch has plenty going for it: a fantastic waterfront setting, an open-air dining lanai with an adjoining beergarden, two bars (you can watch the brewing process from one) and its own German-style lagers—dark and malty Dunkles; Export, a lighter beer for American tastes; and Marzen, an Octoberfest-style beer. The place is big—it seats almost 400—but the kitchen does an amazing job of getting food on the table quickly. Best of all, the San Francisco–based chain has hired one of the best local chefs around, Kelly Degala (we've been fans of his for years at other restaurants), to oversee the kitchen. Degala's menu does not disappoint; the combinations are imaginative, the flavors intense. The pupu menu in the beergarden is an expansion of the appetizer menu; on both, you must try the Gordon Biersch Garlic Fries—if you love garlic, that is. The grilled chicken skewers in a spicy peanut sauce and the garlic lamb and red pepper flatbread are other worthy starters. Salads are lovely, especially the Asian pear with spiced walnuts and blue cheese on baby greens. Main courses offer such possibilities as seafood curry with steamed banana leaf and sticky rice, red curry braised lamb shank, and seared scallops with grilled leeks and red peppers over pasta. At lunch, we usually opt for one of the pizzas, like the rock shrimp with goat cheese, basil, and oven-dried tomatoes. The desserts do tend to lean toward the chocolate decadence syndrome, like the double chocolate brownie sundae and an especially good chocolate espresso crème brûlée.

Just in case you're not into beer, there's a selection of almost 40 California wines, with at least 10 available by the glass.

Live entertainment prevails Wednesday through Saturday after 7pm, usually featuring groups such as Strange Brew (no cover).

BUDGET

For those who don't feel like braving the lines at the other restaurants—and don't mind saving a few bucks—there's the **Fabulous Food Lanai,** big enough to seat 700 hungry souls at tables overlooking the water. The food stalls offer everything from Cajun to Japanese to pizza and pasta to natural foods. My favorite here, the **Cajun Big Easy,** has wonderful combination plates for $6.25; choose among main courses like shrimp etouffée, bourbon chicken, and blackened fish.

5 McCully-Moiliili, University & Kapahulu Areas

EXPENSIVE

✪ Alan Wong's Restaurant

At McCully Court building, 5th floor, 1857 S. King St. ☎ **808/949-2526.** Reservations recommended. Main courses $15–$30. AE, MC, V. Daily from 5pm. PACIFIC RIM.

Honolulu foodies have hardly been able to contain themselves awaiting the opening of Alan Wong's new restaurant. One of Hawaii's most acclaimed young chefs, Wong, who achieved fame for Canoe House and Le Soleil at the Mauna Lani Bay Hotel on the Big Island, has returned to his native Honolulu and opened his own place. This is an intimate restaurant—very much in a kamaaina mode—with wonderful photographs of Hawaii, new and old, on the walls. A casual-yet-elegant atmosphere, interiors are done in subtle earth tones with accents of curly koa and coconut woods. Tempting aromas waft from the open kitchen, setting your expectations for Wong's award-winning, cutting-edge cuisine. Wong's training in classical French cooking (he did a stint at Lutèce in New York) is at the heart of his interpretations of Pacific Rim and other cuisines from around the world. Of course, he uses only the finest and freshest Island ingredients; he is a master of light, healthful low-fat methods of food preparation. The menu will change frequently, but typical dishes include the pan-roasted lamb chops with a coconut macadamia-nut crust; Oriental ratatouille, and star-anise sauce; "Ahi Cake," with layers of grilled eggplant, Maui onion, seared ahi, and Puna goat cheese–lemongrass sauce; and a spicy lobster curry with cilantro macadamia-nut pesto and pineapple-mango salsa. Planned for the near future: wine-maker dinners featuring guest chefs, theme nights, prix-fixe menus, family-style dinners, and a five-course Tasting Dinner.

MODERATE

Phillip Paolo's Seafood-Pasta House

2312 S. Beretania St. ☎ **808/946-1163.** Reservations recommended. Appetizers $5.95–$7.95; main courses $9.95–$26.95. AE, MC, V. Daily 11am–1:30pm, dinner Sun–Thurs 5–9:30pm, Fri–Sat 5–10pm. ITALIAN.

Local friends introduced us to this restaurant, which won an instant and enthusiastic kamaaina following at its opening several years ago. Now it's one of our favorites too. You'll be seated in one of several pretty, Victorian-style dining rooms. You're in for a very pleasant dining experience here: The waiters are knowledgeable and helpful, the crowd is attractive, the wine is delicious. Pastas and seafood are featured on the large menu, with various specialties every day. The crabcakes make a good starter. For the main event, try a dinner for two—either a seafood paella with Italian rice, or cloppino (seafood in a light tomato broth, with pasta on the side). Chicken marsala, steak ruffino, and eggplant/zucchini parmigiana are all very good. Only fresh herbs are used, and all dishes are served with either salad or soup. Everything is cooked to order, so have a drink while you're waiting. For dessert, go with the cheesecake served with the house's own fresh fruit sauce.

There's a much bigger Phillip Paolo's establishment in Kona, on the Big Island; it's called The Seafood Pasta Palace.

Salerno Ristorante Italiano

In the McCully Shopping Center, 1960 Kapiolani Blvd. ☎ **808/942-5273** or 808/946-3229. Reservations recommended. Appetizers $2.90–$9.90; main courses $7.90–$16.90 ($2–$3 less for smaller portions). AE, DC, MC, V. Mon–Sat 11am–2:30pm, daily 5–10pm. ITALIAN.

We first went to Salerno in self-defense, because our friends in Honolulu refused to give us any peace until we tried it; now that we've been there, we return often. It's a very pretty little place with a mirrored bar, comfortable red-velvet chairs, bouquets of orchids on the tables, and seascapes decorating the walls. The food is hearty, delicious, and inexpensive. Nothing unusual about the menu—there's the usual range of pastas, pizzas, chicken and veal dishes, seafood, the staples of Southern Italian cooking. What is unusual is that all of the main courses on the menu (an extensive one for such a small place) are offered in small or regular portions,

Eating as the Locals Eat: Where to Find Honolulu's Best Plate Lunches

The food of Hawaii—like its people—reflects the islands' cultural diversity: Japanese, Chinese, Hawaiian, Korean, Filipino, and other cuisines abound, as does a good deal of American-style eating. The unique down-home cuisine that is an amalgam of these various ethnic styles is known as "local food," and sampling some of it might possibly be the most interesting eating you do in the Islands. Probably the best—and most authentic—way to try the real eats of the Islanders is by ordering yourself a genuine "plate lunch," a Hawaiian-style sampler unto itself.

Some of the foods you'll find as part of your average carbohydrate-filled plate lunch are *lomi-lomi salmon* (well-seasoned, hand-kneaded salmon), *laulau* (ti leaves stuffed with pork, salt fish, bananas, sweet potatoes, and taro shoots, then steamed), *loco moco* (a hamburger patty topped with a fried egg and gravy), and rice, potato salad, and/or macaroni salad—two scoops of one or more of these starchy sides are almost always included. You may want to supplement your plate with the islands' most popular soup, *saimin* (a thin noodle broth topped with bits of fish, shrimp, chicken, pork, and/or vegetables), or a *manapua* (steamed dumplings filled with pork, meat, or bean paste) or two. Enjoy!

- Even before it was immortalized in song by Hawaii's favorite funny man, Frank DeLima, **Grace's Inn** (1296 S. Beretania St.) and the plate lunch were all but synonymous. Specialties at this modest (but immensely popular) eatery include chicken and beef katsu, teriyaki beef, and sweet-and-sour pork—all served with two scoops of rice, of course.
- Restaurant Row's **I Love Country Café** (500 Ala Moana Blvd.) may be the most stylish setting in which you can enjoy a local-style lunch. Here, the traditional Island favorites, such as pork adobo, are accompanied by both rice *and* macaroni.
- If you're near the University, stop in at the unassuming **Aloha Poi Bowl** (2671 King St., in University Square) for an authentic plate lunch. In addition to the regularly featured Hawaiian staples such as kalua pig and tripe stew, there's always a daily special—and the *haupia* (traditional Hawaiian coconut pudding) is great.
- What **Ono Hawaiian Foods** (726 Kapahulu Ave) lacks in size, it makes up for with aloha. This friendly place, easily accessible to Waikiki, includes *pipikaula* (Hawaiian beef jerky), lomi-lomi salmon, poi or rice, and haupia with all of their plates, including the combination kalua pig and laulau.

giving one the opportunity to sample more than one dish, or to dine lightly. House specialties worth knowing about include stuffed eggplant, pollo linguine (boneless chicken sautéed with vegetables and topped with either a pesto or tomato sauce), and deep-fried calamari. For dessert? Heavenly fresh pastries, baked daily (as are the breads) in Salerno's kitchen. The restaurant features an Italian grocery—marinara sauce, meatballs, homemade Italian sausage, and pasta to take away with you. Ask your waiter, then order your favorites.

BUDGET

✪ Keo's Thai Cuisine

625 Kapahulu Ave. ☎ **808/737-8240.** Main courses $8.95–$15.95. AE, DC, DISC, JCB, MC, V. Daily 5–10:30pm. THAI.

Thai food and the name "Keo's" are practically synonymous in Honolulu, ever since Keo Sananikone started opening restaurants and serving his marvelous modern interpretations of classic Thai and Southeast Asian cuisine. To get here, take TheBUS no. 2 (Campbell), get off at Zippy's and walk one block toward the mountains. There are five outposts in the Keo empire, but this is the one you should go to to catch the stars—Hollywood celebrities like Richard Chamberlain, Shirley MacLaine, Diana Ross, and Michael J. Fox. The stars shine in the decor too—tiny lights are strung into the plants in the jungle-garden setting, and there are masses of orchids and ginger everywhere. Umbrellas, ceiling fans, carvings, portraits, and statues add to the ambience.

The stars of the cuisine are Keo's succulent dishes, which use no artificial colorings, preservatives, or MSG, and only the freshest ingredients available. Evil Jungle Prince, an original Keo recipe, a red-chili-and-basil sauté with chicken, shrimp, or vegetables, is a specialty; so, too, are the spring rolls wrapped in rice paper and served with fresh lettuce and mint leaves. Wonderful soups, noodle and rice dishes, tangy curries, and cooling desserts await your pleasure. Let your waiter guide you as to what's spicy, what's very spicy, and what's bearable.

The Kapahulu location is the most fun, but also pleasant are Keo's at Ward Centre, 1200 Ala Moana Blvd. (☎ 808/533-0533); Keo's at King Street, a Thai Bar and Grill, 1486 S. King St. (☎ 808/947-9988); Mekong Restaurant, 1295 S. Beretania St. (☎ 808/523-0014); and Mekong II Restaurant, 1726 S. King St. (☎ 808/941-6184). If you're inspired to learn to cook Thai, buy Keo's cookbook, *Keo's Thai Cuisine,* available at the restaurants, and shop for Thai food at his store, Asian Grocery, 1319 S. Beretania St., and you're on your way.

Rama Thai Restaurant

802 Kapahulu Ave. ☎ **808/735-2789.** Reservations accepted. Main courses $4.95–$9.45; buffet dinner Wed night $11.95. MC, V. Daily 11am–2pm and 5–10pm. THAI.

Be sure to arrive early if you want to have dinner here, as this cozy, 11-table spot is very popular. Arrive by 6:30pm and you're not likely to have a problem, but later it fills up and then some. To get here, take TheBUS no. 2 (Campbell), get off at Zippy's and walk toward the Freeway. The food is delicious and reasonably priced. Most dishes serve two or three people easily, and this applies to appetizers, soups, salads, Thai curries, main courses, and noodle or rice dishes. Vegetarians will be happy here with a complete menu, from spring rolls to soups to main courses like Thai curry mixed with tofu. We started a recent meal here with the classic satay barbecue sticks—your choice of beef, pork, or chicken—to dip in a tangy cucumber-and-peanut sauce. Our ginger chicken soup was a winner: The chicken is simmered in coconut milk with parsley, green onions, and Thai ginger. There is a choice of six curries which can be ordered mild, medium, or hot (we recommend mild), and a score of main courses such as fried shrimp with assorted vegetables, beef with Thai red-gravy sauce, and cashew-nut chicken. We topped off our meal with cool and sweet Thai apple-banana-coconut pudding; next time it will be the Thai corn-and-tapioca pudding. Lunch offers similar main courses at slightly lower prices.

6 Downtown Honolulu

MODERATE

Centre Court

At Executive Centre Hotel, 1800 Bishop St. ☎ **808/539-3000**. Reservations recommended. Main courses $14.95–$22.95. AE, CB, DC, DISC, MC, JCB, V. Mon–Fri 6:30am–8:30pm. ISLAND CONTEMPORARY.

The busy crowds that throng Centre Court every weekday at lunchtime are not limited to the business travelers who stay at the Executive Centre Hotel; the local business community has discovered that there's some wonderfully imaginative cooking going on here. In the evening, people come from a wide radius—including Waikiki—to sample Chef Linda Yamada's creations. And the setting couldn't be sweeter: a light, airy, indoor "garden café" with Italian umbrellas, rattan seats, and island art. Yamada grew up in Hawaii and trained here and on the mainland; her menu reflects some traditional and local touches like homemade beef stew at lunch and dinner, sweet-potato bread French toast and "loco moco" at breakfast, as well as more contemporary fare. The poi-battered shrimp and the smoked salmon rolls are my favorites among the dinner appetizers. For main courses, I'd go with the sautéed shrimp in a chili black-bean sauce over linguine, the barbecued beef with a guava chili sauce, or the Ballyhooed chicken stuffed with roasted garlic and baked in an herb crust. For a full meal salad, the house smoked chicken breast with feta cheese and peppers in a garlic-anchovy vinaigrette is very good, too. Yamada makes her own breads and pastries, the latter served up in a dessert cart at the end of the meal, along with specialty drinks from the Espresso Bar.

Indigo

1121 Nuuanu Ave., in Chinatown. ☎ **808/521-2900**. Reservations recommended for weekend dinners. Small plates $3.90–$7.50; large plates $8.50–$12.50. AE, CB, DC, DISC, JCB, MC, V. Mon–Fri 8–10am, Mon–Sat 11am–9:30pm. EURASIAN.

It's hard to know how to characterize Indigo; it's in Chinatown and the decor is certainly Chinese. Yet, what can one say of a restaurant that fills wontons with goat cheese and tops them with a four-fruit sauce, or offers "Buddhist buns" with sun-dried tomato and eggplant? Not to mention Peking pizzettas, pizzas topped with such classic Chinese dishes as Peking duck with Imperial plum sauce? Whatever one calls this East-West hybrid, there's no disputing the fact that owner-chef Glenn Chu's food is fabulous; newly opened at the time of our visit, the restaurant was already drawing raves, and the word was out among Honolulu foodies that this was the place to go.

Both indoor and outdoor dining areas are lovely. The indoor space is furnished in rattan, and an intricately carved screen hides the compact kitchen. Note the stunning modern portraits of Chinese women; they're Pegge Hoppers, commissioned for the restaurant, and quite different than anything this noted artist has done before. The outdoor area is even more charming; it overlooks one of Honolulu's vest-pocket parks, this one with a rock waterfall and pond. Breakfast and morning tea feature such diverse goodies as granola and fruit or smoked jook with pickled ginger. As for those "small plates" served at both lunch and dinner, it's hard to choose between the likes of roasted Kahuku tomato and garlic crab soup, couscous pilaf potsticker with tangerine sauce, or tea-smoked chicken salad with raspberry hoisin on mixed greens. If you go on to one of those "large plates," you could have Norwegian salmon cakes with smoked chipotle mayonnaise, grilled Mongolian beef with black-bean sauce, or maybe grilled Pacific fish with lilikoi sauce. All are served with marinated salads, chutney and salsa of the day, plus a choice of rice or chive pillow noodle cake (take the latter). Desserts are not what one would associate with a Chinese restaurant: rich, creamy gelatos; fruit sorbets; cheesecake with a lime-ginger sauce; chestnut barquette topped with dark chocolate ganache, and more. The combination of such imaginative food, such a beautiful setting, and such modest prices makes Indigo a real find.

Won Kee Sea Food

In the Chinese Cultural Plaza, 100 N. Beretania St. ☎ **808/524-6877.** Reservations accepted. Main courses $6–$26.50 or more, depending on market prices. CB, JCB, MC, V. Daily 11am–2:30pm and 5–10pm. CHINESE/SEAFOOD.

This is a gourmet seafood place, where specialties like fresh island fish, island prawns, jumbo shrimp, king crab legs, or Maine lobster are prepared artfully—perhaps steamed with ginger-and-soy sauce, braised with ginger-and-garlic sauce, or stir-fried with black-bean sauce—and is a standout among the restaurants in the Cultural Plaza. Specialties depend on the market, but most of the dishes are very reasonable; dishes like fresh clams with black-bean sauce, sautéed shrimp with vegetables, Eight Treasures tofu, roast duck with plum sauce, and cold ginger chicken are mostly under $9.50. Soup of the day (mine was turnip), rice, and tea are included in the price. Don't expect an ornate place; here you have white tablecloths, simple wood paneling, and Chinese-style wrought-iron fixtures. It's the food that's ornate.

BUDGET

✪ Cafe Sistina

1314 S. King St. ☎ **808/526-0071.** Reservations recommended. Main courses $9–$15.75. MC, V. Mon–Fri 11am–2pm; Mon–Thurs 5:30–10pm, Fri–Sat 5:30–10:30pm, Sun 5:30–9pm. ITALIAN.

Sergio Mitrotti is a Renaissance man—a chef, an artist, and an entrepeneur who knows how to put together a terrific restaurant, one that excels in sophisticated, contemporary Italian cuisine. The room is smart looking with square marble tables and two splendid murals by Sergio, one of an Italian street scene, the other of a portion of the Sistine Chapel ceiling. Italian opera playing in the background lends a nice touch. The menu features some wonderful antipasti (bruschetta with grilled tomatoes or with chopped clams in a wine garlic sauce, griglia mista, frittata rustica, and so on), hearty salads like the insalata di mare, half a dozen veal dishes, and a huge variety of pastas. Some favorites are linguine al porcini, penne al formaggi, pollo al limone, rigatoni in caponata, and several unusual seafood pastas like the mussels and shrimp in a saffron porcini sauce or scampi alla vodka. A vocalist (Sergio's wife) entertains most nights, and there's often a jam session on Sundays (call to check).

⦵ Hong Kong Noodle House

In the Chinese Cultural Plaza, 100 N. Beretania St. ☎ **808/536-5409.** Reservations not required. $3.25–$6.50. No credit cards. Daily 10am–2:30pm. CHINESE.

Use your noodle when you're downtown; save money and have a tasty meal for under $7 by visiting the Hong Kong Noodle House. This small, plain restaurant on the mauka-Ewa corner of the Chinese Cultural Plaza, facing the river, is one of about seven in a row that feature Chinese, Japanese, Korean, and Mongolian cooking. Even those who are not noodle fans could be converted. There are 12 different noodle soups, and any one of these is a full meal, like fishball noodle soup or roast duck noodle soup. There are almost as many tossed noodle dishes with soup served separately; the noodles with shrimp are delicious. Brave souls might want to try the noodles with pig's feet. A dozen rice soups include fascinating combos such as preserved eggs with salted pork. Specialties like crispy roast duck, tender boiled pig's liver, and tender boiled pig's stomach are offered in the under-$6 price range.

7 Waialae-Kahala Area

MODERATE

✪ Baci Due Ristorante

3196 Waialae Ave. ☎ **808/735-5899.** Reservations recommended. Main courses $14–$32.50. AE, DC, MC, V. Mon–Fri 11:30am–2:30pm, daily 6–10:30pm. NOUVELLE AND TRADITIONAL ITALIAN.

Chef Shari Sarabi may have closed his wonderful Baci Ristorante in Waikiki (due to stratospheric rents), but never fear: There are two other terrific restaurants under his aegis, and this is the closest to Waikiki (the other, Spiedini, is covered later in this chapter). The surroundings are small and intimate; only 40 lucky diners can be seated at a time. Try for one of the booths, upholstered in French Provincial style. Start with bruschetta, the buffalo mozzarella, or maybe one of the superb risottos as an appetizer. Then on to a special pasta, perhaps fettucine all'Aragosta (half a lobster tail in the shell, atop pasta with fresh tomato), or a main course like the lusty cioppino, the saltimbocca (sautéed veal with prosciutto and mozzarella), or the scampi alla Baci, (large prawns sautéed in garlic butter). Fish presentations are always imaginative; ask about the fresh fish of the day and the other dinner specials. The chef is accommodating of special requests for those eating healthy. For the reckless ones, order dessert: The profiteroles filled with gelato and topped with chocolate sauce are worth writing home about. A moderately priced lunch menu—soup and appetizers $3.50 to $9.95, pastas from $8.25 to $13.75, and main courses from $12.95 to $15.95—is also a delight.

Ikkyu Sushi

3458 Waialae Ave. ☎ **808/732-7938.** Reservations not necessary. Sushi $1–$5.50; plate lunches $5.50. No credit cards. Mon–Sat 10am–4:30pm. JAPANESE/HAWAIIAN.

Known to local folk as "sushi heaven", this shiny-clean, sunny new place really rolls a mean sushi, not to mention the *ono* plate lunches—shrimp, chicken, or beef curry plates served with the usual macaroni salad and rice. A major local favorite is the—believe it or not—Spam musubi for $1. (Culinary trivia note: Did you know that 3¹/₂ times as much Spam™ is consumed in Hawaii as in any other state?) Owner Joanne Takatsugi and her busy staff keep the great kaukau coming and manage to keep everyone happy. My local friends love it, and they're not the only ones—people who work in the burgeoning Waialae Avenue business district come running at lunchtime for goodies to take out. There are only two tables, but there's a park across the street; or, you can assemble a fine beach picnic here. Rumor has it that these people cater some of the finest parties in this classy Waialae-Kahala neighborhood.

BUDGET

Yen King

In the Kahala Mall Shopping Center, 4211 Waialae Ave. ☎ **808/732-5505.** Reservations recommended. Main courses $6.95–$16. AE, MC, V. Tues–Sun 8am–9:30pm, Mon 11am–9:30pm. CHINESE.

This popular Northern Chinese restaurant just keeps getting better, gaining new fans among *kamaainas* and *malihinis* alike. It's an attractive place, with beige colors highlighting the filigreed teak screen dividers, tile ceiling, and murals. The menu is vast, at both lunch and dinner, but there's no way you can go wrong here, as everything is prepared with master-chef expertise. You can choose among some 30 vegetarian dishes (the local vegetarians swear by this place), and about two dozen seafood choices, mostly featuring squid, clams, and shrimp in various styles. Of course there are plenty of beef, pork, and fowl dishes (garlic chicken and roast duck are especially good), and a wide variety of Peking-style dim sum (dumplings and noodles). Hot Mongolian beef is available anytime, but give them three hours' notice if you want to try their beggar's chicken baked in clay—quite unusual. Friday and Saturday from 9:30pm to midnight, the sounds of karaoke—in English, Chinese, and Japanese—will accompany those sounds of sizzling rice.

8 Hawaii Kai & Aina Haina

EXPENSIVE

✪ Hanatei Bistro

6650 Kalanianaole Hwy. ☎ **808/396-0777.** Reservations recommended. Main courses $16–$26; Sun brunch $21.95. AE, MC, V. Daily 5:30–10:30pm; Sun brunch 10am–1:30pm. CONTEMPORARY FRENCH/ASIAN.

A spotlighted bank of orchids at the entrance, immediate attention to your seating by the maître d', understated Japanese decor, soft classical music, decorative pools with miniature falls, and wooden bridges over which you make your way to the dining room with its panoramic view of the sea—all this leads you to expect a special dining experience. And On Jin Kim's restaurant, being hailed as one of the hottest new places in Honolulu, does not disappoint. On Jin Kim, an honored culinary genius and one of the outstanding women chefs in the country, serves up the best contemporary French and Asian cuisine in a serene and lovely setting. The result is nothing less than a world-class dining experience.

The gourmet experience begins with such appetizers as ravioli stuffed with prawns, garlic and basil in a tomato-cognac sauce or the escargots en croute with shiitake mushrooms. Then comes the main course. The liberal portion of boneless salmon is served on a bed of cooked watercress blended with spinach, artfully arranged on a black-and-white platter, surrounded by ginger-sake sauce. Equally beautiful—and delicious—are such main courses as baked chicken breast stuffed with goat cheese, prosciutto, and sun-dried tomatoes; Hawaiian ocean snapper steamed with a delicate Chinese sesame chili sauce; or the house specialty, an exquisite bouillabaisse, with fresh salmon and opakapaka, flavored with saffron, lemon grass, and plum tomatoes. There are also salads and pastas with delectable sauces to choose from. Wonderful home-baked desserts change daily.

There's live classical music or acoustic jazz at Hanatei Bistro every night, but I'd suggest you plan your visit for a Tuesday if possible. That's when Chef

On Jin, a former opera singer, shares her "Repertoire for Romance," a program of beautiful arias; she's accompanied by one of Honolulu's top pianists.

On Jin's Saturday and Sunday brunch is spectacular, with a sushi bar, an omelet station, several hot dishes including roast prime rib carved on the buffet line, many island delicacies, and an irresistable dessert buffet.

✪ Roy's

6600 Kalanianaole Hwy. ☎ **808/396-7697.** Reservations recommended. Main courses $14–$28. AE, CB, DC, DISC, JCB, MC, V. Mon–Thurs 5:30–9:30pm, Fri 5:30–10:30pm, Sat 5–10:30pm, Sun 5–9:30pm. HAWAIIAN REGIONAL.

Roy's is the place where everyone wants to go. Forty-year-old wunderkind chef/owner Ray Yamaguchi is still hailed, after 10 years, as the master for his innovative marriage of Asian and Western cooking styles and ingredients. He recently received The James Beard Award for "Best Chef" in the Pacific and Northwest, and both *Honolulu* magazine and a Zagat survey have named Roy's "Hawaii's Most Popular Restaurant." If you've got wheels, hop in your car and drive the eight miles to Hawaii Kai to see for yourself.

Roy's is a two-level restaurant; downstairs there's a piano bar and lounge with outdoor tables for cocktails. But the main action—and the open display kitchen from which the wondrous dishes emerge—is upstairs. The huge, striking room has a wraparound window affording uninterrupted views of Maunalua Bay, Diamond Head, and Koko Head. The lighting is indirect, the decor elegant and subdued, the service meticulous, and the show-biz crowd can be a show in itself.

The food is exquisite. Since Roy is constantly coming up with new inspirations, there are perhaps 30 specials on the menu every night—and they always include original appetizers, salads, pastas, wood-fired individual pizzas, and many fresh fish dishes, including local spiny lobster. And on the regular menu you'll get a chance to try many of his signature dishes. Our favorites among the appetizers are potstickers in a lobster miso sauce and lemon grass-crusted fish sateh with Thai peanut sauce. As for main courses, you can choose among the likes of a Northern Chinese–style roast duck with Oriental stir-fry vegetables, a smoked lime chicken with rosemary and sausage, black-bean–bell-pepper stuffing in achiote chile sauce, or an Asian pesto mahimahi with shiitake mushrooms, tomatoes, and cranberries in a Thai curry, ginger, basil, and coconut sauce. Preparations of lamb, salmon, and local fish come in endless variations. Desserts are special, too, and change every night. The wine list is well chosen, and not over-priced. There's entertainment—contemporary music and vocals on Thursday and Friday from 8 to 10pm, and Hawaiian slack-key guitar and vocals every Saturday from 8:30 to 10pm.

Note: Call several days in advance to reserve for dinner on weekends. There are two more Roy's on Maui—Kahana Bar & Grill and R.J.'s—a new Roy's at Poipu Shopping Village on Kauai, as well as one in Tokyo and one in Guam.

Tulips

5730 Kalanianaole Highway (Niu Valley Shopping Center). ☎ **808/377-8854.** Reservations recommended on weekends. Main courses $13.95–$22.95. AE, CB, DC, DISC, MC, V. Daily 5:30–9:30 pm. PACIFIC RIM.

Island residents like to come here to celebrate a special occasion because the atmosphere is so festive. The dining room looks like an old-fashioned garden—all yellow and white and green—with floral prints, ivy, even picket fence dividers all around the room. And while the yellow tulips in the buckets and wheelbarrows are silk, there's nothing faux about the cuisine. I especially like their salads, the pear and goat cheese salad with toasted walnut vinaigrette is a nice way to start a meal, as are such appetizers as ginger chicken spring rolls with a spicy coconut-peanut sauce, or the crispy crab and tofu dumpling with Chinese oyster sauce and sesame bok choy salad. For main courses, you can't go wrong with one of the pastas, or the scallops and prawns with black-bean sauce, or the grilled chicken with sizzling lime butter and mashed potatoes. One caveat: The last time we were there, the chef had overwhelmed everything with too much pepper; we literally had to scrape it off to taste the delicious food underneath. Hopefully, that situation has been corrected by the time you read this; if not, just tell the server to tell the chef to hold the pepper—you'll add your own, thanks. Except for that, Tulips is terrific.

MODERATE

✪ Spiedini

7192 Kalanianaole Hwy. (Koko Marina Center). ☎ **808/396-6161.** Reservations recommended. Main courses $11.95–$25.50. AE, DISC, MC, V. Daily 5–10pm. NOUVELLE AND TRADITIONAL ITALIAN.

This elegant yet charmingly homey place is the latest of owner-chef Shari Sarabi's excellent eateries (see Baci Due, listed earlier). It resembles a first-rate Italian country inn. The lighting is soft and romantic; the walls are white; the carpeting, with its muted floral pattern, looks antique; and the windows overlook the marina and the courtyard, and on to the mountains beyond. (Ask for a table overlooking the marina or mountains when you make your reservation.) The soft Italian opera or contemporary music is the perfect background for Chef Shari's *deliziosi* creations. The menu changes every few days, but there will usually be such tasty antipasti as the *gamberetti marinati* (charcoaled shrimp with chilled lime, mint, and feta cheese) and the yummy *panzanella* (bread salad with tomato, artichoke, and onion in a spicy vinaigrette). Pastas are all made in-house and done perfectly; there are at least 16 to choose from. Since *"spiedini"* means grilled, there are a good number of grilled selections, all accompanied by seasonal vegetables and a choice of pasta, risotto, or salad; especially good are the *spiedini di pollo* (grilled fresh chicken breast) and the *saltimbocca alla spiedini* (pounded veal and prosciutto rolled in fresh mozzarella and grilled). There's a grilled fish every day. Lunch also offers tempting—and moderately priced choices: We're partial to the kiawe-grilled sandwiches ($6.95 to $11.50); there are also appetizers, pastas, and a few main dishes, from $3.95 to $14.50. Desserts are freshly made and change daily—gelati, cheesecakes, chocolate decadence, and more where they came from.

Service at Spiedini is extremely pleasant and efficient.

✪ Swiss Inn

5730 Kalanianaole Hwy. (Niu Valley Shopping Center). ☎ **808/377-5447.** Reservations recommended. Main courses $13.50–$20; Sun brunch $13.50. AE, CB, DC, DISC, JCB, MC, V. Wed–Sat 6–10pm, Sun 6–9pm; Sun brunch 10:30am–1pm. SWISS.

Swiss food is a rarity in Honolulu, so should you get the urge, say, for authentic wienerschnitzel or Bündnerfleisch or cheese fondue, the way to satisfy that urge is to get into your rented car, drive out to the Niu Valley Shopping Center (a 15- to 20-minute drive from Waikiki, en route to Hanauma Bay), and stop in at this old favorite. Owner-chef Martin Wyss is a dedicated man who personally cooks every order and really cares about his customers' satisfaction. The place is cozy, with scenic pictures and tole ware on the walls, and several gazebos with hanging plants and tables inside. Begin your meal with the above-mentioned

Bündnerfleisch (thinly sliced, air-dried beef) or escargots, then on to one of the main courses. Everything is good, but I especially like the veal médaillons Florentine, the émincé de veau Zurich-style, the garlic shrimp and scallops Madagascar, and the wienerschnitzel, of course. Cheese fondue is ready on the spot, but give them 24 hours' notice if you want the beef fondue, also delicious. Light dinners are even more reasonable—$5 to $7 for the likes of bratwurst, vegetarian pastas, and Wienerli, European-style frankfurters with Swiss potato salad. Come for Sunday brunch and enjoy a European-style buffet with salads, cold cuts, hot dishes, and many desserts.

BUDGET

Dining Room

Hawaii Kai Golf Course & Links, Hawaii Kai. ☎ **808/395-7900.** Reservations not necessary. Main courses $4.25–$5.75. AE, MC, V. Daily 6am–7pm. AMERICAN.

You don't have to be a golfer, or even know the difference between a golf course and golf links to enjoy this place—the setting is simply beautiful. The dining room is located on the second floor of the clubhouse overlooking the greens, the mountains, and the ocean. The greens are actually smack up against the mountains; some of the holes are partway up the mountains. The room is huge, all glass on the ocean and mountain sides with the kitchen up at the front and a very well-stocked bar, the Nineteenth Hole, at the other end. There's happy chatter from the golfers and the many families who come here to eat and visit. The view far outshines the food, but for the price, it isn't half bad: There are local favorites like corned beef and cabbage, stir-fried chicken with vegetables, chicken teriyaki plate, lots of sandwiches and burgers ($3.25 to $5.15), and a very reasonable breakfast menu. The entire menu prevails all day, except for the pancakes.

Sadec Vietnamese Restaurant

377 Keahole St., on the second floor of the Koko Kai Shopping Center. ☎ **808/396-3020.** Reservations not necessary. Main courses $4.75–$7.95. Thurs–Tues 10am–9pm. VIETNAMESE.

For a taste of Vietnamese food while you're out seeing the island, Sadec is a good choice. The dining room is small, with soft lighting and abundant greenery; from one section of the L-shaped room you can see Maunalua Bay. Prints of Vietnamese scenery adorn the white walls. The staff is hospitable; what they lack in proficiency in English they more than make up for in their eagerness to please. The bill of fare is varied for such a small place, and you can't beat the prices. Sugarcane shrimp, spring rolls, seafood mixed vegetable soup, sautéed fish, sour squid, and a variety of plate lunches are all satisfying. I like their special rice noodles, served with cucumber, mint, lettuce, and bean sprouts, and sprinkled with peanuts and a special sauce—it's the best. The restaurant does a brisk take-out business with the neighborhood folks; you could take your order out for a picnic.

9 Windward Oahu

KAILUA
MODERATE

Assaggio Italian Restaurant

354 Uluniu St. ☎ **808/261-2772.** Reservations recommended, especially on weekends. Main courses $8.90–$17.90. AE, CB, DC, MC, V. Mon–Fri 11:30am–2:30pm, daily 5–10pm. ITALIAN.

A place that's won a big following for its wonderful food at oh-so-reasonable prices, Assaggio is something special. The service is special, too. The whole staff takes care of everyone; there's always someone watching to see if you're happy. At dinner the hot antipasto—which has *everything*—is exceptional. At dinner only, one may order a small or regular portion of pasta or any other main course. Our favorite pasta here—and one you don't see everywhere—is the baked ziti alla siciliano. Chicken, veal, seafood dishes—they're all good, especially the sauces. Lunch main courses are pretty much the same, and go down $1 or $2 in prices. Even if you have to get a take-out bag, don't leave Assaggio without sampling their liqueur-infused cheesecakes ($4); of course, you'd be perfectly safe with the tiramisù or the zabaglione with imported marsala, too, at $3.50. The restaurant is pleasant enough, with changing artwork on the walls—but it's the food that shines here. Our one complaint: Sometimes the baked pastas are overcooked and too soft, not al dente, as I prefer.

Jaron's

Hamakua Drive. ☎ **808/261-4600.** Reservations recommended for dinner. Main courses $9.95–$20.95. DC, MC, V. Mon–Sat 11am–2am, Sun 9am–midnight. ISLAND ECLECTIC.

It's no wonder that Jaron's is always crowded at night—this is one of the Windward side's more attractive and upscale eateries, yet the prices are very reasonable, considering the quality of the food and service. The softly lit dining room, done in rich emerald green, with flowers on every table, is a warm and inviting background for a varied menu that runs from potstickers, nachos, and baked brie among the appetizers, to plentiful pastas, gourmet pizzas, and, best of all, a good selection of fresh Island fish, done in a variety of styles. My favorite presentation is kiawe-grilled fish served with fresh vegetables, brown rice–walnut apricot pilaf, and a curry sauce made with coconut milk and Kaffir lime leaves. Other good possibilities: pan-fried Maryland crabcakes, smoked salmon fettuccine, a delicious bouillabaisse, and a good seafood curry. Main courses come with one of three house salads—Caesar, mixed greens with fresh mint and walnuts, or tossed greens—or homemade soup. There are special choices for "heart-healthy" diners and for vegetarians. If I could find one fault with this place it's that the staff sometimes gets overwhelmed and it can take a while to get your check—but they do try.

BUDGET

Cinnamon's

315 Uluniu St. ☎ **808/261-8724.** Reservations recommended for parties of more than four. Main courses $7.50–$17.95. DISC, MC, V. Daily 7am–2pm, Thurs–Sat 5–9pm. AMERICAN.

Named after the bear in a French children's story, Cinnamon's is an immensely popular restaurant on the ground floor of a neighborhood shopping plaza. Its aim is to provide wholesome, natural, nutritious foods with no preservatives in a smoke-free atmosphere, and this it does—with style. The restaurant is small and cozy; four of the tables are under a pretty white gazebo. And the tab will be very reasonable. For lunch, we like the chicken-cashew salad ($6.50) and the grilled three-cheese deluxe sandwich ($3.95). At dinnertime, pick one of the house specials, such as chicken fantasy, with "made from scratch" hollandaise; kebabs of chicken, beef, or mahimahi; or barbecued ribs. Meals come with soup or salad; rice, fries, or baked beans; vegetables; and hot dinner rolls. On the à la carte dinner menu, the fiesto taco grande salad and the chef's super salad ("a veritable salad bar brought to your table") are inexpensive and fun. Breakfast has its own delights, including eggs Benedict, carrot pancakes, three-egg omelets, and freshly baked cinnamon rolls.

El Charro Avitia

14 Oneawa St. ☎ **808/263-3943.** Reservations recommended. Main courses $7.75–14.50. AE, DISC, MC, V. Daily 11am–9pm. MEXICAN.

It's best to come here on a weekday if you can, because this place is insanely popular and on weekends, even with a reservation, you'll probably still have to wait a little. But it will be worth it. This is some of the best Mexican food you'll find anywhere, prepared with love and care by the Avitia family (they have several successful restaurants in California and Nevada as well), and served in astounding portions; we always leave with doggie bags. The decor is beautiful indoors and out; you can dine outdoors on tables decorated with big clay lanterns and surrounded by ficus trees in mammoth clay pots, or indoors in a room laden with Mexican artifacts, with colorful Mexican pottery and clay lanterns decorating your table. The chairs are carved in ornate Mexican style, and the music is pure south-of-the-border; you'll soon forget that you're in beautiful downtown Kailua and not in old Mexico. Anything you choose on the all-day menu will be good. Huevos Mexicanos—rancheros, colorados, revueltos—are served all day long. Start with a fresh fruit margarita; end with a simple flan or even fried ice cream. A treat.

✪ Harry's Cafe & Deli

629 Kailua Rd ☎ **808/261-2120.** Reservations not required. Main courses $6.95–$11.95. CB, DC, MC, V. Mon–Sat 11am–3pm, daily 5:30–9pm. MEDITERRANEAN.

Back in the 1930s and '40s, Harry Owens was one of the foremost composers of popular Hawaiian music: "Sweet Leilani" (which won him an Academy Award in 1939), "To You, Sweetheart, Aloha," and "Hawaii Calls" are standards of the hapa-haole repertoire. Now his son, Tim, has opened a charming restaurant that recalls the man and the era. Originals of the sheet music of many of his hits adorn the walls, as do superb Hawaiian quilts and changing art exhibits. The attractive young staff is impeccably trained: Servers are able to tell you exactly how each dish is prepared. And they know a good deal about wines, too (only wine and beer are served). The food lives up to the setting: We like to start with the pane formaggi (French bread stuffed with provolone cheese and baked with garlic-and-basil butter) or the rare carpaccio. Then we move on to such main courses as shrimp Provençale, pasta primavera, and chicken breast Medici. As for desserts, it's a hard choice. There are usually four kinds of cheesecakes made on the premises (strawberry, rum, amaretto, and chocolate are among the most popular), and there's always a sour-cream fudge cake with cream-cheese frosting, carrot or banana cake, and chocolate mousse. Relax over your meal as long as you like; no one is going to rush you. Harry's is a hit!

Nana's

201 Hamakua Dr. ☎ **808/261-5546.** Reservations not necessary. Pastas $3–$4.75; sandwiches $4.35; specials $4.50–$5. No credit cards. Mon–Fri 11am–3pm, 5–9pm; Sat–Sun 11am–9pm. ITALIAN.

If you need a picnic lunch for the beach or a quick meal as you drive around the Island, Nana's can oblige. Nana and her three daughters run this tiny little place, with just five tables inside and three outside. Windowboxes of flowers and plants front the kitchen, from which emerges food that's splendid for the price. The baked pastas may be a tad overcooked, but the sauces are very good, especially the clam sauce. Nana and family have another restaurant downtown at 1111 Bishop St., which does a very brisk business at lunch.

Pepper's Place Philadelphia Cheesesteaks

301-A Hahani St. ☎ **808/261-1331.** Reservations not accepted. Sandwiches $4.79–$5.99. No credit cards. Mon–Sat 9am–9pm, Sun 11am–8pm. AMERICAN.

This is just a tiny place—about five tables indoors and one outdoors—but it has really caught on with the local folk and the bed-and-breakfast guests in the area. It has a '50s look about it; there are old Coke posters, a painting depicting Bogey, Marilyn, and James Dean seated at a lunch counter, and behind the counter, none other than . . . Elvis! The specialty is cheesesteaks (their slogan is "6,000 miles to Philly—better eat here!"), but everything is good, especially their baked and french-fried potatoes, both served three different ways (the cheese fries are to die for!), and their sandwich rolls. They also have chicken and vegetarian sandwiches. The menu is over the counter; you order and pay, and they'll give you a holler when your order is ready. We like the bottomless sodas (unlimited refills). This is a favorite spot to pick up lunch to take to the beach.

KANEOHE

Chart House

46–336 Haiku Rd. ☎ **808/247-6671.** Reservations recommended. Main courses $15–$42. AE, DISC, MC, V. Sun–Thurs 5–9pm, Fri–Sat 5–10pm; Sun brunch 10:30am–2pm. STEAK/ SEAFOOD.

Once it was Haiku Gardens, a beloved old restaurant in Windward Oahu, not far from Honolulu. Now it's Chart House, situated in one of the oldest, loveliest gardens on the Island. Like all Chart Houses, this one is handsome: Tiki torches light the walkway from the parking lot; there's a fountain in front of the door; and inside one can pause for drinks in the reception room, so comfortable with rattan furniture and soft, big cushions in a pastel print. The dining room has been totally redone, and the food lives up to the setting. For a mere $12.95, you could have a veritable feast on the fabulous salad bar alone; with it come hot "squaw" and sourdough breads. On the regular menu there are nifty appetizers like poke (an island delicacy of raw fish marinated in soy sauce and red peppers), smoked fish, imported Brie, and a special favorite, coconut crunch shrimp in tempura batter, served with three sauces. Pride of the house is the hand-carved prime rib. There's also a variety of steaks, two chicken selections, and several seafood dishes. With the main course comes a choice of the salad bar or a large bowl of New England clam chowder. Desserts befit the steak-house atmosphere—keylime pie, chocolate mousse pie, and mud pie.

WAIMANALO

Bueno Nalo

41–865 Kalanianaole Hwy. ☎ **808/259-7186.** Reservations not accepted. Main courses $6.95–$9.95. No credit cards. Daily 11:30am–9pm. MEXICAN.

Out in the wilds of beautiful Waimanalo, for which "Nalo" is a local pet name, this restaurant has been around for at least 30 years, and it's still popular with folks from all over the island. Cheerful decorations inside and out—flags, piñatas, sombreros, bright red chilies painted on the tabletops and on the park benches where diners wait to gain admittance—set the scene for fresh and delicious tacos, tostadas, tamales, burritos, and the like. Huevos rancheros is one of their specialties. In addition to the menu items, they have a weekday lunch special of enchiladas or tacos served with rice and beans for $6.50. No liquor, so BYOB. Check out the chile pepper hats and shorts.

10 The North Shore

MODERATE

Jameson's by the Sea

62-540 Kam Hwy., Haleiwa. ☎ **808/637-4336.** Reservations recommended. Main courses $14.95–$22.95. AE, DC, MC, V. Mon–Fri 11am–11pm, Sat–Sun 9am–11pm; brunch Sat–Sun 9am–noon. SEAFOOD.

Jameson's is a wonderfully picturesque spot for lunch or dinner, with sweeping ocean and sunset views. If you're in the area around lunchtime, stop in at the downstairs pub, so inviting with its open-air deck. The menu features hearty fish, seafood, and meat sandwiches; some excellent shrimp, crab and seafood Louie salads; and a variety of interesting pupus. The salmon pâté is an all-time favorite, as is the creamy Boston clam chowder. Better still, plan your trip to be in this area around day's end; this is one of the best sunset scenes on Oahu, especially in the spring and summer months. On Monday and Tuesday evenings, some dinner items are served downstairs, but you can enjoy the full menu Wednesday through Sunday in the spacious upstairs dining room. The seafood comes direct from Hawaiian waters and is market-priced daily. If it's available, have the opakapaka—Hawaiian pink snapper, poached in white wine, and topped with a garlic Hollandaise sauce. Main courses are served with fresh seasonal vegetables and a choice of rice or garlic linguine. Have a homemade chiffon pie to go with your Kona coffee, or, better yet, indulge in a steaming Irish coffee, a Jamesons's trademark.

BUDGET

⑤ Ahi's

Kahuku. ☎ **808/293-5650.** Reservations not accepted. Main courses $8.25–$9.50. No credit cards. Mon–Sat 11am–9pm. SEAFOOD.

If you love seafood—and especially shrimp—don't pass up a chance for a meal at Ahi's; residents drive from all over the island to partake. Ahi's shrimp specials—a choice of scampi, shrimp cocktail, lightly fried shrimp tempura, deep-fried shrimp, or a sampler of all, served with hot vegetables, grilled bread, and either rice or mashed potatoes—have been described as "awesome." The rest of the food is okay, too, but the shrimp is what you come here for. Ahi's looks like a gracefully ageing Hawaiian *hale* (house) halfway down a country road in Kahuku (if you're coming via Kaneohe and you reach the sugar mill, you've gone a bit too far). Look for the weathered old blue building with a green roof, decorated with fishing nets and glass floats. Ahi and his family (sons, nephews, nieces) are friendly and delightful, and treat you like a guest in their own home. This is a real taste of old Hawaii!

Coffee Gallery

In the North Shore Marketplace, 66–250 Kam Hwy., Haleiwa. ☎ **808/637-5571.** Reservations not accepted. Sandwiches $3.75–$6.95; main courses $3.95–$8.95. AE, MC, V. Mon–Fri 6am–9pm, Sat–Sun 7am–9pm. ETHNIC/VEGETARIAN.

It's pleasant to sit at the screened outdoor café and have a cup of freshly roasted gourmet coffee or a light lunch or dinner at this informal place. The emphasis is on healthy, fresh foods; the pastries, baked on the premises, are made without eggs or sugar. Lunch features quiches, waffles, veggie burgers, salads, and chili and rice; a vegetarian specialty is always available at dinner. There's a nice menu for children. The espresso bar has some delightful combinations, like vanilla ice cream topped with espresso. With your coffee, try a "death by chocolate" brownie—if you dare.

Kua'Aina Sandwiches

66–214 Kam Hwy., Haleiwa. ☎ **808/637-6067.** Sandwiches $3.50–$5.40. No credit cards. Daily 11am–8pm. SANDWICHES.

Where can you get the best sandwich on the North Shore, maybe on all of Oahu? We cast our vote for Kua'Aina, a rustic shop across the street from the courthouse in Haleiwa. It's tiny, neat as a pin, with wooden tables; a few are on the porch. The atmosphere is casual; people come in off the beach. We haven't stopped raving yet about the sandwiches we had on our last visit: mahimahi with melted cheese, Ortega pepper, lettuce, and tomato; tuna and avocado, and a great baconburger. Sandwiches are hearty enough to be a whole meal and are served on either a kaiser roll, honey wheatberry bread, or earthy rye. Two years in a row, the Zagat survey voted them as no. 10 in the state for food and no. 2 for best "Bang for the Buck."

Rosie's Cantina

In the Haleiwa Shopping Plaza, 66-165 Kam Hwy., Haleiwa. ☎ **808/637-3538.** Reservations not required. Main courses $4.95–$12.70. MC, V. Daily 7am–10pm. MEXICAN.

This attractive modern spot is a favorite for tasty Mexican food. Rosie's serves all three meals, features delicious tortas (hamburger or chicken on thick bread with fries or beans), as well as generous servings of all the traditional Tex-Mex favorites. It's been famous for its frosty fruit margaritas since it opened 10 years ago. A good stop, before or after the beach.

11 Central Oahu

BUDGET

Anna Miller's

Pearlridge Center, Phase 1, 98-115 Kaonohi St. ☎ **808/487-2421.** Reservations not accepted. Burgers and sandwiches $4.75–$5.95; main courses $7.75–$16.95. AE, MC, V. Daily 24 hours. AMERICAN.

When a restaurant can stay open 24 hours a day, 365 days a year and always be busy—and has been for the past 23 years—you know they're doing something right. Anna Miller's is a local success story, started in 1973 by Stanley Miller in honor of his grandmother, Anna, who was famous for her homemade pies. Anna's signature pies are still here, and they're still good—rocky road, pumpkin, apple, peanut-butter chocolate, macadamia nut, to name a few—available by the slice or pie. Also good are the breakfast items, like the banana pancakes and the Portuguese sweetbread french toast; the entire menu is available all hours of the day and night. You can always get a burger, a Philadelphia cheesesteak, a tomato stuffed with chicken or tuna salad, or local favorites like kal bi ribs, oxtail stew, or several seafood dishes. Kids have their own menu. With generous portions and prices like these, it's no wonder that local families and off-duty military personnel stationed nearby consider this a favorite.

Bravo

Pearlridge Center, Phase 1, 98-115 Kaonohi St. ☎ **808/474-5544.** Reservations only for parties of 8 or more. Pizzas $6.95–$12.95; pastas $7.95; sandwiches $5.95–$6.25; main courses $10.95–$18.95. AE, MC, V. Sun–Thurs 11am–10pm, Sat–Sun 11am–11pm. ITALIAN.

Bravo is an insanely popular place, not only with the people who live nearby, but with kamaainas far and wide. Call the atmosphere psuedo-Mediterranean: Romanesque columns, hanging plants, mirrors, wine-colored booths, Italian prints adorning the walls. No *nuova cucina* at this place—this is your traditional, heavy, home-style southern Italian food, and tasty it is. Pasta is made fresh daily in Bravo's sparkling exhibition-style kitchen; you choose the kind you like and team it with a sauce: marinara, Bordelaise, pesto, pomodoro, or homemade meat sauce. Other Italian specialties include eggplant parmigiana, chicken cannelloni, and ravioli stuffed with Italian sausage, spinach, and ricotta cheese. Desserts come from Bravo's sister restaurant, Anna Miller's, and should not be missed, especially the cappuccino ice cream sundae or any of Anna's fabulous pies.

Shanghai

Pearlridge Center, Phase 2. ☎ **808/488-0419.** Reservations not accepted. Main courses $5.95–$26.50 (most under $6.95). DISC, MC, V. Daily 11am–9pm. SZECHUAN.

This upscale little Chinese boite next to the Pearlridge Four-plex movie theatres always gets a good crowd when the movies break. It's a handsome place, with a "Happiness Gate" between the front and rear dining rooms, a collection of charming fans, and a bas-relief of golden dragons along the wall. Although the restaurant specializes in the fiery Szechuan-style cooking, you can order the dishes mild, and many of them resemble Cantonese-style cooking, which is certainly safe (albeit a bit boring). There are many vegetarian dishes, including Jai, which is not easy to find. Almond custard makes a cooling dessert.

8

Oahu Beaches & Outdoor Activities

by Jeanette Foster

When people usually think of Oahu, the Waikiki skyline, with its rows of hotels, or downtown Honolulu, with its canyons of tall buildings, are the images that immediately come to mind. Oahu, however, is much more than an urban jungle or a tropical Disneyland blighted by overdevelopment; it's also a haven for the nature lover and outdoor enthusiast. With year-round air temperatures in the upper 70s, ocean temperatures in the mid- to high 70s, and miles of verdant and unspoiled landscape, Oahu is perfect for outdoor activities of all kinds—hiking, golf, tennis, biking, horseback riding— Oahu has it all and much more. The island's waters, though, is where the majority of both residents and visitors head for relaxation, rejuvenation, and recreation. Locals don't think of their island or state boundaries as ending at land's edge—rather, they're beyond the reefs, well out into the ocean.

1 Beaches

Oahu has more than 130 beaches of every conceivable description, from legendary white-sand stretches to secluded rocky bays. Waikiki, of course, is the best known of Oahu's beaches, but there are many others—some more beautiful, all less crowded. What follows is a selection of the finest of Oahu's beaches, carefully chosen to suit every need, taste, and interest, from the sunbather in repose to the most ardent diver.

A Note of Caution: Keep in mind—wherever you are on Oahu— that you're in an urban area; never leave valuables in your car. Thefts do occur at Oahu's beaches, and locked cars are no deterrent.

WAIKIKI BEACH

The name of the world-famous two-mile stretch means "spouting water," probably referring to the duck ponds that once occupied this former swamp land. A crescent-shaped beach of imported sand on Oahu's south shore, Waikiki extends—interrupted periodically by sea walls, rock groins, and a yacht harbor—from the Ala Wai Canal to the foot of Mt. Leahi (better known as Diamond Head). Hawaii's most popular beach, Waikiki is nearly always crowded with tourists. You can experience nearly every imaginable type of ocean activity here: One of the best places on Oahu for swimming, Waikiki also offers both board and bodysurfing, outrigger canoeing, diving, sailing, snorkeling, and pole fishing. Every imaginable type of marine equipment and toy is available for rent. The many hotels that line the beach offer an array of food and drink. The best place to park is around Kapiolani Park. Facilities on the beach include showers, lifeguards, public restrooms, and picnic pavilions at the Queen's Surf end of the beach (near the park).

HANAUMA BAY

Formerly a playground for Hawaiian royalty, this beautiful bay is now a Marine Life Conservation District and the most popular snorkeling spot on Oahu for both visitors and residents. The enclosed 2,000-foot beach just east of Koko Head fronts a pristine bay, which is actually a volcanic crater open to the ocean on one side. Hanauma's shallow shoreline waters and bountiful marine life are both a blessing and a curse; the number of visitors to the bay is so overwhelming that some fear that the ecology of the marine preserve is in danger. Because of the existing threat, the government has restricted both parking and access by commercial operators. Since Hanauma Bay is a conservation district, taking anything from the ocean here is prohibited. Facilities include parking, restrooms, a picnic pavilion, grass volleyball court, lifeguard, barbecues, picnic tables, and a food concession. If you're driving, take Kalanianaole Highway to Koko Head Regional Park. To avoid the crowds and ensure yourself a parking space, go early on a weekday morning. Or, take TheBUS to escape the parking problem. The Hanauma Bay Shuttle runs from Waikiki to Hanauma Bay every half hour from 8:45am to 1pm; you can catch it at the Ala Moana Hotel, the Ilikai Hotel, or at any city bus stop on the route. It returns every hour on the hour from noon to 4pm. At this writing, the city regularly closes the bay on Wednesdays for maintenance.

SANDY BEACH

Also part of Koko Head Regional Park, Sandy Beach is one of the best bodysurfing beaches on Oahu. Unless you're experienced, though, you might be restricted to watching the expert bodysurfers and boogie boarders ride the waves and the chiseled bodies strut up and down the shore. This 1,200-foot-long beach is pounded by waves nearly all year long. The steep, quick drop-off underwater adds to the intensity of the waves and produces a strong, forceful backwash. The backwash is especially dangerous for children and weak swimmers; the lifeguards here make more rescues in a year than those stationed at any other beach except nearby Makapuu. Visitors unfamiliar with the beach and its dangers—and fooled by the experienced bodysurfers making wave-riding look so easy—all too often find themselves overwhelmed by the waves. As a result, the lifeguards have developed a flag system warning of the dangers of the day's surf: green means safe, yellow caution, and red indicates very dangerous water conditions. Be sure to check the flags before you dive in. Facilities include restrooms and parking. The best times to avoid the crowds are weekdays; the best times to watch top bodysurfers are weekends. TheBUS no. 22 (Kuhio) will get you there from Waikiki.

MAKAPUU BEACH PARK

At the base of the Koolau Mountains on Oahu's easternmost point is Makapuu Beach Park, the most famous bodysurfing beach in Hawaii. Movie fans will recognize this classically beautiful 1,000-foot-long white-sand beach, bordered by the stark black cliff of Makapuu Point, as a location for the famous Burt Lancaster–Deborah Kerr love scene in *From Here to Eternity*. Picturesque Rabbit Island lies just off the coast. During the summer months the ocean can be as gentle as a backyard pool, making swimming and diving a breeze; but extremely dangerous current and surf can be present from September through April, when the pounding waves erode the beach and expose rocks and boulders in the shorebreak area. Because these conditions are ideal for expert bodysurfers, board surfing is prohibited by state law. Small boards, 3 feet or less with no skeg (bottom fin), are permitted. Facilities include restrooms, lifeguard, barbecue grills, picnic tables, and parking. To get to Makapuu, follow Kalanianaole Highway toward Waimanalo. TheBUS no. 57 or 58 (Sea Life Park) will get you to there from Waikiki.

LANIKAI BEACH

Hidden by the residential area of Mokulua Drive on the windward side of the island, Lanikai is a beautiful mile-long beach that's safe for swimming and—with the prevailing trade winds—excellent for sailing and windsurfing. The fine, hard-packed sand along the shoreline is perfect for jogging. Offshore, the two tiny islands called the Mokuluas (which are sea-bird sanctuaries) are easily reachable by kayak. Because Lanikai is off the main roads, undeveloped, without facilities, and surrounded by residential homes, it's less crowded than other beaches on the windward side. It's the perfect place to claim a remote, isolated spot for a morning of swimming and relaxation. Sun-worshipers should arrive in the morning, as the Koolaus' shadow will block your access to the rays in the afternoon. From Waikiki, take TheBUS no. 56 or 57 (Kailua), then transfer to the shuttle bus.

KAILUA BEACH PARK

A 30-acre public park located on the east end of Kailua Bay, Kailua Beach Park is a broad, grassy area with picnic tables, a public boat ramp, restrooms, a pavilion, a volleyball court, and food stands. The wide, sandy beach area is popular for diving, swimming, sailing, snorkeling, and board and windsurfing. In fact, the dependable winds make this one of the more popular windsurfing areas on Oahu. The water conditions are generally safe, but parents should keep an eye on young children, who are often attracted to the brackish water pond in the middle of the park; the seemingly shallow pond has deep holes and has been the scene of several drownings. The park gets extremely crowded on weekends, when local families come here; the best time to come is weekdays. To get to Kailua Beach Park, take the Kalanianaole Highway or the Pali Highway to Kailua Road, which loops around to Kawailoa Road. Parking is available. From Waikiki, take TheBUS no. 56 or 57 (Kailua) into Kailua, then take the no. 70 shuttle.

KUALOA REGIONAL PARK

This park is listed in the National Register of Historic Places. In ancient Hawaii this was a very sacred spot; Hawaiian chiefs brought their infant children to Kualoa to be raised and trained as rulers. When canoes passed offshore, they lowered their sails in recognition of the sacredness of Kualoa. It is easy to see why this was considered a sacred place: the curtain of the Koolau Mountains provides a spectacular backdrop for this broad grassy park bordered by a white-sand beach, with the islet Mokolii (popularly known as Chinaman's Hat) in the distance. The offshore waters are shallow and safe for swimming year round; they're also excellent for kayaking and fishing. Lifeguards are on duty, and picnic and camping areas are available. Since both residents and visitors frequent this huge beach park, weekdays tend to be less crowded. The park is located on the Kamehameha Highway in Kauloa; you can take TheBUS no. 55 (Circle Island) to get there.

Oahu's Beaches

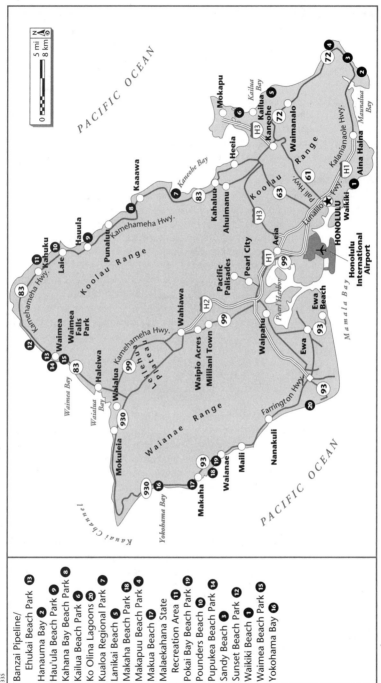

PACIFIC OCEAN

Mokapu

Kailua Bay

Mamalua Bay

Kalanianaole Hwy.

Heeia

Kaneohe Bay

Kaneohe

Waimanalo

Koolau Range

Aina Haina

Waikiki

HONOLULU

Kahaluu

Ahuimanu

Aiea

Pearl City

HONOLULU

Pacific Palisades

Honolulu International Airport

Pearl Harbor

Mamala Bay

Ewa Beach

Koolau Range

Koolau Punaluu

Kaaawa

Kamehameha Hwy.

Hauula

Laie

Kahuku

Waimea

Waimea Falls Park

Haleiwa

Waialua

Kamehameha Hwy.

Wahiawa

Waipio Acres Mililani Town

Waipahu

Ewa

Leilehua Plateau

Waianae Range

Farrington Hwy.

Nanakuli

Maili

Waianae

Makaha

Mokuleia

Waialua Bay

Waimea Bay

Yokohama Bay

Kauai Channel

PACIFIC OCEAN

1335

KAHANA BAY BEACH PARK

This white-sand, crescent-shaped beach is backed by a huge, jungle-cloaked valley with dramatic, jagged cliffs, and protected by ironwoods and *kamani* trees. The bay's calm water and shallow, sandy bottom make it a safe swimming area for children. The bay is famous for the *akule* (big-eyed scad), which come in seasonally. Other fish often taken here include *papio* and goatfish. The surrounding park has picnic areas, camping, and hiking trails, and the wide sand-bottom channel that runs through the park and out to Kahana Bay is one of the largest on Oahu—it's perfect for kayakers. Visitors and residents alike come to this relaxing beach, so weekdays are best. The Beach Park is located right on the Kamehameha Highway in Kahana; if you like, take TheBUS no. 55 (Circle Island) to get there.

HAU'ULA BEACH PARK

The nearby town of Hau'ula was named after the *hau* trees that used to be abundant in the area, and now are less so. During July and August, hau blooms every morning with a bright yellow flower; the yellow flowers change color as the day progresses, until they are a reddish gold by dusk and dark red by night, when they fall to the ground. The cycle is repeated the next day. Hau'ula Beach Park is a straight and narrow park, about 1,000 feet long, fronting the Kamehameha Highway, and shaded by kamani and ironwood trees. An offshore reef protects the waters off the beach, making the area safe for swimming, particularly since the bottom is shallow and rocky. Snorkeling is good along the edge of the coral reef, and fishing for papio and goatfish can be productive. There are picnic and camping facilities. Weekends tend to be more crowded. TheBUS no. 55 (Circle Island) will get you to Hau'ula Beach.

POUNDERS BEACH

Because of its easy accessibility and its great bodysurfing waves, Pounders is a popular weekend beach. The beach used to be called Pahumoa, after a local fisherman who arranged the local *hukilau* (catching fish in a net) and made sure that the elderly living in the area received a portion of the catch. The name change occurred in the 1950s, when a group of students at the Church College of the Pacific (now Brigham Young University-Hawaii) called the beach "Pounders" after the crushing shorebreak that provided brief but spectacular bodysurfing rides; the nickname stuck. Pounders is a wide beach, extending a 1/4-mile between two points. At the west end of the beach, next to the old landing, the waters usually are calm and safe for swimming; at the opposite end, near the limestone cliffs, there's a shorebreak that can be dangerous for inexperienced bodysurfers. The bottom here drops off abruptly, causing strong rip currents. Fishermen catch moi, oio, and papio here. Favored by local residents, weekends and after school are the busiest time for this beach; weekday mornings are the quietest. Park on Kamehameha Highway in Kailua, or take TheBUS no. 55 (Circle Island) to get here.

MALAEKAHANA STATE RECREATIONAL AREA

According to Hawaiian legend, a beautiful young princess, Laieikawai, was hidden here to guard her from mortal men. But word of her beauty got out, and many princes tried to woo her. Like the princess, this beautiful, long (over a mile), curving, sandy beach was once hidden from public access as the domain of wealthy families, who used the area for private beach homes. The state has since reclaimed the area and made it into a state park with public access, picnic areas, and camping. TheBUS no. 55 (Circle Island) takes you right to the park. As you enter through the main gate off Kamehameha Highway, two miles north of the Polynesian Cultural Center, you'll come upon the wooded beach park area; it's excellent for swimming, picnicking, and shore activities. There's no lifeguard here, but the beach is protected most of the year. Mokuauia (Goat) Island, which lies just offshore, is a state bird refuge. You can wade out to the island at low tide to visit secluded Mokuauia Beach, on the island's leeward shore. Surprisingly, very few visitors come to Malaekahana Beach, one of the best on Oahu—it's a true find.

SUNSET BEACH PARK

Surfers around the world know this famous site for the spectacular winter surf—the waves can be huge, thundering peaks reaching up 15 to 20 feet. Oddly enough, this surfing site wasn't really "discovered" until the 1940s; before that, surfers preferred Makaha. During the winter surf season, September to April, swimming is very dangerous here, due to the alongshore currents and powerful rip currents. The "Sunset rip" has been the site of numerous rescues, and has carried numerous surfboards out to sea. The only safe time to swim at Sunset is during the calm summer months. Sunset also features a huge sandy beach adjacent to the street. This is a great place to people watch, but don't go too near the water when the lifeguards have posted the red warning flags. One of the most popular beaches on the island, Sunset is the spot for local surfers, sunbathing beauties, and visitors wanting to get a glimpse of this world-famous surf spot. To avoid the crowds, mid-week is the best time to go. On the other hand, if you're looking for the crowds, try Saturdays and Sundays. Located right on Kamehameha Highway in Paumalu, TheBUS no. 52 (Circle Island) will get you there if you would rather not drive.

BANZAI PIPELINE/EHUKAI BEACH PARK

These are actually three separate areas, but since the sandy beach is just one continuous beach, with only one sign EHUKAI BEACH PARK, most people think of it as one beach park. Located near Pupukea, the actual Ehukai Beach Park is one acre of grass with a parking lot. The long, broad, white-sand beach is known for its winter surfing action. Swimming is good during the spring and summer months, but currents and waves prohibit safe swimming in the winter. The surf in front of Ehukai Beach Park is excellent for body and board surfers.

The park also provides access to Pipeline and Banzai. The Pipeline is actually about 100 yards to the left of Ehukai Beach Park. When the winter surf rolls in and hits the shallow coral shelf, the waves that quickly form are steep—so steep, in fact, that the crest of the wave falls forward, forming a near-perfect tube, or "pipeline." Surfers tried for years to master the pipeline; many were wiped out, suffering lacerations and broken bones on the shallow reef. The first surfer to ride the Pipeline successfully was Phil Edwards in the early 1960s. Even today, the Pipeline still causes injuries and a few fatalities. Just west of Pipeline is the area surfers call "Banzai Beach." The Japanese word *banzai* means "10,000 years"; it's given as a toast or as a battle charge, meaning "go for it." In the late 1950s, filmmaker Bruce Brown was shooting one of the first surf movies ever made, *Surf Safari,* when he saw a bodysurfer ride a huge wave. Brown yelled: "Banzai!" and the name stuck. In the winter, this is a very popular beach with surfers, surf fans, curious residents, and visitors; it's less crowded in the summer months. Ehukai Beach Park is located off Kamehameha Highway on Ke Nui Road, Pupukea. TheBUS no. 52 (Circle Island) will drop you on the highway.

PUPUKEA BEACH PARK

This 80-acre beach park is a Marine Life Conservation District; as such, it has strict rules about the taking of marine life, sand, corals, shells, or rocks. There are two major swimming areas in the Marine Life Conservation District: Sharks Cove and Three Tables. Don't worry: Shark's Cove, near the northern end, is not named for a plethora of sharks that call this home (in fact, it's relatively uncommon to see a shark here); rather, it's a popular snorkeling and dive site. Diving is best outside the cove, where caves promise interesting night diving. During the calm summer months, this is a popular dive site both day and night. At the southern end of the Marine Life Conservation District is Three Tables, which is named for the three flat sections of reef visible at low tide. Snorkeling is good around these tables where the water is about 15 feet deep. Diving outside the tables, where the water is 30 to 45 feet deep, is excellent—there are many ledges, arches, lava tubes, and a variety of marine life. Swimming, diving, and snorkeling are best from May to October, when the water is calm; nevertheless, watch out for surges. In the winter, when currents form and waves roll in, this area is very dangerous, even in the tidepools, and there is no lifeguard present. Summers find this Marine Life Conservation District brimming with visitors weekdays and weekends; this is a very popular site for local dive operators to take their clients. In the winter, it's nearly empty during the week. Located right on Kamehameha Highway in Pupukea; there's a very small parking lot. TheBUS no. 52 (Circle Island) stops at the park.

WAIMEA BEACH PARK

Despite what the Beach Boys' croon in their hit song (why-a-MEE-ah), the name of this famous surfing beach is pronounced why-MAY-ah. Waimea Bay is known in the surfing circuit as the home of some of the biggest ridable surfing waves in the world. During the winter—October to April—huge, pounding waves come rolling in, creating strong rip currents. Even expert surfers think twice when confronted with 30-foot waves. When the surf's up, it seems like everyone on Oahu drives out on Kamehameha Highway to Waimea to get a look at the monstrous waves and those who ride them. It's hard to believe that during the summer this same bay is glassy and calm, a great place for swimming, snorkeling, and diving. Since this beach is popular with local residents, weekdays are best. From Waikiki, take The BUS no. 52 (Circle Island) to get to Waimea Beach Park.

YOKOHAMA BAY

At the end of the paved Farrington Highway, this area abuts the 853-acre Kaena Point State Park, a remote and wild coastline preserve offering picnicking, hiking, swimming, and surfing. Also known as Keawalua Beach and Puau Beach, Yokohama got its name from the Japanese immigrants, originally from Yokohama, who traveled to this bay to fish. This is the last sandy stretch of shore on the northwestern coast of Oahu. There's a fairly wide beach between two rocky points. When the surf is calm (mainly during the summer) this is a good area for snorkeling, diving, swimming, and shore fishing. When the surf's up, the board and bodysurfers are out. Surfing can be dangerous here. There are no lifeguards, no facilities, and no bus service to this beach.

MAKUA BEACH

Visitors rarely sojourn to this long, gently curving sandy beach—known for its diving, fishing, swimming, and limited bodysurfing. Makua was a movie star in the 1960s, when it was used in the movie *Hawaii*. Swimming is good here during the calm summer months, but when the big swells roll in, so do turbulent and dangerous currents. The eastern end of the beach is popular for catching moi. The area off the Makua Cave has the best snorkeling. But be warned: There is no lifeguard here. Mostly local residents use this beach, which really never gets crowded. Located on Farrington Highway, there is no bus service.

MAKAHA BEACH PARK

Makaha means "fierce" or "savage," many people think the name refers to the giant surf and dangerous rip currents, shorebreaks, and backwashes that occur from October through April. But actually it alludes to a community of robbers who lived in the Makaha Valley and would threaten anyone who walked through. Today Makaha still may not be the safest place for visitors to roam, but when the surf's up at Makaha Beach it's spectacular. This is the original home of Hawaii's big-wave surfing championship: When the north or west swells run during the winter, monstrous waves pound the beach here. During the summer months, the waters are perfectly safe for swimming. To get to Makaha Beach from Waikiki, take TheBUS no. 51 (Makaha). You'll not find many visitors here; there's some sentiment in the local community that there are plenty of beaches for visitors and this beach should be reserved for local residents. Chances are good that no one will bother you, but you might want to respect these feelings and stop at another beach for swimming.

POKAI BAY BEACH PARK

This wonderful beach, off the beaten path for most visitors, offers excellent swimming year round, even when the rest of the Waianae shoreline is getting battered by heavy surf. A protected bay, the waters inside are calm enough for children and offer excellent snorkeling. The swimming area is marked by buoys. The Waianae area does have something of a parochial reputation for being xenophobic; however, local residents want the same thing most people want, guests who come with respect for local customs, conscious of being good stewards of the land, and with appreciation of the local resources—do what the natives do, pick up your garbage, don't play loud music, and be friendly. On weekdays, you can practically have the area to yourself. The beach park is located on Waianae Valley Road, off Farrington Highway. The BUS no. 51 will drop you off on the highway, and you can walk the block to the park.

KO OLINA

The developer of the 640-acre Ko Olina Resort has created four white-sand lagoons to make the rocky shoreline more attractive. Only two of these man-made lagoons are currently open. The northernmost lagoon, located adjacent to the Ihilani Resort and Spa, is the best. The nearly circular lagoon, with calm, shallow waters and a powdery white-sand beach bordered by a broad, grassy lawn, is the most attractive of the four lagoons. Lifeguards and restrooms are on the site, and the amenities and restaurants of the hotel are steps away. The other lagoon that's open right now is located three lagoons away from the Ihilani Hotel. There's plenty of public parking, a lifeguard station, and restrooms there. This scenic, calm lagoon is mainly used by local residents, but it doesn't have quite the ambience of the lagoon next to the hotel (only part of which is used by hotel guests). Located off H-1 in Kapolei, there is no local bus service to Ko Olina; the closest bus stop is on Farrington Highway, more than four miles away.

2 Water Sports & Recreation

Every type of water activity is pursued on Oahu, from professional surfers braving giant winter waves on the North Shore to recreational water skiiers enjoying the calm waters of Hawaii Kai. You can kayak from Lanikai Beach to the Mokulua Islands or float above Waikiki on a parasail as a speed boat tows you blissfully through the air. If you have something of an adventurous spirit, you might scuba dive the walls of the Kahuna Canyon, swim with clouds of *ta'ape* (butterfly fish), or view an occasional shark from the comfort of a passenger submarine. Whatever water recreation you might be interested in, whether you're a beginner or an expert, you can find it on Oahu.

BODYBOARDING (BOOGIE BOARDING) & BODYSURFING

Bodysurfing—riding waves without a board, becoming one with the rolling water—is immensely popular in Hawaii. Some bodysurfers just rely on their outstretched hands (or hands at their sides) to ride the waves. Others use handboards (flat, paddle-like gloves). An excellent beach at which to learn bodysurfing is Kailua. The best beaches for experts are Makapuu and Sandy Beach.

For additional maneuverability, try a boogie or bodyboard (also known as belly boards or paipo boards). These three-foot long vehicles, which support the upper part of your body, are easy to carry and very maneuverable in the water. The same open-heel fins that are used in bodysurfing are used in bodyboarding. The best place to learn boogie boarding is in the calm waters of Waikiki or Kailua Beach, under the careful watch of the lifeguards. The consistently gentle waves and generally placid conditions allow beginners to practice under ideal conditions. Once you get the feel of boogie boarding and are ready to test your skills against more aggressive waves, check out those at Point Panic (by Kewalo Basin) or Makapuu. When the waves are right, advanced boogie boarders will relish the challenge at Sandy Beach or Banzai Beach.

Boogie boards can be rented for as little at $8 a day from **Surf & Sea,** 62-595 Kamehameha Hwy., Haleiwa (☎ 808/637-9887), **Aloha Beach Service,** Sheraton Moana Surfrider Hotel, 2365 Kalakaua Ave., Waikiki (☎ 808/922-3111), and at all **Local Motion** locations: 1714 Kapiolani Blvd., Honolulu (☎ 808/955-7873), Koko Marina Shopping Center (☎ 808/396-7873), Windward Mall, Kaneohe (☎ 808/263-7873) and Pearl Kai Center, Aiea (☎ 808/486-7873). These outfitters will rent you the fins you need as well. Other places to rent boogie boards include **Downing Hawaii/Get Wet,** 3021 Waialaie Ave., Honolulu (☎ 808/737-9696), **Barnfield's Raging Isle Sports,** Haleiwa Market (☎ 808/637-7077), and **Leahi Beach Services,** Waikiki Beach (☎ 808/922-5277).

DEEP-SEA FISHING

The waters surrounding Hawaii are known the world over as one of the best places for big game sport-fishing. The largest blue marlin ever captured on rod and reel anywhere on the planet was landed on a charter boat operated by Capt. Cornelius Choy off Oahu. The monstrous fish weighed in at 1,805 pounds! No saltwater fishing license is required in Hawaii.

In addition to marlin (which, unlike other places, are caught in all 12 months of the year in Hawaii), you can try for sailfish, swordfish, various tunas, rainbow runner, mahimahi, wahoo, barracuda, trevally, bonefish, and various snappers, groupers, and other bottom fish. Some 28 current world fishing records were set in Hawaii for marlin, swordfish, tuna, rainbow runner, and trevally.

Charter boats can be contacted through most activities' desks or by walking the docks and talking with the captains; the latter method also allows you to make sure that they do the type of fishing you're interested in—fishing styles can range from bottom fishing to trolling for big game fish. Charter fishing boats range both in size—from small 24-foot open skiffs to luxurious 50-foot-plus yachts—and in price—from a low of less than $50 per person to "share" a boat with other anglers to more than $800 a day to book an entire luxury sport-fishing yacht on an exclusive basis.

Kewalo Basin, located between the Honolulu International Airport and Waikiki, is the main location for charter fishing boats on Oahu. Top sport-fishing boats from Kewalo Basin include the *Coreene-C II,* a 57-foot custom Sampan (☎ 808/226-8421), *Fish Hawk,* a 42-foot Uniflite (☎ 808/596-8338), *Kono Fishing Charters,* a 61-foot custom Sampan (☎ 808/536-7472), and *Sea Hawk,* a 42-foot Tollycraft (☎ 808/591-8888). To get to Kewalo Basin from Waikiki, take TheBUS no. 19 or 20 (Airport).

Boats are also available in Waianae and at Heeia Kea harbors. At Waianae Harbor, the sport-fishing charter-boat operations include: **Live Bait Charters,** a 31-foot Uniflite (☎ 808/695-9990), **Meagan Sport Fishing,** a 33-foot Luhrs (☎ 808/486-4854), and **Miss Makaha Sport Fishing,** a 32-foot Lugar (☎ 808/623-4450). In Haleiwa, you can fish with **Chupu Charters,** a 36-foot Vega (☎ 808/637-5689) or **Kuuloa Kai Charters,** a 26-foot Banana Patch (☎ 808/637-5783).

OCEAN KAYAKING

Gliding along the ocean, with only the sound of your paddle dipping into the water to disturb your peace, is what kayaking is all about. A popular sport on Oahu, there are several kayak clubs that have regularly scheduled outings and can provide visitors with useful information. The three I recommend are **Hui Waa Kaukahi,** P.O. Box 88143, Honolulu, HI 96744; **Kanaka Ikaika,** P.O. Box 438, Kaneohe, HI 96744; and **Women's Kayak Club of Hawaii,** P.O. Box 438, Kaneohe, HI 96744.

Neophytes who want to try this sport should go to **Waimea Valley,** Waimea Falls Park, 59–864 Kamehameha Hwy. (☎ 808/638-8511), on the North Shore for kayak lessons and equipment, at a cost of $15 per person. To get there, take TheBUS no. 52 (Circle Island). The kayaking takes place along the Waimea River and paddles out to the white sands of Waimea Bay, where kayakers can rest or swim.

For a guided kayaking tour, call **Kayak Oahu Adventure,** with locations in Haleiwa and Waikiki (☎ 808/593-4415). During the calm summer months from May to October, they lead 2¹/₂-hour tours along six miles of the North Shore. Starting at Waimea Falls, the kayaks are launched through the estuary and paddled out to the bay. From there, the 6 to 12 paddlers travel downwind, downcurrent, down the coast to finish at Haleiwa. All equipment (including reef walking shoes) is provided along with lessons for $59 per person.

Or, rent a kayak and go exploring yourself. Equipment rental starts at $10 an hour or $37 for a day; try **Prime Time Sports,** Fort DeRussy Beach, Waikiki (☎ 808/949-8952), or **Leahi Beach Service,** Waikiki (☎ 808/922-5277). In

Honolulu, you can rent kayaks from **Go Bananas,** 732 Kapahulu Ave., (☎ 808/ 737-9514). On the other side of the island, try **Kailua Sailboard,** 130 Kailua Rd., Kailua (☎ 808/262-2555) or **'Cuda Kayaks,** 789 Kailua Rd., Kailua (☎ 808/ 261-8424); 'Cuda will also deliver to your beach of choice. A wonderful adventure is to rent a kayak, arrive at Lanikai Beach just as the sun is appearing, and paddle across the emerald lagoon to the pyramid-shaped islands off the beach called Mokulua—it's an experience you won't forget.

PARASAILING

This relatively new ocean adventure sport is something of a cross between skydiving and water skiing. You sail through the air, suspended under a large parachute attached by a tow line to a speedboat. Ten-minute rides are $36 to $49 (*Hint:* book directly with the parasail company and save money; if you book through an activities center, you'll also pay their commission). Hawaii's original parasail company, **Aloha Parasail,** (☎ 808/521-2446) takes you over the Waikiki and Ala Moana coastlines. They also provide free pick-up service. Or, try **Sea Breeze Parasailing,** Koko Marina (☎ 808/396-0100), the largest parasail business on the island; or **Big Sky Parasail,** Koko Marina Shopping Center (☎ 808/396-0564) and Hawaii Kai Shopping Center (☎ 808/396-9224).

SAILING

From a two-hour sunset sail to a day-long adventure on the waves, Oahu offers a variety of sailing activities, including sailing lessons—picture yourself at the helm! **Honolulu Sailing Co.,** 47–335 Lulani, Kaneohe (☎ 808/239-3900), has been in the business for nearly two decades, providing everything from weddings at sea to honeymoon cruises, sailing-snorkeling sails, private lessons, and exclusive charters. The fleet ranges from 36- to 70-foot yachts. Charters start at $50 per person and lessons start at $125 per person per day.

Tradewind Charters, 1833 Kalakaua Ave., Honolulu (☎ 808/973-0311), also provides a range of sailing options, including private sailing lessons on boats ranging from 29 to 36 feet, starting at $39 an hour per student. Their fleet of boats, located at Keehi Marine Center (15 minutes from Waikiki, just off Nimitz Highway at 24 Sand Island Rd. also features sunset and moonlight sails from $65 per person for a three-hour sail, half-day adventure snorkeling sails from $59 per person with snorkeling equipment included, and private interisland and overnight cruises starting at $495 a day. For a snorkel-picnic sail, call **North Shore Catamaran Charters,** Haleiwa (☎ 808/638-8279). From May to January, they offer four-hour sails on their 40-foot catamaran, which holds 25 passengers, with stops for snorkeling and a picnic lunch. The cost for this half-day adventure is $48, including all snorkel gear.

Watch the sunset as you enjoy a five-course continental dinner, drinks, and entertainment aboard the *Navatek I,* off Waikiki (☎ 808/848-6360). The boat's revolutionary SWATH (Small Waterplane Area Twin Hull) design guarantees a smooth, comfortable ride, even for those prone to seasickness. The ride is so smooth that it feels more like a train than a boat. This new technology allows the boat to not only cruise Waikiki's scenic coastline, but to go beyond Diamond Head (where most boats turn around because of rough seas). The Sunset Cruise (which departs from Honolulu Pier 6) costs $150, including transportation to and from Waikiki. *Navatek I* also has a luncheon cruise with Hawaiian entertainment for $45, and a candlelight dinner and moonlight cruise, with entertainment and transportation from Waikiki for $75. Other dinner-cruise boats which sail past Waikiki in the sunset include *Windjammer,* from Honolulu Pier 7 (☎ 808/537-1122), offering a range of dinners priced from $72.50 to $103.75; and the *Ali'i Kai* **Catamaran Sunset Dinner Cruise,** from Honolulu Pier 5 (☎ 808/524-6694), which offers a range of Polynesian shows and dinners starting at $48.

SCUBA DIVING

Scuba (which is the abbreviation for Self-Contained Underwater Breathing Apparatus) involves using a personally carried source of air to allow lengthy exploration underwater. Oahu is a wonderful place to scuba dive, especially for those interested in wreck diving. One of the more famous wrecks in Hawaii is the *Mahi,* a 185-foot former mine sweeper easily accessible just south of Waianae. Abundant marine life makes this a great place to shoot photos—schools of lemon butterfly fish and *ta'ape* are so comfortable with divers and photographers that they practically pose. Eagle rays, green sea turtles, manta rays, and white-tip sharks occasionally cruise by, and eels peer balefully from the wreck.

Right off the shores of Waikiki lies another accessible wreck, the 110-foot long *YO 257.* Built in the 1940s, this former yard oiler was purposely sunk to create an artificial reef in 1989. Almost immediately, the vessel began attracting marine life: amberjacks, trumpet and coronet fish, tangs and surgeon fish, even moray eels. This is a great place for underwater photo buffs, because the ship sits at 100 feet, with the pilot house at 55 feet and the main deck at 85 feet. Other popular wrecks are *Corsair* (off Maunaloa Bay) and Seaplane Wreck (off Pokai Bay).

For non-wreck diving, one of the best dive spots in the summer is Kahuna Canyon. In Hawaiian, *kahuna* translates as priest, wise man, or sorcerer; this massive amphitheater, located near Mokuleia, is a perfect example of something a sorcerer might conjure up: Walls rising from the ocean floor create the illusion of an underwater Grand Canyon. Inside the amphitheater, crabs, octopus, slipper, and spiny lobsters abound (be aware that taking them in the summer is illegal). Giant trevally, parrotfish, and unicorn fish congregate here. Outside the amphitheater, an occasional shark can be seen in the distance.

The North Shore is loaded with magical dive spots with mystical names like Devil's Rock, Waialua Wall, Turtle Heaven, and Waimea Walls. For night dives, stay right on the North Shore. Three Tables, located in the Marine Life Conservation District of Pupukea Beach, features lobsters, eels, octopuses, a variety of tropical fish, and the occasional shark.

But before you can experience all of this you have to become a certified diver. Since vacation time is precious, take a dive class at home so when you arrive in Hawaii you're prepared to dive. If you are unsure if scuba diving is for you, most dive operators offer what is known as an introductory dive. No experience is necessary (the cost ranges from $40 to $95), and you'll learn if this glimpse into the Neptune's world makes you hunger for more.

Since the best dives on Oahu are offshore, we suggest that you book with a dive operator for a two-tank dive from their dive boat. **Atlantis Reef Divers,** 1085 Ala Moana Blvd. (☎ 808/592-5801), offers two-tank dive trips at $74. One dive is in the *YO-257* wreck and the other is in a shallower reef canyon famous for its green sea turtles. Free hotel pick-up is available in the Waikiki area. Atlantis also offers to videotape your dive—a great way to take Hawaii home with you. On the other side of the island, try **Ocean Concepts Scuba,** 94–547 Ukee St., Waipahu (☎ 808/677-7975); they'll take you diving in local lava caves, volcanic ledges, and the *Mahi* wreck. Prices range from $45 to $220, depending on the number of dives you do. Other dive tour operators include: **Dive Waikiki,** Waikiki Beach (☎ 808/949-3483); **Mahi Divers,** 85–371 Farrington Hwy., Waianae (☎ 808/696-7200); **Rainbow Divers,** Waianae (☎ 808/625-7190); and **South Pacific Scuba,** 740 Kapahulu Ave., Honolulu (☎ 808/735-7196).

If you prefer to dive on your own, write for a copy of the *Dive Hawaii Guide* by Dive Hawaii, a non-profit association, and the University of Hawaii Sea Grant Extension Service. Listed are 44 locations, which are also mapped and described. Send $2 to UH/SGES, 100 Pope Rd., MSB 226, Honolulu, HI 96844, attention: Ray Tabata.

SNORKELING

You don't need to take courses to enjoy snorkeling—all you need is a mask, fins, and a snorkel. A word of advice on snorkeling equipment: Many tour operators provide equipment for free, but if your equipment doesn't fit you, it's all but worthless. There's nothing worse than having a snorkeling trip ruined by a leaky mask. You might want to make the investment (about $15 a week) and rent snorkel gear that fits. If you wear eyeglasses, you should be able to rent a suitable prescription mask for an extra charge. The piece of equipment that must fit well is your mask: It should stick to your face without the strap when you inhale (make sure all hair is away from the mask—men with moustaches often have leakages in that area). Fins should fit comfortably and float (you are snorkeling, not swimming great distances, so monstrous fins are not necessarily better, unless you're a swimmer in training).

Snorkel rentals are available at most dive shops and beach activity centers, including **Aloha Dive Shop,** Koko Marine Shopping Center (☎ 808/395-5922), the closest dive shop to the underwater park at Hanauma Bay, and **Leahi Beach Services,** Waikiki Beach (☎ 808/922-5277). For snorkel rental, instruction, and tours, contact **Snorkel Bob's,** also on the way to Hanauma Bay at 700 Kapahulu Ave., Honolulu (☎ 808/735-7944); **Haleiwa Surf Center,** 66–167 Haleiwa Rd., Haleiwa (☎ 808/637-5051); and **Paradise Snorkel Adventure,** Waikiki (☎ 808/923-7766).

Some of the best snorkeling in Oahu is at the underwater park at Hanauma Bay. It's crowded and sometimes it seems there are more people than fish, but Hanauma has clear, warm waters, an abundance of friendly reef fish, scenic beauty, protection from the waves, and it's easy to get there. Go early (by 10am it's packed). Take TheBUS to avoid the crowded parking conditions. For full transit and shuttle information—or directions, if you choose to drive—see "Beaches," above. At this writing, the city regularly closes the bay on Wednesdays for maintenance. Hanauma Bay has two reefs, an inner and an outer—the first for novices, the other for experts. The inner reef is calm and shallow (less than 10 feet; in some places you can wade and put your face in the water). Here you'll experience clouds of reef fish, including Moorish idols, scores of butterfly fish, damsel fish, and wrasses.

Serious snorkelers should send for a copy of the book *Dive Hawaii Guide;* for full details, see "Scuba Diving," above.

SNUBA

This new underwater activity is a cross between snorkeling and scuba diving. It gives you the benefit of being able to stay underwater without the required certification and equipment needed for scuba. Snuba utilizes an air tank floating in a raft on surface. A 20- to 25-foot hose is attached to the air tank and provides air for the diver, so that he or she can stay down without the hassle or responsibility of a bulky air tank on their back. **Snuba Tours of Oahu,** 172 Nawiliwili (☎ 808/922-7762), offers tours from $65 to $95, which includes hotel pick-up, equipment, and instruction.

SUBMARINE DIVING

Here's your chance to play Jules Verne and experience the beauty of the underwater world, all in the comfort (air-conditioned, comfortable seating) of a 65-foot submarine. *Atlantis* **Submarines Hawaii,** 1600 Kapiolani Blvd. (☎ 808/973-9811), will be happy to take you below the surface. A catamaran picks you up at the Hilton Hawaiian Village hotel dock in Waikiki, and takes you to the sub, moored offshore. The submarine (equipped with large portholes) dives to 100 feet for a view of the underwater world. The entire trip is narrated, with professional divers outside the sub feeding the tropical fish so you can get a close look at the critters of the deep. The tour is $79 for adults and $38 for children.

Voyager Submarines Hawaii, 1085 Ala Moana Blvd., Honolulu (☎ 808/592-7850 or 808/592-7851), also offers tours of the deep. Passengers board a 90-foot catamaran at Kewalo Basin for a six-minute ride, with views of Waikiki and Diamond Head, to the submarine moored offshore. As the submarine descends to Kewalo Reef, an ancient lava flow 80 feet beneath the surface, passengers can see the underwater world through 30-inch-wide viewports or via the color video monitors at each seat. For the next 35 minutes, the submarine explores the reef. The first stop is Trumpetfish Cove, a lava outcropping with cauliflower coral and flittering tropical reef fish. Next stop: Urchin Hill, covered with hundreds of red spiny urchins. The sub then begins its trip across the face of the reef, passing volcanic rocks and boulders, clouds of reef fish, colorful corals and, occasionally, dolphins. The 73-foot sub weighs 99 tons and is certified by the U.S. Coast Guard to dive to 150 feet. Price (which includes round-trip bus transfers from Waikiki) is $92.71 for adults and $51.04 for children 12 and under. Children must be at least 36 inches tall to board the submarine.

SURFING

In the summertime, when the water is warm and there's a soft breeze in the air, the south swell comes up. It's surf season in Waikiki, the best place to learn how to surf on Oahu. At last count, Oahu had more than 100 surf sites—this is the place to be when the waves are happening. Winter in Hawaii also means waves—monstrous waves—on the North Shore. These are not the gentle swells of summer, lapping lazily on the shore. These mountains of water, 20-plus feet tall, explode when they collapse on the beach; the ground rumbles.

Surfing is the sport Hawaii has given to the world. The ancient origins of surfing in Hawaii can be seen in carved petroglyphs and in ancient chants traced back to the 15th century. The Hawaiians looked upon surfing not only as a sport (a betting sport, at that, with spectators wagering property on their favorite wave rider), but also as a religious experience. The Hawaiian word for surfing, *he'e nalu,* can be translated literally to mean wave sliding; but a more poetic translation—and one favored by surfers—summons up a metaphor of a newborn baby slipping from a terrifying, roaring, surging saltwater womb.

During the months of November and December, the world championship of surfing, the Triple Crown, is held in Hawaii, a three-event series that concludes the year-long Association of Surfing Professional's World Tour. Even if you've never given surfing much thought, this event is exciting—it's the Super Bowl of surfing; more than 60 surfing competitions held throughout the world lead up to this event. Some $2.5 million in prize money is given away to the men and women, the greatest surfers in the world, who can best the monstrous waves.

While you're in Hawaii, don't pass up the opportunity to experience surfing. To learn to surf, go early to **Aloha Beach Service,** next to the Sheraton Moana Surfrider Hotel in Waikiki (☎ 808/922-3111). The beach boys offer surfing lessons for $25 an hour and board rentals are $8 for one hour and $12 for two hours. The only requirement is that you know how to swim. Surf lessons are also offered in Waikiki by **Leahi Beach Services** (☎ 808/922-5277). In Haleiwa, check out the surf lessons at **Surf & Sea,** 62-595 Kamehameha Hwy. (☎ 808/637-9887), and **Barnfield's Raging Isle Sports,** 66-250 Kamehameha Hwy. (☎ 808/637-7707).

More experienced surfers should check with the myriad surf shops around Oahu, or call **808/596-SURF** (Surf News Network Surfline) or **808/836-1952** to get the latest information on the surfing conditions. A good surfing spot for advanced surfers is The Cliffs, at the base of Diamond Head. The four- to six-foot waves churn in here, allowing high-performance surfing. And the view of Diamond Head is great, which helps to make this place a paradise for surfers.

Surf-board rentals in Honolulu are available at: **Downing Hawaii/Get Wet,** 3021 Waialae Ave. (☎ 808/737-9696); **Local Motion,** 1714 Kapiolani Blvd. (☎ 808/955-7873); **Planet Surf,** 415 Nahua St. (☎ 808/926-2062); and **Recon Surf,** 1652 Wilikina Dr. (808/621-5153).

SWIMMING

For a quiet, peaceful place to swim, **Malaekahana Bay,** near Kahuku, is one of the best Oahu beaches. This mile-long, white-sand, crescent-shaped beach is about a 90-minute drive and a million miles from the crowds at Waikiki. To get there, take Kamehameha Highway past Laie and follow the signs to Malaekahana State Recreational Area. Or, take TheBUS no. 52 (Circle Island). Another good swimming beach is **Lanikai:** Secluded and calm, this beach is great for families. From Waikiki, take TheBUS no. 56 or 57 (Kailua), then transfer to the shuttle bus.

WATER SKIING

Water skiing in Hawaii? Yes, Virginia there is water skiing on Oahu; in fact there's even an Oahu Waterski Club, which sponsors water-skiing competitions. To learn to water-ski or to go out and practice a few turns, call the oldest water-ski center in Hawaii, **Suyderhoud Water Ski Center,** Koko Marina Shopping Center (☎ 808/395-3773). To get there from Waikiki, take TheBUS no. 58 (Sea Life Park). Lessons are $49. Half-day packages for three hours of boat time plus equipment rental are $89 per person, with a four-person limit.

WHALE WATCHING

From December to April, 45-foot humpback whales—Hawaii's most impressive visitors—come to spend the winter. They make the journey from Alaska to calf and mate in Hawaii's calm, warm waters. Once nearly hunted to extinction, humpback whales are now protected by federal law. The animals may not be approached by any individual or watercraft within 100 yards.

Whales can frequently be seen off the island on calm days. If you spot the familiar spout of water—a sign the whale is exhaling—there's a good chance that you'll see the animal on the surface. If you're in a car, please pull over, as numerous accidents have occurred when visitors try to spot whales and drive at the same time.

For whale watching outside of Waikiki, the *Navatek I,* from Honolulu Pier 6 (☎ 808/848-6360), offers 2¹/₂-hour whale-watching cruises from January to April. If you fear seasickness, this is the boat for you. *Navatek I* is designed with a revolutionary technology called SWATH (Small Waterplane Area Twin Hull), which makes the boat very stable with a smooth ride (minimal motion, which prevents seasickness). The whale-watching cruise features an Earthtrust naturalist on board every trip to answer questions and to point out interesting facts about these leviathans. The cost of this morning cruise is $39 for adults and $24 for children ages 5 to 12 years old; children under 5 years old are free.

Tradewind Charter, which operates out of Keehi Marine Center (☎ 808/973-0311), also offers whale-watching charters from late December to early May. The four-hour excursion on one of their sailing yachts is $59 for adults and $20 for children age 12 and under. On the North Shore, **North Shore Catamaran Charters,** Haleiwa (☎ 808/638-8279), offers a three-hour whale-watching cruise on their 40-foot catamaran from January to April; the cost is $30 per person.

WINDSURFING

This is another ocean activity that combines two sports: sailing and surfing. Windsurfers stand on a surfboard that has a sail attached to it, thus bringing the wind and the waves together in a ride that enthusiasts claim is a real adrenalin rush. On Oahu, Kailua Beach Park on the windward side is the home of champion and pioneer windsurfer Robbie Naish. It's also the best place to learn. The oldest and most established windsurfing business in Hawaii is **Windsurf Hawaii,** 156-C Hamakua Dr., Kailua (☎ 808/261-3539). The company offers everything: sales, rentals, instruction, repair, and free advice on where to go when the wind and waves are happening. Lessons start at $37.50 and equipment rental is $25 for a half day and $30 for a full day. Or, you can just venture out to the North Shore to watch the windsurfers dance over the waves. **Kailua Sailboard Company,** 130 Kailua Rd., Kailua (☎ 808/262-2555), also offers instructions, rentals, and sails; they specialize in beginners. In Haleiwa, windsurfing lessons and instructions are available from **Surf and Sea,** 62-595 Kamehameha Hwy. (☎ 808/637-9887).

3 Hiking

Oahu offers much beyond its urban sprawl: carved mountains, verdant valleys, tropical rainforests, secluded beaches. In fact, Oahu has more forest hiking trails than the Big Island of Hawaii, which is six times Oahu's size. The remote beauty of many of the island's forests, waterfalls, and scenic overlooks, though, can only be reached on foot.

For complete information on Oahu's hiking trails and to obtain free trail maps, contact the **Honolulu Department of Parks and Recreation,** 650 S. King St., Honolulu, HI 96813 (☎ 808/527-6343), and the **State Division of Forestry and Wildlife,** 1151 Punchbowl, Room 325, Honolulu, HI 96813 (☎ 808/587-0166). For information on trails, hikes, camping, and permits in all state parks, contact the **Hawaii State Department of Land and Natural Resources,** State Parks

Division, P.O. Box 621, Honolulu, HI 96825 (☎ 808/587-0300). Another good source of information is the *Hiking/Camping Information Packet* from **Hawaii Geographic Maps and Books,** 49 S. Hotel St., Suite 218, Honolulu, HI 96813 (☎ 808/538-3952), for a cost of $7 (postage included).

The **Hawaiian Trail and Mountain Club,** P.O. Box 2238, Honolulu, HI 96804, offers regularly scheduled hikes on Oahu. You bring your own lunch and drinking water and meet up with the club at the Iolani Palace to join them on a hike. They also have an information packet on hiking and camping in Hawaii, as well as a schedule of all upcoming hikes; send $1.25, plus a legal-sized, self-addressed, stamped envelope to the address above. The **Sierra Club,** 1111 Bishop Street, Honolulu, HI 96813 (☎ 808/538-6616), also offers regularly scheduled hikes on which they welcome visitors. The **Hawaii Nature Center** (☎ 808/955-0100) is another group that offers organized hikes, as well as "Sunday Adventures" for children. Some of their activities require a small fee, but some are free.

Some of Oahu's best hikes are:

KAENA POINT

At the very western tip of Oahu lie the dry, barren lands of Kaena Point. The 853 undeveloped acres of Kaena Point State Park consist of a remote, wild coastline of jagged sea cliffs, deep gulches, sand dunes, endangered plantlife, and a wind- and surf-battered coastline. Kaena means "red hot" or "glowing" in Hawaiian; the name refers to the brilliant sunsets visible from the point.

Kaena is steeped in legend. A popular one concerns the demigod Maui: Maui had a famous hook that he used to raise islands from the sea. He decided that he wanted to bring the island of Oahu and Kauai closer together, so one day he threw his hook across the Kauai Channel and snagged the island of Kauai (which actually is visible from Kaena Point on clear days). Pulling with all his might, Maui was only able to pull loose a huge boulder, which fell into the waters very close to the present lighthouse at Kaena. The rock is still called *Pohaku o Kauai* (the rock from Kauai). Like Black Rock in Kaanapali on Maui, Kaena is thought of as the point on Oahu from which souls depart. According to tradition, when someone is near death, their soul leaves their body and wanders around, making sure that all their earthly obligations have been filled. If all is right, then the soul proceeds to Kaena to leap from this world into the next.

To hike out to the place where souls depart, take the clearly marked trailhead from the parking lot of the Makua-Kaena Point State Park. The moderate, five-mile round-trip hike to the point will take a couple of hours. The hike begins with scrub *haole koa,* but then the brilliant yellow flowers of *ilima papa* and the light blue flowers of *pau o hiiaka* appear in the dry weeds. In the seemingly barren dunes, look for the half-crowns of white-flowered *naupaka* and the purple flowers of the *pohinahina* nestled in the gray-green leaves. Occasionally, you can spot the rare *ohai,* a dark orange-red flower with muted green leaves. The trail along the cliff passes tide pools abundant in marine life and rugged protrusions of lava reaching out to the turbulent sea; sea birds circle overhead. During the winter and spring months, Laysan albatrosses nest in the sandy areas of the point.

There are no sandy beaches and the water is nearly always turbulent. During the winter months, when a big north swell is running, the waves at Kaena are the biggest in the state, averaging heights of 30 to 40 feet. Even when seemingly calm, the offshore currents are incredibly powerful, so don't plan to swim. Occasionally

Outdoor Activities On Oahu

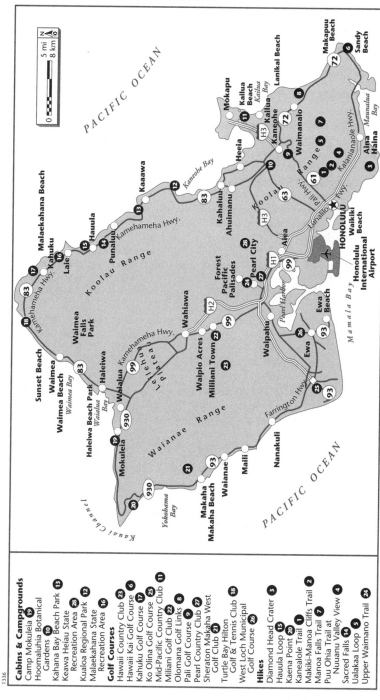

Cabins & Campgrounds
Camp Mokuleia ⑲
Hoomaluhia Botanical Gardens ⑩
Kahana Bay Beach Park ⑬
Keawa Heiau State Recreation Area ㉘
Kualoa Regional Park ⑫
Malaekahana State Recreation Area ⑯

Golf Courses
Hawaii Country Club ㉓
Hawaii Kai Golf Course ⑥
Kahuku Golf Course ⑰
Ko Olina Golf Course ㉕
Mid-Pacific Country Club ⑪
Mililani Golf Club ㉒
Olomana Golf Links ⑧
Pali Golf Course ⑨
Pearl Country Club ㉗
Sheraton Makaha West Golf Club ㉑
Turtle Bay Hilton Golf & Tennis Club ⑱
West Loch Municipal Golf Course ㉖

Hikes
Diamond Head Crater ③
Hauula Loop ⑮
Kaena Point ⑳
Kaneaole Trail ①
Makiki-Manoa Cliffs Trail ②
Manoa Falls Trail ⑦
Puu Ohia Trail at Nuuanu Valley View ④
Sacred Falls ⑭
Ualakaa Loop ⑤
Upper Waimano Trail ㉔

✈ Airport

1336

you'll see a cobblestone "beach" along the rugged lava shoreline. Go early in the morning to see the school of dolphins that frequent the area just offshore.

To get to the trailhead from Honolulu or Waikiki, take the H-1 Freeway west to its end; continue on Hi. 93 past Makaha and follow Hi. 930 to the end of the road. There is no bus service to Kaena Point.

UPPER WAIMANO TRAIL

This is a strenuous, 14-mile round trip with an altitude gain of nearly 2,000 feet. But the rewards are worth it: magnificent views from the top of windward Oahu's Koolau Mountains, and a chance to see rare native Hawaiian plants. Plan a full day for this eight-hour hike. To get there from Waikiki, take TheBUS nos. 8, 19, 20, or 58 to the Ala Moana Shopping Center and transfer to TheBUS no. 53. Tell your driver where you are going and he will take you as far as he can on Waimano Home Road; you'll have to walk the rest of the way to the trailhead. If you have a car, take the H-1 to the Pearl City exit (Exit 10) on Moanalua Road; head north and turn right on Waimano Home Road; follow it to the end, just over 22 miles. Park on the road.

Pick up the trailhead at the dirt path to the left of the gate, outside the fence surrounding the Waimano Home. Follow the trail through swamp mahogany trees to the first junction; turn right at the junction to stay on the upper Waimano Trail. At the second junction, turn right again to stay on the upper trail. The Christmas berry becomes denser, but as you move up the mountain, koa, kukui, hau, mango, guava, mountain apple, and ginger start to appear. You'll know you are getting closer to the stream bed when the mosquitoes begin buzzing. Cross the stream bed and climb the switchbacks on the eucalyptus-covered ridge. More native plants begin to appear: ohia, uluhe, and koa. Just before you reach the crest of the next ridge, look for rarely seen plants like yellow-flowered *ohia lehua, kanawao* (a relative of the hydrangea), and mountain *naupaka*. The trail ends on the sometimes rainy—and nearly always windy—peak of the Koolaus, where you'll have views of Waihee Valley and the entire windward side from Kahaluu to Kaneohe Bay. It's very clear that this is the end of the trail; retrace your steps to the trailhead.

KANEALOLE TRAIL

This is the starting place for some of Oahu's best hiking trails; miles of trails converge through the area. To get a general feel for the hikes in the area, take this 1^1/$_2$-mile round-trip moderate hike, which climbs some 500 feet and takes less than an hour. To get there, take McCully Avenue north out of Waikiki; cross over the H-1 Freeway and turn left on Wilder Avenue. Make a right turn on Makiki Street and continue until the road forks at the park. Take the left fork past the Makiki Pumping Station; the road is now called Makiki Heights Drive. Follow it up to the hairpin turn and make a right on to the small spur road which goes into Makiki Valley; park just beyond the green trailers that house the Hawaii Nature Center. (After parking, you might want to stop in at the Hawaii Nature Center; not only does it have information on the plants and animals of Hawaii, but it also has excellent maps and pamphlets on the nearby trails. The center also sponsors unique hikes through the area.) If you are taking the bus, it's a little trickier: From Waikiki, take TheBUS no. 8, 19, 20, or 58 to the Ala Moana Shopping Center and transfer to TheBUS no. 17. Tell your driver where you're going, and he'll let you off near the spur road just off Makiki Heights Drive; you'll have to walk the rest of the way.

Continue walking uphill past the Hawaii Nature Center, under the protection of kukui and lush vines. The road gets smaller and smaller until it's just a footpath. Along this narrow path, look for the tall, bushy grass-like plant, called Job's Tears. While it's considered a weed in Hawaii, this is no ordinary grass; it can grow up to five feet high and produces a grey, tear-shaped seed. The trail continues through an abandoned valley where there once was a thriving Hawaiian community. Occasionally you'll spot the remains of stone walls and even a few coffee plants; Makiki Valley supported a coffee plantation in the last century. When you meet the Makiki Valley Trail, you can retrace your steps, or choose from the dozens of trails in the area.

MAKIKI-MANOA CLIFFS TRAIL

From rain forests to ridgetop views, this somewhat strenuous loop trail is one you'll never forget. The hike is just over six miles, gains 1,260 feet in elevation, and takes about three hours. To get to the trailhead, follow the directions for the Kanealole Trail (see above). This trail is part of the labyrinth of trails found in this area.

The trail starts by the restrooms of the Hawaii Nature Center. Look for the paved path that crosses Kanealole Stream via a footbridge (Maunalaha Trail). Stay on the trail, following it up the hill into the forest, where you'll pass bananas, Norfolk and Cook island pines, ti plants, even a few taro patches. Cross over Moleka Stream and look for the four-way junction with the Makiki Valley and Ualakaa trails; turn right on the Makiki Valley Trail. This takes you through a dense forest, past a giant banyan tree, and then joins with the Moleka Trail. Turn left on the Moleka Trail—now you're in the rain forest: ancient guava trees reach overhead, maiden hair ferns cling to rocks, tiny white-flowered begonias crop up.

Further on, the kukui and koa give way to a bamboo-filled forest, which opens up to a parking lot on Round Top Drive at the end of the Moleka Trail. Cross Round Top Drive to the Manoa Cliffs Trail, which emerges on Tantalus Drive. Turn right on Tantalus and walk about 100 yards down the street to the Nahuina Trail on the left side of Tantalus. As you walk downhill, you'll have breathtaking views of downtown Honolulu. At the junction of Kanealole Trail, turn right and continue back to where you started.

DIAMOND HEAD CRATER

The entire family can handle this easy walk to the summit of Hawaii's most famous landmark. Children will especially love reaching the top of the 760-foot volcanic cone, where they'll have 360-degree views of Oahu up the leeward coast from Waikiki. The 1.4-mile round trip will take about an hour.

Diamond Head was created by a volcanic explosion about a half-million years ago. The Hawaiians called the crater Leahi (meaning the brow of the *ahi,* or tuna, referring to the shape of the crater). Diamond Head was considered a sacred spot; King Kamehameha offered human sacrifices at a *heiau* (temple) on the western slope. It wasn't until the 19th century that Mt. Leahi got its current name. A group of sailors found what they thought were diamonds in the crater. It turned out they really only found worthless calcite crystals, but the Diamond Head moniker stuck.

Before you begin your adventure hiking to the top of the crater, gather a flashlight (you walk through several dark tunnels), binoculars (for better viewing at the top), water, and your camera (the panoramic view definitely should be captured on film). Go early in the day. To get to the hike, take TheBUS no. 58 from the Ala Moana Shopping Center or drive to the intersection of Diamond Head Road and 18th Avenue. Follow the road through the tunnel (which is closed from 6pm to 6am) and park in the lot. The trailhead starts in the parking lot and proceeds along a paved walkway (with handrails) as it climbs up the slope. You'll pass old World War I and II pillboxes, gun emplacements, and tunnels built as part of the Pacific defense network. Several steps take you up to the top observation post on Point Leahi. The views are indescribable.

PUU OHIA TRAIL TO NUUANU VALLEY VIEW

This moderate hike takes you through a rainforest, up to the top of Tantalus (Puu Ohia) cinder cone, and down through Pauoa Flats to view Nuuanu Valley. Plan nearly two hours for this 3½-mile round-trip hike, which gains about 1,200 feet in altitude. No buses service this area. To get there, follow the directions given to the Kanealole Trail, above, but turn to the right at the park fork in Makiki Street. The fork to the right is Round Top Drive; drive to the top and park in the turn-out.

The Puu Ohia trailhead is located across the street from where you parked. As you head up (a series of switchbacks and, at the steepest, hand-cut stairs in the dirt) you pass night-blooming jasmine, ginger, Christmas berry, and avocado trees. After dense guava trees and bamboo, the vegetation parts for a magnificent view of Honolulu and Diamond Head. Just as quickly, as you continue along the trail, the bamboo once again obstructs the view. At the next junction stay on the main trail by bearing to the left; you'll pass through ginger, koa, and bamboo. At the next junction, bear left again, and climb up the steps around the trunk of an old koa tree. At the top is a paved road; turn right and walk downhill. The road leads to an old telephone relay station, then turns into a footpath. Passing through bamboo, koa, ti, and strawberry guava, turn left onto the Manoa Cliffs Trail. At the next junction, turn right on the Puu Ohia Trail, which leads to the Pauoa Flats and to the view of the Nuuanu Valley. Retrace your steps for your return.

UALAKAA LOOP

The same series of volcanic eruptions that produced Diamond Head and Koko Crater also produced the cinder cones of Round Top (Puu Ualakaa), Sugarloaf (Puu Kakea), and Tantalus (Puu Ohia). Puu, as you may have already guessed, means hill; these three hills overlook Honolulu and offer spectacular views. The easy Ualakaa Loop Trail is a half-hour hike of about a mile that traverses through woods, offering occasional panoramic views of Honolulu. There's no bus service to this trailhead. Follow the directions for the Puu Ohia hike, above, but instead of driving to the top of Round Top Drive, turn off on the fourth major hairpin turn (look for it after a long stretch of panoramic straightaway). The turn will go through the gate of the Puu Ualakaa State Wayside Park. Continue a little more than four miles inside the park; look for a stand of Norfolk Pine trees and park there. The trailhead is on the right side of the Norfolk Pines. The park is open from 7am to 7:45pm from April 1 to Labor Day; after Labor Day, the park closes at 6:45pm.

The loop trail, lined with impatiens, passes through more Norfolk Pines, palm trees, ironwoods, and Christmas berry trees. The once native forest now has many foreign intrusions—including all of the foregoing—as well as native ti, banana, banyan, guava, and mountain apple. At two points along the trail, you emerge on Round Top Drive; just walk about 100 feet to continue on the trail on the opposite side of the road. The loop will bring you back to where you started.

Manoa Falls Trail

This is the most accessible hike through a rain forest and to a waterfall in Honolulu. It's also an easy two-mile round trip that should take about an hour, depending on how much time you spend at the waterfall. This area gets about 100 inches of rainfall a year, so be prepared for rain, muddy trails, and mosquitoes. To get there from Waikiki, take McCully Street, cross over the H-1 Freeway and turn left on Wilder Avenue, then right on Punahou Street. Punahou curves around Punahou School and becomes Manoa Road. At the fork, bear right to stay on Manoa Road. Park by Paradise Park. To get there via TheBUS, take TheBUS no. 5 from the Ala Moana Shopping Center as far as it goes up Manoa Valley; you'll have to walk the rest of the way.

However you've arrived, walk up Manoa Road, past Paradise Park and Lyon Arboretum. Just past Lyon Arboretum, a chain blocks vehicles from continuing on the road; the trailhead starts here. You'll cross over the Aihualama Stream and pass over a sometime muddy trail lined with kukui, African tulip, guava, and mountain apple trees. A series of switchbacks around a huge banyan tree brings you to the falls. At the base of the falls lies a pool big enough for children to wade in. Avoid the pool up high, since rocks are occasionally swept over the falls. The area above the falls is a closed watershed and entry is prohibited.

Sacred Falls

It's easy to see why this place was given the name "Sacred." Clear, cold water, originating from the top of the Koolau Mountains, descends down the Kaluanui Stream and cascades over Sacred Falls into a deep, boulder-strewn pool. The hike to this awe-inspiring waterfall passes under guava and mountain apple trees and through a fern-filled narrow canyon that parallels the stream bed.

A few words of warning before you grab your walking shoes and hiking boots: Do not attempt this hike in wet weather. In fact, the State Parks Division closes the falls if there is a danger of flash floods. This is no idle warning—in 1987, five hikers attempting to reach the falls died in three separate incidents while the normally babbling stream was flooded. In October 1993, a Boy Scout troop had to be rescued by helicopter during a flash flood. Another warning of a more human kind: Go in a group—there have recently been a few muggings along the 2.2-mile trail.

The best time to take this hike is in the morning, when the light is good. Be prepared with rain gear and insect repellent. The easy 4.4-mile round trip will take about two to three hours. To get to the trail, drive north on the Kamehameha Highway (Hwy. 83) to the turn off for Sacred Falls State Park, or take TheBUS no. 20 (Circle Island). The trail begins at the parking lot and heads for the mountains, paralleling the Kaluanui Stream. About a mile into the trail is a grassy area with emergency warning equipment inside a cyclone fence; the trailhead is to the left of the fence. The beginning is a bit rough—the trail is muddy and passes under tangled branches and through a tunnel of Christmas berry. About a half-mile beyond the trailhead, you'll cross the Kaluanui Stream; if the water is high or muddy, don't cross—you could become trapped in the canyon during a flash flood. As you continue up the trail, the canyon becomes increasingly narrow, with steep walls on either side. Be on the lookout for falling rocks. At the end of the trail are the majestic falls and deep pool. The extremely cold pool is home to spidery Malaysian prawns and other species.

HAUULA LOOP

For one of the best views of the coast and the ocean, follow the Hauula Loop Trail on the windward side of the island. It's an easy 2¹/₂-mile loop on a well-maintained path that passes through a whispering ironwood forest and a grove of tall Norfolk Pines. The trip takes about three hours and gains some 600 feet in elevation. To get to the trail, take TheBUS no. 55 (Circle Island) or take Hwy. 83 to Hauula Beach Park. Turn toward the mountains on Hauula Homestead Road; when the road forks to the left at Maakua Road, park on the road. Walk along Maakua Road to the wide, grassy trail that begins the hike into the mountains.

The climb is fairly steep for about 300 yards, but continues on to easier-on-the-calves switchbacks as you go up the ridge. Look down as you climb; you'll find wildflowers and mushrooms among the matted needles. The trail continues up, crossing Waipilopilo Gulch, where you'll see several forms of native plantlife. Eventually you reach the top of the ridge, where the views are spectacular.

The Division of Forestry does permit camping along the trail, but it's difficult to find a place to pitch a tent on the steep slopes and in the dense forest growth. There are a few places along the ridge wide enough for a tent. Contact the **Division of Forestry and Wildlife,** 1151 Punchbowl St., Honolulu, HI 96813 (☎ 808/587-0166), for information on camping permits.

4 Golf

There are numerous golf courses located all over Oahu, from reasonably priced public golf courses (with very long waiting lists for tee times, of course) to spectacularly beautiful resort courses. For the golf courses listed below, cart costs are included in the greens fees, unless otherwise noted.

SHERATON MAKAHA WEST GOLF CLUB COURSE

Some 45 miles west of Honolulu is this challenging golf course, surrounded with tropical beauty (swaying palm trees, brilliantly colored bougainvillea, even strutting peacocks), that will put you in the mood to fine-tune your game. Designed by William Bell, the par-72, 7,091-yard course meanders toward the ocean before turning and heading into the Makaha Valley. With the Waianae range rising in the background, the beauty of the course might make it difficult to keep your mind on the game if it weren't for the challenges of it: eight water hazards, 107 bunkers, and constant wind. Facilities include a pro shop, bag storage, and a snack shop. This course is packed on weekends, so it's best to try weekdays. To get there, take TheBUS no. 51-A (Makaha). Greens fees are $150 for non-residents of Hawaii; they drop to $90 after noon on weekdays. Twilight rates are available. Call **808/695-9544.**

KO OLINA GOLF COURSE

Golf Digest named this 6,867-yard, par-72 course one of "America's Top 75 Resort Courses" in 1992. The Ted Robinson–designed course has rolling fairways and elevated tee and water features. The signature hole—the 12th, a par-3—has an elevated tee that sits on a rock garden, with a waterfall cascading just a few feet away from the tee into a landscaped garden. Wait until you see the 18th hole; you'll see and hear water all around you—seven pools begin on the right side of the fairway and slope down to a lake, and a waterfall is on your left off the elevated green. You'll have no choice but to play the left and approach the green over the water. There is a dress code for the course: Men are asked to wear shirts with a collar. Facilities include a driving range, locker rooms, Jacuzzi/steam rooms, and a restaurant/bar. Lessons and twilight rates are available. This course is crowded all the time. Greens fees are $165. Book in advance by calling **808/676-5300.** There's no bus service to the course.

HAWAII COUNTRY CLUB

This public course, located in central Oahu in Wahiawa, is a modest course where golfers usually have no trouble getting a tee time. The 5,861-yard, par-71 course is not manicured like the resort courses, but it does offer fair play, with relatively inexpensive greens fees ($28 for weekdays and $39 on weekends, cart included). Located in the middle of former sugar cane and pineapple fields, the greens and fairways tend to be a bit bumpy and there are a number of tall monkeypod and pine trees to shoot around, but the views of Pearl Harbor and Waikiki in the distance are spectacular. There are a few challenging holes, like the seventh (a 252-yard, par-4), which has a lake in the middle of the fairway and slim pickings on either side. With the wind usually blowing in your face, most golfers choose an iron to lay up short of the water and then pitch it over for par. Facilities include a driving range, practice greens, club rental pro shop, and restaurant. Call **808/621-5654** for tee times.

MILILANI GOLF CLUB

It's usually easy to get a tee time within a week at this par-72, 6,360-yard public course, located in the suburban residential area of Mililani. The course is popular with nearby residents, so tee times are easiest to get during the week. Situated between the Koolau and Waianae mountain ranges on the Leilehua Plateau, the views of the mountains are breathtaking from every hole. Unfortunately, there are also lots of views of trees—eucalyptus, Norfolk pines, and coconut palms. This is the place to practice staying on the fairways, or you'll suffer the penalty of playing from the trees. In fact, the par-5, 520-yard, 13th hole has a row of African Tulip trees, aflame in brilliant orange-red flowers, bordering the right side of the fairway. Carts are included in the greens fees, which are $83 on weekdays and $91 on weekends; call **808/623-2222** at least a week in advance for tee times. Facilities include a driving range, practice greens, club rental, a pro shop, and a restaurant.

WEST LOCH MUNICIPAL GOLF COURSE

This municipal course is located about 30 minutes from Waikiki in Ewa Beach, surrounded by residential neighborhoods. This 6,615-yard, par-72 course is a very challenging municipal course. The big factors here are water—there are lots of water hazards—and constant trade winds, combined with narrow fairways. In fact, the entire layout of the Robin Nelson and Rodney Wright–designed course is a bit unusual. The first hole plays right in front of the clubhouse; the next 10 holes are located on the other side of the freeway, and holes 12 to 18 are back on the starting side of the freeway. You'll have some help on the water hazards; the course features a "water" driving range, complete with a lake to practice your drives. This is a popular course (greens fees are only $36, including cart) so be sure to call **808/676-2210** at least one week in advance to get a tee time. Facilities include the "water" driving range, practice greens, pro shop, and restaurant.

PEARL COUNTRY CLUB

Looking for a challenge? This popular public course, located just above Pearl City in Aiea, has all the challenges you can imagine. Sure, the 6,230-yard, par-72 looks harmless enough, and the views of Pearl Harbor and the *USS Arizona* Memorial are gorgeous; but around the fifth hole, you'll start to see what you're in for. That par-5, a blind 472-yard hole, doglegs quite seriously to the left (with a small margin of error between the tee and the steep out-of-bounds hillside on the entire left side of the fairway). A water hazard and a forest await your next two shots. Suddenly, this nice public course becomes not so nice. Oahu residents can't get enough of this course, so don't even try to get a tee time on weekends; stick to weekdays—Mondays are usually the best bet. Greens fees are $75, including cart. Call **808/ 487-3802** at least a week in advance. Facilities include a driving range, practice greens, club rental, pro shop, and restaurant.

HAWAII KAI GOLF COURSE

If you're staying in Waikiki, this par-72, 6,350-yard course is reasonably close, located between Sandy Beach and Makapuu Point. To get there, take TheBUS no. 58 (Circle Island). This is a moderately challenging course with scenic vistas, and the greens fees are easy on the pocketbook—$80; rates for the par-3 course are a mere $37. Lockers are available. Call **808/395-2358** for tee times.

OLOMANA GOLF LINKS

This is a gorgeous course located in Waimanalo, on the other side of the island from Waikiki. The low-handicap golfer may not find this course difficult, but the striking views of the craggy Koolau Mountain Ridge are worth the greens fees alone. The par-72, 6,326-yard course is very popular with local residents and visitors. The course starts off a bit hilly on the front nine, but flattens out by the back nine. The back nine have their own special surprises, including tricky water hazards. The first hole, a 384-yard, par-4 that tees downhill and approaches uphill, is definitely a warm-up. The next hole is a 160-yard, par-3 which starts from an elevated tee to an elevated green over a severely banked, V-shaped gully. Shoot long here—it's longer than you think—as short shots tend to roll all the way back down the fairway to the base of the gully. This course is very, very green; the rain gods bless it regularly with brief passing showers. You can tell the regular players here—they all carry umbrellas and wait patiently for the squalls to pass, then resume play. Reservations are a must; call **808/259-7926**. Greens fees are $80, including cart. Facilities include a driving range, practice greens, club rental, pro shop, and restaurant.

PALI GOLF COURSE

This beautiful municipal course sits on the windward side of the island near Kaneohe, just below the historical spot where King Kamehameha the Great won the battle to unite the islands of Hawaii. Built in 1953, this par-72, 6,494-yard course has no man-made traps, but it does have a small stream that meanders through the course. If you're off line on the ninth, you'll get to know the stream quite well. The course, designed by Willard G. Wilkinson, makes use of the natural terrain (hills and valleys that make up the majority of the 250 acres). The challenge of the course is the weather—whipping winds and frequent rain squalls. The views include Kaneohe Bay, the towns of Kailua and Kaneohe, and the verdant cliffs of the Koolau Mountains. Due to the frequent rains, you might want to pay for just nine holes and then check out the weather before signing up for the next nine.

Greens fees are $30, plus another $12 for an optional cart. Call **808/296-7254** for tee times. Facilities include practice greens, club rental, locker rooms, and a restaurant.

MID-PACIFIC COUNTRY CLUB

This is a rare chance for non-members to play on a private course. The public is invited to play this par-72, 6,848-yard course on weekdays (most private golf clubs on Oahu do not allow non-members to play unless accompanied by a member). Don't pass up the opportunity to experience this challenging, unique course, located in the beachside community of Lanikai, on the windward side of the island. The first nine holes were designed by Seth Raynor and opened for play in 1928; 20 years later, the next nine opened. In 1981, William Bell brought the course up to date, but left the basic design alone. The most challenging hole is the fifth, a par-5, 517-yard dogleg left, bordered on the right by a tributary from Enchanted Lakes and by another small lake on the left. The green is on a narrow, 39-yard island in the tributary. *Hint:* use a mid- to long-iron (check the wind conditions). Regular players make the green in two—better two than one in the drink. Greens fees are $120, cash only; no credit cards are accepted. Reservations are taken one day in advance only; call **808/261-9765.** Facilities include a driving range, practice greens, club rental, locker rooms, pro shop, and restaurant.

TURTLE BAY HILTON GOLF & TENNIS CLUB

Chose either the George Fazio–designed 9-hole course—this is the only course he designed in Hawaii—or the 18-hole Links at Kuilima, designed by Arnold Palmer and Ed Seay—*Golf Digest* rated it the fourth best new resort course in 1994. Turtle Bay used to be labeled a "wind tunnel;" it still is one, but the ironwood trees have matured and abated the winds somewhat. But Palmer-Seay never meant for golfers to get off too easy—this is a challenging course. The front nine holes, with rolling terrain, only a few trees, and lots of wind, play like a British Isles course. The back nine holes have narrower, tree-lined fairways and water. The course circles Punahoolapa Marsh, a protected wetland for endangered Hawaiian waterfowl. To get to Turtle Bay, take TheBUS no. 52 or 55 (Circle Island). Facilities include a pro shop, driving range, putting and chipping green, and snack bar. Greens fees are $99 for the Links at Kuilima and $55 for the 18-holes on the 9-hole course. Twilight rates are available. Weekdays are best for tee times; call **808/293-8574.**

KAHUKU GOLF COURSE

Okay, so this is only a nine-hole municipal course and there are no facilities, except a few pull carts that go out with the first few golfers. But this oceanside course has beautiful views, a peaceful country location, and 1950s' prices. This is strictly recreational golf, but you'll get plenty of exercise since you'll most likely have to carry your clubs and walk. Holes 3, 4, 7, and 8 are right on the shoreline, offering gorgeous views of the North Shore. The par-3 holes are not as easy as they look; the greens are small, so you better be accurate right from the tee or you'll be in trouble. No reservations are taken; tee times are available on a first-come, first-served basis (and there are a lot of retired residents who don't mind getting there early). Greens fees are $19 for nine holes; a pull cart (if available) is another $1. No club rentals are available, so be sure to bring your own. *Hint:* if you are staying in Waikiki, call **808/293-5842** to check on the weather, as it can be sunny and clear in Waikiki and rainy and windy in Kahuku.

5 Other Outdoor Activities

Oahu is a great place to fulfill all your outdoor needs, and even a dream or two: You can gallop on horseback over a white-sand beach at sunset or jump out of an airplane and parachute to the island's surface. You can play a game of tennis at dawn or watch international racing yachts cross the finish line at Diamond Head. Oahu even has an ice skating rink. The top professional football players can be seen at the annual Pro Bowl game in Honolulu, and top cowboys from across the country compete in a rodeo competition that draws people from all over the globe.

BICYCLING

For a guided bicycling adventure, try the Bike & Hike at **Kualoa Ranch,** Ka'a'awa (☎ 808/237-7321). Mountain bike through the scenic Ka'a'awa Valley (seen in the movie *Jurassic Park*), then hike to Hakipuu Ridge for a panoramic view of the 4,000-acre Kualoa Ranch, situated between Kaneohe Bay and the Koolau Mountain Range. The adventure ends with a barbecue lunch at the Ranch's private beach retreat. Cost is $59 and includes a complimentary water bottle. Thrill seekers will enjoy the two-hour downhill bike ride at **Waimea Valley,** Waimea Falls Park (☎ 808/638-8511). The $60 fee includes park admission, rental of bike and safety equipment, the two-hour bike tour, and a complimentary water bottle.

For those who prefer to venture out on their own, **Island Triathlon and Bike,** 569 Kapahulu Ave. (☎ 808/732-7227), has mountain-bike rentals complete with lock, pump, repair kit, and helmet for $25 the first day and $10 for each additional day. They are also in the know about upcoming bicycle events or interesting bike rides you can enjoy on your own. Bike rentals are also available in Waikiki at **Blue Sky Rentals,** 1920 Ala Moana Blvd. (☎ 808/947-0101); **Coconut Cruisers,** across from the International Market Place on Kalakaua Ave. (☎ 808/924-1644); and **Wiki Wiki Wheels,** 2310 Kuhio Ave. (☎ 808/923-5544).

If you would like some company while you bike, contact the **Hawaii Bicycle League,** P.O. Box 4403, Honolulu, HI 96812 (☎ 808/735-5756). Not only will they fix you up with someone to ride with, but they can also provide you with a schedule of upcoming rides, races, and outings.

GLIDING

Silently soaring through the air on gossamer-like wings, with a bird's-eye view of Northern Oahu and the multihued reefs below, is an experience you won't want to miss. You can take a glider ride from Dillingham Air Field, in Mokuleia, on Oahu's North Shore. A one- or two-passenger glider is towed behind a plane; at the right altitude, the tow is dropped and you're left to soar in the thermals—it's the ride of a lifetime. The gliders are grounded only 30 days out of the year, when the normal northerly trade winds shift to southerly winds. You can book rides right up to the night before your flight; you can even chance showing up on the day you want to fly, but you may have to wait. To book glider rides, call **Glider Rides** (☎ 808/677-3404 or 808/637-4551); Mr. Bill at Glider Rides has been offering piloted rides longer than anyone else on the island (since 1970). The cost is $60 for one person (plus pilot) for a 20-minute ride, and $90 for two passengers. If you get bit by the gliding bug, Glider Rides also offers instruction at $45 to $70 per session. **Soar Hawaii** (☎ 808/637-3147) also offers glider rides, starting at $70 for one passenger and $75 for two. Be sure not to leave the ground without your camera!

HORSEBACK RIDING

Kualoa Ranch, 49-560 Kamehameha Hwy., Kaneohe (☎ 808/237-8515), has a number of different tours through the 4,000-acre ranch, starting at $45. Be sure to wear long pants and closed-toe shoes. **Senator Fong's Plantation and Gardens,** 47-285 Pulama Rd., Kaneohe (☎ 808/239-6775), has guided horseback rides throughout the park starting in the gardens and venturing up into the rainforest. The tours range from one to three hours, starting at $30. Or, gallop on the beach at the **Turtle Bay Hilton Golf & Tennis Resort,** 57-091 Kamehameha Hwy., Kahuku (☎ 808/293-8811); one-hour tours start at $32. Other horseback trail rides are available through **Happy Trails Hawaii,** Kahuku (☎ 808/948-1235), which has rides with views of Waimea Bay. **Hoku Ranch,** located on the Dole Plantation, 64-1550 Kamehameha Hwy., Haleiwa (☎ 808/622-2100), offers rides through pineapple fields and up into the mountains with views of a lake and a waterfall.

If you've dreamed of learning how to ride, the **Hilltop Equestrian Center,** 41-430 Waikupanaha St., Waimanalo (☎ 808/259-8463), offers lessons in either British or Western riding style from British Horse Society–accredited instructors for $35.

ICE SKATING

Believe it or not, ice skating is popular in Hawaii—there's even a local hockey league. The place to skate is the **Ice Palace** at Stadium Mall, 4510 Salt Lake Blvd. (☎ 808/487-9921). Admission (which includes skate rental) is $6. Weekends and evenings are packed; mid-week afternoons are best.

SKYDIVING

Everything you need to leap from a plane and float to earth can be obtained from **Blue Sky Rentals and Sports Center,** 1920 Ala Moana Blvd. (☎ 808/947-0101), for $225 per jump (including suit, parachute, goggles, plane rental, etc.). For instructions, call **SkyDive Hawaii,** 68-760 Farrington Hwy. (☎ 808/637-9700), which has a first-jump course for $300 (includes equipment), or a seven-jump course for $1,000. If you want to try skydiving first to see if you like it, they also offer a tandem jump (where you're strapped to an expert who wears a chute big enough for the both of you) for $225. There's no doubt about it–this is the thrill of a lifetime. Other skydiving instruction centers at the Dillingham Airfield include **Pacific International Skydiving Center** (☎ 808/637-7472), **Parachutes Hawaii** (☎ 808/623-7076), and **Tandem Hawaii,** (☎ 808/637-8544).

TENNIS

Oahu has 181 free public tennis courts. To get a complete list of all facilities, as well as any upcoming tournaments, contact the **Department of Parks and Recreation,** 650 S. King St., Honolulu, HI 96813 (☎ 808/523-4182). The courts are available on a first-come, first-served basis; playing time is limited to 45 minutes.

If you're staying in Waikiki, the **Ilikai Sports Center** at the Ilikai Hotel, 1777 Ala Moana Blvd. (☎ 808/949-3811), has six courts, equipment rental, lessons, and repair service. Courts are $7.50 per person per hour. If you're on the other side of the island, the **Turtle Bay Hilton Golf & Tennis Resort,** 57-091 Kamehameha Hwy., Kahuku (☎ 808/293-8811, ext. 24), has 10 courts, 4 of which are lighted for night play. You must make reservations for the night courts in advance, as they are very popular. Court rates are $12 for the entire day. Equipment rental and lessons are available. The "Thursday Night Mixer" is a very popular activity where both resort guests and nonguests, including local residents, participate in a clinic from 5pm to 7pm for $9 per person.

Tennis instruction is available through **Alan's Tennis Etc.,** 7534 Muolea Pl. (☎ 808/395-4341); **Peter Burwash International** (☎ 808/735-3661); and **Waipahu Racquet Surf and Sport,** 1831 S. King St. (☎ 808/941-4911).

6 Spectator Sports

Even though Hawaii isn't home to professional football, baseball, or basketball teams, Islanders love these sports and play them in organized leagues. The 50,000-seat **Aloha Stadium,** located near Pearl Harbor (☎ 808/486-9300), is host to high school and University of Hawaii football games. It's also the home of three televised football games a year: the Aloha Bowl (top collegiate teams) during Christmas week, the Hula Bowl in January (an all-star game of the top college senior players), and the Pro Bowl (the National Football League's all-star game) played right after the Super Bowl at the beginning of February. There are usually express buses that will take you to the stadium on game nights; they depart from Ala Moana Shopping Center (TheBUS nos. 47–50 and 52) or from Monsarrat Avenue near Kapiolani Park (TheBUS no. 20). Call TheBUS at **808/848-5555** for times and fares.

The **Neal Blaisdell Center,** at Kapiolani Blvd. and Ward Ave. (☎ 808/521-2911), features the University of Hawaii basketball games—in December you can see the Annual Rainbow Classic, a collegiate basketball invitational tournament—plus professional boxing, Japanese sumo wrestling, and other sporting events. For bus information, call TheBUS at **808/848-5555.**

Another popular spectator sport on Oahu is polo, which is played every Sunday from March through August in Mokuleia or Waimanalo. Bring a picnic lunch and enjoy the game. Call **808/637-7656** for details on times and admission charges.

Hawaiian outrigger canoe racing is an extremely popular local sport that takes place every weekend from Memorial Day to Labor Day at various beach parks around Oahu. The races are free and draw huge crowds. Check the local papers for information on the race schedule.

Motor-racing fans can enjoy their sport at **Hawaii Raceway Park,** in Campbell Industrial Park (☎ 808/682-7139), on Friday and Saturday nights.

Some of the other spectator sports that are scheduled during the year are:

Morey Boogie World Bodyboard Championships. In January at the Bonzai Pipeline, depending on the surf conditions. For information call **808/396-2326.**
Hawaiian Open Golf Tournament. Top professional golfers participate in this nationally televised PGA tournament at the Waialae Country Club in January. For information call **808/526-1232.**
Buffalo's Big Board Surfing Classic. This colorful, old-style surfing competition—on long boards—takes place in February in Makaha. For information call **808/525-8090.**
Hawaiian Ladies Open. Top women golfers from the United States and Japan compete at Ko Olina Golf Course in February for a $500,000 purse. For information call **808/676-9957.**

America's Favorite Pastime, Hawaiian Style: Winter Baseball

Where else in the United States can you indulge in the national pastime beside swaying palms—in the middle of winter? Nowhere else, we suspect, but Hawaii. The winter of 1996 will mark the fourth season for the Hawaii Winter Baseball League. This is professional baseball, played each year from mid-October to mid-December. There are two Oahu-based teams: the Honolulu Sharks, who play at Rainbow Stadium at the University of Hawaii; and the West Oahu Cane Fires, who play on the leeward side at Hans L'Orange Park in Waipahu; These are all top-notch players and prospects from the United States, Japan, and Korea. Each teams plays some 54 games in 60 days, with the championship game at the end of the season, on December 15. While going to a baseball game anywhere is a uniquely—and universally—American experience, we think it's just a multicultural blast in the islands. Ticket prices are extremely reasonable—from $4 to $6—for an entire even-ing of fun. Even if you don't like baseball, go for the food. We hear the chili dogs at Maui's War Memorial Stadium are the best anywhere! And we know there are no other ball parks where you can also get a Japanese Bento or a teriyaki plate.

For schedules, consult the local papers or call the team offices: Honolulu Sharks, 808/973-1935; West Oahu Cane Fires 808/973-7247.

—Faye Hammel

Hawaii Challenge International Sport Kite Championship. Kite fliers from around the world gather in Kapiolani Park in March to compete. For information call **808/922-5483.**

Hawaiian Professional Rodeo. In April cowboys compete in rodeo events in Waimanalo, which are rounded out with barbecue, country music, and dancing in the dirt for a true Hawaiian *paniolo* experience. For information call **808/235-3691.**

Hawaiian Classic Senior Men's Ice Hockey Tournament. Skating aces from Hawaii compete in April at the Ice Palace. For information call **808/487-9921.**

Bankoh Kayak Challenge. This open-ocean kayak race from Molokai to Oahu takes place in May. For information call **808/254-5055.**

Kenwood Cup. This international yacht race is held during July in odd-numbered years only, so you won't be able to catch this one until 1997. Sailors from the United States, Japan, Australia, New Zealand, Europe, and Hawaii participate in a series of races around the state. For information call **808/946-9061.**

Hawaiian Open Ice Skating Competition. Top skaters compete for honors in July at the Ice Palace. For information call **808/487-9921.**

Na Wahine O Ke Kai. This 41-mile, open-ocean Hawaii outrigger canoe race from Molokai to Waikiki, which happens in September, attracts international teams. For information call **808/262-7567.**

Outrigger Hotels Hawaiian Oceanfest. The top lifeguards from around the world compete in various ocean sports in Waikiki during the month of September. For information call **808/521-4322.**

Waikiki Rough-Water Swim. This popular two-mile, open-ocean swim from Sans Souci Beach to Duke Kahanamoku Beach in Waikiki takes place in September. For information call **808/522-7045.**

Bankoh Molokai Hoe. Top outrigger-canoe teams from around the world compete in a 41-mile, open-ocean race from Molokai to Waikiki in October. For information call **808/261-6615.**

Outrigger Top Gun Hydrofest. From the flying Blue Angels performing acrobatics to hydroplane racing, this is a fun week of aerial activities at Pearl Harbor in October. For information call **808/254-6788.**

Triple Crown of Surfing. The top surfing events held in Hawaii, these November to December competitions include the Pipeline Masters, the Hawaiian Pro, and the World Cup of Surfing. For information call **808/623-8409.**

Honolulu Marathon. More than 20,000 runners descend on Honolulu for the world's second largest 26.2-mile race in December. For information call **808/734-7200.**

What to See & Do in Honolulu

This is a city with more than the usual share of diversity and excitement, with a rich cultural past and a stimulating, cosmopolitan present. How to see it need present no problem at all. If time is short or if you want to get an overall bird's-eye view before you begin in-depth exploring, simply take one of the excellent commercial sightseeing tours that hit all the major points (see "Organized Tours and Activities," below). Or you can rent a car and drive to all the things you want to see (details on car rentals can be found in Chapter 5, "Getting to Know Oahu"). But even without benefit of a car or guided tour, you can get around very well indeed. Honolulu is, after all, a major U.S. metropolis, and it has an excellent public transportation system, called TheBUS. For 85¢ cents a ride plus a little ingenuity and determination, you can get almost anywhere in Honolulu you want to go. (For complete information on TheBUS, see "Getting Around" in Chapter 5.)

SUGGESTED ITINERARIES

If You Have 1 Day

Get up early, drive or take TheBUS to the USS *Arizona* Memorial at Pearl Harbor. Spend the rest of the day touring the Bishop Museum or loafing on Waikiki Beach.

If You Have 2 Days

Spend the first day as above, the second day driving around the island of Oahu, seeing the Polynesian Cultural Center and the world-class surfers and other daredevils at Waimea, Sunset, and Banzai beaches. If it's summertime, take a dip in the calm North Shore waters.

If You Have 3 Days

Spend the first two days as above, and on day three spend the morning snorkeling at Hanauma Bay. In the afternoon, take a walking tour of downtown Honolulu. Stop in at the Mission Houses Museum, Iolani Palace, and the Hawaii Maritime Center, and take a stroll through historic Chinatown.

If You Have 5 Days or More

Spend the first three days as above. Then visit the National Memorial Cemetery of the Pacific at Punchbowl Crater. Study the masterpieces at the Honolulu Academy of Arts. Take an easy hike to the summit of Diamond Head for spectacular Waikiki and ocean views. Whatever you do, be sure to save yourself plenty of beach and relaxation time!

1 The Top Attractions

In the pages ahead, we outline for you the major sights of Honolulu. These sights will show you what Hawaiian life was and is like, from the days of the early Polynesian settlers through the missionary period and the era of Hawaiian royalty, through the trying years of World War II, and into Space Age Hawaii of the 1990s.

HISTORIC HONOLULU

✪ Bishop Museum

The State Museum of Natural and Cultural History, 1525 Bernice St. ☎ **808/847-3511.** Admission (including a 1pm daily music and dance presentation and entrance to the Bishop Museum Planetarium—see below) $7.95 adults, $6.95 children 6–17, active military, and seniors; children under 6 free. Daily 9am–5pm. Closed Christmas Day. Take TheBUS no. 2 to School and Kapalama Sts.; walk one block makai on Kapalama, then turn right on Bernice St.; entrance is midblock.

One of the most important natural and cultural history museums of the Pacific, the Bishop Museum makes the world of the early Polynesian settlers come alive. You'll see such Hawaiian artifacts as outrigger canoes, a model **heiau,** the intricate feather cloaks of the **alii,** and other rare treasures. There's an exciting collection of pre-industrial art from Polynesia, Micronesia, and Melanesia. A visit here will give you a basis for understanding Hawaiian life and culture.

Shop Pacifica is laden with attractive items, everything from $3 kukui-nut pendants to a $1,000 Niihau-shell necklace.

If you have access to an Internet web browser, you can take a look at the Bishop Museum's collection before you go. The URL is http://www.bishop.hawaii.org/.

Note: If you plan your visit for a Wednesday, Saturday or Sunday, arrive late in the afternoon and stay to see the evening performance by The Brothers Cazimero. The admission price of $37.50 with dinner, $22.50 without, includes admission to the Bishop Museum; on performance days, the museum stays open until 7pm. (See Chapter 14 for further information.)

Bishop Museum Planetarium

1525 Bernice St. ☎ **808/848-4136.** Admission $3.50 or included with Bishop Museum admission. Sky shows daily 11am and 2pm, additional shows Fri and Sat 7pm.

Learn about astronomy from a uniquely Hawaiian perspective in exciting educational multimedia star shows held daily. Evening shows on Friday and Saturday also include free observatory telescope viewing, weather permitting.

Queen Emma Summer Palace

2913 Pali Hwy. ☎ **808/595-3167.** Admission $4 adults, $1 ages 12–18, 50¢ for those under 12. Daily 9am–4pm. Closed holidays. From Waikiki take TheBUS no 4 (Nuuanu). Ask the driver to let you off at the stop nearest the palace.

"Hanaiakamalama," the country estate of Kamehameha IV and his consort, Queen Emma, has been restored by the Daughters of Hawaii to its mid–19th-century Victorian splendor. Guided tours are available.

Royal Mausoleum

2261 Nuuanu Ave. Admission free. Mon–Fri 8am–4:30pm. Closed most holidays (open March 26, Kuhio Day; and June 11, Kamehameha Day). For directions, see Queen Emma Summer Palace, above.

This is where the alii of the Kamehameha and Kalakaua dynasties are buried.

✪ Mission Houses Museum

553 S. King St. ☎ **808/531-0481.** Admission (including guided tour) $5 adults, $4 seniors and military, $1 ages 6–15, free for children 6 years and under. Tues–Sat 9am–4pm, Sun noon–4pm. Take TheBUS no. 2 to the State Capitol; walk one block down Punchbowl Street to King Street; turn left and walk a half block to the Mission Houses. The Waikiki Trolley also passes within one block.

These historic buildings take you back to the early 1800s, when they served as the homes and headquarters for the first Christian missionaries to Hawaii. Built between 1821 and 1841, the houses were restored and furnished to reflect the daily life and work of American missionaries, their encounter with Hawaiians, and their clashes with Western merchants and traders. An orientation exhibit and video explores the controversy surrounding the Mission and sets the stage for highly personalized guided tours. The museum will give you a fascinating glimpse into the past.

A walking tour of historic downtown Honolulu leaves the museum on select weekdays at 9:30am. The $7 fee includes admission to the museum. Reservations are required; call for availability. Monthly Living History programs feature historical role-playing, hearth cooking, craft and work demonstrations, and candlelit evenings; contact the museum for a current schedule.

There's also a charming gift shop, full of Hawaiiana. Behind the Mission Houses is a library containing the collection of the Hawaiian Mission Children's Society and the Hawaiian Historical Society. Researchers are welcome.

✪ Kawaiahao Church

957 Punchbowl St. ☎ **808-522-1333.** Mon–Fri 9am–3pm, Sat 9am–noon; group tours weekdays by appointment. Take TheBUS no. 2 to Punchbowl and Beretania streets; walk one block to King Street.

The church that the king, his subjects, and missionaries built has been, since its dedication in 1841, the "Westminster Abbey of Hawaii." Even if you don't get to Sunday services (10:30am, conducted partially in Hawaiian; free guided tours afterward), take a look around. Note the fine portraits of Hawaiian royalty that hang in the church. The church is located across Kawaiahao Street from the Mission Houses.

✪ Iolani Palace

S. King and Richards streets. ☎ **808/522-0832.** Admission $4 adults, $1 children 5–12 (children under 5 not permitted on tours). Wed–Sat 9am–2:15pm. Take TheBUS no. 2 to Punchbowl and Beretania streets.

The official residence of Hawaii's last reigning monarchs, Iolani Palace was designed in the European manner for King Kalakaua, "The Merrie Monarch." Royalty resided here for 11 years (1882 to 1893) until the monarchy was overthrown. From 1893 to 1968 Iolani Palace was the capitol of the provisional government and the Republic, Territory, and State of Hawaii. Since 1978 it has been a museum, opened to the public after a $10 million restoration-reconstruction program. Although some areas are unfurnished, the Throne Room, State Dining Room, King's Library, and Privy Council Chamber are complete. Other rooms and areas are partially furnished. A tour of the building is well worth your time

Honolulu Attractions

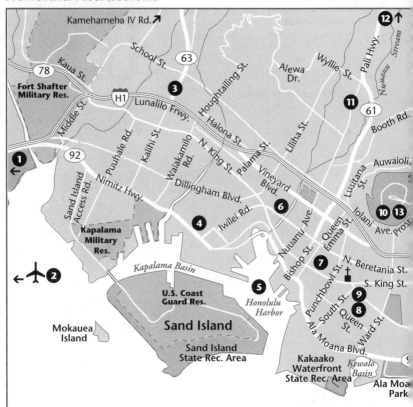

Kamehameha IV Rd.

Kaua St.
School St.
63
Kauai St.
78
Fort Shafter Military Res.
Middle St.
H1
Lunalilo Frwy.
Houghtailing St.
Halona St.
Alewa Dr.
Wyllie St.
Pali Hwy.
Nuuanu Stream
11
61
Booth Rd.

92
Nimitz Hwy.
Sand Island Access Rd.
Puuhale Rd.
Kalihi St.
Waiakamilo Rd.
N. King St.
Palama St.
Vineyard Blvd.
Liliha St.
Auwaioli
Lusitana St.
Iolani Ave.
Prosp
10
13

Dillingham Blvd.
Iwilei Rd.
6
Nuuanu Ave.
Queen Emma St.

Kapalama Military Res.
4
Kapalama Basin

U.S. Coast Guard Res.
5
Honolulu Harbor
Bishop St.
7
N. Beretania St.
S. King St.
9
8
Punchbowl St.
South St.
Queen St.
Ward St.

Mokauea Island
Sand Island
Sand Island State Rec. Area
Ala Moana Blvd.
Kakaako Waterfront State Rec. Area
Kewalo Basin
Ala Moana Park

Mamala   Bay

1337

OAHU
Honolulu

Bishop Museum & Planetarium **3**
Contemporary Museum **14**
Damien Museum **18**
Dole Pineapple Cannery **4**
Foster Botanic Garden **6**
Gandhi Statue **20**
Hawaii Maritime Center **5**

Honolulu Academy of Arts
Honolulu Zoo **19**
Iolani Palace **7**
Kapiolani Park **21**
Kawaiahao Church **9**
Lyon Arboretum **17**
Mission Houses Museum **8**

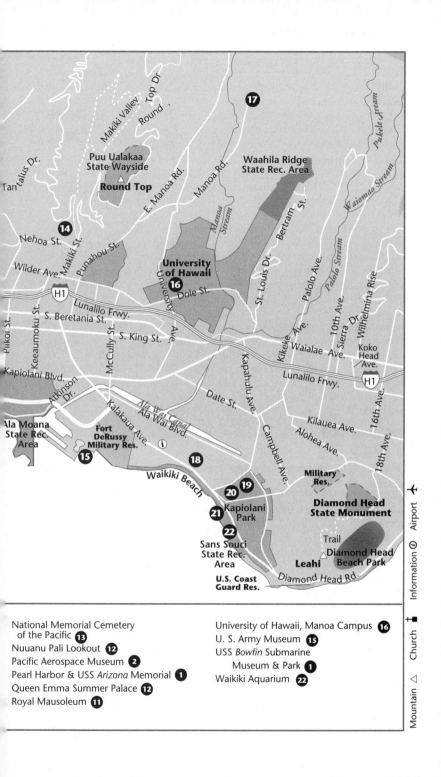

National Memorial Cemetery
  of the Pacific **13**
Nuuanu Pali Lookout **12**
Pacific Aerospace Museum **2**
Pearl Harbor & USS *Arizona* Memorial **1**
Queen Emma Summer Palace **12**
Royal Mausoleum **11**

University of Hawaii, Manoa Campus **16**
U. S. Army Museum **15**
USS *Bowfin* Submarine
    Museum & Park **1**
Waikiki Aquarium **22**

Mountain △   Church ╫   Information ⓘ   Airport ✈

to see the intricate woodwork, the highly polished fir floors, and the shining banisters and mirrors. Guides explain the furnishings and the history of each room. Tours are conducted every 15 minutes by the Friends of Iolani Palace and last 45 minutes. Be sure to make a reservation.

On the same grounds, at King and Likelike streets, are the **Archives of Hawaii,** the largest collection of Hawaiiana extant. Open Monday through Friday from 7:45am to 4:30pm.

✪ Hawaii Maritime Center

Pier 7, Honolulu Harbor. ☎ **808-536-6373.** Admission (including boarding *Falls of Clyde*) $7 adults, $4 ages 6–17, free for children under 6. Daily 9am–5pm. Take TheBUS no. 19 or 20 (Airport) to the Federal Building. The Waikiki Trolley and the free Hilo Hattie shuttle bus also stop here.

This world-class maritime center is dedicated to the preservation of Hawaii's rich ocean heritage. Admission entitles you to visit several attractions. Tour the *Falls of Clyde,* the world's only fully rigged four-masted ship, which, beginning in 1898, plied the waters between Hilo and San Francisco for many years. Visit the *Hokule'a,* a replica of a thousand-year-old Polynesian voyaging canoe which repeats the trip between Tahiti and Hawaii frequently, navigated by the stars and currents, as in ancient times. The $6-million Kalakaua Boathouse is the star attraction, a state-of-the-art museum that traces the maritime history of Hawaii from its original discovery by Polynesians on voyaging canoes right up to the present. Exhibits, audiovisual displays, and life-size dioramas deal with everything from Captain Cook and the sandalwood trade to the days of the whalers, the luxury ships of the Matson line, tsunamis and weather, and sailing and surfing. Kids will love the Observation Tower for sighting harbor traffic, and the *Cory Sause,* a tot-sized replica of a ship.

WORLD WAR II

✪ Pearl Harbor

☎ **808/422-0561.** Admission free. Tours daily 8am–3pm; visitor center hours 7:30am–5pm. From Waikiki, take TheBUS no. 20; from Ala Moana Shopping Center TheBUS no. 51 or 52. If you prefer to take a commercial shuttle bus (round-trip $6), phone 808/926-4747.

It would be unthinkable to visit Hawaii without making a pilgrimage to the USS *Arizona* Memorial at Pearl Harbor. This tomb for some 1,000 American servicemen who died on December 7, 1941, the day Japanese bombs fell on Hawaii, is a silent, stark reminder of the fury and folly of war.

Try to arrive early in the morning at the visitors center, administered by the National Park Service, to avoid huge crowds. While you're waiting for the shuttle boat to take you out to the sunken USS *Arizona* itself—you'll be given a number and time of departure—you can busy yourself with the absorbing exhibits at the visitor center museum. Many of these show the personal mementos of the attack victims, plus photographs, paintings, and historical documents. A 30-minute talk and film precedes your trip to the ship. Children under 12 must be accompanied by adults. Shoes and shirts are required; no bathing suits.

Note: Visiting Pearl Harbor by sea is also a very moving experience. Paradise Cruise's sleek luxury vessel *Star of Honolulu* makes the trip every day at 9am. Cost is $26.50 adults, $13.25 children. For reservations call **808/593-2493,** or 800/334-6191 from the mainland.

USS *Bowfin* Submarine Museum & Park
☎ **808/423-1341.** Admission $8 adults, $5 military, $3 children. Children under 4 admitted to the museum free, but are not allowed on the submarine for safety reasons. Daily 8am–5pm, except Thanksgiving, Christmas, and New Year's Day. For shuttle service from ($3 each way) Waikiki, call 808/732-4436. By public transportation, follow directions to USS *Arizona* Memorial, above.

Adjacent to the USS *Arizona* Memorial Visitor Center, this is the home of the USS *Bowfin,* a World War II submarine launched a year after the attack on Pearl Harbor. Youngsters, especially, will enjoy going aboard to explore below the decks of the submarine where the 80-man crew served. *Bowfin* completed nine successful war patrols and earned the Presidential Unit Citation and Navy Unit Commendation. There are fewer than 20 U.S. World War II submarines in existence today, and USS *Bowfin,* nicknamed the "Pearl Harbor Avenger," was named a National Historic Landmark in 1896.

You can also explore the *Bowfin* Museum, with its impressive collection of submarine-related artifacts, see a 1960s TV film featuring the *Bowfin,* and tour the park grounds to view rare artifacts such as Kaiten, better known as a Japanese suicide torpedo. The Waterfront Memorial honors submariners lost during World War II. Visit the gift shop too, with many nautical souvenirs.

✪ National Memorial Cemetery of the Pacific
Punchbowl Crater. ☎ **808/541-1434.** Admission free. Oct–Feb, daily 8am–5:30pm; Mar–Sept, daily 8am–6:30pm. Take TheBUS no. 2 on Kuhio Avenue heading downtown, get off at Alapai Street, and transfer to no. 15 (Pacific Heights). This leaves every hour on the half-hour, so time your trip carefully. Get off at Puowaina Drive and walk approximately 10 minutes.

Punchbowl Crater, an extinct volcano once named the "Hill of Sacrifice," is the final resting place of some 37,000 American service personnel killed in the Pacific during World War II, the Korean War, and the Vietnam War. One of the most visited graves here is that of astronaut Ellison Onizuka.

Note: Possible federal budget cuts may necessitate closing on certain days; call before going. To preserve the sanctity of the cemetery, no tour buses are allowed to stop here. There's an easy way to get to Punchbowl and also to be guided on a walking tour of the cemetery, thanks to the American Legion. Last year, the organization began to offer $15 one-hour tours that include roundtrip transportation from Waikiki hotels. Inquire at your hotel travel desk, or phone the American Legion at **808/946-6383.**

ART MUSEUMS

✪ Contemporary Museum
At Spalding Estate, 2411 Makiki Heights Dr. ☎ **808/526-1322.** Admission $5 ages 13 and over; free on the third Thurs of each month. Tues–Sat 10am–4pm, Sun noon–4pm. Telephone for driving instructions.

The art collection and the beautiful setting vie for attention here. A 1920s Honolulu mansion and a breathtaking garden, overlooking the city and sea, house a modern collection focusing on 40 years of art in Hawaii, as well as on international artists of note. On permanent view is David Hockney's stage set from the Metropolitan Opera production of *L'Efant et les Sortilèges.* There's an appealing gift shop and an upbeat restaurant, the Contemporary Café.

✪ Honolulu Academy of Arts

900 S. Beretania St. ☎ **808/532-8700.** Voluntary admission $5 general, $2 seniors and students; children under 12 free. Tues–Sat 10am–4:30pm, Sun 1–5pm. Take TheBUS no. 1 or 2 and get off at Ward Avenue and S. Beretania Street.

This supremely graceful building, with intimate galleries overlooking serene courtyards, is a model of what an art museum should look like. While both island artists and masters of Western art—Picasso, Braque, van Gogh, and so on—are well represented, the real glory of the museum is its collections of Asian scrolls, paintings, tapestries, screens, and sculpture from Korea, China, and Japan. Don't miss the awe-inspiring statue of Kuan Yin, a 12th-century representation of the Chinese goddess of mercy. A sculpture garden contains masterpieces from the Academy collection, including some Noguchis and Henry Moores.

Be sure to visit the gift shop, and perhaps have lunch at the Garden Café (closed in August); phone **808/532-8734** for reservations.

FISH, FLORA & FAUNA

✪ Foster Botanic Garden

50 N. Vineyard Blvd. ☎ **808/522-7060.** Admission $1, free for children under 13 with an adult. Daily 9am–4pm. Closed Christmas and New Year's Day. Self-guided brochure available. Guided tours Mon–Fri at 1pm (reservations recommended: call 808/522-7066). Take TheBUS no. 2, 19, or 20 (Airport or Airport/Hickam) toward town (request a transfer). Get off at the corner of Hotel and Bethel streets, and change to no. 4 (Nuuanu/Dowsett); ask the driver to let you off at the garden.

On view are 15 acres of rare tropical plantings from around the world, including many exceptional trees. You can walk through orchid and primitive cycad gardens. Check out the gallery and bookstore. The garden was begun by Dr. William Hillebrand in 1853 on royal land.

✪ Frommer's Favorite Honolulu & Oahu Experiences

The Annual Lei Day/May Day Concert at the Waikiki Shell. On May 1, everybody wears leis and there are contests for the most beautiful, with judging at Kapiolani Park. In the evening, the Brothers Cazimero present a fabulous show, and all Honolulu, in their aloha finery, turns out to attend. A joyous event.

Sunset Cocktails at the Open-Air House Without a Key. At the Halekulani Hotel, as you watch the sun sink slowly into the Pacific, and a beautiful hula girl dances to melodious music, you know picture-postcard Hawaii still exits.

A Walk through Historic Chinatown. Examine the open-air fish and vegetable stalls at the Oahu Market, peek in at herbalists' shops and noodle factories, stop for goodies at the Chinese bakeries, and finish with a visit to some of the town's most sophisticated art galleries.

Snorkeling at Hanauma Bay. This idyllic beach cove, created centuries ago when one side of Koko Head Crater was washed into the sea, is now a marine reserve, and the fish are so gentle that they eat right out of your hand.

A Visit to Byodo-In Temple on Windward Oahu. This exact replica of venerable Byodo-In in Japan has a magnificent carving of Amida, the Buddha of the Western Paradise.

✪ Honolulu Zoo

151 Kapahulu Ave. ☎ **808/971-7171.** Admission $3 adults, free for ages 12 and under. Daily 9am–4:30pm (June–Aug, also Wed to 7:30pm). Closed New Year's Day and Christmas Day. You can walk from most major hotels or take TheBUS no. 8, 19, 20, 58, or 2 (Kapiolani Park), running in a Diamond Head direction.

The big news at the Honolulu Zoo is the opening of their multimillion-dollar African Savanna, which allows you to see wild animals in settings approximating their native habitats. The Asiatic elephants are great favorites with the crowd; call for times of their public demonstrations. With Diamond Head providing the background, plenty of trees and flowers (including orchids, a giant banyan, and date palms), it's one of the most charming small zoos anywhere.

During the summer there's free entertainment on Wednesday starting at 6pm at the stage under the earpod tree, just behind the flamingos. Take a picnic supper and join the fun. Local artists hang their work on the fence outside on Tuesday, Saturday, and Sunday. Be sure to stop in at Zootique, the charming gift shop for imaginative animal gifts.

Kapiolani Park

Take TheBUS no. 2 (Waikiki-Kapiolani Park) from Kuhio Ave. in a Diamond Head direction.

This 99$^{1}/_{2}$-acre park at Kalakaua and Monsarrat avenues, has facilities for just about everything, from tennis, soccer, and rugby to archery and picnicking. The Royal Hawaiian Band plays on Sundays in the bandstand, and major musical events take place in the Waikiki Shell. For a particularly beautiful view, note Diamond Head framed in the cascading waters of the splendid Louise C. Dillingham Fountain.

Bordering the ocean on the right is a stretch of wide, palm-dotted grass lawn with a fringe of sand to let you know you're still at the beach. Swimming here is excellent, since the surf is quite mild; it's a big favorite with local families. **Kapiolani Beach Park,** with restrooms, picnic tables, and snack bar, is just ahead.

✪ Lyon Arboretum

3860 Manoa Rd. ☎ **808/988-7378.** Donations requested. Mon–Sat 9am–3pm, group tours by prior arrangement. Closed Sun and public holidays. Phone for driving directions.

An important research facility for the University of Hawaii, Lyon Arboretum is one of the most beautiful nature spots in Honolulu. A free 1$^{1}/_{2}$-hour guided tour, held at 1pm on the first Friday and third Wednesday of each month and at 10am on the third Saturday of each month, will tell you all you'll ever need to know about exotic and tropical plants, as well as the flora of Hawaii. Reservations for these tours are a must: Call **808/988-7378** between 9am and 3pm weekdays, and inquire, too, about a wide variety of classes, outings, and programs. The Arboretum also maintains a book and gift shop featuring handcrafted notecards, napkins, baskets, pottery, and other unique gifts, as well as a wide selection of books on tropical plants, crafts, Hawaiiana, and culinary arts. Write for schedules or information.

Waikiki Aquarium

2777 Kalakaua Ave. ☎ **808/923-9741.** Admission $6 adults, $4 seniors, $2.50 juniors 13–17; children 12 and under free. Daily 9am–4:30pm. Closed Thanksgiving and Christmas. Take TheBUS no. 2 (Waikiki–Kapiolani Park) from Kuhio Avenue in a Diamond Head direction.

A 19-month, $3.1-million renovation has made the always entertaining Waikiki Aquarium more enthralling than ever. New exhibits include the Sea Visions Theater and accompanying jellyfish display, the outdoor Northwest Hawaiian Islands habitat with endangered Hawaiian monk seals, the Mahimahi Hatchery, and an expanded Hunters on the Reef shark exhibit. You can also see, among other sea creatures, the *lauwiliwilinuknukuoioi:* if you can't pronounce it, just ask for the long-nosed butterfly fish. An outdoor display, Edge of the Reef, is a simulated living-reef environment that includes hundreds of colorful fish, live coral, and a tidal surge. Stop in to see their attractive gift shop, the Natural Selection. Everything for sale relates to the ocean and its life-forms. They have a good selection of children's toys and books, too.

2 More Attractions

University of Hawaii

The University of Hawaii at Manoa, pride of Hawaii's nine-campus public system of higher education, is well worth your visit—not only for a theatrical presentation, a concert, an experimental film, or a presentation of Asian folk dancing, but to see the campus itself.

Located in lush, tropical Manoa Valley, with verdant mountains as a backdrop, the campus is just a short drive or bus ride from Waikiki, where a number of university students live. Originally a small, land-grant agricultural college, the university has grown the way everything in Hawaii has since statehood. It's now become an important center of higher learning for some 21,000 students, many from far beyond the islands. The campus itself is a flower garden, art is prevalent everywhere, and the buildings are beautiful.

Guided tours of the campus leave from Manoa Campus Center at 2pm on Mondays, Wednesdays, and Fridays, but visitors are welcome to explore on their own. Maps and directions for self-guided tours are available at the University Relations Office (Hawaii Hall, Room 2). If you're an art enthusiast, be sure to see Jean Charlot's two-story mural of the history of the island in Bachman Hall and Juliette May Fraser's *Makahiki Ho'okupu* in Hamilton Library. There are other important murals by island artists at Bilger and Keller halls and in the Music Building, ever-changing art exhibitions are on view at the Campus Center and the gallery in the Art Building, and there are occasional exhibits at Burns Hall. For nature lovers, rare varieties of tropical plants and trees are everywhere. But for us, the most interesting sights of the university are the students, especially the ones in native garb who are studying at the East-West Center. This important institute accepts graduate students from both East (Asia and the Pacific Islands) and West (the mainland), trains them in each other's cultures, and then sends them on fieldwork to those areas. Free tours of the East-West Center leave from Thomas Jefferson Hall every Wednesday at 1:30pm.

Take TheBUS no. 4 (Nuuanu-Dowsett) from the corner of Kapahulu and Kalakaua directly to the university.

Nuuanu Pali Lookout

The Pali is one of the most dramatic spots on Oahu; the view from the top is one of the best vistas on the island. Back in 1795, atop these jagged cliffs, Kamehameha the Great toppled thousands of Oahuans to their deaths in the final battle before he consolidated his power. The view of Windward Oahu is spectacular. Remember to take a jacket or windbreaker, as the winds are chilling up here. And remove all valuables from your car, as it's a prime spot for petty thieves.

Note: Nuuanu Pali is included in our driving tour of Southeast Oahu (see Chapter 13); however, to get there directly from downtown Honolulu, turn left off

Nimitz Highway (Hi. 92) onto Nuuanu Avenue or Bishop Street. Follow it to Pali Highway (Hi. 61), which will take you to the Pali.

U.S. Army Museum

Fort DeRussy Park. ☎ **808/438-2821.** Admission free. Tues–Sun 10am–4:30pm. Take TheBUS no. 8 (Ala Moana Center) from Kuhio Avenue, in an Ewa direction.

Housed in Battery Randolph, built in 1909 as a key installation in defense of Honolulu and Pearl Harbor, this museum contains military memorabilia dating from ancient Hawaiian warfare to the present. On the upper deck, the Corps of Engineers Pacific Regional Visitors Center graphically shows how the corps works with the civilian community in managing water resources in an island environment.

Damien Museum

130 Ohua St. ☎ **808/923-2690.** Donations accepted. Mon–Fri 9am–3pm, Sat 9am–noon. Closed holidays. Within walking distance of most major hotels, or take TheBUS no. 8, 19, or 20 running in a Diamond Head direction.

In the Diamond Head area, behind St. Augustine's Catholic Church, this small museum presents a moving account of Father Damien's work with the victims of leprosy on the island of Molokai. The museum contains prayer books used by Father Damien in his ministry as well as his personal items. A continuously running video recounting Damien's story is narrated by Terence Knapp, a local actor who has portrayed Father Damien in award-winning performances on stage and TV. He fittingly honors one of Hawaii's heroes.

Gandhi Statue

An impressive statue of Mahatma Gandhi, located in front of the Honolulu Zoo, created by New York artist Zlatko Paunov, was a gift to the people of Hawaii from the Jhamanadas Watumull Fund. The statue is accompanied by a plaque quoting from Gandhi's philosophy: "It is possible to live in peace."

Dole Pineapple Cannery

Although the Dole Pineapple Cannery is no longer in operation, you can still take a free bus out to Cannery Square to see a multimedia show on the role of Dole in Hawaiian history, and to shop and browse at Cannery Courtyard. By the time you read this, there will be a huge (44 acres eventually) outlet shopping complex—to be constructed in five phases—here. Unfortunately, the names of the shops (up to 100 of them) are not for publication as we go to press, but we can tell you this: The Horizon Group, the developers, are committed to preserving the history of this important Hawaii landmark. A self-guided tour of the area is planned and much of the actual cannery equipment will be on view as sculpture, in tribute to this major era of the economic history of Hawaii.

For bus information (pickups are made every hour at 10 Waikiki hotels), see local tourist papers or call **808-548-6601.** You can also take TheBUS no. 19 (Airport/Hickam) to Cannery Square.

Pacific Aerospace Museum

At Honolulu International Airport. ☎ **808/839-0777.** Admission $4 adults, $1 children 6–12. Usually open Sun 10am–6pm, Mon–Tues 9am–6pm, Wed–Thurs 9am–7pm, Fri–Sat 9am–9pm.

If you've got a long wait at the airport between planes, here's something of interest that might amuse older children. Located in the central waiting area of the main terminal, the museum has a three-dimensional multimedia theater that traces the history of flight in Hawaii. There's also a full-scale space shuttle flight deck. Kids will like the mission control computer program that traces flights in the Pacific.

3 Organized Tours & Activities

GUIDED SIGHTSEEING TOURS

Certainly the easiest way to see the sights of Honolulu and the island of Oahu is to take a guided tour—especially if your time is limited. The smaller companies are usually the most fun. **E Noa Tours** (1110 University Ave., Room 306, Honolulu, HI 96826; ☎ 808/591-2561), for one, takes you out in a 21-passenger minibus and provides delightful, personalized looks at the island sights.

WALKING TOURS

The people at ✪ **Honolulu Time Walks,** 2634 S. King St., Suite 3 (☎ 808/943-0371) would like to take you for a walk. In the course of their popular 2¹/₂-hour walking tours, which leave from various points, you can meet with the ghosts of Honolulu, relive the events of December 7, 1941, or follow in the footsteps of Mark Twain. Many of these tours are led by master storyteller Glen Grant, who has been collecting tales of the supernatural in Hawaii for over 25 years. (You may have seen him last year on NBC's "The Other Side" talking about the prevalence of ghosts in Hawaii.) In addition to the walking tours, special showings are held at the Hawaii Heritage Theater in the International Marketplace on such subjects as "Obake . . . Japanese Tales of the Dead" and "Ghosts of Hawaii." Special tours are available for children. Most tours cost between $7 and $10; trolley tours can go up to $50. Call the number above for timely information and reservations. Local friends rave about these tours!

Kapiolani Community College presents a unique series of walking tours into Hawaii's past, including visits to Honolulu's famous cemeteries, the almost vanished "Little Tokyo" neighborhood, the old plantation community of Waialua, and many more fascinating destinations. Tours cost $5; for information and reservations, call 808/734-9245.

The Mission Houses Museum presents a walking tour of "Historic Downtown Honolulu" on selected weekdays at 9:30am. The cost of $7 also includes admission to the museum. Call 808/531-0481 for tour days and reservations.

The Hawaii Geographic Society (☎ 808/538-3952) offers several unusual and highly worthwhile tours from April through September. One is "A Temple Tour," including Chinese, Japanese, Christian, and Jewish temples, cathedrals, and other houses of worship; another is an archeology tour in and around downtown Honolulu. Each is guided by an expert from the Hawaii Geographic Society. A brochure is available on request. Cost is $10 per person; a minimum of three persons required. Call for details and reservations.

The society's brochure, "Historic Downtown Honolulu Walking Tour," is a fascinating self-guided tour of the 200-year-old city center. It's $3, including postage, from Hawaii Geographic Maps and Books, 49 S. Hotel St., Suite 218 (P.O. Box 1698), Honolulu, HI 96808.

The **Moanalua Gardens Foundation** (☎ 808/839-5334) offers walking tours of Kamananui Valley on the second Saturday and fourth Sunday of every month, from 9am to 1pm. Donations are requested.

Two different organizations offer walking tours of Chinatown. The three-hour "Walk-A-Tour," run by the **Chinese Chamber of Commerce** only on Tuesday mornings at 9:30am, is an old favorite. It includes visits to shops, markets, and historic sites. The price is $5, and lunch can be arranged. The tour leaves from the Chinese Chamber of Commerce headquarters at 42 N. King St. (☎ 808/ 533-3181 for reservations).

The **Hawaii Heritage Center** at 1168 Smith St. (☎ 808/521-2749) conducts walking tours which focus on the history and cultural uniqueness of the Chinatown area. Tours assemble at 1128 Smith St., outside the Ramsay Gallery, on Fridays at 9:30am. The requested donation is $4 per person. Reservations are required only for groups of 15 or more, and may be arranged on other weekdays.

MORE HAUNTED HAWAII

After the success of Glen Grant and his Hawaiian ghost tours and books (see above), it was inevitable that more and more sightings of tour companies offering similar spectral events would appear. Among these is a new company called **Ghost Tours Hawaii,** which offers an engaging three-hour bus excursion to haunted spots in town and on Windward Oahu, stopping at among other places, cemeteries known for "ghost lights" and a "moving" statue; at the Royal Mausoleum, where a tree is thought to be haunted; and at the Pali Lookout, from whose cliffs Kamehameha the Great toppled thousands to their deaths in a bloody battle in 1795—surely, there must be a ghost or two still there. The trip, which is held every Saturday, often on Sunday, and sometimes on weekdays as well, costs $35; phone 808/596-2052 for information and reservations.

Gray Line has gotten into the act with a program called "Legends and Spirit Tales of Old Hawaii." Here, guests dine at the picturesque Crouching Lion Inn on Windward Oahu while they're regaled with an evening of storytelling of Hawaiian legends, myths, and, of course, ghost stories. Cost is $43, for adults, $34.50 for children (ages 2 to 12), which includes dinner and transportation. For information and reservations, phone Gray Line at **808/833-8000** or **800/367-2420.**

HISTORIC HARBOR TOURS

✪ Historic tours of Honolulu Harbor aboard the former municipal fireboat *Abner T. Longley* are great fun for those with or without children to entertain. Built in 1951 as Honolulu's first bonafide fireboat, the *Abner T. Longley* served the community for over 40 years. It is able to pump over 30 tons of water per minute through its five water cannons while maintaining a speed of seven knots. Its 25-foot tall red smokestack and the steamwhistle from the old Libby Pineapple Company make it quite a presence on the waterfront.

There are nine daytime cruises, from 10:15am to 4pm, each lasting 45 minutes and costing only $7.50, free for children under 5 when accompanied by an adult (one child per adult)—a bargain for an activity of this sort. The Early Evening Sunset Cruise, 5:30 to 6:30pm, adds a cocktail and pupus; cost is $15 for adults, $11.50 for children ages 5 to 12, free for those under 5. The niftiest of all are the two Evening Water Show Extravaganzas, which give passengers the opportunity to operate the water cannons (maintained to original fire-fighting standards). Both cruises conclude with a computer-controlled water show featuring lighted water cannons synchronized with sound effects. The cost for this one-hour tour (including a free cocktail), offered at 7pm and again at 8:30pm, is $15 for adults, $11.50 for children ages 5 to 12, free for those under 5.

CULTURAL ACTIVITIES

There's a tremendous interest these days in reviving the traditions of the Hawaiians; all over the state, people are learning to speak Hawaiian; make Hawaiian quilts; do featherwork; weave lauhala baskets; and, of course, dance the hula. If any of these activities appeal to you and you have the time to take some classes, your best one-stop resource is the **Atherton Halau** of the Bishop Museum, 1525 Bernice St., ☎ 808/847-3511, where classes in Hawaiian crafts are held Monday through Saturday from 9am to 3pm at a nominal charge (usually $5, plus materials). It's usually quilting on Monday and Friday, fresh flower lei-making on Tuesday, lauhala weaving and hula-implement making on Wednesday. One of the most rewarding aspects of taking a class here is meeting the truly lovely "Aunties" and "Uncles" who teach these classes. Atherton Halau is also the site of special events, usually held on weekends.

Aspiring quilters can also watch demonstrations and take classes at **Kwilts 'n' Koa**, a delightful shop at 1126 12th Ave. in Kaimuki (☎ 808/735-2300).

Should you be in Honolulu for the summer, consider the wide variety of offerings in the Summer Session at the University of Hawaii.

As for learning the hula, be advised that hula dancers study for many years to master their craft; hula *halaus* demand tremendous discipline and dedication from their students. You can learn a few basic steps, of course, in hula classes given at local hotels and shopping malls, but for something more organized, try the classes at the **Waikiki Community Center** (☎ 808/955-0100).

4 Highlights for Kids

Hawaii is a wonderful place for a family vacation. There are loads of places and activities to keep the keikis amused, including the following (full details on each place can be found earlier in this chapter, unless otherwise noted):

- **The Beach.** This is the best of Honolulu's kid-friendly activities, hands down. At Waikiki Beach, the waves are gentle, swimming safe (except for occasional deep holes at Kuhio Beach; be sure to supervise non-swimmers), and there are potential playmates aplenty. Kids can take surfing lessons or go boogie-boarding; the whole family can go out on an outrigger canoe and ride the waves back to shore—almost as thrilling, and a lot less risky, than surfing. (See Chapter 8 for details.)
- **Bishop Museum Planetarium.** Older children will love the sky shows and looking through the telescope at the night skies. The Bishop Museum hosts regularly changing exhibits for families on a wide range of topics, such as ecology and archeology.
- *Bowfin* **Submarine Museum Park.** Close to the USS *Arizona* Memorial at Pearl Harbor (good for older children), this interactive museum gives kids a chance to explore below the decks of the *Bowfin* submarine, to see where its 80-man crew served during some of the fiercest naval battles of World War II.
- **Fireboat Cruises.** Kids love the tours of historic Honolulu Harbor on the retired fireboat *Abner T. Longley,* especially if they get to operate one of the water cannons on the nighttime cruises.

- **Ghost Tours.** Honolulu Time Walks is known for its "Ghosts of old Honolulu" tour. They even have one especially for the kids (but don't worry—it won't keep them up at night).
- **Hawaii Maritime Center.** Young skippers love to steer the *Cory Sause,* a tot-size replica of a ship, and climb to the Observation Tower to sight harbor traffic.
- **Honolulu Zoo.** Kids like just about everything at the zoo, especially the elephant show and the petting zoo.
- **Kapiolani Park.** Should the kids get impossible, tell them go fly a kite—and Kapiolani Park is the place to do it.
- *Magic of Polynesia.* Master illusionist John Hirokawa's show at the Hilton Hawaiian Village is a big favorite with kids, even though—or maybe because—it can be pretty scary. (See Chapter 14 for details.)
- **Oceanarium Restaurant,** in the Pacific Beach Hotel. While they're eating, kids can eyeball thousands of tropical fish swimming in the three-story, 280,000 gallon aquarium. (See Chapter 7 for details.)
- **Pacific Aerospace Museum.** Technologically oriented youngsters will be fascinated by the mission-control computer program that traces actual flights at this museum in the Honolulu International Airport.
- **Submarine Diving.** A dive 100 feet below the waters off Waikiki on the submarine *Atlantis* could well be the thrill of a youngster's lifetime. (See Chapter 8 for details.)
- **Waikiki Aquarium.** Everything in this exemplary aquarium is fascinating to little ones—especially the sharks!

   Note: The excellent Hawaii Children's Museum was "on vacation" as of this writing, but should reopen sometime this year as the Children's Discovery Center in the as-yet unbuilt Kakaako Waterfront Park. Check local papers for information or phone **808/592-5437.**

10 City Strolls

If you want to know what makes the 50th state tick, you must explore the city of Honolulu. And if you really want to experience the sights, sounds, and feel of a city, the best way to do it is to get out and walk. Happily, it's also the cheapest way and the most fun.

Commercial tours are expensive and can touch only on the highlights. We think the city merits more attention. Local buses, a good pair of walking shoes, and the instructions that follow will get you to the major places. And, more important, you can go at your own pace, devoting the most time to what most interests you—and you alone.

WALKING TOUR 1
Downtown Honolulu

Start: Honolulu Academy of Arts.

Finish: Kalanimoku (Ship of Heaven).

Time: Approximately 3 hours including time for museum-browsing.

Best Time: Tuesday through Saturday.

Worst Time: Sunday and Monday, when the Academy of Arts and Mission Houses Museum are closed.

TheBUS no. 2 in Waikiki will take you right to the:

1. **Honolulu Academy of Arts,** at the corner of Ward Avenue and South Beretania Street—a low, graceful building where magnificent art treasures await you.

   Retrace your steps across Thomas Square to King Street and you'll see:

2. **Neal S. Blaisdell Center,** 777 Ward Ave., known as "NBC" to the locals. It's a giant $1.25-million complex with an arena, a concert theater (it's home to the Hawaii Symphony), and a convention hall. There are no official tours, but apply at the administration office if you are interested in seeing it; they will have someone show you around. Don't forget to ask for a schedule of upcoming events. Kids will enjoy feeding the tame ducks and geese that live in the ponds on the grounds.

   Cross Ward Avenue on the Ewa side of the center, turn left onto King Street, and walk Ewa three short blocks to King and Kanaiahao Streets. There you will come to the:

Walking Tour—Downtown Honolulu

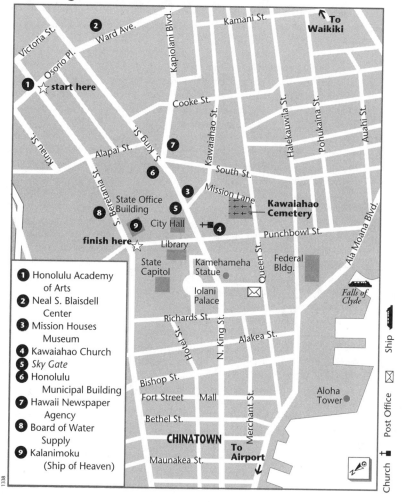

Map labels:

Victoria St.
Ward Ave.
Kamani St.
To Waikiki
Osorio Pl.
Kapiolani Blvd.
Kinau St.
Cooke St.
start here
S. King St.
Alapai St.
Kawaiahao St.
Halekauwila St.
Pohukaina St.
Auahi St.
South St.
S. Beretania St.
Mission Lane
Kawaiahao Cemetery
State Office Building
City Hall
Punchbowl St.
Ala Moana Blvd.
finish here
Library
State Capitol
Kamehameha Statue
Federal Bldg.
Falls of Clyde
Iolani Palace
Queen St.
Richards St.
N. King St.
Alakea St.
Hotel St.
Bishop St.
Fort Street Mall
Aloha Tower
Bethel St.
Merchant St.
CHINATOWN
To Airport
Maunakea St.

Ship
Post Office
Church

1 Honolulu Academy of Arts
2 Neal S. Blaisdell Center
3 Mission Houses Museum
4 Kawaiahao Church
5 *Sky Gate*
6 Honolulu Municipal Building
7 Hawaii Newspaper Agency
8 Board of Water Supply
9 Kalanimoku (Ship of Heaven)

1338

3. **Mission Houses Museum,** 553 South King St. These three 19th-century buildings provide a glimpse of the historic encounter between the New England missionaries and the native Hawaiians in early 19th-century Honolulu. It was here that James Michener did much of his research for *Hawaii*.

Outside the Mission Houses Museum, turn left and cross Kawaiahao Street to:

4. **Kawaiahao Church,** 957 Punchbowl St. This is Hawaii's "Westminster Abbey," the church of its royal families and the scene of their coronations, weddings, and funerals. It's considered the most architecturally significant work of the missionary period. Explore the graveyard and look for missionary tombstones. Behind the church is an adobe schoolhouse, one of the oldest school buildings in the state.

On the sidewalk outside Kawaiahao Church, walk across King Street to the neo-Spanish City Hall to see some of the architectural highlights of the Civic

Center, called Honolulu Hale, 530 South King St. Its Mediterranean-influenced architecture of the California Mission style works particularly well in Hawaii. Walk inside to see the splendid central courtyard open to sun and sky; changing art and other exhibits are held here; it's particularly festive at holiday times. In a Diamond Head direction of Honolulu Hale are two very attractive New England–style red-brick buildings with white trim. These house such city and county departments as municipal reference and records. Continuing in a Diamond Head direction, on the expanse of rolling lawn between these buildings and the towering gray-stone monolith beyond, you'll see:

5. *Sky Gate,* a highly controversial piece of art acquired by the city and county at a cost of $120,000. Created by famed sculptor Isamu Noguchi, it consists of four pieces of what is apparently a gigantic stove pipe, painted flat black and welded together.

The aforementioned gray-stone monolith is the:

6. Honolulu Municipal Building, 650 South King St. This is the home of the departments of transportation, buildings, and public works, and much more. Like *Sky Gate,* this building was greeted with something less than unmitigated joy by Honolulu's citizenry, many of whom feel that its architecture is out of keeping with the rest of the Civic Center.

When you stand in front of the municipal building by the flagpoles, the very attractive gray building with terra-cotta roof that you see is the:

7. Hawaii Newspaper Agency, 618 Kapiolani Blvd., which houses the two daily newspapers. Many consider it one of the loveliest Monarchy-style buildings in the city.

Walk through the municipal building and out the other side, cross the little park area, and on the other side of Beretania Street you'll see:

8. Board of Water Supply, 630 South Beretania St., a lovely pale-green building with a beautiful lawn and a lighted fountain. Pop inside to see its six-foot aquarium in the lobby.

Now retrace your steps in an Ewa direction, this time along Beretania Street; the beautiful new building you see across from the rear of Honolulu Hale is the:

9. Kalanimoku (Ship of Heaven), 1151 Punchbowl St., a state office building at the Civic Center. It houses the state departments of land and natural resources, fish and game, and forestry, among others. The building has a cool, wonderfully open design, and at night, softly colored lights filter through the cutout designs at the top. It is gorgeously landscaped.

WALKING TOUR 2
The Honolulu Waterfront & Hawaii's Wall Street

Start: Aloha Tower.
Finish: Fort Street Mall.
Time: 2 or 3 hours, including time for museums, shopping, and refreshments.
Best Time: Any day before 5:30pm, when the Maritime Center closes.

From Waikiki take TheBUS no. 19 (Airport or Airport/Hickam) or no. 20 (Airport/Halawa Gate), and get off at the Federal Building on Ala Moana Boulevard. Then walk toward the water to the first component of the Hawaii Maritime Center, the:

The Honolulu Waterfront & Hawaii's Wall Street

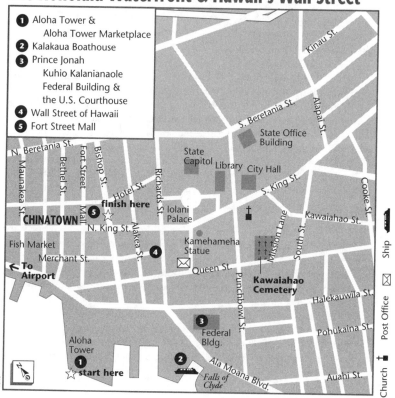

1. Aloha Tower &
   Aloha Tower Marketplace
2. Kalakaua Boathouse
3. Prince Jonah
   Kuhio Kalanianaole
   Federal Building &
   the U.S. Courthouse
4. Wall Street of Hawaii
5. Fort Street Mall

1. **Aloha Tower,** at Pier 9, on the waterfront. Once the tallest building in Hawaii, it still provides a great view of the city in all directions. It's adjacent to the new Aloha Tower Marketplace, a vast shopping and dining bazaar with ongoing entertainment and cultural events. You can take a tour of Honolulu Harbor on a historic fireboat for just $7.50. This is also your best place to:

   TAKE A BREAK The Food Lanai seats 700 in a picturesque over-the-water location, offering everything from Cajun to Chinese to natural foods. Better yet, sample the beers brewed in Hawaii's first microbrewery, Gordon Biersch, and have a tasty lunch in its indoor/outdoor café, presided over by renowned gourmet chef Kelly Degala.

   Once you're done relaxing, visit the:

2. **Kalakaua Boathouse,** an absorbing museum full of exhibits that highlight the maritime history of Hawaii. This is the centerpiece of the Hawaii Maritime Center. From the Kalakaua Boathouse, you can step right onto the *Falls of Clyde,* the only four-masted, fully-rigged sailing ship still in existence. If it's in port, you can also see the *Hokule'a,* an authentic replica of an ancient Hawaiian double-hulled canoe, similar to those that brought the first Hawaiians to these shores.

Leave the Maritime Center and walk across Ala Moana Boulevard to see some of the newer buildings of the State Civic Center Mall, including the:

3. **Prince Jonah Kuhio Kalanianaole Federal Building** and the **U.S. Post Office, Custom House, and Courthouse,** two unusual low-lying structures with terraced roofs in the style of Nebuchadnezzar's Hanging Gardens of Babylon. (They are situated makai of the Civic Center; the state capitol is mauka, and Iolani Palace is the middle.) Two outdoor sculptures here have also caused quite a stir: **Two Open Angles Eccentric** (and that's just what they are–two huge stainless steel open and transparent frames that slice through the air but never collide as they frame buildings and sky) and **Barking Sands** (Peter Voulkos), composed of serpentine and geometric forms. Be an art critic and express your own opinion. Some lovely fiberworks by Ruthadell Anderson and Sharyn Amii Mills can be seen in the lobby and on the fourth floor of the courthouse.

Two blocks mauka of the federal building is Merchant Street, known as the:

4. **Wall Street of Hawaii.** The "Big Five"—the great financial powers of the islands—have their offices here. You'll see the handsome office of Dole, Davies Pacific Center, Dillingham Transportation, AMFAC Center (at Merchant and Bishop), and the Alexander and Baldwin, Ltd., building with its Hawaiian and Asian motifs, considered to be one of the most splendid commercial buildings in Honolulu.

Turn left on Merchant Street, and across Bishop Street you will come to the:

5. **Fort Street Mall,** a lively shopping thoroughfare lined with fast-food stands and throngs of local people. You'll find Liberty House here, one of Hawaii's leading department stores, as well as a big fascinating Woolworth's, with plenty of souvenirs.

WALKING TOUR 3
The State Capitol & Iolani Palace

Start: State Capitol.
Finish: Iolani Palace.
Time: Approximately 2 to 3 hours, including time for visiting Iolani Palace.
Best Time: Wednesday through Saturday before 2:15pm.

Take TheBUS no. 2 from Waikiki to the corner of Punchbowl and Beretania streets. Across from you will be the:

1. **Hawaii State Capitol,** on Beretania Street between Punchbowl and Richard streets. This magnificent structure, completed in 1969 at a cost of $25 million, has an open-air roof that sweeps skyward like the peak of a volcano, reflecting pools representing the state's ocean environment, and Hawaiian murals and motifs throughout. Hopefully, the renovation of the building will have been completed by the time you read this, so you can see the state legislature in session or "experience" the offices of Hawaii's governor and lieutenant governor. Should the building not yet be open when you arrive (I'm keeping my fingers crossed!), then visit the temporary Capitol District Visitor Center at 510 South Beretania St., diagonally across the intersection from the capitol. Here you can see an elaborate multimedia presentation about the construction of the capitol; an accompanying videotape about the interior appointments,

Walking Tour—The State Capitol & Iolani Palace

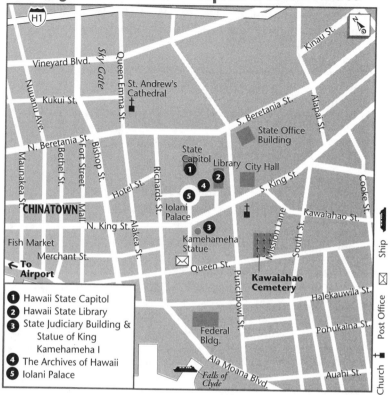

1. Hawaii State Capitol
2. Hawaii State Library
3. State Judiciary Building & Statue of King Kamehameha I
4. The Archives of Hawaii
5. Iolani Palace

statuary, and other works of art; and occasional touring exhibits. Open 8am to 4pm.

In front of the capitol building itself, note Marisol's controversial statue of Father Damien, as well as the other works of art facing Beretania Street. (Replicas of the Damien statue, and that of King Kamehameha outside the State Judiciary Building, represent Hawaii in the Hall of Statuary in the United States Capitol Building in Washington, D.C.) Just outside the makai side of the building are two relatively new works: a replica of the Liberty Bell and a statue of Hawaii's last reigning monarch, Queen Liliuokalani. Admirers of the Hawaiian monarchy (and those who have dreams of restoring it) often place flowers and leis in her hand and on her outstretched arm.

As you stand at the statue facing makai (toward King Street), you'll see the central building of the:

2. **Hawaii State Library,** 478 King St. This Greco-Roman edifice has a delightful open-air garden court. Visit the Edna Allyn Children's Room to see Hawaiian legend murals by Juliette May Fraser. Other paintings worth a look are hung throughout the library. Directly across King Street is the:

3. **State Judiciary Building.** Right in front is the famous statue of King Kamehameha I, dressed in a royal feathered cape and a helmet that looks curiously Grecian. A symbol of Hawaii (you'll see it in countless pictures and

on postcards), this larger-than-life statue of the leader who unified the islands is not a great work of art, but it's appropriately heroic. On Kamehameha Day, June 11, the local citizenry decks the statue with huge leis.

Just ewa of the library, you'll see a streamlined building; its:

4. **The Archives of Hawaii.** Inside are valuable documents, journals, photographs, and other records—it's the largest collection of Hawaiiana in existence. The archives are on the grounds of:

5. **Iolani Palace,** which is Diamond Head of the building (at King and Richards streets). This is the high point and end of the tour: Plan your walking tour so that you will arrive here in time to tour the only royal palace on American soil (☎ 808/522-0382 for reservations).

WALKING TOUR 4
Historic Chinatown District

Start:　Oahu Market.
Finish:　Kuan Yin Buddhist Temple.
Time:　Approximately 1 to 2 hours.
Best Time:　Daylight hours.

From Waikiki, take TheBUS no. 19 (Airport or Airport/Hickam) or no. 20 (Airport) toward downtown Honolulu. Get off at Mauankea Street and you'll find yourself in the midst of the Historical Chinatown District. With its jumble of shops laden with crafts, herbs, and Chinese groceries, and with many recently arrived merchants from Vietnam, Thailand, and other parts of Southeast Asia, the area is more fascinating and exotic than ever before. It's still a mixture of sleaze and sophistication, of tattoo parlors and opulent temples. There are several Chinese acupuncturists and Hong Kong herb doctors here (many locals swear by them) and it's fun to look in their windows and try to figure out what those weird ingredients—powdered deer hooves or reptile skins or whatever—could do for you.

On King Street, near the waterfront, you'll want to stop in at an old Chinatown fixture, the:

1. **Oahu Market.** Open-air stalls overflow with dizzying arrays of fish, poultry, and unidentifiable vegetables. The sights, sounds, and aromas provide an authentic glimpse at supermarket Hawaii.

From Oahu Market, turn left and then right on River Street. When you get to the mauka side of Beretania Street, you'll see an impressive statue of Sun Yat Sen, the father of modern China, who spent some years in Hawaii. You're now at the:

2. **Chinese Cultural Plaza.** Many cultural events take place here. There are several restaurants and a number of small shops that may be worth a quick browse, but beware—we've usually found the goods here to be overpriced. The biggest new development in Chinatown, which you can reach by exiting the Cultural Plaza from the Maunakea Street side and turning right, is the:

3. **Maunakea Marketplace,** in the block bounded by Hotel, Puahi, and Maunakea streets. There's a statue of Confucius, a clock tower, and thousands of bricks engraved with personal messages. The office of the Historic Hawaii Foundation is here, as is the Chinese Visitor Center, where you can pick up self-guided tour maps and tapes of Chinatown, and see a historical presentation of old Chinatown.

Walking Tour—Historic Chinatown District

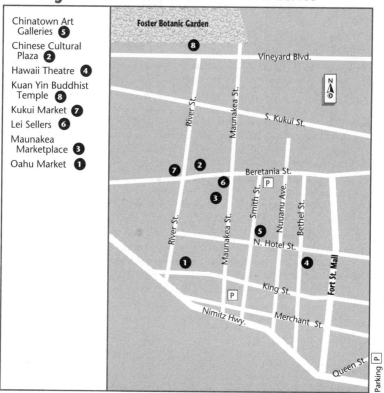

Chinatown Art Galleries **5**

Chinese Cultural Plaza **2**

Hawaii Theatre **4**

Kuan Yin Buddhist Temple **8**

Kukui Market **7**

Lei Sellers **6**

Maunakea Marketplace **3**

Oahu Market **1**

Foster Botanic Garden

Vineyard Blvd.

River St.

Maunakea St.

S. Kukui St.

Beretania St.

Smith St.

Nuuanu Ave.

Bethel St.

N. Hotel St.

Fort St. Mall

King St.

Nimitz Hwy.

Merchant St.

Queen St.

Parking P

☕ **TAKE A BREAK** The Maunakea Marketplace Food Court has a truly international array of fast-food stands, with a central courtyard for dining. You can sample the foods of Thailand, Korea, the Philippines, even Puerto Rico, as well as China, of course. Directly behind the Food Court is a fresh seafood market, wholesale and retail; many restaurants get their seafood here.

As you wander through Chinatown's little streets, you'll notice that Old Chinatown is giving way to several new buildings, a park, and continued upgrading of historic older buildings. To see a good example of this architectural revival, exit the Maunakea Marketplace on Maunakea Street. Turn left, walk to Hotel Street, then right to Bethel Street. Make another left and there, at no. 130, is the:

4. Hawaii Theatre, newly restored to its original 1920s art deco splendor. The theater has hosted everything from beauty pageants and band concerts to the Hawaii International Film Festival and political functions.

Go back down Hotel Street; turn right on Nuuanu, and you can spend a little time browsing at the:

5. Chinatown Art Galleries. Something of an artistic renaissance is going on here. There are perhaps a half-dozen galleries in the neighborhood, and they're well worth your time. Two of the major ones are those of Pegge Hopper, at 1164 Nuuanu St., whose works are seen all over the islands, and Ramsay,

1128 Smith St., the renowned pen-and-ink artist who was in the process of creating a new restaurant in the adjacent space at the time of this writing.

Leaving the Ramsay Gallery, turn left on Pauahi Street. Walk to Maunakea Street and visit the shops of the:

6. **Lei Sellers.** There are at least a dozen of them in these few blocks, and they offer the best prices and finest lei work in Honolulu. Cindy's, Violet's, and Jenny's are a few of the best.

You could end your tour here, or you might want to walk another few blocks to climax your trip with an exotic sight. Walk three blocks mauka from King Street to Beretania Street; turn left and walk ewa a block or two to the Nuuanu Stream. Much of the old Japanese neighborhood that used to be here—scrubby little saimin stands and pool halls, fish and grocery stores under quaint Asian roofs—has been torn down to make way for new construction. You'll see the Kukui Market, with its distinctive blue roof. Now follow River Street toward the mountains—you're likely to see local people fishing for tilapia, a nutritious fish that breeds rapidly in such brackish water—then cross Vineyard Boulevard and you'll be at the:

7. **Kuan Yin Buddhist Temple,** 170 North Vineyard St. Slip off your shoes and walk inside. Joss sticks and incense burn at the altar, food offerings calm the ancestral spirits, and America seems far, far away. (There is another statue of Kuan Yin—one far more splendid—in the Honolulu Academy of Arts.)

Ask anyone who's been there: Honolulu is a great place to shop. In fact, if you walk along Kalakaua Avenue any afternoon or evening, it sometimes seems that tourists are doing nothing else. For even though prices on many items are just about what you'd expect to pay back home, there are so many good buys and so many interesting things that just about everybody gets caught up in the shopping fever. New shopping complexes have blossomed all over Honolulu, with scads of temptations right in or very near Waikiki. Indulge and enjoy yourself—it can't be helped.

Spend an hour or two in the shops that line Kalakaua Avenue, in the Ala Moana Shopping Center, or at the Royal Hawaiian Shopping Center, and you'll have a pretty good idea of the things that everybody wants to bring back from the islands. Clothing is undoubtedly the most popular item—island resort wear, both vintage and new, in bright, bold Hawaiian prints, the colors of the sun and tropical landscape. And then there are fragrant, flowery perfumes, beautiful works of island art, tapas (bark cloth printed with primitive religious symbols), kitschy dolls with grass skirts, genuine Hawaiian-made ukuleles, rare Niihau-shell leis, and other fanciful island jewelry. And you can't forget the food—macadamia nuts, Hawaiian jams, coconut syrup, Kona coffee, not to mention the pineapples and coconuts that you'll want to have or send back home. All these are typical of the islands and they are on sale everywhere.

Note: Most shopping malls are open from 9 or 10am to 9pm Monday through Friday, to 5:30pm on Saturday, and usually to 4pm on Sunday. Non-mall shops keep similar hours, though many are closed on Sunday; you might telephone in advance for a shop's hours.

1 Vintage Aloha Shirts

✪ Bailey's Antique & Aloha Shirts, Inc.
517 Kapahulu Ave. ☎ **808/734-7628.**

You can buy a good aloha shirt anywhere for around $30 to $50 or even less. So why should anyone want to spend up to $1,000 for one? Many people do, since vintage rayon shirts from the 1930s,

'40s, and early '50s have become hot collectors' items. Bailey's is where celebrities and collectors go for their $100-to-$1,000 finds; but if you have only $5, $10, or $20 to spend, they have plenty for you too. Great browsing here among literally thousands of shirts as well as other collectibles, including art deco and retro jewelry and Levi jeans dating back to the 1920s.

Claire de Lune
At Ward Warehouse. ☎ **808/596-0808.**

Antique aloha shirts from the '30s, '40s, and '50s sometimes find their way to this delightful antique shop.

Kula Bay
In the Royal Hawaiian Hotel, 2259 Kalakaua Ave. ☎ **808/923-0042,** and at the Hilton Hawaiian Village, 2005 Kalia Rd., ☎ 808/943-0771.

Kula Bay does some clever work; they take authentic prints from shirts of the 1930s, '40s, and early '50s, have them painted on long-staple cotton in more muted colors, and turn out handsome, very well-tailored, brand-new aloha shirts for about $50 to $60. For photos of the originals, and a history of the aloha shirt, read *The Hawaiian Shirt,* by H. Thomas Steel (Abbeville Press), available at many local bookstores.

Reminisce
2139-A Kuhio Ave. ☎ **808/921-9056.**

This charming vintage clothing shop, a block from the Kuhio Theater, has an eclectic collection of authentic 1950s Aloha shirts, amazing cravats, fascinating, one-of-a-kind cufflinks, mint-condition bathing suits, and other treasures from more gracious days.

2 New Aloha & Resort Wear

Could you possibly go back home without at least one Hawaiian muumuu, aloha shirt, or bathing suit? Unthinkable! Let us first, however, tell women a little bit about the Hawaiian fashion scene. Since every kind of contemporary fashion idea has hit Hawaii, it's a great place to shop for sophisticated resort wear, with many of the stores carrying lovely clothes by California designers. And it's easy to find lovely things from Bali here. But after all, this is Hawaii, and we still think the most beautiful Hawaiian dresses are the graceful, full-length muumuus that Hawaiian women have been wearing for over a century. You'll find them perfect for evening; and "shorty muus" are great for daytime. Everybody, of course, will want an aloha shirt—boldly printed and cut fuller than men's ordinary sport shirts, since they are designed to be worn outside the trousers. You can find Hawaiian clothing just about anywhere, but we'll give you a few hints on our own special favorites, where we feel the quality is the best for the money. Reasonably priced aloha wear may also be found at such chains as J.C. Penney and Sears at Ala Moana Shopping Center.

Andrade
In the Sheraton Princess Kaiulani Hotel, 2342 Kalakau Ave. ☎ **808/971-4266.**

A very respectable old-timer, Andrade's also has an excellent selection of men's aloha and sports shirts, and women's fashions as well. There's another Andrade's across the street at the Sheraton Waikiki.

Carol and Mary
Royal Hawaiian Hotel, 2355 Kalakaua Ave. ☎ **808/971-4262.**

One of the better women's fashion stores, Carol and Mary handles the top Polynesian lines and a large selection of beautiful sportswear from mainland designers as well.

⊛ Hilo Hattie Fashion Center
700 Nimitz Hwy. ☎ **808/537-2926.**

Vast selections of aloha wear for men, women, and children are available here. They are all for sale at factory prices with free refreshments, free hemming, and a shell lei greeting. They'll bus you to their factory free of charge; phone the above number.

Liberty House
2314 Kalakaua Ave. ☎ **808/941-2345.**

Liberty House is one of Honolulu's most exclusive department stores—it's the Bloomingdale's of Hawaii, if you will. They have a superb collection of men's and women's aloha wear and resort wear, showing some of the top designers. In addition to the Waikiki location, Liberty House is at Ala Moana Shopping Center, in downtown Honolulu, and at many other locations throughout the islands.

Mamo Howell
At Ward Warehouse, 1050 Ala Moana Blvd. ☎ **808/522-0616.**

Mamo Howell, a former Christian Dior model, takes the inspiration for her stunning muumuus from Hawaiian quilt motifs. Her elegant clothing is worn by some of the best-dressed women in Honolulu.

Noa Noa
At Ala Moana Shopping Center. ☎ **808/947-4451.**

No need to travel all the way to the Big Island to get some of that wild and wonderful tropical clothing for which Noa Noa is so well known—owner Joan Simon now has a store at Ala Moana Shopping Center. In addition to original batik designs using all natural fabrics, she carries exotic gift items, such as wall hangings, masks, ceramics, chests, and basketry from China.

Pomegranates in the Sun
At Ward Warehouse. ☎ **808/531-1108.**

Pomegranates in the Sun has established a loyal following of fashion-conscious women. It features local artists and designers inspired by the Hawaiian atmosphere. Many of the items in stock are one-of-a-kind. Look for the smashing Pomegranates in the Sun in Haleiwa, on the North Shore, when you journey around the island.

Princess Kaiulani
1222 Kaumaulii St. (call for driving directions). ☎ **808/847-4806.**

This muumuu manufacturer was the first to start using pretty, small-figured, calico prints in pastel colors. Their dresses are ultra-feminine, with eyelet, lace, or ruffles, and the fabrics are top-quality. This attractive factory showroom offers its own line and others at about 30% less than retail. Long muumuus, selling here in the $75-to-$80 range, would be well over $100 at most stores.

Reyn's
Sheraton Waikiki, 2255 Kalakaua Ave. ☎ **808/923-0331**.

No doubt about it, Reyn's offers the most distinctive designs in men's aloha and sports shirts. Patterns and colors are muted and subtly understated. Reyn's also carries a small selection of women's clothing. Other shops are at Ala Moana Shopping Center, Kahala Mall, and many other locations throughout the Islands.

Tahiti Imports
At Ala Moana Shopping Center. ☎ **808/941-4539**.

In business for many years, Tahiti Imports takes Tahitian prints of their own design and makes them into muumuus, aloha shirts, bikinis, and pareaus. They also sell their exquisite hand-printed fabrics by the yard.

Victoriana Luxe
At craft fairs and at A Crafter's Dream, 1365 Nuuanu Ave. ☎ **808/521-6611**.

Paige Lawes, who designs under the name Victoriana Luxe, makes dresses in charming country and floral prints. If you see a dress you like but it isn't in your size and or you really prefer one of the other fabrics, Paige will whip it up for you at the same price as the one on the rack—she won't let you buy something that doesn't become you.

3 Wearable Art

Hawaiian Heritage
810 Bannister St. (call for driving directions). ☎ **808/847-5855**.

Allen James's exquisite creations for women—he designs not only the clothes but the fabrics as well—sell for $200 and up in places like Liberty House. Last time we visited his factory showroom, we saw muumuus in kukui nut-and-leaf patterns, lehua, crown flower, puakenikeni, ilima, and quilt patterns. At the showroom, things are 20% less than retail; if you want your own custom-made dress or suit, the 20% goes back on. Mr. James's pieces are classics; women in Hawaii wear them for years, and many use them as wedding dresses. They're sold under the Hawaiian Heritage label and the Mango's label, depending on the fabric. If you don't see what you want, ask to see the book; anything in it can be made just for you. Recently they've added a line of superb aloha shirts in cotton and silk.

Montsuki
1148 Koko Head Ave. ☎ **808/734-3457**.

All of the beautiful clothing in this sunny shop is created by Janet Yamasaki and her daughter, Patty, out of Japanese kimonos, mostly silk. Skirts, jackets, pants, tops, and dresses are planned to show off each kimono design to its best advantage: The placement of a delicate spray of flowers or a bold leaf turns the appearance of a simply cut jacket or top into a glorious piece of wearable art. Styles are classic and elegant, and the fabrics make each one look different. I love their jacket and skirt ensembles; Pair one with a Montsuki top, classic shoes, and a great pair of earrings (the shop is full of them), and you'll turn heads. If you can't manage a complete silk ensemble—anywhere from $250 to $500 or more—there are some lower-priced jackets and pants made from cotton yukatas or Kasuri cotton in colorful prints. At the very least, you're sure to find a fabulous hair ornament fashioned from antique obis or made of chopsticks with beads;

a pair of earrings by Misono, charming little kimono-clad girls to dangle from your ears; earrings by Margaret Realica of California; enameled fancies by Hawaii jewelry artist Leighton Lee; or shimmering beaded baubles by Carole Ikeda. Check out the baskets brimming with belts and sashes made from obis, and don't miss Helen Hamada's exquisite one-of-a-kind cards.

Nake'u Awai

1613 Houghtailing St. (not far from the Bishop Museum). ☎ **808/841-1221.**

Joel Nake'u is a young Hawaiian designer whose beautiful silk-screened fabrics are a blend of the traditional and the contemporary. He turns his textiles into long skirts, shirts, muumuus, bags, and sundresses, which are worn by some of the most fashion-conscious women in Honolulu.

4 Consignment Shops

Comme Çi Comme Ça

2484 Waialae Ave. ☎ **808/734-8869.**

Well-known hula dancer Sweetie Moffat presides over this tiny, eclectic shop filled with goodies. Everything here is one of a kind. Sweetie and her husband, Tom (an entertainment promoter who brings big-name shows to Hawaii), travel a great deal, particularly in France and Italy. When Sweetie sees something she likes, she buys it for the shop—but only one of each item, so if you see a wonderful French designer dress and it isn't your size, well, comme çi comme ça. The other side of the coin here is the consignment side. Sweetie takes great clothes and decorative items—they must be in mint condition—on consignment. There are designer duds, vintage jewelry, and children's clothes that must have cost a fortune. I especially liked a toddler party dress with an exquisite cutwork collar for $12.50. There are old entertainment posters, vintage pillbox hats, lots of Italian pottery, new Flavia address books, beaded collars, and much more.

The Ultimate You

851 Pohukaina St., Blvd. C., Bay 4. ☎ **808/591-8388.**

This designer's consignment store is full of surprises: You could even pick up an Armani or a Kamali here, because this is where Hawaii's best-dressed women send their designer duds when they're bored with them. You'll often find designer muumuus—the kind that sold originally for $150 to $200—for as little as $25. (I scooped up three on my last visit.) Owner Kelsey Sears also discounts brand-new merchandise: costume jewelry, accessories, scarves, and many lovely Island clothes.

5 Antiques

Antique Alley

1347 Kapiolani Blvd. ☎ **808/941-8551.**

Hawaiian mementoes of the '30s, '40s, and '50s can be found at some of the dealers who show their wares at this mini-mall. There are often old photos, menus from Matson Liner days, funky jewelry, vintage Hawaiian "Nodder" hula dolls, and lots more. Paké Zane has the best selection.

Claire de Lune

At Ward Warehouse. ☎ **808/596-0808.**

Nostalgia buffs seek out Claire de Lune, where they snap up everything from rattan furniture to outrigger canoe models to framed prints, old sheet music and books, antique aloha shirts, vintage bark cloth, dishes, boxes, candlesticks, even Hawaiian quilt design earrings.

6   Hawaiian & Polynesian Crafts

Little Hawaiian Craft Shop and Wood Gallery
At the Royal Hawaiian Shopping Center. ☎ **808/926-2662**.

Almost everything at this outstanding shop is handmade in Hawaii by craftspeople using natural Island materials and working in both traditional and contemporary styles. Replicas of museum pieces sit among hand-carved tikis and barrels of raw materials. Niihau-shell necklaces, authentic kukui-nut leis, feather hatbands, sandwood necklaces, handpainted totebags, and Hawaiian quilting pillows and patterns are among the treasures. The Wood Gallery specializes in hand-carved replicas of Hawaiian artifacts as well as in collector's items—spirit figures, tapas, weavings, war clubs, drums, masks, spears—from Fiji, the Solomon Islands, New Guinea, Tonga, and Micronesia.

Pakipika Trading Company
At Aloha Tower Marketplace. ☎ **808/537-5511**.

Strangely enough, shops showing authentic Hawaiian and Polynesian crafts are a rarity in Hawaii. Pakipika is a happy exception. Among their excellent collection: tikis, tapa cloths, real kukui-nut leis, lauhala woven baskets, pareaus, petroglyph earrings, lava "eggs," and much more.

South Seas Mercantile & Trading Co.
2310 Kuhio Ave. ☎ **808/923-5509**.

Everything in this exemplary Waikiki shop is handmade by Hawaiian and Polynesian craftspeople, employing whenever possible the same techniques used in ancient times. The focus is on Hawaiian crafts, but Polynesia and Micronesia are also represented. There are museum replica hand-carved tiki figures, tapa cloths, Tahitian dance skirts, authentic hula instruments, kukui-nut leis, and much more. Of special interest to collectors are the Polynesian ceremonial masks and hand-carved weapons, one in the traditional woods and styles. Owner Joseph Berardy's own tie-dyed pastel pareaus, which he creates in his North Shore home using a sun-sensitive heliographic process, make great all-occasion garments for women; many island residents use them as tropical tablecloths and wall hangings. There's another South Seas Mercantile location at Dole Cannery Square, 650 Iliwei Rd.

7   More Arts & Crafts

Artlines
At Ala Moana Shopping Center. ☎ **808/941-1445**.

Here's a highly tasteful collection of jewelry, animal masks, carving, statuary, crystals, bells, Tiffany-type lamps, and the like, collected from all over the world—particularly from Egypt, Morocco, India, Indonesia, Greece, and Africa. There's an exotic collection of sterling silver earrings. Prices begin at $1 for unpolished stones and go as high as $3,500 for a superb Buddha.

Honolulu's Craft Fairs

Craft fairs are very, very popular in Honolulu; there's one going on almost all the time, all year long. Local craftspeople are on hand, happy to show and discuss their works with you. Notables are the **Mission Houses Museum Fair,** held the weekend after Thanksgiving; the **Honolulu Theatre for Youth Fair,** the weekend after Halloween; and the **Pacific Handcrafters Christmas Fair** at Thomas Square, the first weekend in December. Fairs are always listed in the local newspapers under "Things to Do" or in the calendar section.

You will, of course, find your own favorite artists and artisans as you wander through a fair; these are some of the talented people I like best:

Probably the sterling silver and gold petroglyph reproductions that Tom Cohen, jeweler *extraordinaire,* makes are his biggest sellers since the prices are so reasonable, but his one-of-a-kind creations in gold or silver and gemstones are truly spectacular. His wife, Dharma, makes enchanting gold and silver angels. Darlene Mandel creates beautiful, one-of-a-kind pieces of jewelry. Darlene buys jewelry from the '20s through the '50s, pulls them apart, and creates her own totally unique pieces. She also has beautifully embellished denim jackets.

Aunty Mary Louise Kekuewa is the doyenne of Hawaiian featherwork; she makes wondrous feather leis, combs, and other pretty things, and gives instruction at the Bishop Museum's Atherton Halau. Aunty has a shop on Kapahulu Avenue where she also sells feathers in bulk.

The pretty dresses in country and floral prints that go under the "Victoriana Luxe" label are made by Paige Lawes, who can custom-make them in your size and color in a jiffy. Kerstin, a Swedish beauty who lived for many years in Hawaii and now calls Florida home, comes back for all of the major craft fairs. Her graceful, fluttery muumuus embellished with hand crocheting are exquisite. Makaki'i is the creator of exquisite, gorgeously costumed porcelain Hawaiian dolls. Any one of them would make a great remembrance of Hawaii. Deb Aoki's creations in Fimo—jewelry, magnets, notepads, and the like—are unique and adorable. One by One's T-shirts are hand-screened and feature designs such as Daruma (the founder of Zen) and the maneki neko (welcoming cat); you'll see them in shops all over Hawaii. Look for the pretty Aloha Angels, made from the monstera plant, near Yuletide.

A bubbly English lady, Denise Reid, a.k.a. Cesta, imports clothing, jewelry, and decorative items from far-flung places like you'll see nowhere else in Hawaii. Rebecca, of Rebecca's Chachkies, uses luminous, semiprecious beads to create her lovely jewelry. Bye-Bye Birdies makes handcrafted birds whose wings move and create the illusion of flight, Lono and Kay Smith of Kauai bring them over for all of the major fairs. Dudley, a young potter, makes delightful things; we are partial to her little turtles, which make great gifts.

If the craft fair fever descends upon you at mid-week or on a weekend when no fairs are going on, head straight for A Crafter's Dream at 1365 Nuuanu Ave. (☎ **808/521-6611**), which features items on consignment from crafters all over the state.

Craft Flair

At Ward Centre. ☎ **808/592-1800.**

Owner Valerie Tanabe set out to combine the uniqueness and variety of a local craft fair with the convenience and service of a retail store. The result: Craft Flair, whose name says it all. Over 150 artists, both local and mainland, are featured in a delightful collection of one-of-a-kind handcrafted clothing, accessories, and gift items. Prices go from just a little to quite a lot. Treasures include porcelain earrings, baby blankets, marbled silk ties, and kimono vests.

Following Sea

At Kahala Mall. ☎ **808/734-4425.**

Following Sea is one of Honolulu's oldest and most respected craft galleries. It presents the work of many American craftspeople in ceramics, glass, jewelry, fiber, and woodwork. Each piece is more glorious than the next; many Island artists are represented.

From Ed and Friends

2563 S. King St. ☎ **808/943-8680.**

This is a mesmerizing hodgepodge of the work of 60 to 70 artists and craftspeople from Hawaii and the mainland. Owner Ed Higa is a master potter, and his ceramic pieces are treasures. Also represented are a glassblower, several jewelry artisans, and woodworkers.

Magic Attic

At Aloha Tower Marketplace. ☎ **808/536-7771.**

Weird, wild, unconventional, handpainted furniture is the stock in trade at Magic Attic, run by a colorful lady named Elsha. Prices start at $50 for a small stool and go up to about $1,600. Jeweler Liddy provides an extraordinary collection of earrings with clock faces.

Nohea Gallery

At Ward Warehouse. ☎ **808/599-7927.**

With the work of more than 450 island artists and craftspeople in handcrafted jewelry, paintings, koa boxes, chests and furniture, basketry, featherwork, quilts, pottery, glass, and sculpture, Nohea offers just about the widest and best selection of fine arts and crafts in the islands.

8　Hawaiiana

For antique Hawaiiana, see Bailey's Aloha Shirts, Claire de Lune, and Antique Alley, listed above.

Mission Houses Museum Gift Shop

553 S1 King St. ☎ **808/531-0481.**

This tasteful shop has an excellent collection of Hawaiiana, including hard-to-find tapa cloth that can be framed, koa-wood bracelets, and Christmas ornaments made of lauhala and other local materials, as well as appliqué kits with Hawaiian quilt motifs and T-shirts with Mission Houses of Hawaii quilt patterns or flowers.

Shop Pacifica

1525 Bernice St. (in the Bishop Museum). ☎ **808/847-3511.**

Shop Pacifica is a fine place to shop for Hawaiian gifts. It's a cut above the usual museum-shop fare, with books on Hawaiian and other Pacific cultures, handcrafted feather leis and native koa-wood boxes and bowls, reproductions of Polynesian artifacts, fascinating photographs of old Hawaii, and rare and unique Island jewelry.

9 Fine Art

AMFAC Plaza Exhibition Room
AMFAC Center, Fort Street Mall and Queen Street. ☎ **808/531-0444.**

Group exhibitions of contemporary paintings, crafts, sculpture, and photography are held here on a regular basis.

Art a La Carte
At Ward Centre, 1200 Ala Moana Blvd. ☎ **808/536-3351.**

This is a cooperative gallery featuring the work of a dozen local artists who take turns "sitting" the gallery, and often work right here.

Arts of Paradise
At the International Market Place, 2nd floor, ☎ **808/924-2787.**

This well-thought-out, artist-owned gallery features work in all mediums by Hawaii's top professional artists. There are frequent free demonstrations and talks by participating artists. Call for information.

Honolulu Advertiser Gallery
First floor of News Building, 605 Kapiolani Blvd. ☎ **808/526-1322.**

A long-time showcase for the works of both local and mainland artists.

Images International of Hawaii
Ala Moana Shopping Center. ☎ **808/926-5081.**

Internationally acclaimed artists such as Hisashi Otsuka, Caroline Young, Tatsuo Ito, and Robert Lyn Nelson, as well as the unique leather sculptor, Liu Miao Chan, are featured here.

Chinatown's Best Art Galleries

A small art colony flourishes in this gentrified part of Chinatown. Of the dozen-or-so galleries here, the ones you want to be sure to see are:

Ramsay, 1128 Smith St. ☎ 808/537-2787. Pen-and-ink artist Ramsay, who has achieved national and international fame (an exhibition of her masterful architectural drawings appeared at the Senate Rotunda in Washington, D.C. in 1988), exhibits her own work and also shows work by prominent artists in other media.

Pegge Hopper, 1164 Nuuanu Ave. ☎ 808/524-1160. Hopper's images of Polynesian women are seen everywhere in the Islands. The gallery features her original paintings, drawings, and collages, in addition to her posters, limited-edition prints, calendars, and gift items.

Gateway Gallery, 1050 Nuuanu Ave. ☎ 808/599-1559. This upbeat gallery features fine arts and unique gift items. They specialize in floral- and tropical-themed paintings and sculpture.

Rosalie's Studio
Aloha Tower Marketplace. ☎ **808/533-4866.**

This charming gallery is devoted exclusively to the works of the owner's mother Rosalie Rupp Prussing, who does delightful, colorful paintings, lithographs, and seriographs of island scenes.

Tennent Art Foundation
203 Prospect St. (on the slopes of Punchbowl; call for directions). ☎ **808/531-1987.**

A great lady of the arts in Hawaii was Madge Tennent, who came to Hawaii at the turn of the century via South Africa and Paris. She broke away from the academy and its conventions to record on canvas her massive portraits of the Hawaiian people; her works are collector's items now. You can visit her gallery, now presided over by her niece, from 10am to noon Tuesday through Saturday, 2 to 4pm on Sunday, or by special appointment.

10   Jewelry

Bernard Hurtig
Hilton Hawaiian Village. ☎ **808/949-2828.**

Bernard Hurtig, one of Honolulu's most respected fine jewelers for many years, has a tremendous local following. He's known for his golf watches, antique jade, netsukes, and beautiful pieces in 18-karat gold.

Hawaiian Heirloom Jewelry Factory
Royal Hawaiian Shopping Center. ☎ **808/924-7972.**

This is one of the best sources for those hand-carved, heavy gold bracelets and pendants inscribed with your name or a saying in Hawaiian letters that you see so many local people wearing; they have been a tradition in Hawaii since the days when Queen Liliuokalani journeyed to the court of Queen Victoria. The Hawaiian Heirloom Jewelry Factory conducts free tours every hour on the hour, from 10am to 4pm weekdays. You'll learn something of the history of Hawaiian heirloom jewelry, and see how these beautiful pieces are made today. Favorite inscriptions: Kuu Ipo (Sweetheart), Tutu (Grandma), and the name of the family's newest baby.

Kim's Fashion
96 N. King St. ☎ **808/599-7721.**

If you're looking for freshwater pearls, this little Chinatown shop is *the* place. Owner Kim Phung offers beautiful freshwater pearls at prices that are often lower than wholesale on the mainland; strands run $2 to $70, and they're beautiful. People come from all over for Kim's pearls and, once home, they keep calling for reorders. She has a nice selection of handbags and cloisonné as well.

Liberty House
2314 Kalakaua Ave. ☎ **808/941-2345.**

An excellent source for both costume and fine jewelry. The works of many leading craftspeople are shown. There's another Liberty House at Ala Moana Shopping Center, and at many other Island locations.

Maui Divers Jewelry Design Center
1520 Liona St. ☎ **808/949-6729.**

Maui Divers were the first to mine black coral—Hawaii's official state gemstone—in the deep waters off Lahaina some 30 years ago. Pink and gold coral were next. Today, they combine coral with diamonds, gold, pearls, rubies, and other precious gems to create some unique jewelry. There are thousands of pieces to choose from, and all come with lifetime guarantees. Shop the showroom after you've taken their free tour, which really is interesting and educational, and includes a film and a walk through a manufacturing center to see their skilled artisans at work. The factory is within walking distance of Ala Moana Shopping Center; or, for free shuttle bus service from Waikiki, call the number above.

11   Flower Leis

When local people need to buy leis, they usually head for Chinatown—and so should you. Although leis are sold at several other places, especially at the airport and on the ocean side of Kalakaua Avenue, the best prices and finest quality can usually be found among the Chinatown lei sellers. Some of my favorites, all on Maunakea Street, are **Cindy's Lei Shoppe,** at no. 1034; **Violet's** at no. 1165; **Jenny's Lei Stand** at no. 1151; and **Lin's** at no. 1107. **Lita's Leis** is around the corner at 59 N. Beretania St., and **Aloha Leis** is at the corner of Puuahi.

12   Quilts

Kwilts 'n Koa

1126 12th Ave., in Kaimuki. ☎ **808/735-2300.**

Hawaiian quilts are among the treasures of the islands; old ones hang in museums, new ones can cost thousands. Along with other elements of Hawaiian culture, the art is blossoming again today. If you want to learn to quilt, buy a quilt pattern, or a quilt itself, visit Kathy Tsark, the owner of this store, her daughter Leanne, and her nephew Robert; avid quilters all three. They sell pillows and quilts in stocks—from $150 for pillows, up to $3,500 for a king-size quilt—and will also take commissions. A commissioned quilt will take up to a year to make; a small piece, about a month (remember, this is intricate handiwork). They also give classes and demonstrations. The shop also carries koa wood products— boxes, calabashes, mirrors—plus Hawaiian gifts like dolls, shirts, jewelry, hula implements, and more.

13   Gifts & Souvenirs

You will, of course, have to buy lots of gifts and souvenirs for the folks back home. I've found gifts of Kona coffee and chocolate-covered macadamia nuts to be hands-down favorites. T-shirts are welcome, too, but please don't patronize the vendors who line many of the side streets in Waikiki; they pay no rent or taxes or insurance, they're an eyesore, and they're in unfair competition with reputable merchants, whose offerings are of much better quality. (They are, however, cheap—they often sell four T-shirts for $10.) Crazy Shirts, which has locations all over town, including one in King's Village (see below) offers an imaginative, whimsical selection. Should you want to give key chains, letter-openers, money clips, and the like, all decorated with some Hawaiian symbol or figure, as well as Hawaiian perfumes and food products, the The ubiquitous ABC Discount Stores, in addition to Sears at Ala Moana Shopping Center, will be your best bets.

14 Shopping Centers

IN WAIKIKI

Hyatt Shops, Hyatt Regency Waikiki
2424 Kalakaua Ave. ☎ **808/923-1234.**

This exquisite skyscraper hotel houses a beautiful shopping complex, with fountains, waterfalls, sculpture, and greenery, all in a stunning Hawaiian monarchy setting. Sixty shops are located in the three-story shopping and dining arcade that surrounds the hotel's open-air atrium. The range goes from exclusive designer shops to those that specialize in one-of-a-kind creations, jewelry, affordable gifts, souvenirs, and sundries. Popular chains **Benneton, Esprit,** and **Crazy Shirts** all have outposts here. **Hunting World** can outfit you for your next safari. And there's a great selection of swimsuits and beachwear at **Swim Inn.**

Between shopping chores, catch some of the free events that take place all day—classes in Hawaiian quilt-making, lei-making, and hula-dancing. There's entertainment in the Great Hall everyday. Open daily from 9am to 11pm.

International Market Place
2330 Kalakaua Ave. ☎ **808/923-9871.**

Waikiki's oldest "shopping center" and still its most popular, this is an open-air bazaar with scores of booths selling jewelry, candles, T-shirts, beach cover-ups, pearls-in-the-oyster, resort wear, kitschy souvenirs, and more. Shops come and go, so our best advice is to browse, bargain, and comparison-shop. Special favorites include **Ball Designs,** which imports lovely clothing for men and women directly from Indonesia, and **Arts of Paradise,** showing original work by island artists. Be sure not to miss the all-Elvis shop. Open daily from 9am to 11pm.

King's Village
131 Kaiulani Ave. ☎ **808/944-6855.**

As much fun to browse through as to shop at, King's Village recaptures the flavor of Hawaii's monarchy period with its cobblestoned streets and classic architecture. You'll sense the British feeling as soon as you pass through the gate. There's a changing-of-the-guard ceremony nightly at 6:15. The tiny shops might suggest Victorian London at first glance, but their wares are definitely international, with a smattering of Polynesia. The **Royal Peddler** has all sorts of gift items, and all kinds of candles in whimsical shapes are available at **Candle Odyssey.** The ubiquitous **Crazy Shirts** has a large store here. **Casa de Europe** features European men's and women's accessories and clothing.

In keeping with the British atmosphere of King's Village, there's an English pub: **Rose and Crown** is perfect for a glass of ale, a meal or snack, a sing-along at the piano, or even a game of darts. Japanese treats are available at **Tanaka of Tokyo** and **Odoriko.** Open daily from 9am to 11pm.

Kuhio Mall
2301 Kuhio Ave. ☎ **808/922-2724.**

Located directly behind the International Market Place, Kuhio Mall is very similar, with scads of booths selling tourist stuff. Both Kuhio Mall and the International Market Place provide direct access to the International Food Court, with fast-food stands from many nations surrounding a central eating area. There's a free hula show every night at 7 and 8pm on the second floor. Open daily from 9am to 11pm.

✪ Royal Hawaiian Shopping Center
2201 Kalakaua Ave. ☎ **808/922-0588.**

One of the newer shopping centers in town, this is also one of the biggest and most grandiose: $40 million and 6¹/₆ acres of the most valuable real estate in Hawaii went into its making. Fronting the entrance to the Royal Hawaiian and Sheraton-Waikiki hotels, it is three city blocks full of Island shops and restaurants set in a tasteful and still-growing tropical environment. More than 150 shops and restaurants can provide hours of amusement.

There's so much to see here that you should wander around as fancy leads you. If price is no object, join the crowds who sometime wait in line to get into designer shops like **Lancel, Cartier,** and **Chanel.** Boutiques bearing such European fashion names as Giorgio Armani, Ferragamo, Hermès, DKNY, Burberry, and the like, are all part of the **McInerny Galleria** on the first and second floors. But another McInerny shop here features a "Sale Studio," where prices are marked way down.

One of our favorite places is the ✪ **Little Hawaiian Craft Shop,** where everything is handmade in Hawaii. Rare Niihau-shell necklaces, authentic kukui nuts, feather hatbands, and the like are among the traditional handcrafts found here. Prices are modest, beginning at $3 to $5, and the people couldn't be nicer. The shop includes an outstanding wood gallery specializing in hand-carved replicas of Hawaiian artifacts as well as collectors' items.

Using only silk, cotton, and other natural fabrics, and dying them the subtlest and softest colors, designer Marlo Shima creates women's clothing of great beauty at ✪ **Boutique Marlo, Sunshine Kids** has some adorable clothing for the keikis. You'll want all the soft, marvelous leather goods at **Raku Leather**—and maybe a music box or two from **Ekiki's Hawaiian Music Boxes. Van Brugge House** has a smashing selection of Australian-designed sportswear and everything for the surfing set. Open Monday through Saturday from 9am to 10pm, Sunday from 9am to 9pm.

Waikiki Shopping Plaza
2250 Kalakaua Ave., corner of Seaside Avenue. ☎ **808/923-1191.**

Some of the outstanding shops here include European fashion favorites like **Bally of Switzerland, Paloma Picasso,** and **Hunting World.** There are also outposts like **Yokohama Okadaya** for Japanese folk crafts, with many handmade objects. **Ala Baba Imports,** a major source for eelskin products, has a huge store here, offering handbags, wallets, belts, billfolds, and the like, at wholesale prices. **Hawaii Cloisonné Factory** makes its own inexpensive jewelry, offering fashion artifacts not available elsewhere in the United States. Art lovers will enjoy the **Art Forum Gallery,** which also has branches in Tokyo, Osaka, and Los Angeles. **Island Casuals** is known for wide selections and good bargains. There's a nice array of swimsuits at **Beach Avenue,** and **Treasure Island** is the place to find **Hawaiian Heirloom Factory Jewelry.**

You can use the center's elevators, but it's more fun to ride the escalators all the way to the top, admiring the five-story-high, million-dollar waterfall, with dancing waters and changing colors. Open daily from 9am to 11pm.

AROUND HONOLULU

✪ Ala Moana Shopping Center
Ala Moana Blvd. ☎ **808/946-2811.**

Ala Moana is for those who hate shopping centers. It's 50 acres of Island architecture at its best, laced with pools and gardens, plantings and sculptures, fountains and wide shady malls. In between are the shops—and what shops! An international array from East and West, as dazzling a selection of goods as can be found anywhere, in as wide a price range as possible—a fascinating barometer of how far the 50th state has come into the modern world of merchandising.

The big names are here: **Sears Roebuck, J.C. Penney,** and **Liberty House's** flagship store. **Reyn's** is tops for men's wear. Join the throngs of local citizens who flock to the Japanese department store, **Shirokiya. Hopaco Stationers** sells all sorts of tasteful gifts, Hawaiian specialties, and stationery.

You'll find something at **Slipper House** to soothe your feet, something to read at **Honolulu Bookshop,** and something to wear at **Tahiti Imports. Paniolo Trading Company** is the place for cowboy togs and **Alexia** for women's clothing in natural fabrics from Greece. **Noa Noa** has wild and wonderful tropical clothing in natural fabrics. Jewelry, carvings, statuary, crystals, bells, and animal masks—mostly from Egypt, Morocco, India, Indonesia, Greece, and Africa—are in plentiful supply at fascinating ✪ **Art Lines,** one of the most successful stores at Ala Moana. There's plenty of health food at **Vim and Vigor,** and plenty of everything edible at the gigantic **Foodland Supermarket,** an international food fair under one roof.

Californians who miss Rodeo Drive now have Center Court here at Ala Moana. Designed for an affluent crowd, the newest area features such shops as **Chanel, Gucci, Jaeger, Adrienne Vittadini, Emporio Armani, Christian Dior, Escada, Kenneth Jay Lane, Royal Copenhagen,** and **Polo/Ralph Lauren.**

Open Monday through Saturday from 9:30am to 9pm, Sunday from 10am to 5pm. There are acres of parking. To reach Ala Moana from Waikiki, take either TheBUS no. 8 or 19 from Kalakaua Ave.; it's about a 10-minute ride.

Aloha Tower Marketplace

1 Aloha Tower Dr. ☎ **808/528-5700.**

A combination festival, celebration, cultural experience, and shopping bazaar, the new Aloha Tower Marketplace is one of the most engaging places in Honolulu, situated right out on the downtown waterfront next to the revitalized Aloha Tower. Mediterranean-style architecture with Hawaiian accents evokes the Hawaii of the '30s and '40s, when local residents gathered here on Boat Days to greet the Matson Line passenger ships. Shopping the more than 100 high-quality stores and kiosks here provides plentiful entertainment today, no matter what else is going on. **Pakipika Trading Company** has a splendid collection of authentic Hawaiian crafts, including carvings, textiles, jewelry, and beautiful pareaus. **Pacifically Yours** is the place for sheepskin items, New Zealand straw-fired bowls, and wonderful carvings. **Handblock** has clothing, household accessories, and more, all in their unique handblocked prints. Whimsical handpainted furniture plus unusual jewelry is the stock in trade at **Magic Attic** (see above). The custom-made furniture at **Martin & MacArthur** uses many native Hawaiian woods; it's extraordinary—and expensive. Distinctive clothing, bedding, and gift items by the talented Sig Zane of the Big Island are also shown here.

Rosalie Rupp Prussing's delightful artwork based on island scenes is shown at **Rosalie's Studio.** To get an overall perspective of Hawaiian crafts, a visit to **Hawaiian Crafters Factory Store,** stocked with many antiques and collectibles, is in order.

Want to swing in a hammock? The people at **Swing Song** can sell you a nice one made in Puerto Rico for $59; hammock chairs are $79.

Nifty places to eat at Aloha Tower Marketplace include a Food Court that seats 700 in a handsome waterfront setting, plus half-a-dozen regular restaurants, all with waterfront views. **Gordon Biersch,** Hawaii's first microbrewery and beer garden, is one of the best.

Open daily from 10am to 10pm. Restaurants and bars are open from 11am to midnight, often until 2am. The Aloha Tower Express Trolley operates daily from 8:45am to 2am; the cost is $1 each way. In Waikiki, there are frequent stops along Kuhio Avenue and Kalakaua Avenue. Trolleys run every 30 minutes; after 9:45pm, once an hour.

Kahala Mall
Waialae Kahala Shopping Complex. ☎ **808/732-7736.**

This is an upscale, indoor, air-conditioned, fully carpeted suburban shopping center, without the frenetic pace of Ala Moana. There are many intriguing specialty shops here. It's difficult to know whether to call **Following Sea** a shop or a crafts gallery, but this striking place is such a beautiful visual experience that it should not be missed. You'll see no mass-produced tourist junk here: Everything is one of a kind, created by outstanding American craftspeople, and truly unusual. Jewelry, woodwork, paperweights, stained-glass items, carvings, ceramics, and so on, are priced from a little to a lot. There's beautiful ethnic jewelry and unique contemporary clothing at **Juma.** And **Corner Loft Kahala** is a good source for antiques, collectibles, jewelry, and gift items. Beautiful clothes from Mexico and India, among other places, can be found at **Cotton Cargo, Paradizzio** is a lovely boutique filled with wonderful items for the home, shipped from around the world.

Open Monday through Saturday from 10am to 9pm, Sunday from 10am to 5pm. Take TheBUS no. 58; or, by car, take the Waialae exit from the Lunalillo Freeway East; it's about a 15-minute drive from Waikiki.

Pearlridge Shopping Center
Aiea. ☎ **808/488-0981.**

Out in Aiea, about a half-hour drive from Waikiki, this multi-million-dollar complex is a huge favorite with the local people. Pearlridge boasts 170 stores, 16 theaters, two food courts, and three "phases." It's built on opposite sides of an 11-acre watercress farm. Shoppers travel between Phase I and Phase II in Hawaii's only monorail train, which affords a panoramic view of Pearl Harbor. Both kids and grownups will enjoy Pearlridge, it's a good place to keep in mind for a rainy-day excursion.

As at most of the shopping centers catering to the local trade, familiar names such as **Liberty House, Sears, J.C. Penney, Long's Drugs,** and **Woolworth's** dominate the scene. **Shirokiya** shows the Japanese influence, with many art objects from Asia. In addition, many of your favorite specialty shops are on hand.

Point your kids in the direction of **Fernandez Fun Factory's Flagship** in Pearlridge Phase II; this must surely be one of the world's fanciest "penny arcades," featuring the newest and most elaborate electronic games.

Official store hours at Pearlridge are 10am to 9pm Monday through Saturday and 10am to 5pm on Sunday. You can easily squeeze your visit to Pearlridge into your trip to Pearl Harbor. If you're driving to Pearl Harbor on Kam Highway, you see it on your right just after you reach Pearl Harbor's entrance to the USS *Arizona* Memorial. If you're driving out the H1 Freeway, take the Aiea exit. When driving out the Lunalillo Freeway from downtown, you'll see Pearlridge on the freeway directory signs. By bus, take TheBUS no. 20 from Waikiki to Pearlridge.

Note: You can combine your visit to Pearlridge with one to the **Kam Super Swap Meet,** which is held at the Kam Drive-In, across from the shopping center, Wednesday and on weekends, beginning at 6am.

✪ Ward Centre

1200 Ala Moana Blvd. ☎ **808/531-6400.**

Not far from Ward Warehouse, Ward Centre is Island shopping with elegance. There are swimsuits and aerobic wear galore at **Allure.** Local craftspeople make all the items at **Craft Flair:** wonderful children's dresses and T-shirts, jewelry, dried flowers, and more. **Art à la Carte** has an excellent collection. Collectors—of plates, dolls, miniature cottages, music boxes, paintings, and more—will have a field day at **Our House Collectibles.** Wonderful breads and divine pastries emerge from the ovens at **Mary Catherines.** Gourmet food items (including the best pastas and cheeses flown in from Europe), plus fine wines and spirits, are offered at **R. Field Wine Co.**

Open Monday through Friday from 10am to 9pm, Saturday from 10am to 5pm, Sunday from 11am to 4pm. Take TheBUS no. 8 from Waikiki (except those marked "Waikiki Beach and Hotels") or buses no. 19 or 20.

✪ Ward Warehouse

1050 Ala Moana Blvd. ☎ **808/591-8411.**

A shopping center with class and charm, Ward Warehouse is just 15 minutes from Waikiki, across from Fisherman's Wharf. This is one shopping center equally as popular with sophisticated Honolulu residents as with visitors.

Many shops sell fine and decorative art. **Nohea Gallery** is a stunner: Many local artists show glass, hardwoods, sculpture, jewelry, paintings, prints, and much more. Prices vary, beginning modestly. The art of neon comes alive at **Neon Leon:** You're invited to custom-design your own logos, names, frames, or whatever in this art medium. American folk art—woodcarvings, arks, building signs, weathervanes, quilts, Steiff bears, boxes, glassware and more—shine at **Crescent Gallery.** Hand-carved chess sets, wind chimes, bells, furniture, textiles, quilts and some lovely clothing, all from Indonesia, are shown in the handsome **Indo Pacific Trading Company** store. **Claire de Lune** is a favorite with collectors for '20s, '30s and '40s memorabilia.

The artistic impulse at Ward Warehouse also translates into clothing at shops like ✪ **Pomegranates in the Sun,** which features the work of local artists and designers inspired by the Hawaiian atmosphere. Many items are one of a kind. Highly artful, too, is the clothing at shops like **Blue Ginger Designs,** with its delicate hand-blocked batik fabrics, and **Mamo Howell,** where striking muumuus, long and short, are based on designs derived from Hawaiian quilt patterns. **Imports International** has scads of good buys in clothing, as well as Balinese masks, carvings, and Asian arts and crafts.

Open Monday through Friday from 10am to 9pm, Saturday from 10am to 5pm, Sunday from 11am to 4pm. Take TheBUS no. 8 from Waikiki (except those marked "Waikiki Beach and Hotels").

12

What to See & Do Around the Island

As you may already know, there's much more to Oahu than what's within the city boundaries. Listed below are some of Oahu's attractions beyond Waikiki and Honolulu.

1 Southeast Oahu

Hanauma Bay State Underwater Park

Snorkelers feel like they've died and gone to heaven when they see Hanauma Bay. During the last eruption on Oahu (volcanologists say it was at least 10,000 years ago), one side of Koko Head Crater was washed into the sea; the result is an idyllic beach, one of the most popular in the islands. Since the placid turquoise waters cover a cove in the purple coral reef, it's a perfect place for both beginners and advanced snorkelers. The best place to enter the water for both swimming and surfing is a large sandy break in the reef called Keyhole. A path along the sea cliff leads to Toilet Bowl, a natural pool that, like a flushing toilet, rises up and falls down with the tides. Hanauma Bay is now a marine reserve, and so gentle have the fish become that parrot fish, bird wrasses, and others will eat bread from a swimmer's hand. For details, see "Beaches" in Chapter 8.

Admission $19.95 adults, $10.95 seniors (65+), $8.95 juniors ages 6–12, $13.95 children 4–5, free for children under 4. (Prices, subject to change, include tax).

Daily 9:30am–5pm, to 10pm on Friday; on Friday nights, Hawaiian entertainment is included in the regular price of admission. For information on free roundtrip shuttle transportation from Waikiki, call **808/955-FISH.** Public buses make hourly runs to the park (☎ 808/848-5555). Also consider the Oahu Nature Bound Circle Island Express, which provides transportation to both Sea Life Park and to Waimea Falls Park and includes admission to both for $29.95. For information, call **808/947-OAHU.**

Ulupoa Heiau State Monument
In Kailua, near the YMCA Building.

This building foundation of lichen-covered lava rocks is the remains of an ancient temple dedicated to the sacred birth of the *alii* (chiefs). The intricate stone construction work is credited to the Menehunes—the amazing race of "little people" who were supposedly here before the Polynesians (they did most of their construction jobs on Kauai). If you step onto the ground nearest the entrance, the entire surface of the heiau is visible, and you can see all the way to Kaneohe and the Kawainui marsh bird refuge. Walk the width of the heiau, around it, and down the path; here, on the far side, it stands 30 feet high. Don't disturb the ti-leaf wrapped *ho'okupu* (gifts) of fresh fruit that the faithful still leave here. Stop to rest and meditate in the small terraced park on the edge of the forest, with a stream, banana trees, ti leaf, enormous shade trees, and everywhere the song of forest birds—it's enchanting. Perhaps, like a friend of ours who has lived in this area half her life, you'll be moved by the *mana* of the place; certainly, it's magical when there's a light mist and a rainbow. But perhaps not—to some, it's just a pile of moldy rocks.

2 Windward Oahu

Byodo-In

In the Valley of the Temples, 47-200 Kahekili Hwy. ☎ **808/239-8811**. Admission $2 adults, $1 children. Open during daylight hours. To get there from Honolulu, take Likelike Highway, turn left at Kahekili Highway, and watch for signs to the Valley of the Temples.

Situated in the Valley of the Temples, in the verdant Ahuimanu Valley, Byodo-In is a $2.6-million replica of the 900-year-old Byodo-In Temple that has been proclaimed a national treasure by the government of Japan. There's no doubt that this is one of the treasures of Hawaii. It was dedicated on June 7, 1968, almost 100 years to the day after the arrival of the first Japanese immigrants to the islands. The grounds are beautifully landscaped, with the temple sitting in the midst of a Japanese garden planted with plum, pine, and bamboo. Before you enter the temple itself, ring the bell for good luck and the blessings of the Buddha. Inside the temple is an immense, imposing golden carving of Amida, the Buddha of the Western Paradise, an important work of sacred art, as are the filigree screens and panels. When you finish gazing at the treasures within, you can buy some fish food to feed the carp in the two-acre reflecting lake. You can also shop for Far Eastern souvenirs, walk through the tranquil gardens, and recharge yourself with the almost palpable serenity.

Heeia State Park

Kaneohe. ☎ **808/247-3156**. Admission free. Daily 7am–6:45pm; staff on hand Mon–Fri 8am–4pm. Located a few miles after Windward Mall in Kailua, on your right.

This is a highly educational and enjoyable excursion, and a big favorite with kids. The park was the site of an ancient heiau that was destroyed by a sugar plantation in the 1850s. The site was said to be a *leina-a-ke-akua*—a place from which spirits leaped out into the nether world; many believe the *mana* is still there. An ancient fishpond borders the park on the south end; the Heeia Kea Boat Harbor is to the north. Geologically, the park is the end "finger" of a lava flow, offering a panoramic view of the sea and the mountains. The plants in the park represent staples of the ancient Hawaiian diet—sugarcane, taro, breadfruit, banana, coconut. The highlight of the exhibition hale, with its displays on marine life, botany, and ecology, is the 225-gallon, one-ton, high-tech saltwater aquarium. The Friends of Heeia State Park hold an annual luau in March to which the public is invited featuring name entertainers like Pekelo and the Kipapa Rush Band (Admission is $12.50 adults, $7.50 children; phone the Park for information.)

Island Attractions at a Glance

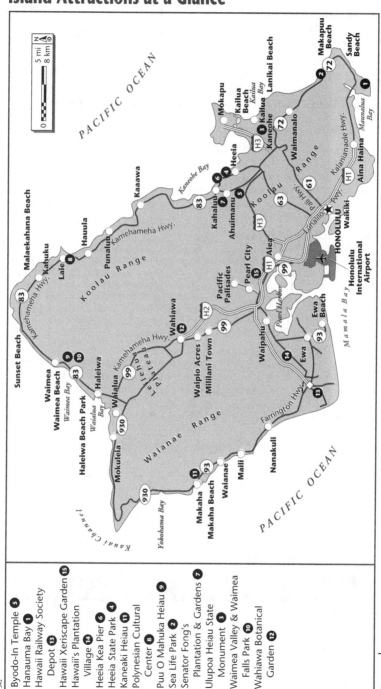

Byodo-In Temple **5**
Hanauma Bay **1**
Hawaii Railway Society
  Depot **13**
Hawaii Xeriscape Garden **15**
Hawaii's Plantation
  Village **14**
Heeia Kea Pier **6**
Heeia State Park **4**
Kaneaki Heiau **11**
Polynesian Cultural
  Center **8**
Puu O Mahuka Heiau **9**
Sea Life Park **2**
Senator Fong's
  Plantation & Gardens **7**
Ulupoa Heiau State
  Monument **3**
Waimea Valley & Waimea
  Falls Park **10**
Wahiawa Botanical
  Garden **12**

Airport ✈

1342

Glass-Bottom Boat Tours

Heeia Kea Pier. ☎ **808/235-2888** for advance reservations. Admission $7.50 adults, $3.50 children under 12.

What goes on beneath Hawaii's waters? If you're not into snorkeling or scuba diving, try a glass-bottom boat trip out of Heeia Kea Pier to see the coral gardens beneath Kaneohe Bay. Plan this expedition for a day when the water is clear.

Senator Fong's Plantation and Gardens—The Adventure Center

47-285 Pulama Rd. ☎ **808/239-6775**. Admission $8.50 adults, $5 children 5–12. Daily 10am–4pm; last tram tour departs at 3pm.

Former U.S. Senator Hiram Fong has opened his magnificent 725-acre estate to the public. Visitors are taken on guided tours in open-air trams through five gardens, each named for one of the five U.S. presidents under whom Fong served in his 17 years in Congress. After the tour, stop at the Visitors Center, perhaps have lunch, or take a class in lei making (for a $5 charge). Check out the Banana Patch gift shop. Plan on an hour or so for this delightful excursion.

Polynesian Cultural Center

Laie. ☎ **808/293-3333**. Villages and afternoon highlights, $25 adults, $13 children. Add to this the buffet and admission to the evening production, "Mana," and cost is $42 adults, $25 children. For $54 adults and $35 children, you get a luau package, which also includes the IMAX presentation, "Polynesian Odyssey." Reservations can be made at the center's ticket office on the ground floor of the Royal Hawaiian Shopping Center in Waikiki; call the number above or toll free from the mainland at 800/367-7060. Open Mon–Sat; closed Thanksgiving and Christmas. If you're driving directly to Laie from Honolulu, take the Pali Highway (Hi. 61) and turn north on Kamehameha Highway (Hi. 83). Plan on at least an hour's drive.

This top tourist attraction was built more than 30 years ago to provide work and scholarships for Polynesian students and to revitalize the ancient Polynesian cultures. All in all, barring a mite too much commercialism in their evening show, they do a terrific job. Seven authentic Polynesian villages have been re-created at the center—Hawaiian, Tongan, Fijian, Samoan, Maori, Marquesan, and Tahitian. They are staffed by Polynesians who came here from their respective islands for just this purpose. They demonstrate crafts, perform ancient songs and dances, and explain their culture to you. In addition to the villages, demonstrations, and hands-on activities, the center stages a variety of vibrant shows: "Mana! The Spirit of Our People," a 90-minute evening extravaganza with a cast of over 100 islanders; the "Pageant of the Long Canoes," a colorful half-hour waterborne introduction to the young people of Polynesia; a brass-band concert; an island farewell festival; even a "Keiki Polynesian Show" in which visiting keikis can watch their friends perform. Since a visit here could take up to eight hours, you may want to plan accordingly by arriving no later than 2pm.

3 The North Shore

Puu O Mahuka Heiau

A mountain road leads up to the ruins of this ancient heiau, where it's easy to imagine the days when human sacrifice was practiced here. When Captain Vancouver put in at Waimea Bay in 1792, three of his men were captured and offered to the bloodthirsty gods. Today, though, all is tranquil here, and the faithful still come, offering stones wrapped in ti leaves in homage to the ancient gods. Drive up if only to see the sweeping views of the coast from this vantage point; they are among the best on this side of the island.

Waimea Valley

Home of Waimea Falls Park. ☎ **808/638-8511** or 808/923-8848. Admission $19.95 adults, $10.95 seniors (65+), $8.95 juniors ages 6–12, $3.95 children 4–5, free for children under 4. Daily, including holidays, 10am–5pm. The Shortest direct route from Honolulu is via Hwy. 99 (Kam Highway) or Interstate H-2 to Hwy. 83. The Oahu Nature Bound Circle Island Express takes passengers to both Waimea Falls and Sea Life parks; cost of $29.95 includes admission to both parks and a coastal trip along Windward Oahu. For Information, call 808/947-OAHU.

Just across the road from Waimea Bay, situated in a lush, 1,800 acre valley rich in the history of old Hawaii, the park includes one of the world's finest arboretums and botanical gardens, a wildlife preserve and bird sanctuary, miles of hiking trails, and magnificent plants and flowers—many of them rare and endangered (photographers, take note). You can play the ancient sports of old Hawaii—spear throwing, lawn bowling, Hawaiian checkers—at the Hawaiian Games site, and watch the park's resident hula troupe present ancient hulas several times daily. You may also catch the Acapulco-style diving from the cliffs at Waimea Falls. Picnic in the meadow, pick up something to eat at one of the snack bars, or have a lovely lunch at the open-air Pikake Pavilion. Twice each month the park opens its gates for free walks to the waterfall and back by the light of the moon. Incidentally, this is one of the most popular spots for Hawaiian weddings. (For planning information, write Wedding Department, 59-864 Kamehameha Hwy., Haleiwa, HI 96712.)

Waimea Falls Park also offers a series of activities allowing guests to explore "never before seen" areas of Waimea Valley: They include guided all-terrain vehicle rides along 10 miles of wilderness trails; downhill mountain-bike tours through the North Valley; and kayak rides along Waimea River and out to Waimea Bay. Fees vary; for information, phone the park.

4 Central Oahu

Wahiawa Botanical Garden

1396 California Ave. ☎ **808/621-7321**. Admission free. Daily, except Christmas and New Year's, 9am–4pm. From Ala Moana Shopping Center, take TheBUS no. 52, Wahiawa Heights; the bus stops on California Avenue directly across from the garden.

Less than a mile east of Kamehameha Highway, hidden within the dreary town of Wahiawa, is a splendid garden that you can see on a self-guided tour. There are 27 splendid acres to walk through, home to a variety of beautiful trees (including fragrant camphor trees from China and Japan), tropical flowers, and shrubs.

5 Leeward Oahu's Waianae Coast

The Hawaii Xeriscape Garden

Halawa. ☎ **808/527-6113**. Admission free. Wed and Sat 10am–2pm. Call for information or to request tours on other days of the week. From Honolulu, follow the H-1 to the Halawa cutoff.

Located the the very end of Iwaena Street in the Central Park industrial area of Halawa, this is the three-acre pride and joy of the Honolulu Board of Water Supply. When I was told that it was designed to display plants which need very little water to thrive, I expected to see three acres of cactus and succulent plants and very little color. Was I surprised? Yes! The garden explodes with color—bougainvillea, ilima, birds of paradise, varieties of lilies—and cacti and succuents

Take the Train: Historic Hawaii Railway Society Tours

Attention railroad buffs: Between the years of 1890 and 1947, the narrow-gauge tracks of the Oahu Railway and Land Company were busy transporting passengers and freight for the sugar mills from Honolulu to as far away as Kahuku. The stalwart members of the Hawaii Railway Society (who come from all over the world) have worked for more than 30 years, restoring engines and maintaining the existing railway track so that the beautifully restored little train is once more back in business. Every Sunday at 1 and 3pm, the train leaves from Ewa Beach, west of Pearl Harbor for a 13-mile roundtrip across the Ewa plain to the Ka Olina resort and back. The rail trip takes 1 1/2 hours, since the train can only go 17 m.p.h. (downhill) and it has to stop for *everything*—including golf carts. The most recent addition is Ben Dillingham's private parlor car, which, in its heyday, carried such VIPs as Queen Liliuokalani, Prince Kuhio, and President William Howard Taft. Passengers can sit either in an open gondola or in a covered car, where they will hear a narration about the history of trains on Oahu.

The fare is $7 for adults, $4 for children; seating is on a first-come, first-served basis. Take H-1 West, Exit 5A, drive south 2 1/2 miles, turn right onto Renton Road, drive 1 1/2 miles to the end. For information, phone **808/681-5461.**

with brilliant flowers. The garden illustrates the benefits of grouping plants with similar needs together, the thirsty and the not-so-thirsty, the sun-lovers and the ones that crave shade. There are natural footpaths to lead you from one area to another, and the staff is happy to answer questions.

Hawaii's Plantation Village

Waipahu. ☎ **808/676-6727**. $5 donation suggested; $3 seniors and children. Mon–Sat 9am–3pm, Sun 10am–3pm, reservations requested; guided tours given on the hour. From Honolulu, take the H-1 Freeway west to the Waikele-Waipahu exit; take Paiwa Street at the end of the exit ramp onto Farrington Highway; drive about 1 1/2 miles, and turn onto Depot Road toward the Oahu Sugar Mill; the village is just below the mill.

Not far from Pearl Harbor (you can easily combine visits to the two if you're driving) is one of Oahu's newest and most unusual attractions: Hawaii's Plantation Village, an outdoor, non-profit museum, a collection of 30 restored and replica buildings dating from 1840 to 1903. The living history museum provides a vivid picture of the lives of the first immigrants—Chinese, Japanese, Portuguese, Filipino, Puerto Rican, Okinawan, and Korean—who came to Hawaii to work the great sugar plantations alongside the native Hawaiians. Created and cared for by members of each ethnic community, the homes come alive with the traditional ceremonies and events of day-to-day life. You'll see everything from a Japanese tofuya (a building where tofu is made) and a Shinto shrine to an authentic Hawaiian *hale*, a large taro patch, a restored Chinese cookhouse—even a Puerto Rican celebration of Christmas. Plan on spending an hour or two here.

Kane'aki Heiau

In Makaha Valley. Tues–Sun 10am–2pm. Stop at the Sheraton Makaha Resort to get driving directions to the heiaua. It's on private property; access is through a tended gate. To get there, take the H-1 west directly to Makaha.

Throughout Hawaii, ancient heiaus are mostly ruins—piles of rocks where one has to use a good deal of imagination to recall the past. Not so with this one: It has been splendidly restored by the Bishop Museum, the National Park Service, and the Makaha Historical Society. Because it's tucked away deep in a valley an hour's drive from Waikiki, and because it's on private property, it doesn't get a great deal of attention. That's a pity, because, for those who have a serious interest in ancient Hawaii, this is one sight you will not want to miss.

The heiau was originally constructed between 1450 and 1640 A.D. and was modified and enlarged three times; each modification reflects the efforts of the alii and his kahunas (the chiefs and priests), to strengthen the relationship between the people and the gods. Originally, the temple was used for agricultural worship. The third, and final modification, however, is believed to have transformed it into a *luakini heiau*, or a place of human sacrifice. It was probably used by Kamehameha the Great to honor the war god, Kukailimoku, when he was attempting to consolidate his kingdom in the years between 1795 and 1812.

6 Highlights for Kids

Complete details on each kid-friendly place listed below are found earlier in this chapter, unless otherwise noted.

- **Hanauma Bay.** Most everybody snorkels at this wonderful beach, but even if kids just stand in the water, fish will come up to them and eat right out of their hands.
- **Hawaii's Plantation Village.** Older children will enjoy this time-trip back to the early days of Hawaii's immigrant groups at this indoor-outdoor living museum.
- **Hawaii Railway Society Train Rides.** Kids of all ages who remember the Little Engine that Could will identify with this little train that also does its utmost; they'll love the way it chugs along at a maximum speed of 17 m.p.h.—downhill.
- **Jungle River Mini Golf Village.** Kids get a thrill and a chill—and a chance to play miniature golf here. The course is landscaped to look like a real jungle village, complete with banana trees, hibiscus, bamboo, even shrunken heads, skeletons, a huge dinosaur (all bogus, of course). Recorded bird calls fill the air. None of the individual holes of the 18-hole course are terribly intriguing—although one has a big waterfall, several have water hazards, and another requires you to shoot right through the chief's hut. Most of the hazards and rocks are strategically placed to make things difficult. Open from 10am to 10pm Sunday through Thursday and 10am to midnight on weekends. "Greens fees" are $6 for adults, $5 for kids. You can combine this with a shopping excursion, as it's in Phase III of Pearlridge Center. For information, call **808/488-8404.**
- **Polynesian Cultural Center.** Kids are made to feel very welcome at this family-oriented attraction. They love the guided canoe tours and the chance to see their own friends perform in the "Keiki Polynesian Show."
- **Sea Life Park.** This is perhaps the top children's attraction in Hawaii. It's hard to tear Kids away from this place; they especially adore the shows where the dolphins and penguins—and even a killer whale—are put through their paces performing amazing feats.

7 Shopping Around the Island

Outside of the greater Honolulu area, the two best areas for specialty shopping are:

KAILUA

Elizabeth's Fancy, 7876 Kailua Rd. (☎ 808/262-7513), is a must for lovers of fine Hawaiian quilts. A nationally known quilter and designer, Elizabeth offers superb quality at very respectable prices—pillows from $60, full-size quilts from $995. Many of the over 400 products bearing Elizabeth's designs can be seen in shops throughout the state, but you'll find them *all* here: Hawaiian quilt–design bookmarks, ornaments, jewelry, ready-made pillows, wall hangings, appliqué tops, kits, and pattern books. The store also features Hawaiian wood products and a host of items made in Hawaii, some exclusively for the shop.

In front of Elizabeth's and just a few doors down is **The Creative Collection,** 761 Kailua Rd. (☎ 808/261-7080), full of fun things like unusual umbrellas printed with fish or flowers, great T-shirts, cards, toys, jewelry, bears, cookie jars, and more. It's hard to leave without at least one irresistible bauble.

Another wonderful place is **The Garden Art Shop,** 404 Uluniu St. (☎ 808/261-1463). It features hand-painted furniture, rare plants, fresh flowers, and unique artifacts. Also displayed are stained-glass pieces by Kelene Blaine and magical, mystical paintings by artist Lola Stone. In its tiny quarters you'll find wood carvings, collector-quality Hawaiian dolls, and its petite owner, Cindi Tomei, at work decorating one of her popular garden benches.

Art lovers may also want to stop in at **Oceanic Gallery,** 108 Heikil St. (☎ 808/262-3267), where the work of artist Richard Pettit, internationally known for his realistic watercolors of marine animals, is on display. The gallery is attached to the artist's studio.

THE NORTH SHORE

Not far from Kahuku, the restored Old Tanaka Plantation Store, 56-901 Kam Hwy., houses two engaging shops. **The Only Show in Town** (☎ 808/293-1295) has one of the best collections of Hawaiiana around, from stone artifacts to just about everything through the 1950s. This engaging antique emporium also has a fine collection of old bottles, antique jewelry, ivory netsukes, vintage political buttons, and American trade memorabilia. The other shop is **Patagonia Forest,** filled with exotic pretties from Indonesia, South America, and points in-between, including gorgeously colored caftans, beaded bustiers, leather purses, and custom swimwear in stunning batik fabrics, designed by the shop's owner.

In Haleiwa, **Outrigger Trading Company,** 62-540 Kam Hwy., in Jameson's By the Sea (☎ 808/637-4737), has an outstanding collection of works by local artists: hand-thrown pottery, leaded glass and seashell boxes, Hawaiian quilt–pattern pillows, unique toys—starfish, sea horses, mermaids—and much more. **Silver Moon Emporium** is tucked away behind a garden with picnic tables at 66-037 Kam Hwy. (☎ 808/637-7710). This is the place for very feminine clothes, jewelry, and accessories that you won't see elsewhere, much of it handmade and one-of-a-kind. Prices start at $10.

Hand-painted dresses and original designs, most of them made in the area, are offered by Inge Jausel at **Oogenesis Boutique,** 66-249 Kam Hwy. (☎ 808 /

Oahu's Vibrant Art Scene: The Best Galleries Beyond Honolulu

Many young artists are busy cultivating their talents on Oahu and throughout the Hawaiian Islands. Perhaps because of the natural beauty that surrounds them, their works tend to be more representational than those currently coming out of other international art centers. But this is no lagging group—the Hawaiian artists' perspectives are as modern as those of their counterparts in Paris or New York. What's more, as yet another example of the fortuitous cross-fertilization that goes on in every arena of Hawaiian life, not a few of these up-and-coming young artists and craftspeople have intriguingly—and successfully—married Eastern atmosphere with Western techniques. You'll find many of these talents working around the island, beyond the confines of the city:

The ✪ **Ko'olau Gallery,** located on the second level of the Windward Mall Shopping Center in Kaneohe, is a co-op gallery, staffed by the artists themselves, showing a variety of locally produced artworks in many media. More than 40 artists from around the island are represented. You can say hello to the gallery artists daily from 9:30am to 9pm. Also in Kaneohe, serious lovers of art and beauty must not miss a visit to ✪ **Hart, Tagami & Powell Gallery and Gardens,** 45-754 Lamaula Rd., where painters Hiroshi Tagami and Michael Powell open their gallery and tranquil botanical garden to visitors on Saturday, Sunday, and Monday from around 10am to 3:30pm. An appointment is necessary: Call 808/239-8146. The **Fettig Art Studios.** 61-427A Kamehameha Hwy. in Haleiwa, shows work by artist Beverly Fettig, by appointment only (☎ 808/637-5340).

The **Waimanu Street Gallery,** at 66-521 Kamehameha Hwy. in Haleiwa (☎ 808/293-5000), features the works of Jerry Kermode, whose bowls, made of Hawaiian woods, are examples of the woodmaster's art par excellence. Each and every creation is different, sometimes two woods are combined into one piece. Potter Bob McWilliams is also represented by his functional, Oriental-influenced pieces, as is Janet Holaday, with her wonderful screen-printed shirts, cards, and bags. Open Monday through Friday from 10am to 6pm, Sunday from 10am to 5pm.

637-4580). Japanese-inspired designs grace tops, pants ensembles, and simple dresses that can be worn belted or unbelted, all at reasonable prices. These garments are now being sold in mainland stores under the "Inge Hawaii" label.

We always like to make a stop at the **North Shore Marketplace,** 66-250 Kam Hwy., especially to visit **Pomegranates in the Sun,** (☎ 808/637-9260) with a smashing collection of clothing by Hawaiian artists and designers, inspired by the sun-drenched colors of Hawaii. Then there's **Jungle Gems,** (☎ 808/637-6609) where you can shop for jewelry, crystals, and a variety of arts and crafts at very good prices. Opals, personally collected by the owners in Australia and set in unusual and unique jewelry designs, are the specialty of the shop. **Things at Twelve Tribes International** (☎ 808/637-7634) come from all over the world, especially Africa, Indonesia, Guatemala, and Hawaii. There are Rastafarian hats and posters and some lovely and very reasonably priced clothing bearing the Twelve Tribes label.

13 Driving Around the Island

The beach was beautiful, the urban sights of Honolulu were exciting, but there's still more, much more, to see before you leave the island of Oahu. For on the other side of the mountains that border Waikiki is a verdant landscape almost as diverse as the city itself. There you'll find quiet country towns jostling bustling suburbs that feed commuters into the central city; ruins of old religious *heiaus* where sacrifices were made to the ancient gods near the modern meccas of the surfing set; cliffs thrusting skyward along the shores of velvety beaches where children play and campers set up tents, not far from an enormous concentration of military muscle; acres of pineapple plantations using the most modern agricultural methods; and places where the taro is still cultivated the way it was in the old days. Hotels are as peaceful as they should be, picnic spots are around every bend, and restaurants are scenic attractions in themselves. And, of course, there are sightseeing centers—some of the most unique and interesting in the state. You'll have to tour the island of Oahu.

If your time is short, you might want to pick out just one or two of the important sightseeing attractions windward and make a short, direct trip there. You can reach the Polynesian Cultural Center, the Byodo-In Temple, or most of the sights beyond the city in less than an hour. (For complete details on the top attractions around the island, see Chapter 12.)

If you have the time and a car, however, it is eminently rewarding to head out Diamond Head way and circle the island slowly, basking in the omnipresent natural beauty and stopping at places that interest you. Plan on a full day's trip.

Even without a car, though, you can make this trip, thanks to TheBUS no. 55 (Circle Island), which departs daily from Ala Moana Shopping Center at 5 and 35 minutes after the hour, beginning at 6:05am. This bus can take you around the island, albeit quite slowly. The fare is 85 cents, payable each time you board or reboard the bus.

You might also take a sightseeing limousine, which is easy and comfortable, but your own wheels promise the most fun. So choose one of the driving tours below, get yourself a good road map, and prepare for a memorable adventure.

DRIVING TOUR 1
The Windward Coast, North Shore & Central Oahu

If you have only one day to see Oahu, this is the tour to take.

Start: Kalakaua Avenue in Waikiki.

Finish: Same.

Time: 6 to 8 hours, depending on time spent along the way. Begin early in the morning.

Begin by following Kalakaua Avenue to Kapahulu Avenue; take the lane at the end of Freeway West—this is the H1—to Likelike Highway to Wilson Tunnel. Once you've gone through the tunnel, which takes you through the Koolau range, you'll be amazed at how different everything looks: the jagged, windswept, verdant Koolaus will be to your left, the ocean to your right. The natural beauty on this side of the island is nothing short of extraordinary. From the Wilson Tunnel, drive past four intersections to Haiku Road. Turn left, following the signs for the Chart House Restaurant. Park in their lot, walk around the restaurant, and go down a steep hill to:

1. **Haiku Gardens.** For years, Haiku Gardens Restaurant occupied this lovely kamaaina estate; now it's a handsome Chart House Restaurant. The gardens are open to the public for free during daylight hours. A lily pond dominates all; from it, trails lead off to, among other things, a lovely grove of golden bamboo from Java, a palm grove, grass huts, a bird sanctuary, fragrant ginger and anthurium, and an exotic fish pond. The gardens are closed on Monday.

Go back Kahekili Highway and proceed north about two miles to:

2. **Byodo-In Temple** in the Valley of the Temples. Here you'll see an exact replica of the venerable Byodo-In, reputed to be the most beautiful temple in Uji, Japan. Pay your respects, ring the massive bell, wish for good fortune, and proceed on. (See p. 234).

Now we backtrack just a bit, since we need to get to Heeia, alongside the Kamehameha Highway (Hi. 83) which you'll follow for the majority of this trip. (Kahekili Highway and Kamehameha Highway run parallel to each other for a short distance)

From the Valley of the Temples, going back the way you came, take a left to the junction with Kamehameha Highway, turn right around an immense banyan tree, and you'll arrive at:

3. **Heeia Kea Pier.** Here you may want to board one of the glass-bottom boats to view the coral gardens beneath the sea. The charge is $7.50 for adults, $3.50 for children under 12, for an hour's trip. (For advance reservations, which are suggested, phone **808/235-2888** before you leave Honolulu; don't bother with this trip unless the water is clear that day.)

From the pier, go right, and soon, on your left, you'll see:

4. **Heeia State Park.** Exhibits of marine life, botany, ecology, and, best of all, a 225-gallon, one-ton, high-tech aquarium filled with colorful creatures of the reef will make this a worthwhile stop, especially if you have older children in tow. Open daily (see p. 234).

Come out of the park, turn right, drive to the intersection, then continue a few miles. Soon, on your left, you'll see the signs pointing to:

5. **Senator Fong's Plantation and Gardens.** You'll need an hour or so to tour these splendid gardens by open-air tram. (See p. 236). Art lovers may want to make a special stop in these parts:

6. **Hart, Tagami & Powell Gallery and Gardens.** This combination art gallery and botanical garden is the home and studio of two of Hawaii's leading painters, Hiroshi Tagami and Michael Powell. A visit here is a rare privilege, an extraordinary entry into a world of beauty. Open *only by appointment* on Saturday, Sunday, and Monday from 10am to 3:30pm. Phone **808/239-8146** in advance; ask for directions when you call.

Now it's one awesome view after another as you drive north on Hi. 83 along the coast, weaving along past acres of tropical flowers and trees whose branches frequently arch across the entire width of the road. Keep your eyes peeled for the island that looks like its name, Mokoli'i (little lizard), more popularly known as:

7. **Chinaman's Hat.** Don't be tempted to wade out to this island from Kualoa Beach, even though some sources suggest it. Not only can the water be treacherous if a surge comes in at low tide (there have been drownings here), and it's sometimes full of Portuguese man-of-wars, but the island itself is a nesting place for the wedge-tailed Shearwater birds. Please don't disturb their refuge; look respectfully, and drive on. On the other side of the road, a sign, covered by weeds, points to the ruins of a century-old:

8. **Kualoa Sugar Mill Ruins.** Cane grown here was once shipped to "distant" Honolulu. There's not much to see here now, so keep heading north, unless you want to make a stop at Kualoa Ranch (☎ 808/237-7321), a good place for horseback riding. You'll come to a rocky cliff that seems to look like a:

9. **Crouching Lion.** With a little effort, you could imagine this rock formation springing at you. But it's really not menacing—in fact, it's home to the Crouching Lion Inn, a pleasant place to stop and rest for a while. The area is fine for a picnic or a swim at nearby Kaaawa Beach or Swanzy Beach Park. Art lovers might want to check out Punaluu Gallery, a longtime favorite showing the works of local artists.

☕ **TAKE A BREAK   Crouching Lion Inn,** 51-666 Kamehameha Hwy. (☎ 808/237-8511) is one of Windward Oahu's loveliest restaurants. Sit out on the covered lanai and enjoy the view along with the catch of the day or fixings from the all-you-can-eat soup and salad bar. If you come back at night, sit indoors by the enormous stone fireplace and feast on the house's special steak.

Now, as you approach Hauula, you will see a marker pointing to a side road, which leads to the 87-foot:

10. **Sacred Falls.** You can stop for an hour-long hike along a rather rough path, lined with impressive trees and flowers, leading to the falls and a mountain pool below. (For details, see "Hiking" in Chapter 8.) Shoppers may want to stop at the Sacred Falls Gallery, which has pareaus out front and some nice silver jewelry (in addition to the regular tourist junk) inside. Keep going until you reach one of the high points of this sojourn, the picturesque village of:

11. **Laie.** Laie is Salt Lake City with palm trees. No slouches at missionary work, the Mormons arrived in Hawaii not long after the first Protestants: More than 100 years ago, they founded a large colony populated with Hawaiian and Samoan members of the Church of Jesus Christ of Latter-day Saints, whose

Driving Tour—The Windward Coast

1. Haiku Gardens
2. Byodo-In Temple
3. Heeia Kea Pier
4. Heeia Kea State Park
5. Senator Fong's Plantation & Gardens
6. Hart, Tagami & Powell Gallery & Gardens
7. Chinaman's Hat
8. Kualoa Sugar Mill Ruins
9. Crouching Lion
10. Sacred Falls
11. Laie
12. Polynesian Cultural Center
13. Hawaiian Temple
14. Laie Point
15. Malaekahana State Recreation Area

descendants still live here. In 1919, the Mormons established the Hawaiian Temple, the first Mormon house of worship outside the mainland. In 1955, the Brigham Young University–Hawaii campus, a fully accredited liberal arts institution opened; and in 1963, the:

12. Polynesian Cultural Center came into being. This loving re-creation of Polynesia is one of the top visitor attractions in Hawaii. (See p. 236.) It is suggested you arrive by 2pm to experience everything at the center, which could take up to eight hours; you may want to schedule this for another day, driving directly to the center or taking their transportation from town. Whether or not you stop here on your drive, you should take a look at the:

13. Hawaiian Temple. It stands back from the road on high ground, above a pond and an illuminated fountain, and at the head of a long avenue of royal palms. A complimentary Historical Laie Tour is available. The best approach for a Taj Mahal–like vista is to leave the highway at Halelaa Boulevard.

You won't want to leave Laie without a drive out to:

14. Laie Point. The turnoff is just past the entrance to the cultural center; from here you get a dramatic view of the rugged coastline. Walk out over the porous lava rock as far as you can safely go for the best view of all. Some old Hawaii hands swear it's the best vista in the islands. Sunset devotees shouldn't miss this one.

Just past Laie, you may wish to make a stop at:

15. Malaekahana State Recreation Area. This is one of Oahu's most popular camping areas. When the tide is out, you can walk out to tiny Goat Island, a sea-bird sanctuary, for a swim and a beachcomber's stroll; you're likely to find driftwood and seaworn glass balls or shards—and you're likely to be alone. (*Note:* Goat Island is accessible from the camping area of the park only; there is another island that is not accessible in the section of the park reserved for day use. Look for the brown steel gate and the sign reading (MALAEKAHANA STATE RECREATION AREA).

You've now covered the major sightseeing points on the windward side. If it's getting late, you may want to drive back to Honolulu; you'll be at your hotel in about an hour. If, however, you're still game for more—especially for some breathtaking scenery—keep going. Pull in at the:

16. Turtle Bay Hilton Hotel and Country Club. It's lovely just to walk around this beautiful seaside spot where the president of the United States and the premier of Japan once met for talks. If it's lunchtime, you can stop in at the Palm Terrace, overlooking the pool and ocean, for a buffet lunch. If it's around sunset, go to the cocktail lounge overlooking the ocean, the Bay View Lounge; relax while the sun slips below the horizon and disappears behind the giant surf.

Now you're at Oahu's famed North Shore; a short drive down the coast, with its huge breakers crashing in on your right, is:

17. Sunset Beach. Safe enough for summer swimming, Sunset is a wild and windy stretch in the winter, exciting to walk along. In the wilder months, you may be lucky enough to see some spectacular surfing here, for the North Shore is *the* place for the surfing set. Traffic may be jammed for miles from here south to Haleiwa if there's an important surfing contest going on. If you're wondering whether or not you should try it yourself, be advised that the surfing areas range from pretty tough to very dangerous to almost impossible. **Waimea Bay,** just below Sunset, has the distinction of having Hawaii's biggest waves, sometimes as high as 30 feet. However, in the summer months, Waimea Bay is tranquil, the waves are gentle, and the swimming is close to perfect. **Pupukea Beach**

Driving Tour—The North Shore

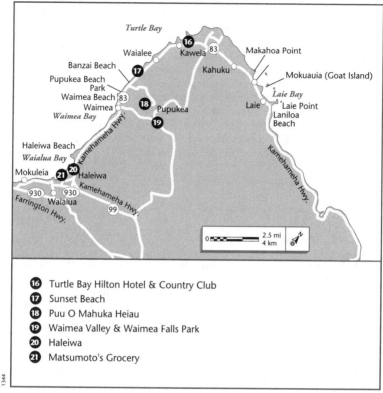

16 Turtle Bay Hilton Hotel & Country Club
17 Sunset Beach
18 Puu O Mahuka Heiau
19 Waimea Valley & Waimea Falls Park
20 Haleiwa
21 Matsumoto's Grocery

Park, for instance, has good swimming and outstanding snorkeling in the summer months. (For details on all these North Shore beaches, see "Beaches" in Chapter 8.)

While the surfers on Waimea Bay are tempting fate, you can survey another site of human sacrifice by turning left onto Pupukea Road—one of the few paved roads here—opposite a fire station and next to a marker. As soon as the road begins its ascent up the hill, take your first right and continue up to:

18. Puu O Mahuka Heiau. Here, on a bluff overlooking Waimea Bay (another great vista) are the ruins of a temple where human sacrifice was practiced (see p. 236).

For a refreshing change of pace, head to:

19. Waimea Valley, Home of Waimea Falls Park. Just across the road from Waimea Bay, this splendid park, which contains an arboretum, botanical garden, a wildlife preserve, bird sancutary, and miles of hiking trails, is one of the major visitor attractions of Oahu and could easily be a full day's adventure in itself (see p. 237).

There's a distinctively artsy atmosphere—small gift shops, art galleries, restaurants, and boutiques—at our next stop, the quaint town of:

20. Haleiwa. This is a browsing, shopping, and gallery-hopping heaven. Some of the most creative people or the island live and work here. (For information on shopping, see p. 240.) **Galerie Lassen,** 62-540 Kamehameha Highway, shows high-quality work, such as sea paintings by Christian Riese Lassen, reproduced by a process called Artagraph, so that each picture is three-dimensional and looks like an original; fascinating prints using ancient Egyptian symbols by Maui artist Andrea Smith; superb whale sculptures by Douglas Wylie, who actually spends three months a year as a boat driver for a whale research team to give him an opportunity to study the magnificent creatures that are his subjects. Then there's a branch of **Wyland Gallery** (there are many throughout the islands), 66-150 Kamehameha Hwy., which specializes in the work of noted marine artist Wyland (everything from originals to posters), and also shows photographs. Before you leave Haleiwa, you should stop at:

21. **Matsumoto's Grocery.** A beloved local institution in these parts, Matsumoto's Grocery at 66-087 Kamehameha Hwy. (across from the intersection of Emerson Street) is the place for the ultimate shave ice experience. Local people come from all over the island to line up here, while no fewer than four workers form an assembly line to shave and season the ice. We won't swear that you'll really love shave ice with ice cream and azuki beans on the bottom, but you can't leave Hawaii without trying it. Aoki's, just down the road, is an alternative if the lines are just too long.

Haleiwa is also one of our favorite places to:

☕ **TAKE A BREAK   Jameson's by the Sea,** overlooking the harbor at 62-540 Kamehameha Hwy., is a wonderfully picturesque spot for lunch and dinner. Great sunsets and food and drink, with an emphasis on fresh fish and seafood. **Kua'Aina Sandwiches,** 66-214 Kamehameha Hwy., is a surfer's hangout and the home of the very best sandwiches on the North Shore.

Now the road turns inward, giving you a chance to see something of Central Oahu. (Note: You cannot completely circle the island of Oahu, since there is no paved road around rugged Ka'en a Point. You've got to go inland and start out from Honolulu again if you want to see the other coast.) Pick up Hwy. 83, Kamehameha Highway, make a left, and soon you're in the midst of the largest pineapple plantation in the world:

22. **Leilehua Plateau.** At the top of the road is a stand where you can buy what will undoubtedly be the finest Hawaiian pineapple you've ever tasted.

Just before you reach the town of Wahiawa, still in the pineapple fields, look for a sign leading you to:

23. **Helemano Plantation.** This center provides many mentally handicapped people with training and vocational opportunities. It has a gift shop, a bakery, and a country store, and serves an inexpensive buffet lunch between 11am and 2:30pm.

As you approach Wahiawa, pass the entrance to the town and continue toward:

24. **Schofield Barracks.** You recognize the name—it was made famous by James Jones in the novel *From Here to Eternity.* Visitors are welcome at the Tropic Lightning Museum, depicting the history of the 25th Infantry Division and Schofield Barracks (open Tuesday through Saturday, 10am to 4pm; admission is free). *Tip:* Park at Kemoo Farm and walk to Schofield; there is only limited parking at the barracks and the streets are congested. Now walk back to:

25. **Kemoo Farm.** Next to historic Kemoo Farm (which now houses a Korean barbecue, a pub serving 130 kinds of beer, and a Mexican restaurant) is the Kemoo Farm Visitor's Center, full of antiques, old photos, and historical memorabilia of the area. Their famous "Mauna Loa Happy Cakes" and macadamia-nut brownies are ready to take home. Browsing here is always a

Driving Tour—Central Oahu

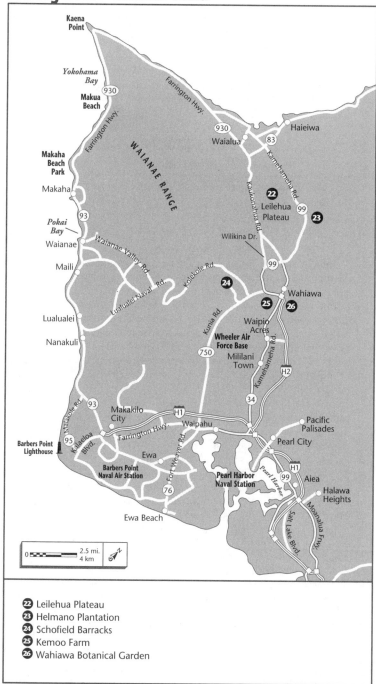

Kaena
Point

*Yokohama
Bay*

**Makua
Beach**

930

Farrington Hwy.

W A I A N A E   R A N G E

930

Waialua

83

Haieiwa

Kamehameha Rd.

22

Leilehua
Plateau

99

23

Farrington Hwy.

**Makaha
Beach
Park**

Makaha

93

*Pokai
Bay*

Waianae

Maili

Waianae Valley Rd.

Kolekole Rd.

Wilikina Dr.

99

24

Kunia Rd.

25

Wahiawa

26

Waipio
Acres

**Wheeler Air
Force Base**

Lualualei Naval   Rd.

Lualualei

Nanakuli

750

Mililani
Town

Kamehameha Rd.

H2

34

Makakilo
City

H1

Waipahu

Pacific
Palisades

Pearl City

93

Malakole Rd.

Farrington Hwy.

**Barbers Point
Lighthouse**

95

Kalaeloa
Blvd.

Ewa

Fort Weaver Rd.

H1

99

Aiea

**Barbers Point
Naval Air Station**

76

**Pearl Harbor
Naval Station**

Pearl Harbor

Halawa
Heights

Salt Lake Blvd.

Moanalua Frwy.

Ewa Beach

0   2.5 mi.
        4 km
N

22 Leilehua Plateau
23 Helmano Plantation
24 Schofield Barracks
25 Kemoo Farm
26 Wahiawa Botanical Garden

1345

delightful interlude. If you have the energy for one more stop (and if it's well before 4pm) the next one should be the:

26. Wahiawa Botanical Gardens. You can wander free of charge through 27 splendid acres. (See p. 237).

From Wahiawa, take either Hwy. 99, to the left, or Interstate H-2. At the intersection with Interstate H-1, you can turn left and drive past Pearl Harbor. At Middle Street, cross to the right side of Hwy. 92 (Nimitz Highway), and it's nonstop past Honolulu Harbor and on to Waikiki.

DRIVING TOUR 2
Southeast Oahu

If you have a second day to drive around Oahu, try this tour of the southeast area.

Start: Kalakaua Avenue in Waikiki.

Finish: Pali Lookout or Round Top Drive.

Time: 2 to 4 hours or more, depending on how long you want to stay on Kailua Beach. Early morning or early afternoon are best.

Begin by taking Kalakaua Avenue to Diamond Head Road and, if you have the time and inclination, stop for a drive into, and maybe even an easy hike (see p. 181)—to the summit of:

1. Diamond Head Crater. The unofficial symbol of Hawaii, Diamond Head Crater was known as Leahi ("casting point") by the ancient Hawaiians, until, back in the days of King Kamehameha I, a group of English sailors thought they saw diamonds reflecting off its slopes. The king declared the place *kapu* until it was realized that the "diamonds" were worthless calcite crystal; the name, nevertheless, stuck. To drive into the crater, turn left onto Paki Avenue, then make a right onto Monserrat; a road leads through the tunnel. Inside the crater, military installations and EAA air traffic controller share space with a state park. The trail will take you up to the 760-foot summit in less than an hour; from there, you'll have panoramic views of half of Oahu. Leaving the crater, Diamond Head Road runs right into:

2. Kahala Avenue. This is the gold coast of Honolulu, a sumptuous residential area. Sculptor Kate Kelly's monument to aviatrix Amelia Earhart is near Black Point, on a lookout point just beyond the Diamond Head Lighthouse. On your right, a paved trail leads to the cliffs, where you can watch some fancy surfing. You may want to drive down some of the side streets that run right to the water's edge to have a look at the homes and the views. This is the area where a Japanese tycoon drove up and down the streets in his limo some years back, snapping up homes that weren't even for sale; he offered so many millions for each that the owners just couldn't refuse. For a while, there was a whole group of homeless millionaires, the "Kahala Refugees," in Honolulu. (If you have time, come back and drive this road at night; it's especially beautiful with moonlight and starlight on the water.)

At the end of Kahala Avenue, where the road hits the Waialae Golf Course, turn left onto Kealaolu Avenue; follow this road to Kalanianaole Highway (Hi. 72—the entrance will be on the right). Before you turn, you come to:

3. Waialae Beach Park. The park has modern facilities, covered pavilions, and wide, wide beaches. It's right next door to the prestigious Waialae Country

Driving Tour—Southeast Oahu

1. Diamond Head Crater
2. Kahala Avenue
3. Waialae Beach Park
4. Hawaii Kai
5. Hanauma Bay
6. Halona Blowhole
7. Sea Life Park
8. Waimanalo
9. Bellows Field Beach Park
10. Kailua
11. Hoomaluhia Botanical Garden
12. Ulupoa Heiau State Monument
13. Nuuanu Pali Lookout
14. Puu Ualaka'a Park

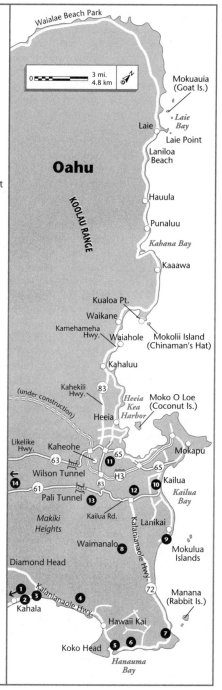

Club. The swimming here is not very good, since the water is full of rocks. Next door is the splendid Kahaila Mandarin Oriental Hotel (in its past incarnation, the legendary Kahala Hilton); you might want to have a look at the lovely grounds and excellent beach.

Just before you reach Koko Head, you'll pass the entrance to Henry Kaiser's once-controversial:

4. **Hawaii Kai.** This 6,000-acre, $350-million housing development is a small suburban city in itself, not as ritzy as Kahala by any means, but still very upscale. You can drive in for your own inspection if you like. There's a beautiful view at the top of the hill past the Hawaii Kai Golf Course over-looking the ocean and the south end of Windward Oahu. While you're in this area, you may want to stop in at Waterfront Village, a charming small shopping complex perched right out on the waters of Koko Marina, tied in by walks and a shared parking lot with the much larger Hawaii Kai shopping center.

Koko Head and Koko Crater, now coming into view ahead, are reminders that Oahu, like all the Hawaiian Islands, is the summit of an underwater volcanic mountain. During Oahu's last eruption (volcanologists say it was at least 10,000 years ago), these craters and the one that houses Hanauma Bay, the next big attraction coming up, were born.

5. **Hanauma Bay.** Snorkelers rate this turquoise beach (closed Wednesdays) at the bottom of Koko Head Crater as one of the best spots on the island. Fish are so tame that they'll eat right out of your hand (see p. 164). The Islanders love this place; the only problem is that you've almost always got to share it with quite a lot of them.

Unless you stay at Hanauma Bay for a swim (or for the day), you'll soon be proceeding along one of the most impressive stretches of rocky coastline in the islands. The black lava cliffs hurtle down to the sea to meet a surging purple Pacific, all set against a brilliant blue-green background of sky, trees, and flowers. Drive slowly to enjoy the beauty—the colors are spectacular. Just ahead is a favorite spot for photographers, the:

6. **Halona Blowhole.** Here geysers shoot into the air through an underground vent in the lava cliffs. The areas just before the Blowhole are just as pretty and much less crowded. It's easy to lose yourself in the wind and spray before returning to the business of living in the 1990s. Just ahead, the Island's daring expert bodysurfers are forgetting their problems in the giant waves of Sandy Beach and, a few miles down the road below the lighthouse, Makapuu Beach. You probably won't want to join them at either of these beaches, as the waves and undertow are fierce. Drive on, instead, and join what seems like half the island's families at:

7. **Sea Life Park.** This is one of Hawaii's biggest sightseeing attractions, with plenty of entertainment, education, and fun for the entire family; kids adore it. (See p. 239.) Although there is a fairly steep admission charge, entrance to the interesting Pacific Whaling Museum is free.

Continuing north on Hi. 72, you soon see Rabbit Island and its sur-rounding turquoise waters. The inland view along this coast is also spectacular, thanks to the towering Koolau range; its corrugated slopes (the result of erosion) provide a soothing balance to the restless sea on your right.

Just past Sea Life Park, you'll find:

8. Waimanalo. This little town has fallen on hard times ever since the sugar plantation that was its economic mainstay closed back in the 1940s. Now its small farms produce anthuriums, papayas, and bananas. Drive any of the country roads and you'll see stables, pig farms, and lots of vegetable and fruit gardens. Waimanalo Beach stretches 3¹/₂ miles around Waimanalo Bay; many Island families consider this their favorite beach on Oahu: pleasant surf, grassy knolls, picnic tables, the works. (Incidents with gangs of local toughs have been reported, you may want to stop, or drive on for *alas,*) a few more miles.)

East of Hi. 72, you'll come upon what was long considered one of Oahu's most magnificent beaches by the few people lucky enough to enjoy it—the military.

9. Bellows Field Beach Park. Nestled against the mountains, this 46-acre strip of fine sand, lively (but not dangerous) surf, and groves of palms and pines is at last open to the public, but on weekends only, from Friday noon to midnight Sunday, and on federal and state holidays. There are public bathouses. Bellows is a perfect place for a picnic lunch (bring your own, as there's nothing to buy) or a swim. Occasionally, Portuguese man-of-wars are spotted here.

Now stay on Hi. 72 until it intersects with Hi. 61, turn right (east) onto Hi. 61 and continue until it reaches one of Honolulu's most pleasant suburbs and the home of two of the best beaches on the island:

10. Kailua. Kailua Beach Park has gentle waves, white sands, and much smaller crowds than those you find at Waikiki. Because of its onshore winds and calm seas, it's become a favorite place for windsurfing, sailboarders, jetskiers, and Kayak racers. Happily, bouys keep them in their own area, so swimming is still good for families. The beach has restrooms, showers, lifeguards, picnic facilities, and food concessions; Lanikai Beach, a few miles further away, has none of these, as it is a private residential area, but it's accessible to the public and it's absolutely wonderful.

Now, if you can tear yourself away from the beach, and would like to see how suburban folks live in Oahu, you can visit the impressive Windward Mall or some tasteful gift shops and galleries.

If it's the weekend and you're in the mood for a hike, you should know about:

11. Ho'omaluhia Botanical Garden in Kaneohe, at 45-680 Luluku Rd. Here, at the foot of the Koolau Mountains, are pleasant hiking trails, a Hawaiian garden, a lake, and much more. At the center, you'll find a small art gallery and exhibit hall. Free two-hour, two-mile long guided nature walks are offered on Saturdays at 10am Sundays at 1pm. Call in advance (☎ 808/233-7233) to make reservations for these hikes.

Before you head back to Honolulu and the scenic highlight of this trip, the Nuuanu Pali, you'll want to fortify yourself. Kailua is the perfect place to:

☕ **TAKE A BREAK**   **Harry's Café,** 629 Kailua Rd. (☎ 808/261-2120), is run by the son of Harry Owens, one of the foremost composers of Hawaiian popular music back in the 1930s and '40s ("Sweet Leilani" was his); the café is full of collectibles from that period. It serves up delicious Mediterranean-inspired fare—shrimp Provnéçale, pasta primavera, and chicken breast Medici are popular choices—at very reasonable prices. Desserts are stellar, especially the sour cream fudge cake. Or, if you prefer Mexican, be prepared to wait a little on weekends to get into **El Charro Avitia,** 14 Oneawa St. (☎ 808/263-3943);

it will be worth it. The setting is smashing indoors and out, the music is pure south-of-the-border, and the moderately priced food is some of the best Mexican fare around.

There's one more spot in Kailua worth checking out. Next to a lovely small park are the remains of a little-known ancient heiau. Driving Honolulu-bound on the Pali Highway, turn right on the first unmarked street past the YMCA sign, then right on Manu-Mele Street; at the end of the road, make another right on Manu-o'o Street, which ends in the YMCA parking lot. Park on your left near the white brick building, walk down the narrow road to your left, and you'll come to the:

12. **Ulupoa Heiau State Monument.** The Hawaiians believed that his sacred place was built by the Menehunes, a race of little people who are better known for their works on Kauai. (See p. 233.)

Back on the Pali Highway, Honolulu bound, follow the signs to the:

13. **Nuuanu Pali Lookout.** This is the most spectacular scenic attraction on Oahu, and one of its prime visitor spots. At the top of these jagged cliffs back in 1795, Kamehameha the Great toppled thousands of Oahuans to their deaths in the final battle that consolidated his power. The view of Windward Oahu, which Mark Twain called the most beautiful vista in the world, is spectacular. Remember to take a jacket or windbreaker, as the winds are chilling up here. And remove all valuables from your car, as it's a prime spot for petty thieves.

This could well be the end of your trip, but if you want to see one more scenic vista before you head for home, follow these directions to:

14. **Puu Ualaka'a Park.** At the town end of Pali Highway, stay in the left lane and take the ramp to the H-1 Freeway. Exit at Kinau Street; the first controlled intersection will be Ward Avenue; turn left and go up the steep hill, turn left onto Prospect, which will become Nehoa Street. At the intersection with Makiki Street, turn left. Turn left on the second street past the school (on the other side of the Board of Water Supply park); this will be Round Top Drive. Halfway up is Puu Ualaka'a Park, from which you get a gorgeous panoramic view from Diamond Head all the way to Pearl Harbor. This is the scene of many local weddings, and several scenes of "Magnum P.I." were filmed here. To return to Waikiki, go down Round Top Drive, down Makiki Street, left on Wilder, and past Punahou School, one of the tonier private schools (whose grounds, incidentally, boast some splendid architecture). Follow Wilder to Metcalf, left on Metcalf to University, right on University to King, left on King to Kapahulu, right on Kapahulu to the ocean—and you're back in Waikiki.

DRIVING TOUR 3
Leeward Oahu's Waianae Coast

Start: H-1 Freeway in Waikiki.

Finish: Same.

Time: 3–5 hours, depending on stops along the way. Any day is good except Monday, when there is no access to Kaneaki Heiau. Plan to arrive at the heiau (about an hour's drive from Honolulu) between 10am and 2pm.

The rugged Waianae Coast is the part of Oahu that few tourists get to see. Not that it doesn't offer some of the most spectacular scenery and first-class surfing beaches on the island; it's just that this is Oahu's backyard, its least-developed commercial area, and the last bastion of ethnic Hawaiians and Samoans. Many of the locals here live on small homestead farms or in shacks, almost every house has a few pigs or chickens in the backyard, and fishing still helps to put food on the table. If you know people here and are lucky enough to be invited into their homes for one of their celebrated wedding or first-birthday luaus, you're in for an unforgettable experience of aloha; but if you're a stranger, you're likely to find the attitude strongly territorial and some of the locals a little less than friendly. Petty thievery can be a problem, especially if you're driving a shiny new rental car. A Honolulu friend advises that you keep nothing of value in your car or trunk if you park at a beach. Should you decide to stop at a beach and should you encounter a group of toughs, leave them alone and they'll leave you alone. It's also advisable that you not go off the main road into the small towns. The Waianae Coast is not dangerous if you exercise these sensible precautions. And it's worth seeing this last outpost of rural Oahu now, as the long arm of "progress" is reaching westward. The Ewa area of the island—that leading to the Waianae Coast—is already home to the new subdivision of Kapolei, a "second city," where hundreds of new homes, shopping malls, and other accoutrements of civilization are being built in response to the needs of Honolulu's ever-growing population. Nearby, Ka Olina, the first planned destination resort outside Waikiki, is already open for business with a golf course and a major luxury resort hotel.

Begin your trip on the H-1 Freeway headed west. When you see the Halawa cutoff, you might want to pull in for a brief tour of a place that will greatly interest horticulturists. That's the:

1. **Hawaii Xeriscape Garden,** which does surprising things with plants that require very little water to grow. (See p. 237.)

Back on the freeway, there's another possible sightseeing stop. Take the Waikele-Waipahu exit, and follow the signs to:

2. **Hawaii's Plantation Village.** This outdoor, non-profit museum turns the clock back over a century for an insightful look at the lives of the immigrants who came to work the great sugar plantations. This living-history museum is highly recommended for families with older children (See p. 238.) Do note, however, that you need an hour or two to do this place justice.

To get back to the H-1, follow Waipahu Street to Kunia Road (Hi. 750) and head west. The road takes you past acres of cane that are gradually being phased out to make room for suburban development. If you'd like to join the rich and beautiful folks at the Ihilani Resort & Spa at Ko Olina for a round of golf or a visit to the spa or for lunch, follow the signs to Ko Olina. Otherwise, continue along H-I until it joins Farrington Highway and head northward up the Waianae Coast. This is a beautiful coastal stretch—if you're lucky you might see some playful dolphins in the turquoise waters.

There are beaches galore along this coast (see "Beaches" in Chapter 8), but a few words of precaution are necessary here. During the winter months, October to March, and often in summer, too, storm swells from the northwest produce high surf and strong currents along this coastline; swimming can be hazardous. (So, too, can the hot sun and lack of shade trees in many places; hats and sunscreen are in order.) One beach that is generally considered safe for winter swimming—but always ask first—and one of the nicest on the coast is:

3. **Pokai Beach Park.** Not only is this park well maintained, clean, watched over by lifeguards, and frequented by local families, it's also home to the remnants

of a 15th- or 16th-century temple, Kuiloloa Heiau, which you can reach by walking past the lifeguard station to the peninsula on the end. Built of coral and lava rock, this heiau has not been restored; not much of it remains, but you will probably see offerings—ti leaves wrapped around rocks—left by local people. Enjoy the atmosphere and the wonderful view of the coast.

Back in the car, head for the high point of our trip, a visit to:

4. **Makaha Valley and Kane'aki Heiau.** Makaha Valley is spectacular, with white pheasants strutting about (the best time to see them is in the months of March, April, and May) and glorious views. It's no wonder that the famed Makaha Inn was built here over 25 years ago as a golf resort. Now it's the Sheraton Makaha Golf Club, and it's very pleasant, indeed. Stop in to ask for precise directions to the heiau, which is on private property in the midst of Mauna 'Olu Estates, a group of luxury homes tucke discreetly into the valley. The heiau is open to the public from 10am to 2pm only every day except Monday. Restored by the Bishop Museum and the National Park Service, this 15th-century temple is one of the best-preserved heiaus in Hawaii, one of Oahu's best-kept secrets (See p. 238).

After the heiau, it's time to:

☕ **TAKE A BREAK**   The lovely **Kaala Room at the Sheraton Makaha Golf Club** serves a very generous lunch buffet for around $10. The views of the grounds from the window tables are beautiful, the food is excellent, and the serving staff could not be sweeter. You can't do better than stopping for a rest and a bite here.

After lunch, drive down to the coast for a look at famed:

5. **Makaha Beach.** In Hawaiian, "makaha" means "fierce" or "savage." The beach got its name not from the rough surf, but from the bands of robbers who used to prey upon travelers here. The robbers are long gone, but the "fierce" and "savage" epithets are still good descriptions for the waves at Kephu Point, where the Makaha International Surfing Championship began back in 1952. Many of the big surfing competitions are now held on the even fiercer waves of the North Shore, but one event, Buffalo's Big Board Surfing Classic, has been drawing the fans here every February to watch old-timers surf with the huge, heavy wooden surfboards used in early Hawaii. (For further details, see p. 169.)

Past Makua, the scenery becomes more rugged, the cliffs more jagged. You may want to have a look at:

6. **Makua Beach.** This photogenic spot is one of those "disappearing beaches" that you see now and then in the Islands. Sometimes, it's a nice sandy beach; other times, big swells come up and take the sand out to sea—thus, making the beach temporarily "disappear."

The paved road ends a few miles from here at:

7. **Yokohama Bay.** The area got its name back in the days of the old Oahu Railway, when the train would let Japanese fishermen off at this deserted spot. The fishing is still good, and so is the snorkeling, but swimming here can be treacherous at times (for details, see p. 168). Tiny puka shells can sometimes be found on the beach.

In all likelihood, this will be the end of your trip, unless you wish to hike 2¹/₂ rugged miles (it will take one to three hours, depending on your pace), to see:

Driving Tour—Leeward Oahu's Waianae Coast

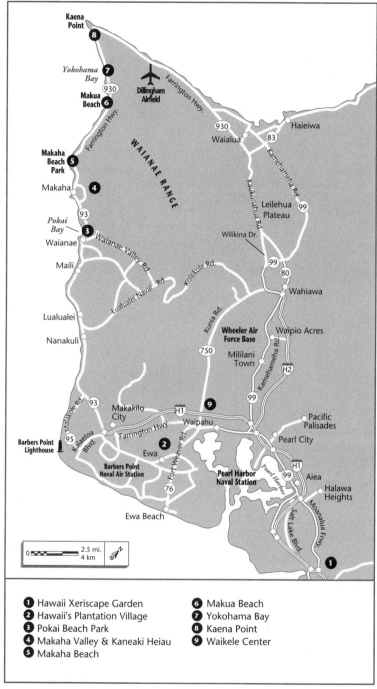

1 Hawaii Xeriscape Garden
2 Hawaii's Plantation Village
3 Pokai Beach Park
4 Makaha Valley & Kaneaki Heiau
5 Makaha Beach
6 Makua Beach
7 Yokohama Bay
8 Kaena Point
9 Waikele Center

8. Ka'ena Point. This is the westernmost promontory of Oahu. The place where, according to legend, the souls of deceased Hawaiians made the jump off into the other world. On a clear day, you can see Kauai from the point. You can also visit the Ka'ena Point Natural Area Reserve, created in 1983 to protect one of the state's best examples of coastal lowlands and dune ecosystems. It's a favorite spot for school groups.

Head back the way you came, taking Farrington Highway until it reaches the H-1, then proceed on to Honolulu. For a total change of pace, you might want to get off the freeway at Waikele and visit:

9. Waikele Center. The factory-outlet-store craze has hit Honolulu, and the local people just love it. Waikele looks like a little country shopping village, with green-roofed, well-designed buildings and its own trolley to take you from store to store. Although we doubt there are any major bargains here, considering the cost of transporting goods from the mainland or Europe, but shopping is fun and prices are competitive. The Saks Fifth Avenue Clearinghouse is the big draw here, but also entertaining are such places as Mikasa, The Fragrance Outlet, Villeroy & Boch, Oshkosh B'Gosh, and Local Motion. You can shop til you drop, then repair to Borders, a big, beautiful book-and-music store that has everything—including a super coffee bar, with great cookies and some awesome pastries (you may have your very own branch of Borders at home).

From here, it's the H-1 heading east, all the way back to Honolulu.

Honolulu After Dark

14

Nightlife on Oahu, as you might expect, is centered in the city. Even if you're staying on another part of the island, you'll have to head to Honolulu for some after-dark action. But never fear—the short journey will be worth it. There's enough going on in Honolulu to make any visitor to Oahu happy. The streets of Waikiki are thronged at night and the bars and clubs are jammed to the gills. On a night out in Honolulu you might catch anyone from Charo to The Brothers Cazimero. You could see a hula show or a Tahitian revue, hear some contemporary Hawaiian sounds, drink beer with students at a University area rock club, check out the dance club scene, or just stroll through a quiet oceanside garden with someone you love and watch the sun set over the Pacific. You may spend a few dollars, or you may go all out and blow the budget for the big-time shows. Happily, though, the cost of nightlife is much cheaper here, than, say, in New York or Las Vegas.

1 The Performing Arts

Sure, Oahu is home to plenty of hula shows and slack-key music. But there's plenty more going on in the arts and entertainment scene; we encourage you to join the locals in enjoying it. Most of the shows and events are inexpensive, compared with mainland prices, and the quality is generally high—Oahu is home to some fabulous performers.

CLASSICAL MUSIC

There's more to Hawaiian music than the ukulele and old island songs, much more, for Hawaii is a music-minded community. The local people flock to the concerts of the great orchestras and soloists who play engagements here en route to the Far East (or vice-versa), and they take great pride in their own splendid **Hawaii Symphony Orchestra.** Nationally and internationally acclaimed artists join the orchestra throughout the August to May season. **Chamber Music Hawaii,** another worthy group, presents about 20 concerts a year at various locations, including the Honolulu Academy of Arts. If you're on Oahu in January, February, or March, you may be able to see the yearly Opera Festival at the Neil S. Blaisdell Concert Hall. And world-renowned opera stars sing with local choruses under the auspices of the **Hawaii Opera Theater.**

HULA SHOWS

Hawaii's unique contribution to the art of the dance is, of course, the hula, a dance of spiritual significance as well as entertainment. As you travel through the Islands you may become aware of the importance the natives placed on the dance of Laka, the goddess of hula and the sister of the volcano goddess, Pele. You can still see the remains of a *heiau* on the Na Pali Cliffs of Kauai, to which devotees from all over Hawaii—men (who were the original hula dancers) as well as women—came to be trained in the *meles,* chants, and dances sacred to Laka.

Seeing the hula danced in Hawaii is always fun, if not always wholly authentic. You should plan to see the **Kodak Hula Show,** which is a good, solid presentation of Hawaiian dance. The hour-long free show is presented Tuesday through Thursday at 10am in Kapiolani Park. You can watch songs and dances of Polynesia, free or for the cost of a drink, at the poolside terrace of the **Sheraton Princess Kaiulani Hotel** every evening between 5:30 and 9:45pm. Dancers and musicians from the **Polynesian Cultural Center** perform at the **Royal Hawaiian Shopping Center** Friday and Saturday between 6:30 and 8pm, and on Saturday between 10:30am and noon. The **Hilton Hawaiian Village** presents the King's Jubilee, a tribute to King David Kalakaua, every Friday night at 6:30pm, with hula dancing beginning around 7pm. Not only hula shows, but also ballet performances, choral and band concerts, martial-arts demonstrations, and fashion shows are held frequently at Centerstage at Ala Moana Shopping Center. More than 500 free programs a year are presented by island talent and international performing groups. Check the tourist papers for exact times of all shows, as they change frequently.

If you have a yen to learn the dance yourself, that can usually be arranged. Perhaps your own hotel will be giving hula classes, and series of classes are often given by the city's Department of Parks and Recreation. Check the local papers for exact dates. There's usually a small admission charge.

Observe the hula dancer carefully. You're supposed to keep your eyes on the hands, which tell the story, but you might be distracted by the wind-blown grass skirts (actually made of ti leaves), the flashing slit-bamboo rods used to beat out a tattoo, the featured gourds (*uliui*) that sound like maracas, the clatter of koa-wood sticks against each other, or the click of smooth stones (*iliili*). And remember, if you see any really violent hula dancing, it's probably Tahitian, *not* Hawaiian. The Hawaiian hula is smooth as the trade winds, graceful as the swaying palms.

THEATER

Now it's easy to find out what's going on in Honolulu's busy theater scene. Phone **808/988-3255** any time day or night and you'll reach the **Theater Hotline,** sponsored by the Hawaii State Theatre Council. It provides information on all plays and musicals currently showing on Oahu, including dates, places, and numbers to call for ticket information. Oahu's major theaters are listed below.

Major Broadway and off-Broadway shows are the fare at the **Diamond Head Theater** (☎ 808/734-0274), and you see them sooner than you'd expect, since the rights are easier to secure 2,500 miles out in the Pacific than on the road-show touring circuit. Sometimes name performers come out to join the local acting company. Check the local papers or phone for specific attractions and prices.

The University of Hawaii's Department of Theatre and Drama, internationally known for its productions of Beijing Opera, Kabuki, and other Asian

---

Partying in Paradise: Oahu's Best Luau

Luaus are fun affairs—everyone arrives dressed in aloha shirts and muumuus, a great ceremony is made of taking the pig out of the imu (camera buffs have been known to go wild with joy at this part), there's lively Polynesian entertainment, and the mai tais flow freely.

Honolulu offers a number of luaus, but one that's most consistently praised is the **Paradise Cove Luau** (☎ 808/973-LUAU, or toll free 800/775-2683 in the mainland U.S.), held in a Hawaiian theme park 27 miles from Waikiki, on a 12-acre beachfront site in the town of Ewa. (Nearby is Oahu's newest resort development, Ko Olina, home to the exquisite Ihilani Resort & Spa.) Guests can wander through a village of thatched huts, learn ancient Hawaiian games and crafts, enjoy the spectacular sunset over the ocean, help pull in the fish in the nets during the hukilau, and watch a program of ancient and modern hula at the imu ceremony. Then it's a buffet meal and a Polynesian show: The fire dancer alone is worth the price of admission. Bus fare from Waikiki is included in the admission prices of $47.50 or $55 adults (upgrade-better seating adults, $27.50 or $32.50) $25 children 6 to 12. The luau is held every night of the week.

---

theater in English, performs at the **John F. Kennedy Theatre** (☎ 808/956-7685). Productions throughout the year also include touring companies, Western classics, musical theater, dance, and contemporary plays.

The top-notch, non-profit **Manoa Valley Theatre** (☎ 808/988-6131) bills itself as "Honolulu's off-Broadway playhouse." MVT has an intimate 150-seat theater and produces an annual season of plays and musicals. Established in 1969, MVT has earned an excellent reputation for its exciting recent hits from Broadway and off-Broadway.

The nationally acclaimed **Honolulu Theatre for Youth** (☎ 808/839-9885) puts on excellent productions for children, but adults enjoy them too. Most shows are aimed at those aged 6 and up.

2 The Club & Music Scene

THE TOP NIGHTCLUB SHOWS

Because nightclub entertainers have a way of moving around a bit, it's always wise to check the local tourist papers and phone ahead to get details on prices before going to a show. Be sure to check the papers for coupons and discount deals. On a recent off-month, we found $50 shows being advertised for as low as $25. Reservations are required.

✪ The Brothers Cazimero

At the Bishop Museum, 1525 Bernice St. ☎ **808/847-5311.** $37.50 with dinner; $22.50 without. Prices include admission to the Bishop Museum.

We'd give up almost anything to catch a show by the Caz. They're beloved champions of authentic Hawaiian music and dance, and many of their songs—and the dances of their company, featuring the incredible Lein'ala—are truly from the heart of Hawaii. After many years at the Royal Hawaiian Hotel, the Caz have relocated to what, at first, seems an unlikely venue, the Bishop Museum; actually, it works perfectly. Surrounded by the ancient artifacts of the Islands, the Brothers delve even more deeply into their love for Hawaiiana. Seating is theatre style. Since the museum does not close before the show (7pm Wednesday, Saturday, and Sunday), you can come early, tour the museum, have a picnic supper out on the lawn, and then spend an evening with the Caz. The picnic supper, included in the higher-priced admission tickets, comes in a lauhala basket that you can keep.

✪ Frank DeLima

Polynesian Palace Showroom, Outrigger Reef Towers Hotel, 227 Lewers St. ☎ **808/ 923-SHOW.** Cocktail show $27.50, plus two-drink minimum.

A huge favorite with the local folks, DeLima is a singing comedian whose outlandish parodies and skits can usually be counted upon to keep patrons more or less rolling in the aisles.

Loyal Gardner and Glenn Medeiros—and Charo!

At the Polynesian Palace Showroom, Outrigger Reef Towers Hotel, 227 Lewers St. ☎ **808/922-SHOW.** Cocktail show $29.50 18 and over, $23.50 students 12 to 18, $18.50 12 and under; dinner show $47.50 12 and over, $38.50 under 12.

The early show at the Polynesian Palace alternates every three months. You might get to see Loyal Gardner and Glen Medeiros, two of the best voices in Hawaii, making mellow music. Then again, you might catch Charo!, the non-stop bundle of Latin energy who sings, dances, tells dirty jokes, and plays the flamenco guitar superbly. The show is on Thursday through Saturday at 7pm.

John Hirokawa

In the *Magic of Polynesia* at the Hilton Hawaiian Village Dome Showroom, 2005 Kalia Rd. ☎ **808/949-4321,** ext. 25. Cocktail show $29.50 adults, $20.50 children; dinner show $49.50 adults, $34.50 children.

Hawaiian-born illusionist John Hirokawa is a modern-day Harry Houdini. How he performs his daring feats of illusion—whatever did happen to the woman who disappeared in mid-air?—nobody knows, but he's a great showman. The show is fine for older children, but it might be a bit scary for really tiny tots.

Don Ho

At the Waikiki Beachcomber Hotel, 2300 Kalakaua Ave. ☎ **808/931-3034.** Cocktail show $28 adults, $14 for those 5 to 20; dinner show, $46 adults, $23 for children 5 to 11.

Don Ho has been called the "Frank Sinatra of Hawaii" and in one respect, at least, the comparison is apt: Like Ol' Blue Eyes, Don just keeps getting mellower all the time. An international star for over 30 years, Don still sits center stage at his organ, telling stories, singing island music, and calling up local talent to perform. It's a heartwarming show, different every night, and one that his legions of old-time fans—who line up to take pictures with him before and after the performance—simply adore.

Legends

Royal Hawaiian Shopping Center, 4th floor, Building B, 2201 Kalakaua Ave. ☎ **808/ 971-1400.** Cocktail show $32 adults, $25 children 3 to 11; dinner show $69 adults.

Talented impressionists take the audience back in time to some of the exciting moments of yesteryear. Jonathon von Brana steals the show as "Elvis Presley"; "Prince," "Madonna," "Marilyn Monroe," and "Michael Jackson" are some of the other featured artists.

✪ Society of Seven

Main Showroom, Outrigger Waikiki, 2335 Kalakaua Ave. ☎ **808/922-6408** or 808/923-0711. Dinner show $50.50 adults, $39.50 children under 12; cocktail show $29.50 adults, $23.50 students 12 to 20, $20 children.

Seven of the most talented performers in Hawaii, headliners for many a year, make up this group. They sing, act, play a variety of musical instruments, and even reprise Broadway musicals. Great fun!

HAWAIIAN AND POLYNESIAN REVUES

Sheraton's Spectacular Polynesian Revue

At the Princess Kaiulani Hotel. ☎ **808/971-5305.** 5:15pm dinner show, $56, $49, cocktail show, 5:45 and 8:30pm, $27.50.

One of the most professional revues in the islands, this one pulls out all the stops. The sensational Tahitian shimmy, the gentle Maori slap dances, the heart-stopping Samoan fire dance, and, of course, the languid Hawaiian hulas are performed by top artists. They're on twice nightly in the stunning Ainahu Showroom; while you're watching the fireworks on stage, you can feast on a bountiful buffet.

Pau Hana Show

At the Hyatt Regency Waikiki, 2424 Kalakau Ave. ☎ **808/923-1234.**

On Friday at 5pm, when local people are done for the day, they like to head for this spot; so should you. Traditional Hawaiian music, dances, and songs are presented for the cost of a few drinks. You can also stand by the giant waterfall and just watch.

DANCE AND ROCK CLUBS

Although clubs come and clubs go (check the local papers when you're there), you can usually count on a few stalwarts:

Kentos

In the Hyatt Regency Waikiki, 2424 Kalakaua Ave. ☎ **808/923-7400.** Cover $10.

The Copycats are usually the featured artists, and they draw the crowds for a lively evening of '50s to '70s "oldies but goodies." The rocking and rolling goes on from 7pm to 2am nightly.

Maharaja Restaurant and Disco

At the Waikiki Trade Center, 2255 Kuhio Ave. ☎ **808/922-3030.** Cover $5 or $29 (the higher charge includes "house money").

An international clientele makes the scene at the posh Maharaja Club, the first of its kind outside Japan. An opulent mood, an international crowd, and all types of music, including Top-40 hits.

Rumours

At the Ala Moana Hotel, 410 Atkinson Dr. ☎ **808/955-4811.** Cover $5 weekends after 9pm; free at other times.

Music videos, a light show complete with special effects, laser karaoke on Tuesdays, and four of the islands best DJs are featured at this smart spot, which has a fancy feeling and a dress code to match.

Scruples

In the Waikiki Marketplace, 2310 Kuhio Ave. ☎ **808/923-9530.** Cover $5 after 9pm.

This is one of Waikiki's hottest nightspots. Scruples' DJs spin Top-40 hits every night from 8pm to 4am.

Studebaker's

At Restaurant Row, 500 Ala Moana Blvd. ☎ **808/526-9888.** Cover $1–4, plus one-drink minimum.

The action here is "bop till you drop" seven nights a week. From 5:30 to 7:30pm Monday through Friday and 6 to 8pm Sunday, they have a terrific buffet included in the cover charge.

Wave Waikiki

1877 Kalakaua Ave. ☎ **808/941-0424.** Free until 10pm; then $5 cover.

Hawaii's biggest, brassiest live rock 'n' roll nightclub features hot mainland bands Wednesday through Sunday, a local band on Tuesday, and a dance contest every other Monday. Dancing and cocktails till 4am. Over 21 only.

3 The Bar Scene

ROOMS WITH A VIEW

Hanohano Room of the Sheraton Waikiki

2255 Kalakaua Ave. ☎ **808/922-4422.**

It's hard to imagine a more romantic spot than this spectacular dining room, where the view is uninterrupted from Diamond Head to Pearl Harbor and the sunset is unforgettable. There's piano music nightly from 6:30pm.

✪ House Without a Key

In the Halekulani Hotel, 2199 Kalia Rd. ☎ **808/923-2311.**

The perfect place for a Waikiki sunset, this open-air waterfront cocktail lounge affords a fabulous view of the sun sinking over the water. While you're enjoying that spectacle, you'll also enjoy relaxing music by either the Islanders or the Hiram Olsen Trio, plus hulas by Kanoe Miller, a former Miss Hawaii. There is Hawaiian music from 5 to 8:30pm daily. Loverly.

Papeete Bar

In the Tahitian Lanai Restaurant, Waikikian on the Beach Hotel, 1811 Ala Moana Blvd. ☎ **808/946-6541.**

This "old Hawaii" hotel boasts a cocktail garden overlooking the lagoon. A lively crowd hangs out at the bar, known for its sing-a-longs, from 5pm.

BARS WITH LIVE MUSIC

Beach Bar

In the Sheraton Moana Surfrider, 2365 Kalakaua Ave. ☎ **808/922-3111.**

One of the nicest places for a drink near the water's edge, this bar is tucked into one of Waikiki's classic oceanfront hotels, which has recently undergone a magnificent period restoration. Music by name artists begins very early—they play from 7 to 11am, take a break, and then hold forth again, from 2 and 11pm.

Gordon Biersch Brewery Restaurant

At Aloha Tower Marketplace, 101 Ala Moana Blvd. ☎ **808/599-4877.** No cover.

Hawaii's first microbrewery is the best place in town for beer. The hugely successful combination restaurant and open-air beer garden is also the place to catch live entertainment every Wednesday through Saturday, from 7pm on. Strange Brew, an engaging group, will probably be playing contemporary music. The brewing vats are fully visible. The food is great.

Mai Tai Bar

In the Royal Hawaiian Hotel, 2259 Kalakaua Ave. ☎ **808/923-7311.**

Keith and Carmen Haugen, a highly admired local couple, make music Tuesday and Wednesday evenings from 5:30 to 8:30pm at this magical spot right on the sands of Waikiki.

Sloppy Joe's

At Aloha Tower Marketplace, 101 Ala Moana Blvd. ☎ **808/528-0007.** No cover, except for special events such as Mardi Gras.

Modeled after the original in Key West, Florida, and bedecked with Hemingway memorabilia, Sloppy Joe's offers a variety of live entertainment every day from noon to closing.

4 Sunset Cruises

Combining a show with a sail and a view of Waikiki's fabled skyline is such a good idea that there is a multitude of dinner cruises to tempt the visitor. The following cruise ships offer the ultimate in entertainment at sea:

✪ *Navatek I*

Royal Hawaiian Cruises. ☎ **808/848-6360,** or 800/852-4183.

Imagine a floating first-class restaurant with breathtaking views of the Honolulu skyline and a cabaret show with beautiful hula and jazz dancers and a terrific band, headlined by multiple Hoku Award–winner Nohelani Cypriano, and you're imagining the *Navatek I* Sunset Dinner Cruise, nightly from 5:30pm until 7:45pm. The dining room is softly lit, and the cruise (thanks to the unique construction of the vessel, which virtually eliminates the possibility of seasickness) is as smooth as even the most sensitive sailor could hope for. The five-course European-style dinner is gourmet all the way, and includes five drinks. Nohelani and her talented troupe put on a fast-paced, energetic show featuring island music and top Hawaiian guest entertainers. The cost is $150 adults, $110 for children 2 to 11.

The *Navatek I* Skyline Dinner Cruise is also a delight, and costs half the price: $75 for adults, $55 for children 2 to 11. Jazz by vocalist Joanne Miles and her group and a candlelit three-course, three-cocktail dinner are the features of this moonlight cruise, which takes place every night except Monday from 8:15 to 10pm.

Both cruises depart from Pier 6, next to Aloha Tower.

✪ *Star of Honolulu*

Paradise Cruises. ☎ **808/536-3641** or 800/334-6191.

The largest cruise ship of its kind in the United States, *Star of Honolulu* is a state-of-the-art vessel whose unique construction all but banishes the possibility of motion sickness. A variety of cruise options is available, from $65 Star Sunset Dinner (dinner, "The Spirit of America" show, round-trip transportation from Waikiki) to the $100 Three Star Sunset Dining (a more elaborate dinner, the show, and jazz music) to the $190 Five Star Dining luxury evening, featuring a chauffeur-driven limousine to take you to the ship, a special VIP captain's reception, white-glove service, a French dinner, live jazz, and full open bar in a private nightclub atmosphere.

Celebrating "Aloha Friday" at Sea

Aloha Friday is a once-a-week celebration of Hawaii's intangible spirit of warmth and affection and welcoming, otherwise known as *aloha*. That's the day when lots of local businesspeople come to work in aloha shirts and muumuus, and special festivities are held. One of the best of these is the weekly Aloha Friday concert held by the venerable **Auntie Irmgard Alului** and her family group, Paumana, aboard the cruise ship *Navatek I.* Auntie Irmgard—84 this year—is one of Hawaii's most prolific songwriters, a "living treasure" of Hawaii, the winner of numerous awards including a Na Hoku Hanohano Award (Hawaii's own version of the Grammys) for her contribution to Hawaiian music. To hear Auntie Irmgard is a special privilege. If you're not in town on a Friday, try one of the *Navatek*'s Sunday through Thursday cruises with popular singer-songwriter Jerry Santos alternating with Brother Greg. Cruises depart from Pier 6, next to Aloha Tower.

The luncheon cruises, which run from noon to 2pm, include a delicious international buffet and two cocktails; the Friday, Saturday, and Sunday buffets feature Hawaiian fare. The cost is $45. For information, call **808/848-6360** or **800/852-4183.**

Index

ACCOMMODATIONS

Key to Abbreviatons VE=Very Expensive; E=Expensive; M=Moderate; B=Budget.

Now Save Money on All Your Travels by Joining

Frommer's
T R A V E L   B O O K   C L U B

The Advantages of Membership:

1. Your choice of any **TWO FREE BOOKS.**

2. Your own subscription to the **TRIPS & TRAVEL** quarterly newsletter, where you'll discover the best buys in travel, the hottest vacation spots, the latest travel trends, world-class events and festivals, and much more.

3. A **30% DISCOUNT** on any additional books you order through the club.

4. **DOMESTIC TRIP-ROUTING KITS** (available for a small additional fee). We'll send you a detailed map highlighting the most direct or scenic route to your destination, anywhere in North America.

Here's all you have to do to join:

Send in your annual membership fee of $25.00 ($35.00 Canada/Foreign) with your name, address, and selections on the form below. Or call 815/734-1104 to use your credit card.

Send all orders to:

FROMMER'S TRAVEL BOOK CLUB
P.O. Box 473 • Mt. Morris, IL 61054-0473 • ☎ 815/734-1104

YES! I want to take advantage of this opportunity to join Frommer's Travel Book Club.

[ ] My check for $25.00 ($35.00 for Canadian or foreign orders) is enclosed.
   All orders must be prepaid in U.S. funds only. Please make checks payable to Frommer's Travel Book Club.

[ ] Please charge my credit card: [ ] Visa or [ ] Mastercard

   Credit card number: _____

   Expiration date: ___ / ___ / ___

   Signature: _____

   Or call 815/734-1104 to use your credit card by phone.

Name: _____

Address: _____

City: _____ State: _____ Zip code: _____

Phone number (in case we have a question regarding your order): _____

Please indicate your choices for TWO FREE books (*see following pages*):

   Book 1 - Code: _____   Title: _____

   Book 2 - Code: _____   Title: _____

For information on ordering additional titles, see your first issue of the *Trips & Travel* newsletter.

Allow 4–6 weeks for delivery for all items. Prices of books, membership fee, and publication dates are subject to change without notice. All orders are subject to acceptance and availability.

AC1

The following Frommer's guides are available from your favorite bookstore, or you can use the order form on the preceding page to request them as part of your membership in Frommer's Travel Book Club.

FROMMER'S COMPLETE TRAVEL GUIDES

(Comprehensive guides to sightseeing, dining and accommodations, with selections in all price ranges—from deluxe to budget)

FROMMER'S $-A-DAY GUIDES

(Dream Vacations at Down-to-Earth Prices)

FROMMER'S COMPLETE CITY GUIDES

(Comprehensive guides to sightseeing, dining, and accommodations in all price ranges)

Amsterdam, 8th Ed.	S176	Minneapolis/St. Paul, 4th Ed.	S159
Athens, 10th Ed.	S174	Montréal/Québec City '95	S166
Atlanta & the Summer Olympic		Nashville/Memphis, 1st Ed.	S141
Games '96 (avail. 11/95)	S181	New Orleans '96 (avail. 10/95)	S182
Atlantic City/Cape May, 5th Ed.	S130	New York City '96 (avail. 11/95)	S183
Bangkok, 2nd Ed.	S147	Paris '96 (avail. 9/95)	S180
Barcelona '93–'94	S115	Philadelphia, 8th Ed.	S167
Berlin, 3rd Ed.	S162	Prague, 1st Ed.	S143
Boston '95	S160	Rome, 10th Ed.	S168
Budapest, 1st Ed.	S139	St. Louis/Kansas City, 2nd Ed.	S127
Chicago '95	S169	San Antonio/Austin, 1st Ed.	S177
Denver/Boulder/Colorado Springs,		San Diego '95	S158
3rd Ed.	S154	San Francisco '96 (avail. 10/95)	S184
Disney World/Orlando '96 (avail. 9/95)	S178	Santa Fe/Taos/Albuquerque '95	S172
Dublin, 2nd Ed.	S157	Seattle/Portland '94–'95	S137
Hong Kong '94–'95	S140	Sydney, 4th Ed.	S171
Las Vegas '95	S163	Tampa/St. Petersburg, 3rd Ed.	S146
London '96 (avail. 9/95)	S179	Tokyo '94–'95	S144
Los Angeles '95	S164	Toronto, 3rd Ed.	S173
Madrid/Costa del Sol, 2nd Ed.	S165	Vancouver/Victoria '94–'95	S142
Mexico City, 1st Ed.	S175	Washington, D.C. '95	S153
Miami '95–'96	S149		

FROMMER'S FAMILY GUIDES

(Guides to family-friendly hotels, restaurants, activities, and attractions)

California with Kids	F105	San Francisco with Kids	F104
Los Angeles with Kids	F103	Washington, D.C. with Kids	F102
New York City with Kids	F101		

FROMMER'S WALKING TOURS

(Memorable strolls through colorful and historic neighborhoods, accompanied by detailed directions and maps)

Berlin	W100	Paris, 2nd Ed.	W112
Chicago	W107	San Francisco, 2nd Ed.	W115
England's Favorite Cities	W108	Spain's Favorite Cities (avail. 9/95)	W116
London, 2nd Ed.	W111	Tokyo	W109
Montréal/Québec City	W106	Venice	W110
New York, 2nd Ed.	W113	Washington, D.C., 2nd Ed.	W114

FROMMER'S AMERICA ON WHEELS

(Guides for travelers who are exploring the U.S.A. by car, featuring a brand-new rating system for accommodations and full-color road maps)

Arizona/New Mexico	A100	Florida	A102
California/Nevada	A101	Mid-Atlantic	A103

FROMMER'S SPECIAL-INTEREST TITLES

Arthur Frommer's Branson!	P107	Frommer's Where to Stay U.S.A.,	
Arthur Frommer's New World		11th Ed.	P102
of Travel (avail. 11/95)	P112	National Park Guide, 29th Ed.	P106
Frommer's Caribbean Hideaways		USA Today Golf Tournament Guide	P113
(avail. 9/95)	P110	USA Today Minor League	
Frommer's America's 100 Best-Loved		Baseball Book	P111
State Parks	P109		

FROMMER'S BEST BEACH VACATIONS

*(The top places to sun, stroll, shop, stay, play, party, and swim—with each
beach rated for beauty, swimming, sand, and amenities)*

California (avail. 10/95)	G100	Hawaii (avail. 10/95)	G102
Florida (avail. 10/95)	G101		

FROMMER'S BED & BREAKFAST GUIDES

*(Selective guides with four-color photos and full descriptions of
the best inns in each region)*

California	B100	Hawaii	B105
Caribbean	B101	Pacific Northwest	B106
East Coast	B102	Rockies	B107
Eastern United States	B103	Southwest	B108
Great American Cities	B104		

FROMMER'S IRREVERENT GUIDES

*(Wickedly honest guides for sophisticated travelers
and those who want to be)*

Chicago (avail. 11/95)	I100	New Orleans (avail. 11/95)	I103
London (avail. 11/95)	I101	San Francisco (avail. 11/95)	I104
Manhattan (avail. 11/95)	I102	Virgin Islands (avail. 11/95)	I105

FROMMER'S DRIVING TOURS

*(Four-color photos and detailed maps outlining
spectacular scenic driving routes)*

Australia	Y100	Italy	Y108
Austria	Y101	Mexico	Y109
Britain	Y102	Scandinavia	Y110
Canada	Y103	Scotland	Y111
Florida	Y104	Spain	Y112
France	Y105	Switzerland	Y113
Germany	Y106	U.S.A.	Y114
Ireland	Y107		

FROMMER'S BORN TO SHOP

*(The ultimate travel guides for discriminating
shoppers—from cut-rate to couture)*

Hong Kong (avail. 11/95)	Z100	London (avail. 11/95)	Z101